Foundations of ITIL®

Other publications by Van Haren Publishing

Van Haren Publishing (VHP) specializes in titles on Best Practices, methods and standards within four domains:
- IT management
- Architecture (Enterprise and IT)
- Business management and
- Project management

Van Haren Publishing offers a wide collection of whitepapers, templates, free e-books, trainer material etc. in the **Van Haren Publishing Knowledge Base**: www.vanharen.net for more details.

Van Haren Publishing is also publishing on behalf of leading organizations and companies: ASLBiSL Foundation, CA, Centre Henri Tudor, Gaming Works, Getronics, IACCM, IAOP, IPMA-NL, ITSqc, NAF, Ngi, PMI-NL, PON, Quint, The Open Group, The Sox Institute, Tmforum.

Topics are (per domain):

IT (Service) Management / IT Governance	Architecture (Enterprise and IT)	Project/Programme/ Risk Management
ABC of ICT	Archimate®	A4-Projectmanagement
ASL®	GEA®	ICB / NCB
BiSL®	SOA	MINCE®
CATS CM®	TOGAF®	M_o_R®
CMMI®		MSP™
CoBIT	**Business Management**	P3O®
Frameworx	Contract Management	PMBOK® Guide
ISO 17799	EFQM	PRINCE2®
ISO 27001	eSCM	
ISO 27002	ISA-95	
ISO/IEC 20000	ISO 9000	
ISPL	ISO 9001:2000	
IT Service CMM	OPBOK	
ITIL®	Outsourcing	
ITSM	SAP	
MOF	SixSigma	
MSF	SOX	
SABSA	SqEME®	

For the latest information on VHP publications, visit our website: www.vanharen.net.

Foundations
of ITIL®

2011 Edition

Colophon

Title:	Foundations of ITIL® 2011 Edition
Authors:	Pierre Bernard
Copy editor:	Jane Chittenden
Publisher:	Van Haren Publishing, Zaltbommel, www.vanharen.net
Design & layout:	CO2 Premedia Bv, Amersfoort – NL
ISBN Hardcopy:	978 90 8753 674 9
ISBN eBook:	978 90 8753 923 8
Edition:	First edition, first impression, April 2012
Copyright:	© Van Haren Publishing, 2012

Foreword

ITIL® is the world's leading framework on IT Service Management. Over the years its adoption has been encouraged by the credibility of its independent owners (the UK Government, specifically the Cabinet Office) and the professional contribution of many international experts. It has become the *'lingua franca'* of the IT Service Management world: a means by which practitioners can develop a first-class service using well understood terms and processes.

The *Foundations of ITIL®* book (and its predecessors) was drafted to create a portable reference book that documented the essentials of the framework. Reflecting the needs of many students and newcomers to the field, it captures the essence of ITIL and shows its context within the wider business. Throughout the years this title has followed the development of the ITIL framework and new revisions have accurately communicated to a global audience the benefits of following this approach.

This latest revision reflects the ITIL® 2011 edition. It follows the established 'Lifecycle Approach' and describes the five key stages and the processes within them. As with all previous editions this title has been the quality result not only of an expert author but also of many QA colleagues around the world who have refined and honed the text. Its quality is reflected in the formal license granted to it by APMG, the official accreditation body of ITIL.

As an independent Advisory Board we always encourage the Publisher to develop products that provide real benefit to the market. We always encourage innovation balanced by the traditional elements of quality and usability. We believe that this book will assist you in achieving your ITIL V3 Foundations Qualification and establishing best practices in IT Service Management in your organization.

Van Haren Publishing IT Management Advisory Board

Jacques Cazemier, VKA NL
Bill Hefley, University of Pittsburgh and ITSqc, LLC
Kevin Holland, NHS Connecting for Health
Brian Johnson, CA
David Jones, Pink Elephant UK
Alan Nance, Independent
Eric Rozemeijer, Quint Wellington Redwood
Gad J Selig, University of Bridgeport
Abbas Shahim, Atos Consulting
John Stewart, Independent

Acknowledgements

The Foundations of ITIL® is one of the very first publishing concepts we had at Van Haren Publishing. In 2002 ITIL was still in its infancy – yet its potential was clear to many in the industry. A concise reference book was in demand and Van Haren Publishing made the effort to create and publish what was one of the first of many such titles in the marketplace. Since that time Van Haren Publishing has revised and updated its basic title to reflect the new editions of ITIL. On visiting clients and customers we will often see these editions (current and old) well-thumbed and sitting on desk tops or on bookshelves.

So we would like to thank and acknowledge all the contributors to this very special product.

Firstly we would like to thank the author Pierre Bernard. Pierre is a dedicated Service Management expert well known and respected throughout the industry. It is always an honour and privilege to work with such a professional writer – and his great sense of humour makes this project even more of a pleasure.

The reviewers to this title took much time and effort to review an extensive piece of work. Their attention to detail was very professional and the resulting text is, we believe, a very high quality offering thanks to their work. So the Publisher would like to express deep thanks to the following:

Claire Agutter ITIL Training Zone
Martin Andenmatten, Glenfis AG
Kevin Holland, NHS Connecting for Health
Mart Rovers, Interprom
Marianna Ruocco, Independent
Luigi Restaino, BITIL
Rob van der Berg, Microsoft

Contents

1 Introduction

1.1 Background

During the last decade (2001 – present), technological developments such as smartphones, tablets, cloud services, near-field-content, Wi-Fi, and especially social media have had a tremendous effect on the world we live in. With the emergence of extremely powerful hardware, highly versatile software and super-fast networks, organisations worldwide have been able to develop their information-dependent products and services to a greater extent, and to bring them to the market much faster. These, as well as many other socio-economic and political developments, have marked the superimposition of the **information age** upon the industrial age. In the so-called "*information age*", where everything is connected, the dissemination of data and information has become faster, more dynamic, as well as a worldwide phenomenon.

Quoting one of Bob Dylan's[1] songs titled "*The Times They Are A-Changin*" is quite appropriate here, as indeed the traditional view and role of the Information Technology organisation (IT) is dramatically altered based on the above. In order to be successful, organisations will need to be as nimble as possible to react to rapidly changing market demands and technologies. First, there is a movement concerning renaming IT to Information Services (IS). Second, cloud computing is becoming both a more viable option and a more common solution. This is a result of organisations realising that technology is not always their core competency and that outsourcing provides them with a more accurate and predictable cost structure.

Organisations should also start considering the significant impact of the arrival in the workplace of extremely technology-savvy employees. These new employees have been using technology basically since birth and have also been not only the early adaptors of mobile technologies but of social media as well. Information is now at their fingertips and they will expect the same in the workplace. In addition to this new generation of employees, organisations need to consider how they will handle the same demands from their existing and potential customers.

There are a lot of books, whitepapers, and articles[2] regarding the need to breakdown vertical business silos and shift the business model to more horizontal **processes** thus "flattening" the organisation. The authors of these documents are advocating that decision-making powers be increasingly bestowed on the employees. Again, according to these various sources, an important advantage of process-oriented organisations is that processes can be designed to support a **customer-oriented approach**. This has made the alignment between the IT organisation (responsible for supplying information) and the customer (responsible for using these information

---

1 Bob Dylan – American singer, songwriter, musician (1941 –)
2 See References section for some examples

systems in their business) increasingly significant. This is usually known as **Business-IT Alignment (BITA)**.

It is against this background that the world of IT Service Management (ITSM) has arisen and gained in popularity.

The above authors are not wrong, nor are they lacking vision; on the contrary. As organisations gained more experience with the **process-oriented approach** of IT service management, it became clear that these processes must be managed coherently. Moreover, it became obvious that the introduction of a process-oriented work method meant a big change for the primarily line and project-oriented organisations. Culture and change management are crucial elements for a successful organisational design. Change management here refers to business change, as well as changes in attitudes, aptitudes, behaviours, and the adoption of frameworks and methodologies adapted to suit the organisational needs.

The truth is that organisations have always used processes and IT is no different. However, one must acknowledge that processes are often conducted in isolation by a few individuals or groups. Processes are often neither shared nor documented. One of the causes for the above is that many people believe that "knowledge is power[3]".

Another important lesson learned is that the IT organisation must not lose itself in a process culture. Just like the one-sided project-oriented organisation, a one-sided process-oriented organisation is not the optimum type of business. Balance is, as always, the magic word. In addition, it has become clear that the customer-oriented approach requires that an **end-to-end** and **user-centric** approach must be followed: it is of no help to the user to know that "the server was still in operation" if the information system is not available at the user's workplace. IT services must be viewed in a larger context. The need for the recognition of the **Service Lifecycle**, and the management of IT services in light of that lifecycle, has become a concern.

Due to the fast growing dependency of business upon information, the quality of information services in companies is being increasingly subjected to stricter **internal and external requirements**. The role of **standards** is becoming more and more important, and **frameworks** of "best practices" help with the development of a management system to meet these requirements. Organisations that are not in control of their processes will not be able to realise great results on the level of the Service Lifecycle and the end-to-end-management of those services. Organisations that do not have their internal organisation in order will also not achieve great results. For these reasons, all these aspects are handled alongside each other in the course of this book.

---

3   Attributed to Sir Frances Bacon (Viscount of St Alban) 1561 – 1626

1.2   Why this book

This book offers detailed information for those who are responsible for strategic information issues, as well as for the (much larger) group who are responsible for setting up and executing the delivery of the information services. This is supported by both the description of the Service Lifecycle, as documented in ITIL (2007 and 2011 editions), and by the description of the processes and functions that are associated with it. The ITIL core books are very extensive, and can be used for a thorough study of contemporary best practices. This Foundations book provides the reader with an easy-to-read comprehensive introduction to the broad library of ITIL core books, to support the understanding and the further distribution of ITIL as an industry framework. Once this understanding of the structure of ITIL has been gained, the reader can use the core books for a more detailed understanding and guidance for their daily practice.

1.3   Organisations

Several organisations are involved in the maintenance of ITIL as a description of the "best practice" in the IT service management field.

The Cabinet Office

ITIL was initially developed by CCTA, a UK Government Organisation, to help UK Government organisations develop capability, improve efficiency and deploy best practice for IT Service Management. ITIL is now owned by the Cabinet Office, part of the UK Government. The UK Government has made significant investments in developing and maintaining this portfolio of guidance. The Cabinet Office also develops and owns best practice products for portfolio, programme, project, and risk management.

itSMF

The target group for this publication is anyone who is involved or interested in IT service management. A professional organisation, working on the development of the IT service management field, has been created especially for this target group.

In 1991 the Information Technology Service Management Forum (itSMF), originally known as the Information Technology Infrastructure Management Forum (ITIMF), was set up as a UK association. In 1994, a sister association was established in the Netherlands, following the UK example.

Since then, independent itSMF organisations have been set up in more than forty countries, spread across the globe, and the number of "chapters" continues to grow. All itSMF organisations operate under the umbrella organisation, itSMF International (itSMF-I).

The itSMF is aimed at the entire professional area of IT service management. It promotes the exchange of information and experiences that IT organisations can use to improve their service provision. The itSMF is also involved in the use and quality of the various standards and methods that are important in the field. One of these standards is ITIL. The itSMF-I organisation has an agreement with the Cabinet Office and the APM Group on the promotion of the use of ITIL.

> The **IT Service Management Forum (itSMF)** is a global, independent, internationally recognised not-for-profit organisation dedicated to IT Service Management. The itSMF is wholly owned and principally run by its membership. It consists of a growing number of national chapters, each with a large degree of autonomy, but adhering to a common code of conduct .The itSMF is a major influence on, and contributor to, industry best practices and standards worldwide, working in partnership with a wide international range of governmental and standards bodies.
>
> itSMF International is the controlling body of the itSMF national chapters and sets policies and provides direction for furthering the overall objectives of itSMF, for the adoption of IT Service Management (ITSM) best practice and for ensuring adherence to itSMF policies and standards.

APM Group

In 2006, OGC contracted the management of ITIL rights, the certification of ITIL exams and accreditation of training organisations to the APM Group (APMG), a commercial organisation. APMG defines the certification and accreditation for the ITIL exams, and published the new certification system (see 2.1: ITIL exams).

Examination institutes

The Dutch Examen Instituut voor Informatica (EXIN) and the English Information Systems Examination Board (ISEB, part of the BCS: the British Computer Society) cooperated in the development and provision of certification for IT service management. For many years they were the only bodies that provided ITIL exams. With the contracting of APMG by OGC in 2006, the responsibility for ITIL exams is now with APMG. To support the world-wide delivery of these ITIL exams, APMG has accredited a number of examination institutes: APMG-International, BCS-ISEB CERT-IT, CSME, DANSK IT, DF Certifiering AB, EXIN, , LCS (Loyalist Certification Services), PEOPLECERT Group and TÜV SÜD Akademie. See www.itil-officialsite.com for the most recent information.

1.4   Differences from previous editions

The *"Foundations of ITIL®"* book has played a key role in the distribution of ideas on IT service management and ITIL for years. The title has been translated into thirteen languages and is recognised as the most practical introduction to the leading "best practices" in this field. Earlier editions of the Foundations book focused on the content of three books from the ITIL series (version 2): Service Support, Service

Delivery, and Security Management, and placed them in a broader context of quality management.

The main difference between ITIL version 2 and 3 lies in the service lifecycle, introduced in version 3. Where the Foundations scope of version 2 focused on single practices, clustered in Delivery, Support, and Security Management, the scope in version 3 takes the entire Service Lifecycle into account.

As a result of continuous development of best practices, some terms have disappeared between the introduction of ITIL version 2 and 3, and a significant number of new terms have been added to version 3. As many of these concepts are part of the scope of an IT service management training or exam, they have been included in the relevant descriptions. For a definitive list of concepts, readers should refer to the various training and exam programs. In 2011 a second edition of ITIL V3 was published. This new edition is comprised mostly of cosmetic, grammatical, and syntactic modifications. The list of these changes is summarised in Appendix B – ITIL 2011 Summary of Updates.

For the purpose of simplification, it is highly recommended to use the generic term ITIL instead of ITIL V3 or ITIL V3:2007 or ITIL V3:2011. Although this book is indeed about the ITIL V3:2011 edition, the term ITIL is used throughout the book to simplify matters and to lighten the text.

1.5   Structure of the book

This book starts with an introduction on the backgrounds and general principles of IT service management and the context for ITIL (**Chapter 1**). It describes the parties involved in the development of best practices and standards for IT service management, and the basic premises and standards that are used.

The body of the book is set up in two major parts:

Part 1, made up of *Chapters 2 and 3*, introduces the Service Lifecycle, in the context of IT service management and IT governance. It discusses principles of organisational maturity, and the benefits and risks of following a service management framework. It introduces and discusses the functions involved in service management good practices. This enables the reader to better relate the processes in Part 2, and their related concepts and activities back to the people aspect of service management.

In **Part 2**, made up of **Chapters 4 to 8**, each of the phases in the Service Lifecycle is discussed in detail, in a standardised structure: Service Strategy, Service Design, Service Transition, Service Operation, and Continual Service Improvement. These chapters provide a detailed view on the characteristics of the Service Lifecycle, its construct and its elements. The main points of each phase are presented in a consistent way to aid readability and clarity, so that the text is clear and its readability is promoted.

Each of these processes and functions is described in terms of:
• Introduction
• Basic concepts
• Activities, methods and techniques
• Management information and interfaces
• Triggers, inputs, and outputs
• Critical Success Factors and metrics
• Challenges and risks

The **Appendices** provide useful sources for the reader. A reference list of the sources used is provided, as well as the official ITIL Glossary. The book ends with an extensive index of terms that will support the reader in finding relevant text elements.

1.6   How to use this book

Readers who are primarily interested in the Service Lifecycle can focus on Part 1 of the book, and pick whatever they need on functions from Part 1 and processes from Part 2.

Readers who are primarily interested in the functions and processes and are not ready for a lifecycle approach yet, or who prefer a process approach, can read the introductory chapters, and then focus on the functions and processes of their interest.

Readers who want a thorough introduction to ITIL, exploring its scope and main characteristics, can read Part 1 on the Lifecycle, and add as many of the processes from Part 2 as they need or like.

In this way, this new edition of the Foundations book aims to provide support to a variety of approaches to IT Service Management based on ITIL.

PART 1: THE ITIL SERVICE LIFECYCLE

2 Introduction to the service lifecycle

2.1 Introduction to ITIL®

In 2007 a new edition of the ITIL framework, known as version 3, was published. This new version took a dramatic new approach for service management. In addition to the process approach, ITIL V3 incorporated the concept of the service lifecycle. Then in 2011 a revision of the 2007 edition was published.

ITIL 2011 is an update and is also designed to:
- Resolve any errors or inconsistencies in the text and diagrams, both in content and presentation
- Improve the publications by addressing issues raised in the Change Control Log, as analysed and recommended by the change advisory board (CAB) and approved by the Cabinet Office. These are largely to do with clarity, consistency, correctness and completeness
- Address suggestions for change made by the training community to make ITIL easier to teach
- Review the ITIL Service Strategy publication to ensure that the concepts are explained in the clearest, most concise and accessible way possible

ITIL offers a systematic approach to the delivery of quality of IT services. It provides a detailed description of most of the important processes for an IT organisation, and includes information about procedures, tasks, roles, and responsibilities. These can be used as a basis for tailoring the framework to the needs of individual organisations.

At the same time, the broad coverage of ITIL also provides a helpful reference guide for many areas, which can be used to develop new improvement goals for an IT organisation, enabling it to grow and mature.

Over the years, ITIL has become much more than a series of useful books about IT service management. The framework for the "best practice" in IT service management is promoted and further developed and influenced by advisors, educators, trainers, and suppliers. These suppliers include a wide variety of technological solutions such as hardware, software, and cloud computing products. Since the 1990s, ITIL has grown from a theoretical framework to the de facto approach and philosophy shared by the people who work with it in practice.

Being an extended framework of best practices for IT service management itself, the advantages and disadvantages of frameworks in general, described in Section 2.4, are also applicable to ITIL. Of course, ITIL was developed because of the advantages mentioned earlier. Many of the pointers from "best practices" are intended to avoid potential problems or, if they do occur after all, to solve them.

ITIL examinations

Due to the new 2011 edition of ITIL, the syllabuses for all qualifications have been updated. The most significant changes relate to new/modified section numbers as well as improved wording and/or clarification for some learning objectives and section details.

At the publication date of this book, well over two million people worldwide have achieved one or more levels of ITIL certification.

There are four qualification levels in regards to the ITIL framework. They are:
• Foundation Level
• Intermediate Level (Lifecycle Stream & Capability Stream)
• ITIL Expert
• ITIL Master

For more information about the ITIL Qualification Scheme, please see:

http://www.itil-officialsite.com/Qualifications/ITILV3QualificationScheme.asp

2.2 IT governance

As the role of information, information services, and ITSM grows, so do the management requirements for the IT organisation. These requirements focus on two aspects. The first is the compliance with internal and external policies, laws, and regulations. The second is the provision of benefits (value-add proposition) for the stakeholders of the organisation. Although it is a relatively young discipline, IT governance is receiving far greater scrutiny than already established standards and frameworks. A definition for IT governance receiving a lot of support is from Van Grembergen:

> **IT governance** consists of a comprehensive framework of structures, processes, and relational mechanisms. Structures involve the existence of responsible functions such as IT executives and accounts, and a diversity of IT Committees. Processes refer to strategic IT decision-making and monitoring. Relational mechanisms include business/IT participation and partnerships, strategic dialogue and shared learning.

From the definition above we can see that governance enables the creation of a setting in which others can manage their tasks effectively[1]. IT governance and IT management, then, are two separate entities. Since ITSM is focused on managing quality IT services it can be considered to be part of the IT management domain. That leaves IT governance in the business or information management domain.

Although many frameworks are characterised as "IT Governance frameworks", such as CoʙiT® and even ITIL, most of them are in fact management frameworks. The International Organisation for Standardisation (ISO®) introduced in 2008 a standard for corporate governance of information technology; ISO/IEC38500:2008.

The ITIL framework approaches governance from the following perspective.

> Governance is the single overarching area tying IT and the business together. Governance defines the common directions, policies, and rules used by the whole organisation to conduct business.
>
> **ITIL's definition of governance**
> *"Governance ensures that policies and strategy are actually implemented and that required processes are correctly followed. Governance includes defining roles and responsibilities, measuring and reporting, and taking actions to resolve any issues identified."*

2.3 Organisational maturity

From the moment Richard Nolan introduced his "staged model" for the application of IT in organisations in 1973 many people have used stepwise improvement models. These models were quickly recognised as suitable instruments for quality improvement programs, thereby helping organisations to climb up the maturity ladder.

Dozens of variations on the theme can easily be found, ranging from trades such as software development, acquisition, systems engineering, software testing, website development, data warehousing and security engineering, to help desks and knowledge management. Obviously the *Kaizen* principle (improvement works best in smaller steps) was one that appealed to many people.

After Nolan's staged model in 1973, the most appealing application of this modelling was found when the Software Engineering Institute (SEI) of Carnegie Mellon University, USA, published its Software Capability Maturity Model (SW-CMM®). The CMM® was copied and applied in most of the cases mentioned above, making CMM something of a standard in maturity modelling. The CMM was later followed by newer editions, including CMMI® (CMM Integration).

---

1   Sohal & Fitzpatrick

Later, these models were applied in quality management models, such as the European Foundation for Quality Management (EFQM®). Apart from the broad quality management models, there are several other industry accepted practices, such as Six Sigma and Total Quality Management (TQM®) which are complementary to ITIL.

The available standards and frameworks of best practice offer guidance for organisations in achieving "operational excellence" in IT service management. Depending upon their stage of development, organisations tend to require different kinds of guidance.

Maturity model: CMMI

In the IT industry, the process maturity improvement process is best known in the context of the **Capability Maturity Model Integration (CMMI)**. This process improvement method was developed by SEI. CMMI provides both a staged and a continuous model. In the continuous representation, improvement is measured using capability levels and maturity is measured for a particular process across an organisation.

The capability levels in the **CMMI continuous representation** are shown in the table below.

Table 2.1 CMMI Capability levels

1. **Incomplete process**	A process that either is not performed or partially performed
2. **Performed process**	Satisfies the specific goals of the process area
3. **Managed process**	A performed (capability level 1) process that has the basic infrastructure in place to support the process
4. **Defined process**	A managed (capability level 2) process that is tailored from the organisation's set of standard processes according to the organisation's tailoring guidelines, and contributes work products, measures and other process improvement information to the organisational process assets
5. **Quantitatively managed process**	A defined (capability level 3) process that is controlled using statistical and other quantitative techniques
6. **Optimising process**	A quantitatively managed (capability level 4) process that is improved based on an understanding of the common causes of variation inherent in the process

In the staged representation, improvement is measured using maturity levels, for a set of processes across an organisation. The **CMMI staged representation** model defines five maturity levels, each a layer in the base for the next phase in the on-going process improvement, designated by the numbers 1 through 5:

Table 2.2 CMMI maturity levels

1. Initial	Processes are ad hoc and chaotic
2. Managed	The projects of the organisation have ensured that processes are planned and executed in accordance with policy
3. Defined	Processes are well characterised and understood, and are described in standards, procedures, tools and methods
4. Quantitatively managed	The organisation and projects establish quantitative objectives for quality and process performance, and use them as criteria in managing processes
5. Optimising	Focuses on continually improving process performance through incremental and innovative process and technological improvements

Many other maturity models were based on these structures, such as the Gartner Maturity Models. Most of these models are focused at capability maturity. Some others, like KPMG's World Class IT Maturity Model, take a different approach.

Standard: ISO/IEC 20000®

Developing and maintaining a quality system which complies with the requirements of the ISO 9000 (ISO-9000:2000®) series can be considered a tool for the organisation to reach and maintain the system-focused (or "managed" in IT Service CMM) level of maturity. These ISO standards emphasise the definition, description, and design of processes. For IT service management organisations, a specific ISO standard was produced: the ISO/IEC 20000 (see Figure 2.1). This does not replace ISO 9000; it

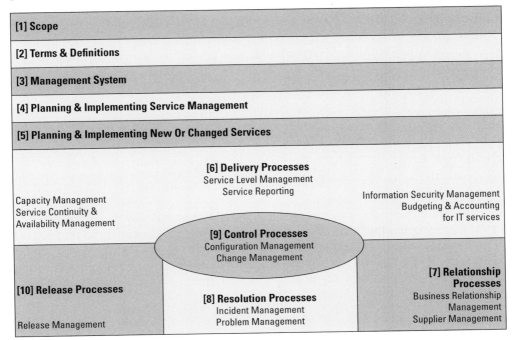

Figure 2.1 Overview of the ISO/IEC 20000 service management system

complements it by focusing on the specific requirements of a management system for IT service management.

Customer maturity

When assessing the maturity of an organisation, we cannot restrict ourselves to the service provider. The **level of maturity of the customer** is also important. If there are large differences in maturity between the provider and the customer, then these will have to be considered to prevent a mismatch in the approach, methods, and mutual expectations. Specifically, this affects the communication between the customer and the provider.

2.4   Benefits and risks of ITSM frameworks

The list below identifies some benefits and possible problems of using IT service management best practices. This list is not intended to be definitive, but is provided here as a basis for considering some of the benefits that can be achieved and some of the mistakes that can be made when using common process-based IT service management frameworks:

Benefits to the customer/user:
- The provision of IT services becomes more customer-focused and agreements about service quality improve the relationship
- The services are described better, in customer language, and in more appropriate detail
- Management of service quality, availability, and reliability and service costs is improved
- Communication with the IT organisation is improved by agreeing on the points of contact

Benefits to the IT organisation:
- The IT organisation develops a clearer structure, becomes more efficient, and is more focused on the corporate objectives
- The IT organisation is more in control of the infrastructure and services it has responsibility for, and changes become easier to manage
- An effective process structure provides a framework for the effective outsourcing of elements of the IT services
- Following best practices encourages a cultural change towards providing services, and supports the introduction of quality management systems based on the ISO 9000 series or on ISO/IEC 20000
- Frameworks can provide coherent frames of reference for internal communication and communication with suppliers, and for the standardisation and identification of procedures

Potential problems/mistakes:

- The introduction can take a long time and require significant effort, and may require a change of culture in the organisation; an overambitious introduction can lead to frustration because the objectives are never met
- If process structures become an objective in themselves, the service quality may be adversely affected; in this scenario, unnecessary or over-engineered procedures are seen as bureaucratic obstacles, which are to be avoided where possible
- There is no improvement in IT services due to a fundamental lack of understanding about what the relevant processes should provide, what the appropriate performance indicators are, and how processes can be controlled
- Improvement in the provision of services and cost reductions are insufficiently visible, because no baseline data was available for comparison and/or the wrong targets were identified
- A successful implementation requires the involvement and commitment of personnel at all levels in the organisation, particularly the executives and the senior management teams; leaving the development of the process structures to a specialist department may isolate that department in the organisation and it may set a direction that is not accepted by other departments
- If there is insufficient investment in appropriate training and support tools, justice will not be done to the processes and the service will not be improved; additional resources and personnel may be needed in the short term if the organisation is already overloaded by routine IT service management activities which may not be using "best practices"

2.5 Service Lifecycle: concept and overview

The information provision role and system has grown and changed since the launch of ITIL version 2 (between 2000 and 2002). IT supports and is part of an increasing number of goods and services. In the business world, the information provision role has changed as well: the role of the IT organisation role is no longer just supporting, but has become the baseline for the creation of business value.

ITIL intends to include and provide insight into the new role of IT in all its complexity and dynamics. To that end, a new service management approach has been chosen that does not centre on processes, but focuses on the Service Lifecycle.

Basic concepts
Before we describe the Service Lifecycle, we need to define some basic concepts.

Best practice
ITIL is presented as a best practice. This is an approach or method that has proven itself in practice. These best practices can be a solid backing for organisations that want to improve their IT services. In such cases, the best thing to do is to select a generic standard or method that is accessible to everyone, ITIL, CobiT®, CMMI, PRINCE2®, and ISO/IEC 20000, for example. One of the benefits of these freely accessible generic

standards is that they can be applied to several real-life environments and situations. There is also ample training available for open standards. This makes it much easier to train personnel.

Another source for best practice is proprietary knowledge. A disadvantage of this kind of knowledge is that it may be customised for the context and needs of a specific organisation. Therefore, it may be difficult to adopt or replicate and it may not be as effective in use.

Service

A service is about creating value for the customer. ITIL defines a service as follows:

> *"A service is a means of delivering value to customers by facilitating outcomes customers want to achieve without the ownership of specific costs and risks."*

The following table provides further explanations regarding the above definition.

Table 2.3 Definition of key terms in the service definition

Means:	The actual "physical" product the customer can actually see, touch, or use
Value:	The customer defines value based on desired business outcomes, their preferences and their perceptions
Outcome:	The business activity or result to be used by the business or delivered to the external customer.
Specific costs:	The customer does not want to worry about all costs regarding the end-to-end provision of the service. The customer prefers to consider IT as a utility which is a more predictable expense.
Specific risks:	The IT organisation takes on most of the risks on behalf of the customer allowing the latter to focus on their core business competencies.

Outcomes are possible from the performance of tasks, and they are limited by a number of constraints. Services enhance performance and reduce the pressure of constraints. This increases the chances of the desired outcomes being realised.

Value

Value is the core of the service concept. From the perspective of the IT organisation value consists of two core components: utility and warranty. Utility is what the customer receives, and warranty is how it is provided. The concepts utility and warranty are described in the section "Service Strategy".

Service management

ITIL defines service management as follows:

> *"Service management is a set of specialised organisational capabilities for providing value to customers in the form of services.*
>
> *Service provider: An organisation supplying services to one or more internal or external customers."*

Service management is also a body of knowledge through all of the existing books, whitepapers, articles, studies, and conferences. It is also a professional practice based on proven practices which includes multiple frameworks and methodologies

Systems

ITIL's definition of a system is:

> *"A system is a group of, interrelating, or interdependent components that form a unified ensemble, operating together for a common purpose."*

Feedback and learning are two key aspects in the performance of systems; they turn processes, functions, and organisations into dynamic systems. Feedback can lead to learning and growth, not only within a process, but also within an organisation in its entirety.

Within a process, for instance, the feedback about the performance of one cycle is, in its turn, input for the next process cycle. Within organisations, there can be feedback between processes, functions, and lifecycle phases. Behind this feedback is the common goal: the customer's objectives.

Functions and processes

It is of the utmost importance for anyone in an organisation, especially in the IT organisation, to understand the difference between a function and a process.

> A **function** is a subdivision of an organisation that is specialised in fulfilling a specified type of work, and is responsible for specific end results. Functions are semi-autonomous groupings with capabilities and resources that are required for their performance and results. They have their own set of tasks, roles, and areas of responsibility as well as their own body of knowledge.

What is a process?

> A **process** is a structured set of activities designed to accomplish a defined objective. Processes result in a goal-oriented change, and utilise feedback for self-enhancing and self-corrective actions. Processes simply group together related activities to simplify and unify their execution and accomplishment.

Processes possess the following characteristics:

Table 2.4 The four characteristics of processes

Measurable	They are measurable because it is possible to set specific targets related to the process performance and measure against them: i.e.: they are performance-oriented
Specific results	They produce specific results In the form of defined outputs at the right time and the right level of quality
Customers and/or stakeholders	They provide results to identified customers and/or stakeholders
Respond to specific trigger	They respond to specific triggers. A process is indeed continual and iterative, but it always originating from a certain identified trigger.

For some people, it may be difficult to differentiate between a function and a process. The difficulty arises when an organisation already has a group of people called by the name of a process. This group is usually dedicated primarily to the execution of what appears to be a single process. However, every group of people is involved in the execution of process activities.

Basically, in and of themselves, processes do nothing. People (and tools) execute the activities of various processes.

Based on the above definitions, a function (group of people) performs the activities of various processes. A good example of a function is a service desk; a good example of a process is change management.

A poor coordination between functions combined with an inward focus leads to the rise of silos. This does not benefit the success of the organisation. Processes run through the hierarchical structure of functions; functions often share many processes. This is how processes contribute to an ever improved coordination between functions.

The Service Lifecycle
ITIL approaches service management from the lifecycle of a service. The Service Lifecycle is an organisation model providing insight into:
• The way service management is structured
• The way the various lifecycle components are linked to each other
• The impact that changes in one component will have on other components and on the entire lifecycle system

ITIL focuses on the Service Lifecycle, and the way service management components are linked. Each phase of the lifecycle describes the processes most relevant to that phase.

The Service Lifecycle consists of five phases. Each core volume describes one of these phases:

Table 2.5 The five stages of the service lifecycle

Service Strategy	The phase of defining the guidelines for creating business value and achieving and maintaining a strategic advantage
Service Design	The phase of designing and developing appropriate IT services, including architecture, processes, systems and tools for ITSM, measures and metrics, policy and documents, in order to meet current and future business requirements
Service Transition	The phase of planning and managing the realisation of new and modified services according to customer specifications
Service Operation	The phase of managing and fulfilling all activities required to provide and support services, in order to ensure value for the customer and the service provider
Continual Service Improvement	The phase of continual improvement of the effectiveness and efficiency of IT services against business requirements

Service Strategy is the axis of the Service Lifecycle (Figure 2.2) that "binds" all other phases. This phase defines perspective, position, plans, patterns, and policies. The phases Service Design, Service Transition, and Service Operation transform the strategy into reality; their continual theme is adjustment and change. The Continual Service Improvement phase stands for learning and improving, and embraces all phases. This phase analyses and initiates improvement programs and projects, and prioritises them based on the strategic objectives of the organisation.

The Service Lifecycle is a combination of many perspectives on the reality of organisations. This offers more flexibility and control.

The dominant theoretical pattern in the Service Lifecycle is the succession of Service Strategy to Service Design, to Service Transition and to Service Operation, and then, through Continual Service Improvement, back to Service Strategy, and so on. In practice, all phases occur iteratively for the management of a particular service. Moreover, the cycle encompasses many concurrent patterns as organisations already have services in stages. All organisations have services at the concept/idea stage, while some are being designed (either new or modified), some are in transition, some are in operation, and some are being investigated for improvement opportunities.

Regardless of tasks, roles, or responsibilities all IT personnel should focus on the service lifecycle first, and foremost. In order to accomplish that they will have to use a process approach to their day-to-day activities; this will include dealing with various technologies and applications. It is important for all IT personnel, including management, to understand what the present deliverables are. At different times, people are involved with various processes in all five phases. More details are provided later in this book.

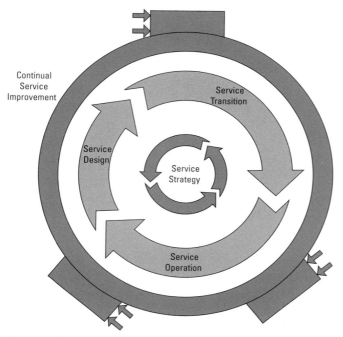

Figure 2.2 The service lifecycle
Source: The Cabinet Office

ITIL Library
The IT Infrastructure Library[2] (ITIL) encompasses the following components:

Core Library – the five Service Lifecycle publications:
- Service Strategy
- Service Design
- Service Transition
- Service Operation
- Continual Service Improvement

Each book covers a phase from the Service Lifecycle and encompasses various processes. The processes are always described in detail in the book in which they find their key application.

---

2   The use of the complete definition for the ITIL acronym has been discontinued.

3 Introduction to service management

3.1 Service management as a practice

Before we define what a service is, a few terms need to be defined first. The difficulty with trying to describe terms in a framework is their circular nature. As a term is defined, it often introduces terms yet undefined.

Utility and warranty

From the customer's point of view, value is subjective. Although at its core value consists of achieving business objectives, it is influenced by the customer's perceptions and preferences. From a service provider point of view, the value of a service is created by combining two primary elements: utility (fitness for purpose) and warranty (fitness for use). These two elements work together to achieve the desired outcomes upon which the customer and the business base their perceptions of a service.

The value of a service can be considered to be the level to which that service meets a customer's expectations. It is often measured by how much the customer is willing to pay for the service, rather than the cost to the service provider of providing the service or any other intrinsic attribute of the service itself.

Utility is the functionality offered by a product or service to meet a particular need. Utility can be summarised as 'what the service does', or 'fit for purpose'. Utility refers to those aspects of a service that contribute to tasks associated with achieving outcomes; the removal of constraints and an increase in performance.

Warranty is an assurance that a product or service will meet its agreed requirements. Warranty refers to the ability of a service to be available when needed, to provide the

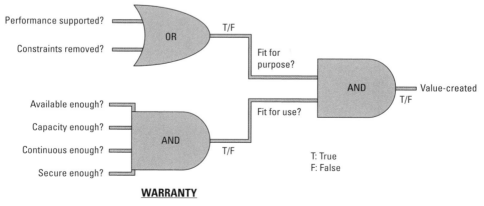

Figure 3.1 Services: designed, built and delivered with both utility and warranty

Source: The Cabinet Office

required capacity, and to provide the required reliability in terms of continuity and security. Warranty can be summarised as 'how the service is delivered' or 'fit for use'.

Services and service management

A service is a means of delivering value to customers by facilitating outcomes customers want to achieve without the ownership of specific costs and risks. To increase the probability of the desired outcomes, services enhance the performance of associated tasks and reduce the effect of various constraints.

Outcome: The result of carrying out an activity, following a process, or delivering an IT service etc. The term is used to refer to intended results, as well as to actual results.

Service: A means of delivering value to customers by facilitating outcomes customers want to achieve without the ownership of specific costs and risks.

IT service: A service provided by an IT service provider. An IT service is made up of a combination of information technology, people, and processes.

Services can be discussed in terms of how they relate to one another and their customers, and can be classified as core, enabling or enhancing.

Core services: delivers the basic outcomes desired by one or more customers. The core services solidify the customer's value proposition and provide the basis for the continued optimisation of the service thus leading to customer satisfaction.

Enabling services: are services required for the successful delivery of a core service. Although enabling services may or may not be visible to the customer, the customer does not perceive them as services in their own right but as being component of the core service.

Enhancing services: are services that are added to a core service to make it more exciting or enticing to the customer. Although enhancing services are non-essential for the successful delivery of a core service, they add value to the core service.

To achieve economies of scales as well as increasing cost effectiveness, services are often "bundled" or "grouped" together. The service provider thus offers various *service packages*. A service package is a collection of two or more services (that can consist of a combination of core services, enabling services and enhancing services) which have been combined to help deliver specific business outcomes.

A service or a service package can be offered with different levels of utility and warranty to create service options. These different service options are called *service level packages*.

Service management

In order to offer and provide services, the service provider must effectively and efficiently manage the entire lifecycle of the services. This can be accomplished by using an approach called service management. Service management is a set of specialised organisational capabilities for providing value to customers in the form of services. Transforming the service provider's capabilities and resources into valuable services is the core of service management. Service management is also a professional practice supported by an extensive body of knowledge, experience, and skills.

> **Service management:** A set of specialised organisational capabilities for providing value to customers in the form of services
>
> **Service provider:** An organisation supplying services to one or more internal or external customers

IT service management

An IT organisation is, by definition, a service provider. It uses the principles of service management to ensure the successful delivery of the outcomes desired by the customers.

> **IT service management (ITSM):** The implementation and management of quality IT services that meet the needs of the business. IT service management is performed by IT service providers through an appropriate mix of people, process, and information technology.
>
> **IT service provider:** A service provider that provides IT services to internal or external customers.

The IT service provider must utilise ITSM effectively and efficiently. By managing IT from the business perspective (as opposed to simply being a technology broker) the IT service provider will generate higher organisational performance and create greater value.

Service providers

There are three main types of service provider. Although almost all aspects of service management apply equally to all types of service provider, there are certain aspects that take on different meanings depending on the type of provider. These aspects include terms such as customers, contracts, competition, market spaces, revenue, and strategy.

Table 3.1 Service provider types

Type I **Internal service provider**	An internal service provider that is embedded within a business unit. There may be several Type I service providers within an organisation
Type II **Shared services unit**	An internal service provider that provides shared IT services to more than one business unit
Type III **External service provider**	A service provider that provides IT services to external customers

Stakeholders in service management

A stakeholder is an individual or a group that has a vested interest in an organisation, project, service, etc. Of interest to the stakeholders are such service management deliverables as activities, targets, resources, etc.

Table 3.2 Stakeholders

Customers	Those who buy goods or services. The customer of an IT service provider is the person or group who defines and agrees the service level targets.
Users	Those who use the service on a day-to-day basis. Users are distinct from customers, as some customers do not use the IT service directly.
Suppliers	Third parties responsible for supplying goods or services that are required to deliver IT services
Internal customers	These are customers who work for the same organisation as the IT service provider. Any internal department is an internal customer of the IT organisation because it uses IT services.
External customers	These are customers who work for a different organisation from the IT service provider. External customers typically purchase services from the service provider by means of a legally binding contract or agreement. External customers may also be customers of the organisation. They directly interact with the technological aspect of the service.

Assets, resources, and capabilities

The use of assets forms the basis for the relationship between service providers and their customers. Each relationship involves an interaction between the assets of each party.

Asset: Any resource or capability

Customer asset: Any resource or capability used by a customer to achieve a business outcome

Service asset: Any resource or capability used by a service provider to deliver services to a customer.

Without customer assets, there is no basis for defining the value of a service. The performance of customer assets is therefore a primary concern of service management.

Resources and capabilities are two types of asset used by both service providers and customers. Resources are direct inputs for production; they are "consumed" or "modified". Capabilities represent an organisation's ability to coordinate, control, and deploy the resources.

Processes

Process: A process is a structured set of activities designed to accomplish a specific objective. A process takes one or more defined inputs and turns them into defined outputs.

Processes define actions, dependencies, and sequence. Process characteristics include:

Table 3.3 Process characteristics

Measurability	We are able to measure the process in a relevant manner. It is performance-driven. Managers want to measure cost, quality and other variables while practitioners are concerned with duration and productivity.
Specific results	The reason a process exists is to deliver a specific result. This result must be individually identifiable and countable.
Customers	Every process delivers its primary results to a customer or stakeholder. Customers may be internal or external to the organisation, but the process must meet their expectations.
Responsiveness to specific triggers	While a process may be on-going or iterative, it should be traceable to a specific trigger.

A process is organised around a set of objectives. The main outputs from the process should be driven by the objectives and should include process measurements (metrics), reports, and process improvement.

3.2 Organising for service management

There is no single best way to organise service management, and best practices described in ITIL need to be tailored to suit individual organisations and situations.

Functions
A function is a team or group of people and the tools or other resources they use to carry out one or more processes or activities.

ITIL defines four functions as follows.

Table 3.4 The four functions

Service desk	This function acts as the single point of contact and communication to the users and a point of coordination for several IT groups and processes
IT operations management	This function executes the daily operational activities needed to manage IT services and the supporting IT infrastructure. IT operations management has two sub-functions; IT operations control and facilities management.
Technical management	This function provides detailed technical skills and resources needed to support the on-going operation of IT services and the management of the IT infrastructure. Technical management also plays an important role in the design, testing, release, and improvement of IT services.
Application management	This function is responsible for managing applications throughout their lifecycle. The application management function supports and maintains operational applications. Application management also plays an important role in the design, testing, release, and improvement of IT services.

Roles

Roles are often confused with job titles. However, they are not the same. Each organisation must define appropriate job titles and job descriptions to suit their needs. Individuals holding these job titles can perform one or more of the required roles.

Role: A role is a set of responsibilities, activities, and authorities granted to a person or team. A role is defined in a process or function. One person or team may have multiple roles.

An organisation needs to define clearly the roles and responsibilities required to undertake the processes and activities involved in each lifecycle stage. Roles are assigned to individuals, and a structure of teams, groups, or functions.

Table 3.5 Organisational structure breakdown

Group	A group is a number of people who are similar in some way
Team	A team is a more formal type of group. These are people who work together to achieve a common objective, but not necessarily in the same organisational structure
Department	Departments are formal hierarchical, organisational-reporting structures which exist to perform a specific set of defined activities on an on-going basis
Division	A division refers to a number of departments that have been grouped together, often by geography or product line

Organisational culture and behaviour

Organisational culture is the set of shared values and norms that control the interactions between a service provider and all stakeholders, including customers, users, suppliers, internal personnel etc. An organisation's values are desired modes of behaviour that affect its culture. Examples of organisational values include high standards, customer care, respecting tradition and authority, acting cautiously and conservatively, and being frugal.

Constraints such as governance, standards, values, capabilities, resources, and ethics play a significant role in shaping and/or influencing the culture and behaviour of an organisation. The management structure and styles may impact positively, or negatively, the organisational culture. Organisational structures and management styles are also contributing factors to the behaviour of people, process, products, and partners.

Adopting service management practices and adapting them to suit the organisation will affect the culture and it is important to prepare people with effective communication plans, policies, procedures, education, training, coaching, and mentoring to achieve the desired the new attitudes and behaviours.

While improving the quality of their services, organisations will eventually be confronted with their current organisational culture. The organisation will have to identify and address any changes to this culture as a consequence of the overall improvement initiative. The organisational culture, or corporate culture, refers to the way in which people deal with each other in the organisation; the way in which decisions are made and implemented; and the attitude of employees to their work, customers, service providers, superiors, and colleagues.

Culture, which depends on the standards and values of the people in the organisation, cannot be controlled, but it can be influenced. Influencing the culture of an organisation requires leadership in the form of a clear and consistent policy, as well as a supportive personnel policy.

The corporate culture can have a major influence on the provision of IT services. Businesses value innovation in different ways. In a stable organisation, where the culture places little value on innovation, it will be difficult to adjust its IT services in line with changes in the organisation of the customer. If the IT department is unstable, then a culture which values change can pose a serious threat to the quality of its services. In that case, a "free for all" culture can develop where many uncontrolled changes lead to a large number of faults.

Processes, projects, programs and portfolios

Activities can be managed from a process perspective, from an organisational hierarchy (line) perspective, from a project perspective, or from any combination of these three. Organisations that utilise only one of these management systems seldom realise the greater potential synergies of leveraging any combination of the approaches. The practical choice often depends upon history, culture, available skills and competences, and personal preferences. The optimum choice may be entirely different, but the requirements for applying this optimum may be hard to realise and vary in time.

There are no "hard and fast laws" for the way an organisation should combine processes, projects, and programs. However, it is generally accepted that there are some consequences attached to modern practices in IT service organisations, since the most widely accepted approach to service management is based on process management. This means that whenever the organisation works with projects or programs, it should have established how these approaches work together.

The practical relationship between projects and processes is determined by the relative position of both in terms of "leading principles for the management of the organisation": if projects are considered more important than processes, then decisions on projects will overrule decisions on processes; as a consequence, the organisation will not be able to implement a stable set of processes. If it is the other way around, with projects only able to run within the constraints of agreed processes, then project management will be a discipline that will have to adapt to new boundaries and definitions (e.g. since projects always change something from A to B, they will most likely fall under the regime of change, release and deployment Management).

The most suitable solution is dependent upon the understanding of the role of IT service management in the organisation. To be able to find a solution for this management challenge, it is recommended that a common understanding of processes, projects, programs, and even portfolios is created. The following definitions may be used:

Process – A process is a structured set of activities designed to accomplish a defined objective.

Project – A project is a temporary organisation, with people and other assets required to achieve an objective.

Program – A program consists of a number of projects and activities that are planned and managed together to achieve an overall set of related objectives.

Portfolio – A portfolio is a set of projects and/or programs, which are not necessarily related, brought together for the sake of control, coordination, and optimisation of the portfolio in its totality.

Note: In ITIL, a service portfolio is the complete set of services that are managed by a service provider.

There are also other portfolios such as the customer portfolio, the customer agreement portfolio, the application portfolio, etc.

Since the portfolio/program/project grouping is a hierarchical set of essential project resources, the issue can be downscaled to that of a relationship between a project and a process.

The most elementary difference between a process and a project is the one-off character of a project, versus the continuous character of the process. If a project has achieved its objectives, it means the end of the project. Processes can be run many times, both in parallel and in sequence. The nature of a process is aimed at its repeatable character: processes are defined only in case of a repeatable string of activities that are important enough to be standardised and optimised.

Projects are aimed at changing a situation A into a situation B. This can involve a simple string of activities, but it can also be a very complex series of activities. Other elements of importance for projects include money, time, quality, organisation, and information. Project structures are normally used only if at least one of these elements is of considerable value.

Actually, projects are just ways of organising a specific change in a situation. In that respect they have a resemblance with processes. It is often a matter of focus: processes focus at the specific sequence of activities, the decisions taken at certain milestone stages, and the quality of the activities involved. Processes are continuously instantiated and repeated, and use the same approach each time. Projects focus more at the time and money constraints, in terms of resources spent on the change and the projects end, and projects vary much more than processes.

A very practical way of combining the benefits of both management systems might be as follows:
- Processes set the scene for how specific series of activities are performed.
- Projects can be used to transform situation A into situation B, and always refer to a change.
- If the resources (time, money, or other) involved in a specific process require the level of attention that is normally applied in a project, then (part of) the process activities can be performed as a project, but always under the control of the process: if changes are performed, using project management techniques, the agreed change management policies still apply.

This would allow organisations to maintain a continuous customer focus and apply a process approach to optimise this customer focus, and at the same time benefit from the high level of resource control that can be achieved when using project management techniques.

The service portfolio

The service portfolio is the complete set of services that is managed by a service provider. It provides information regarding the commitments and investments across all customers and market spaces. The service portfolio includes present contractual obligations, and description of services at the concept, development and improvement stages of the lifecycle. A link to third-party services may be included as they are often a key component part of the service offerings.

It is a three parts database or structured document.

Table 3.6 The three sections of the service portfolio

Service pipeline	All services that are under consideration or development, but are not yet available to customers. The service pipeline provides a business view of possible future services. The pipeline is not normally available to customers.
Service catalogue	All live IT services, including those available for deployment. It is the only part of the service portfolio published to customers, and is used to support the sale and delivery of IT services.
Retired services	All services that have been phased out or retired. Retired services are normally not available to new customers or for "ordering". Retired services are sometimes known as "legacy systems".

Service providers often find it useful to distinguish customer-facing services from supporting services:

Table 3.7 The two major types of services

Customer-facing services	The IT services which are visible to the customer. These services support the customer's business processes and facilitate one or more desired business outcomes. An analogy is to consider them "front-end" services.
Supporting services	IT services that support or 'underpin' the customer-facing services. These are typically not visible to the customer, but are essential to the delivery of customer-facing IT services. An analogy is to consider them "back-office" services.

Knowledge management

Quality data, information and knowledge enable people to perform process activities. It supports the flow of information between service lifecycle stages and processes. It is the responsibility of the knowledge management process in understanding, defining, establishing, and maintaining data and information.

A central repository for the data and information in the form of a tool is desirable. This tool is known as the service knowledge management system (SKMS). In reality, the SKMS is a federated model consisting of multiple tools and repositories using numerous platforms and file structures and formats. A four layers model is a popular approach to represent logically the SKMS. The bottom (first) layer represents the "raw" data from all platforms, file structures, and formats. The second layer represents the information which provides context to the raw data. The third layer represents knowledge in the form of different views which are then analysed for trends, and cause and effect, for example. The analysis determines the "why" of something. Finally the fourth layer represent the presentation layer in the form of different views for various audiences such as operational, tactical and strategic personnel.

3.3 Governance and management systems

Governance

Governance is the single overarching area that ties IT and the business together. Services are only one way of ensuring the organisation is able to execute and achieve governance. Governance is what defines the common directions, policies and rules that both the business and IT use to conduct business.

Governance ensures that policies and strategy are actually implemented, and that required processes are complied with. Governance includes defining roles and responsibilities, measuring and reporting, and taking actions to resolve any issues identified.

Governance works to apply a consistent, managed approach at all levels of the organisation. This starts by setting a clear strategy that defines the policies whereby the strategy will be achieved. The policies define boundaries: what is in or out of scope of organisational operations.

Management systems

A system is a number of related components that work together to achieve an overall objective. Systems should be self-regulating for agility and timeliness. In order to accomplish this, the relationships of all components within the system must influence one another for the sake of the whole. Key components of the system are the structure and processes that work together.

A service provider can deliver many benefits (see list below) by understanding the structure, the relationships between components and the effects of changes over time.

- Adaptability to the ever fluctuating needs of customers and markets
- Sustainable performance
- Defined approach to managing services, risks, costs, and value
- Effective and efficient service management
- Less conflict between processes and personnel
- Reduced duplication and bureaucracy

Management system (ISO 9001): the framework of policy, processes, functions, standards, guidelines, and tools that ensures an organisation or part of an organisation can achieve its objectives. An organisation may use multiple management system standards, such as:

Table 3.8 ISO Management systems aligned with ITSM

ISO 9001	Quality management system
ISO 14000	Environmental management system
ISO/IEC 20000	Service management system
ISO/IEC 27001	Information security management system
ISO/IEC 19770	Management system for software asset management
ISO/IEC 31000	Risk management
ISO/IEC 38500	Corporate governance of information technology

ISO/IEC 20000: ISO specification and code of practice for IT service management. ISO/IEC 20000 is aligned with ITIL best practices.

Specialisation and coordination across the lifecycle

A collaborative approach to service management is of utmost importance to an organisation.

An analogy that can be used to illustrate this is a high-performing sport team.
- Every player positions themselves to support the goal of the team
- Every office personnel positions themselves to support the goal of the team
- Each player and each office personnel has a different specialisation that contributes to the whole
- Every player and every office personnel work together toward the same goal of the team
- The team matures over time, taking into account feedback from experience, best practice, current process, and procedures to become an agile high-performing team

Specialisation and coordination are necessary aspects for a successful lifecycle approach. Specialisation combined with coordination helps to manage expertise, improve focus, and reduce overlaps and gaps in processes. Specialisation and coordination together help to create a collaborative and agile organisational architecture that optimises utilisation of assets.

Service management is most effective when people understand both the service lifecycle and the interactions between the various parties involved, the organisation, the customers, the users, and the suppliers.

Process integration across the service lifecycle depends on the understanding by the service owners, the process owners, the process managers, the process practitioners and other stakeholders of:
- The context of purpose, scope, limitations and use of each process
- The strategies, policies and standards influencing and governing the service management and the processes
- The levels of authority, accountability, and responsibility of those involved in each process
- The information flow between integrated processes, who produces what and why and how it will be used

3.4 Monitoring and control

Monitoring and control of services is based on a continuous cycle of monitoring, reporting, and initiating action. This cycle is crucial to providing, supporting, and improving services.

Introduction

Basic concepts

Three terms play a leading role in monitoring and control:
- Monitoring
- Reporting
- Control

Monitoring: refers to the observation of a situation to discover changes that occur over time.

Reporting: refers to the analysis, production, and distribution of the output of the activity that is being monitored.

Control: refers to the management of the usefulness or behaviour of a device, system, or service. There are three conditions for control:
1. *The action must ensure that the behaviour conforms to a defined standard or norm*
2. *The conditions leading to the action must be defined, understood and confirmed*
3. *The action must be defined, approved, and suitable for these conditions*

The monitoring/control loop

The best-known model for the description of control is the monitoring/control loop. Although it is a simple model it has many complex applications in IT service management. In this section we describe the basic concepts of the model. Next we will show how important these concepts are for the service management lifecycle. Figure 3.2 reflects the basic principles of control.

This cycle measures an activity and its benefits by means of a pre-defined norm or standard to determine whether the results are within the target values for performance or quality. If this is not the case, action must be taken to improve the situation or resume the normal performance.

There are two types of monitoring/control loops:
- **Open loop systems** – are designed for a specific activity, irrespective of the environmental conditions; making a backup, for instance, can be initiated at a specified moment and be completed regardless of other conditions.
- **Closed loop systems** – Monitoring of an environment and responding to changes in this environment; if, in a network, the network transactions exceed a certain number, the control system will redirect the "traffic" via a backup circuit in order to regulate the network transactions.

Figure 3.3 shows a sample **complex monitoring/control loop**: a process that consists of three important activities. Each activity has an input and output and in turn this output is the input for the next activity. Every activity is controlled by its own monitoring/control loop with the aid of a series of norms for that specific activity.

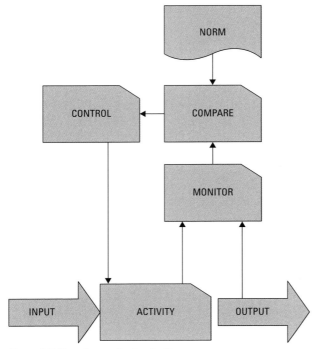

Figure 3.2 Sample monitor/control loop
Source: The Cabinet Office

A coordinating monitoring/control loop monitors the entire process and ensures that all norms are suitable and are being complied with.

The monitoring/control loop concept can be used to manage:
• The performance of activities in a process or procedure
• The effectiveness of the process or procedure as a whole
• The performance of a device or a series of devices

Answer the following questions to determine how the concept of monitoring/control loops can be used in service management:
• How do we define what we need to monitor?
• How do we monitor (manually or automated)?
• What is a normal process?
• What do we depend on for a normal process?
• What happens before we receive the input?
• How often do we need to measure?

Figure 3.4 shows a sample **IT service management monitoring/control loop** and shows how the control of a process or the components of that process can be used to provide a service.

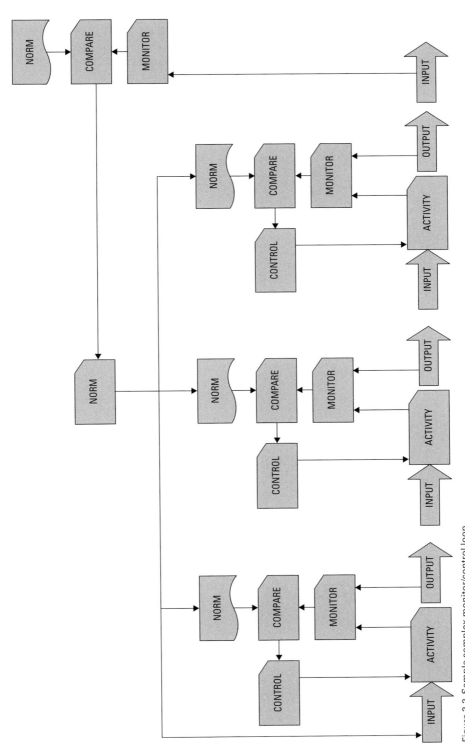

Figure 3.3 Sample complex monitor/control loop
Source: The Cabinet Office

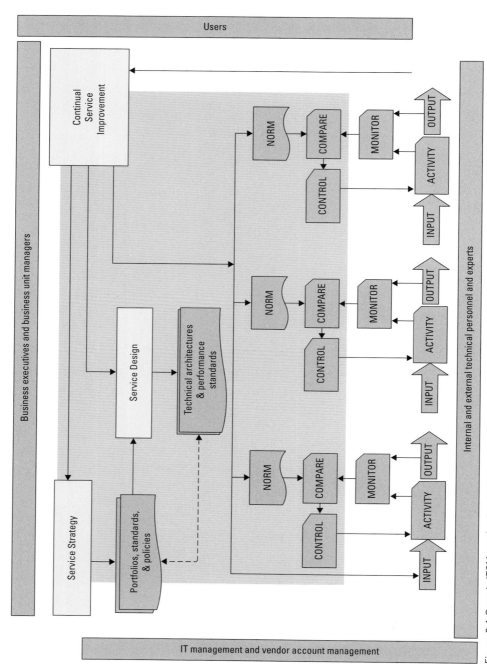

Figure 3.4 Sample ITSM monitor/control loop
Source: The Cabinet Office

There are two levels of monitoring:

- **Internal monitoring and control** – focuses on activities and items that take place within a team or department, for instance a service desk manager who monitors the number of calls to determine how many members of personnel are needed to answer the telephones
- **External monitoring and control** – the server management team monitors (on behalf of other groups) the CPU performance on important servers and keeps the workload under control; this allows essential applications to perform within the target values set by the application management

This distinction is important. If Service Operation focuses only on internal monitoring the infrastructure is well organised, but the organisation has no idea what the quality of the services is or how they can improve this quality. If the organisation focuses only on external monitoring it understands how bad the quality of the service is, but it does not know what causes this or how it can change this. In practice, most organisations use a combination of internal and external monitoring, but in many cases they are not linked.

Monitoring without control is irrelevant and ineffective. Monitoring must always be aimed at achieving the service and operational objectives. If, therefore, there is no clear reason for the monitoring of a system or service, there should be no monitoring.

In order for an organisation to determine what it wants to monitor, therefore, it must first define the desired outcome: **monitoring and control objectives**. Ideally this process should start with the definition of *Service Level Requirements*. These will specify how the customers and users measure the quality of the service. In addition, these Service Level Requirements provide the input for the Service Design processes. Availability management, for instance, will determine how the infrastructure must be configured to achieve the fewest possible disruptions.

An important part in determining what Service Operation will be monitoring and how it will get the processes under control is identifying the stakeholders of each service. A stakeholder can be defined as being anyone who has an interest in IT services being successfully supplied and received. Each stakeholder will consider, from their own perspective, what is necessary to provide or receive an IT service. Service Operation must know what these perspectives are in order to determine what needs to be monitored and what needs to be done with the output.

Tools
There are different types of monitoring tools, whereby the situation determines which **type of monitoring** is used:
- **Active versus passive monitoring**:
  - *Active monitoring* refers to the continual "interrogation" of a device or system in order to determine its status.

- ○ *Passive monitoring* is more commonly known and refers to generating and passing on events to a device or monitoring agent.
- **Reactive versus proactive monitoring**:
  - ○ *Reactive monitoring* is designed to request an action after a certain type of event or disruption.
  - ○ *Proactive monitoring* is used to trace patterns of events that indicate that a system or device may break down. Proactive monitoring is generally used in more mature environments, where these patterns can be detected earlier.
- **Continuous measuring versus exception-based measuring**:
  - ○ *Continuous measuring* is aimed at the real-time monitoring of a system to ensure that it complies with a certain performance norm.
  - ○ *Exception-based* measuring does not measure the current performance of a service or system, but discovers and reports exceptions. An example is the generation of an event if a transaction is not completed. It is used for less essential systems or for systems where costs are important.
- **Performance versus output** – There is an important distinction between reporting on the performance of components, or personnel versus reporting on the *output* – service quality objectives – that have been achieved.

Metrics

It is important that organisations have robust measuring techniques and values that support their objectives. In this context, the following concepts are relevant:

- **Measuring** – Refers to all techniques that evaluate the scope, dimension, or capacity of an item in relation to a standard or unit. Measuring is only useful when it is possible to measure the actual output of a system, function, or process against a standard or desired level. For instance, a server must be capable of processing a minimum of 100 standard transactions per minute.
- **Metrics** – Concern the quantitative, periodic evaluation of a process, system, or function, together with the procedures and tools that are used for this evaluation, and the procedures for interpreting them. This definition is important because it not only specifies what must be measured, but also how the measuring must be done, what the acceptable lower and upper performance limits are and what actions are necessary in the case of normal performance or an exception.
- **Key Performance Indicators (KPIs)** – Refer to a specific, agreed performance level to measure the effectiveness of an organisation or process. KPIs are unique to each organisation and are related to specific input, output, and activities.

4 Functions

4.1 Basic concepts

ITIL defines a function as *"a team or group of people and the tools they use to carry out one or more processes or activities"*; for example, the service desk.

Additionally, the term function can be used to mean:

An intended purpose of a configuration item, person, team, process, or IT service; for example, one function of an email service may be to store outgoing mails, one function of a business process may be to dispatch goods to customers
To perform the intended purpose correctly, "the computer is functioning"

However, for the purpose of this book, the former definition (highlighted above) will be used.

ITIL defines a process as *"a structured set of activities designed to accomplish a defined objective"*.

In and of themselves, processes do nothing; people and tools execute the activities of processes.

It is important to note that although some organisations may have departments with the same name as an ITIL process these people are unlikely to execute only the activities of that process. Each function is an organisation in itself and has a hierarchical structure which includes strategic, tactical, and operational activities. This implies that each function has personnel primarily involved in strategic, or tactical, or operational activities.

Groups, teams, departments, and divisions
The Service Operation book refers, with various terms, to the way people are organised to fulfil processes or activities:

Table 4.1 Definitions for units of people

Group	A group is a number of people who are similar in some way
Team	A team is a more formal type of group. These are people who work together to achieve a common objective, but not necessarily in the same organisational structure
Department	Departments are formal hierarchical, organisational-reporting structures which exist to perform a specific set of defined activities on an on-going basis
Division	A division refers to a number of departments that have been grouped together, often by geography or product line

Achieving balance in Service Operation

Procedures and activities take place in a continually changing environment. This can give rise to a conflict between maintaining the current situation and reacting to changes in the business and technical environment. Consequently, one of the key roles of Service Operation is handling these conflicts. It must try to achieve a balance between conflicting priorities. (See Figure 4.1)

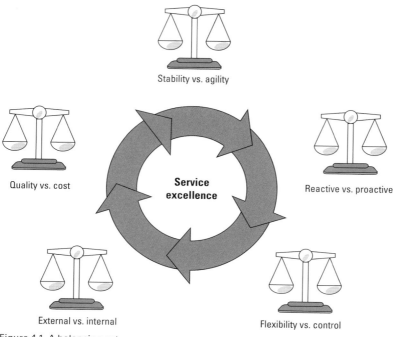

Figure 4.1 A balancing act
Source: The Cabinet Office

The internal IT view versus the external business view

The view that IT is part of IT services (the external business view) is the opposite of the idea that IT is a series of technological components (the internal IT view). This causes the key conflict in all phases of the IT service management lifecycle.

The external IT view is about the way users and customers experience services. The internal IT view is about how the IT organisation manages IT components and systems to provide services.

Both views are necessary to provide services. The organisation that is exclusively focused on business requirements without thinking about how they will provide services will eventually only make promises they are unable to live up to. An organisation that is exclusively focused on internal systems, without thinking about which services they will support, will eventually support expensive services that are of little use. It is a matter of achieving a balance between these two extremes.

Stability versus responsiveness

On the one hand, Service Operation must ensure that the IT infrastructure is stable and available. At the same time, Service Operation must recognise that business and IT requirements change.

Some changes take place gradually and can be planned. They do not jeopardise stability. The platform functionality, performance, and architecture will change over a number of years.

However, other changes can happen very quickly, sometimes under extreme pressure. For example, a business department wins a contract that suddenly requires additional IT services and more capacity.

To achieve an IT organisation in which stability and response are in balance:

- Invest in adaptable technologies and processes, for example, virtual server and application technology.
- Build a strong service level management process that is active from the Service Design phase to the Continual Service Improvement phase of the IT Service Management Lifecycle.
- Encourage integration between service level management and the other Service Design processes, so that business requirements match the operational IT activities and components of the IT infrastructure.
- Initiate changes in the IT Service Management Lifecycle as soon as possible; they can be taken into account in the functional and management requirements.
- Involve IT as soon as possible in the change process in case of business changes; this helps ensure scalability, consistency, and IT services that include the business changes.
- Have the Service Operation teams provide input for the design and the refining of architecture and IT services.
- Implement and use service level management to prevent the business and IT managers and personnel from negotiating agreements informally.

Service quality versus service costs

Service Operation must provide IT services to customers and the users continually, and to the agreed level. At the same time, they have to keep the costs and use of resources at an optimal level. Many organisations are strongly pressured to enhance the service quality, while they have to reduce costs.

Achieving an optimal balance between costs and quality is a key task of service management. Many organisations leave this to the Service Operations team, who lack the authority, but the Service Strategy and Service Design phase are more appropriate for this. Service level requirements and a clear understanding of the goals and dangers of service business can help ensure that the service is provided with the right costs.

Being reactive versus being proactive

A reactive organisation does nothing until an external stimulus forces it to act. For instance, it only develops a new application when a new business requirement arrives. A proactive organisation always looks for new opportunities to improve the current situation. Usually, proactive behaviour is viewed positively, because it enables the organisation to keep a competitive advantage in a changing environment. However, an over-proactive attitude can be very costly, and can create distracted personnel. For an optimal result, reactive and proactive behaviour must be well-balanced.

Providing a service

All Service Operation personnel members must be aware that they are providing a service to the business. Do not only train personnel to provide and support IT services, but also teach them the attitude with which they should provide these services.

Involving operational personnel in design, transition and CSI

It is very important that the Service Operation personnel are involved in Service Design, Service Transition and Continual Service Improvement, and, if necessary, in Service Strategy.

One way to achieve a balance in Service Operation is an effective set of Service Design processes. This will provide IT operations management with:
* A clear definition of IT service goals and performance criteria
* A link between IT service specifications and the IT infrastructure performance
* A definition of the operational performance requirements
* Service and technology planning
* The ability to model the impact of changes in technology and business requirements
* An appropriate cost model to review the return on investment (ROI), and cost reduction strategies

Operational health

An organisation can determine its operational health by isolating some "vital characteristics" of devices or services that are essential to the execution of a critical business function. Consider, for example, the bandwidth usage on a network segment, or the memory usage on an important server. If the value of these characteristics lies within the normal system range, the system is sound, and will not require any additional attention.

From time to time though, it is necessary to check the systems thoroughly for problems that do not directly affect the vital characteristics. The operational soundness also depends on the ability to prevent incidents and problems. Invest in a reliable and well-maintainable infrastructure for this. Create a solid availability design and practice proactive problem management.

Finally, the operational health depends on the ability to identify and effectively locate defects once they have occurred, so that they have little impact on the service. This also requires effective incident and problem management processes.

Communication

People, process, partners, and technology provide the main "machinery" of any organisation, but they only work well if the machine is oiled: **communication** is an essential element in any organisation. If the people do not know about the processes or use the wrong instructions or tools, the output may not be as anticipated. By the way, communication is a closed-loop system (two-way street, so to speak). It requires a feedback mechanism in order to be successful.

It is often heard from senior business leaders in advertising, articles, and interviews that *"our people are our greatest assets"*. Indeed, people are core assets of any organisation. They need to be in place to perform certain activities or to take decisions, but also because people have the good habit of communicating. When an organisation applies highly detailed instructions for all its activities, it will end up in a bureaucracy. On the other hand, an organisation without any rules will most likely end up in chaos. Whichever balance an organisation is trying to find here, it will always benefit enormously from communication between the people in the organisation. A regular and formal meeting culture will support this, but organisations should not underestimate the important role of informal communication: many projects have been saved by means of a simple chat in the tea room, or in the car park.

Note: It is up to the organisation to decide if they will create a CI type for people or not.

In the author's opinion, people are not configuration items. They are attributes of the document CI called "job description". There already exists a database containing the information about people anyway; it is called the Human Resources database.

Formal structures on communication include:

Table 4.2 Formal communication structures

Reporting	Internal and external reporting, aimed at management or customers, project progress reports, alerts
Meetings	Formal project meetings, regular meetings with specific targets
Online facilities	Email systems, mobile devices, social media, document sharing systems, teleconferencing, and videoconferencing
Notice boards	Near the coffee maker, water cooler, at the entrance of the building, in the company cafeteria/restaurant

IT teams and departments, as well as users, internal customers and all operational teams, indeed all teams at all levels, including project teams must communicate well with each other. The **stakeholders** for communication can thus be found among all managers and employees who are involved in service management, in all the layers of the organisation, and with all customers, users, and service providers. Good communication can prevent problems. All communication must have a particular goal or result. Every team, process and every department must have a clear **communications policy**.

IT service management includes several types of communication, such as:
- Routine operational communication
- Communication between teams
- Performance reports
- Communication during projects
- Communication when there are changes
- Communication in case of exceptions
- Communication in case of emergencies
- Training for new or adapted processes and service designs
- Communication with service production teams regarding service strategies and design

Documentation

IT operation management and all technical and application management teams and departments are involved in recording and maintaining the following documents:
- Process manuals for all the processes they are involved with
- Technical procedure manuals
- Planning documents such as capacity and availability plans
- Service portfolio, customer portfolio
- Work instructions for the service management tools, in order to comply with the reporting requirements

4.2 Management of processes

Every organisation aims to realise its strategy through its perspective, position, patterns, and plans; the four Ps of Service Strategy. These are also referred to as the vision, mission, goals, and objectives of the organisation. As a starting point toward achieving their strategies, organisations define, document and publish policies in an attempt to drive the appropriate attitudes and behaviours of their personnel. Having policies in place is not sufficient. The personnel must undertake the appropriate activities in order to achieve the strategy.

For example, a restaurant will have to purchase fresh ingredients, the chefs will have to work together to provide consistent results, and there should be no major differences in style among the waiting personnel. A restaurant will only be awarded a three-star rating when it manages to provide the same high quality over an extended period of time. This is not always the case: there will be changes among the waiting personnel, a successful approach may not last, and chefs often leave to open their own restaurants. Providing consistently high quality means that the component activities have to be coordinated: the more effectively and more efficiently the kitchen operates, the higher the quality of service that can be provided to the guests.

In the example of the restaurant, appropriate activities include buying vegetables, bookkeeping, ordering publicity material, receiving guests, cleaning tables, peeling potatoes, and making coffee. With just such an unstructured list, something will be left out and personnel will easily become confused. It is therefore a better idea to structure the activities. Preferably these will be structured in such a way as to allow us to see how each group of activities contributes to the objectives of the business, and how they are related to other activities.

Such groups of activities are known as **processes**. If the process structure of an organisation is clearly described, it will show:
- What has to be done
- What the expected inputs and results are
- How we measure whether the processes deliver the expected results
- How the results of one process affect those of another process

Processes can be defined in many ways. Depending upon the objectives of the creator, more or less emphasis will be on specific aspects. For example, a highly detailed process description will allow for a high level of control. Superficial process definitions will illustrate that the creator does not care much about the way in which the steps are executed.

Once the processes are defined, the roles, responsibilities, and people can be assigned to specific aspects, bringing the process to the level of a *procedure*.

Processes
Processes are *internal* affairs for the IT service provider. An organisation that is still trying to gain control of its processes therefore has an **internal focus**. Organisations that focus on gaining control of their systems in order to provide services are still internally focused. The organisation is not ready for an **external focus** until it controls its services and is able to vary them on request. This external focus is required to evolve into that desirable customer-focused organisation.

Because organisations can be in different stages of maturity, IT managers require a broad orientation in their discipline. Most organisations are now working on the introduction of a process-focused or customer-focused approach, or still have to start working on this. Process control is therefore a vital step on the road towards a **mature customer-focused organisation**.

Organisations all around the world require access to good information and best practices concerning the **business processes of IT organisations**. Fortunately, the information regarding service management is now quite abundant.

The **process model** is at least as important as the processes because processes must be deployed in the right relationships to achieve the desired effect of a process-focused approach. There are many different process models available. The experiences gained with these processes and process models in recent years have been documented comprehensively in books, magazines and whitepapers, and have been presented at countless conventions/conferences.

When arranging activities into processes, we do not use the existing allocation of tasks, nor the existing departmental divisions. This is a conscious choice. By opting for a process structure, it often becomes evident that certain activities in the organisation are uncoordinated, duplicated, neglected, or unnecessary.

Instead, we look at the **purpose** of the process and the **relationships** with other processes. A process is a series of activities carried out to convert input into an output, and ultimately into an outcome. The **input** is concerned with the resources being used in the process. The (reported) **output** describes the immediate results of the process, while the **outcome** indicates the long-term results of the process (in terms of meaningful effect). Through **control** activities, we can associate the input and output of each of the processes with **policies and standards** to provide information about the results to be obtained by the process. Control regulates the input and the **throughput** in case the throughput or output parameters are not compliant with these standards and policies. This produces chains of processes that show the input that goes into the organisation and what the result is, and it also monitors points in the chains in order to check the quality of the products and services provided by the organisation.

The standards for the output of each process have to be defined in such a way that the complete chain of processes in the process model meets the corporate objective. If the output of a process meets the defined requirements, then the process is **effective** in transforming its input into its output. To be really effective, the outcome should be taken into consideration rather than merely focusing on the output. If the activities in the process are also carried out with the minimum required effort and cost, then the process is **efficient**. It is the task of process management to use **planning and control** to ensure that processes are executed in an effective and efficient way.

We can study each process separately to optimise its quality. The **process owner** is responsible for the process results. The **process manager** is responsible for the realisation and structure of the process, and reports to the process owner.

The logical combination of activities results in clear transfer points where the quality of processes can be monitored. In the restaurant example, we can separate responsibility for purchasing and cooking, so that the chefs do not have to purchase anything and can concentrate on their core activities.

The management of the organisation can provide control based on the process quality of the process as demonstrated by data from the results of each process. In most cases, the relevant **performance indicators** and standards will already be agreed upon. In this case the process manager can do the day-to-day control of the process. The process owner will assess the results based on a **report** of performance indicators and checks whether the results meet the agreed standard. Without clear indicators, it would be difficult for a process owner to determine whether the process is under control, and if planned improvements are being implemented.

Processes are often described using **procedures** and **work instructions**.

A **procedure** is a specified way to carry out an activity or a process.

A **procedure** describes the "how", and can also describe "who" carries the activities out. A procedure may include stages from different processes. A procedure can vary depending on the organisation.

A set of **work instructions** defines how one or more activities in a procedure should be carried out in detail, using technology or other resources.

ISO/IEC 20000 defines a process *"as a logically related series of activities executed to meet the goals of a defined objective. Processes are composed of two kinds of activities: the activities to realise the purpose (operational activities concerned with the throughput), and the activities to manage these (control activities). The control activities make sure the operational activities (the workflow) are performed in time, in the right order, etc."* (For example, in the processing of changes it is always ensured that a test is performed *before* a release is taken into production and not *afterwards*.)

Processes and departments

As previously mentioned processes do nothing; *people* execute the activities of processes. However, simply defining, and documenting a process will not achieve any results. The process approach must be "sold" to the personnel through various means of communication. In return the personnel must "buy" into the process approach. For this the personnel must display the right attitudes and behaviours. This can only be accomplished if the organisation fosters a process-oriented culture. This means that the organisation must establish a system that rewards and recognises people and groups that provide a set of service- and process-oriented attitudes and behaviours instead of recognising the so-called "heroes".

A process-oriented organisation means the personnel are primarily focused on being proactive instead of reactive. Organisations should recognise there will still be situations requiring a reactive approach. However, these situations should be limited to urgent or emergency situations. Just to be clear, procrastination should not be acceptable because someone prefers to be reactive and be seen as the hero.

Processes should span several departments (teams) in order to adequately measure the end-to-end quality of a service by monitoring the utility and warranty aspects of the service. These aspects include the removal of constraints on the enhancement of performance, availability, capacity, continuity, security, as well as costs and stability. A service organisation will try to match these quality aspects with the customer's demands. The structure of such processes can ensure that good information is available about the provision of services, so that the planning and control of services can be improved.

Most businesses are hierarchically organised. There are departments that are responsible for the activities of a group of employees. There are various ways of structuring departments, such as by customer, product, region, or discipline. IT services generally depend on several departments, customers, or disciplines. For example, if there is an IT service to provide users with access to an accounting program on a central computer, this will involve several disciplines. The computer centre has to make the program and database accessible, the data and telecommunications department has to make the computer centre accessible, and the PC support team has to provide users with an interface to access the application.

IT service management and processes

IT service management has been known as the process and service-focused approach of what was initially known as Information Technology management. The shift of management from infrastructure to processes has paved the way for the term IT service management as a process and customer-focused discipline. Processes should always have a defined objective. The objective of IT service management processes is to contribute to the quality of the IT services. Quality management and process control are part of the organisation and its policies.

By using a process approach, best practices for IT service management describe how services can be delivered, using the most effective and efficient series of activities. The Service Lifecycle is based on these process descriptions. The structure and allocation of tasks and responsibilities between functions and departments depends on the type of organisation; these structures vary widely among IT departments, and they often change. The description of the process structure however, provides a common point of reference that changes less rapidly. This can help to maintain the quality of IT services during and after reorganisations, and also among service providers and partners as they change. This makes service providers far less sensitive to organisational change, and much more flexible: providers can continually adapt their organisation to changing conditions, leaving the core of their processes in place. In this way the shop can stay open during reconstruction work. However, reality may pose some practical problems, making this more difficult in practice than it seems in theory.

Applying the best process definitions of the industry allows IT service providers to concentrate on their business. As with other fields of industry, the processes in the IT industry are similar for all organisations of the same nature. Many of the process descriptions documented in ITIL have been recognised as the best that the industry could hope to adopt.

4.3   About the functions

Introduction

To deliver the services as agreed with the customer, the service provider will first have to manage the technical infrastructure that is used to deliver the services. If no new customers are added and no new services have to be introduced, if no incidents occur in existing services, and if no changes have to be made in existing services – even then, the IT organisation will be busy with a range of Service Operations. These activities focus on actually delivering the agreed service as agreed. Figure 4.2 represents the four ITIL functions.

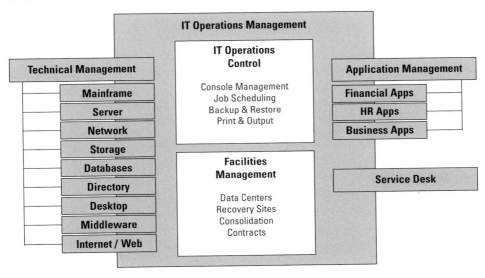

Figure 4.2 Sample service operation functions

Source: The Cabinet Office

IT operations

IT Operations activities refer to the day-to-day operational activities that are needed to manage the IT infrastructure.

IT Operations Control

The IT Operations Control is a central point of coordination that manages various events and routine operational activities, and reports on the status or performance of technological components.

An IT Operations Control brings together all vital observation points in the IT infrastructure so that they can be monitored and managed with minimum effort in a central location.

The IT Operations Control combines many activities such as console management, event handling, first-line network management, job scheduling, and support after regular office hours. In some organisations, the service desk is part of the operations bridge.

Activities, methods, and techniques

Job scheduling

IT Operations executes standard routines, queries or reports that technical and application management teams have handed over as part of the service or of routine daily maintenance tasks.

Backup and restore

Essentially, backup and restore is a component of good continuity planning. Service Design must therefore ensure that there are good backup strategies for every service. Service Transition must ensure that they are tested correctly. The only point of taking backups is to ensure that information can be restored.

Furthermore, some organisations – such as financial service providers and listed companies – must implement and monitor a formal backup and restore strategy as required by the law and regulations. The precise requirements vary per country and industry.

An organisation must protect its data, which includes **backup** and storage of data in reserved locations where it is protected and, if necessary, accessible.

A complete backup strategy must be agreed with the business, which must cover the following elements:

- What data should the backup include, and how often must it be made?
- How many generations of data must be retained?
- The backup type and the checkpoints that are used
- The locations used for storage and the rotation schedule
- Transport methods
- Required tests
- Planned recovery point: the point to which data must be recovered after an IT service resumes
- Planned recovery time: the maximum allowed time to resume an IT service after an interruption
- How will it be checked that the backups are functional when they need to be restored?

In all cases, the IT operations personnel must be qualified in backup and restore procedures. These procedures must be documented properly in the procedure manual of IT operations. Where necessary, you should include specific requirements or targets in the OLA or UC, and specify user or customer obligations and activities in the relevant SLA.

A **restore** can be initiated from several sources, varying from an event indicating data corruption to a *service request* from a user or customer. A restore may be necessary in case of:

- Corrupt data
- Lost data

- A calamity plan / IT service continuity situation
- Historical data required for forensic investigation

Print and output

Many services provide their information in **print** or electronic form (**output**). The service provider must ensure that the information ends up in the right places, correctly and in the right form. Information security often plays a part in this respect.

The customer should notify the service provider in good time of a temporarily increased need for print and output.

Laws and regulations may play an important part in print and output. Archiving important or sensitive data is particularly important.

Service providers are generally deemed to be responsible for maintaining the infrastructure to make the print and output available to the customer (printers, storage). In this case, that task must be laid down in the SLA.

Other operational activities

The remainder of this section focuses on a number of operational activities which ensure that the technology matches the service and process goals. Sometimes these activities are described as processes, but they actually concern a series of specialised technical activities that help to ensure that the technology needed for providing support to the services works effectively and efficiently.

Mainframe management

Mainframes form the central part of many services, and their performance forms a baseline for service performance and user and customer expectations.

The way in which mainframe management teams are organised varies substantially. In some organisations a specialised team fulfils all aspects of mainframe management. In other organisations this is done by several teams or departments.

Server management and support

Most organisations use servers to offer flexible and accessible services for hosting applications or databases, fulfilling client/server services, storage, print and file management.

The server team or department must fulfil the following procedures and activities:
- Supporting the operating system
- Licence management for all configuration items
- Third-line support
- Procurement advice
- System security
- Definition and management of virtual servers
- Capacity and performance

Server and mainframe support activities
Note that the support activities for servers are generally the same as those for mainframes. Although the technologies and skill sets needed are different in how support activities are actually performed, the types of activity needed to support these are essentially similar.

Network management
Since most IT services are dependent on connectivity, network management is crucial to service provision. Service Operation personnel access important service components, via network management.

Network management is responsible for all Local Area Networks (LANs), Metropolitan Area Networks (MANs), and Wide Area Networks (WANs) within an organisation.

Storage and archiving
Many services require that data must be stored for a specific time. Often, such data must be made available as an offline archive when it is no longer required on a daily basis. This is not only for compliance with external regulations and legislation, but also because data may be invaluable internally to an organisation for a variety of other reasons.

Storage and archiving does not only demand infrastructure component management, but also policy that prescribes where data must be stored, for how long, in which form, and who can access the data.

Database administration
Database administration must work closely together with key application management teams or departments. In some organisations the functions can be combined or can be brought under one management structure.

Database administration must ensure optimal database performance, security, and functionality. Database administrators have, among others, the following responsibilities:
• Designing and maintaining database standards and policies
• Database design, creation, and testing

Directory services management
A directory service is a specialised software application that manages information about the available resources on a network, and to which users it is accessible. It is the basis for providing access to those resources, and for detecting and preventing unauthorised access.

Directory services look at every resource as an object of the directory server, and name them. Every name will be linked to a resource network address, so that users do not have to remember confusing and complex addresses.

Desktop support

Many users have access to IT services through a desktop or laptop. Desktop support is responsible for all desktop and laptop hardware, software and peripheral equipment in an organisation. Specific responsibilities include:

Table 4.3 Specific desktop responsibilities

Desktop policy and procedures	for example, license policy, personal use of laptops and desktops, etc.
Desktop maintenance	such as release implementation, upgrades, patches and hot fixes
Support of connectivity problems (together with network management)	for home-workers and field personnel

Middleware management

Middleware connects software components, or integrates them with distributed or unlike applications and systems. Middleware enables effective data transfer between applications. For this reason middleware is important for services that depend on multiple applications or data resources. This is especially relevant in the context of service orientated software/architecture (SOA).

Internet/web management

Many organisations use the internet for their business operations, and are therefore heavily dependent upon the availability and performance of their websites. In such cases, a separate internet/web support team is required. This team has, among others, the following tasks:

- Designing internet and web services architecture
- The specification of standards for the development and management of web based applications, content, websites, and web pages; this is usually addressed during Service Design
- Maintaining all web development and management applications
- Supporting interfaces with back-end and legacy systems
- Monitoring and managing web based performance, such as user experience simulation, benchmarking, and virtualisation

Facility and data centre management

Facility management refers to management of the physical environment of IT operations, usually located in data centres or computer rooms. This is an extensive and complex subject. Service Operation only provides an overview of the most important roles and activities, and emphasises the role of facility management in data centre management.

Data centre strategies

Managing a data centre is much more than hosting an open room where technical groups install and manage equipment for which they use their own approach and procedures. It requires a series of processes and procedures; it involves all IT groups in every phase of the IT service management lifecycle. Data centre activities are determined by strategic and design decisions about management and control, and are fulfilled by operators.

Information security management and Service Operation

Service Design discusses information security management as process. Information security management is responsible for setting policy, standards, and procedures that ensure protection of organisation assets, data, information and IT services. Service Operation teams play a role in fulfilling these policy regulations, standards and procedures, and work closely together with the teams or departments that are responsible for information security management. The role of a service operation team consists of:

Table 4.4 Role of a service operation team

Policing and reporting	Operational personnel check system journals, logs, event/monitoring alerts, hacker detections and actual or potential security breach reports; to do this, they work closely with information security management. This is how a "check and balance system" comes into existence, which ensures effective detection and control of security issues.
Technical assistance	Sometimes IT security personnel need support for their security incident research, for report creation or for gathering forensic evidence that will be used for disciplinary actions or criminal prosecution.
Operational security management	For operational reasons technical personnel need access to important technical areas (root system passwords, physical entry into data centres or communication rooms, etc.); it is crucial that all these activities are checked and recorded so that security events can be detected and prevented.
Screening and vetting	To ensure that every member of the Service Operation personnel will meet the security requirements of the organisation, each member's background is checked; the background of service providers and third parties may also need to be security cleared.
Training and awareness	Service Operation personnel must be trained regularly in the security policy and the procedures of an organisation; this cultivates awareness. This training must include details on disciplinary actions.

Operational activity improvement

Service Operation personnel must be looking continually for process improvement opportunities in order to achieve a higher service quality or a more efficient service provision. This can be done with the following activities:
- Automating manual tasks
- Reviewing makeshift activities or activities
- Operational audits
- Utilising incident and problem management
- Communicating
- Education and training

Functions

A function is a logical concept that refers to the people and tools that execute a defined process, an activity, or a combination of processes and activities.

Functions and activities

Due to the technical character and special nature of certain functions, teams, groups, and departments are often named after the activities that they undertake. Thus network management is often fulfilled by a network management department. However, this is not an absolute rule. There are a few options available when assigning activities to a team or department:

- An activity can be performed by several teams or departments
- A department can perform several activities
- An activity can be performed by groups

Basically all four functions perform the same type of activities because they are often involved with the same processes albeit from a different focus. All four functions are responsible for the following:

- Ensure the knowledge and the expertise related to designing, testing, implementing, managing, and improving the IT Infrastructure is in place. This includes documenting, educating, training, mentoring, and coaching others as required
- Provide the actual resources (funds, infrastructure, applications, information, and people) to design, build, implement, operate, and improve the required delivery and support of IT services
- Provide guidance about on-going operational management of services
- Help plan, implement and maintain stable services to support the organisation's business processes through:
  - Well designed and highly resilient, cost-effective services
  - Use of adequate knowledge and skills to maintain the services in optimum condition
  - Use of knowledge and skills to speedily diagnose and resolve any service issues as required

4.4   IT operations management

IT operations management is the **function** that is responsible for performing the day-to-day operational activities. They ensure that the agreed level of IT service is provided to the business.

IT operations management plays a dual role:

- It is responsible for implementation of activities and performance standards that have been defined during Service Design and have been tested during Service Transition. In this sense, the role of IT operations focuses on maintaining the status quo, whereby stability of the IT infrastructure and consistency of IT services are the most important tasks of IT operations.

- Simultaneously, IT operations are part of the process that adds value to the business and supports the value network (see Service Strategy). IT operations must be capable of continual adaptation to business requirements and demands.

IT operations management objectives

Objectives of IT operations management are:
- Maintaining the existing situation to achieve stability in the processes and activities of the organisation
- Continual research and improvement to achieve better service at lower costs while maintaining stability
- Rapid application of operational skills to analyse operational failures and to resolve them

IT operations management organisation

IT operations management is seen as a separate function, but in many cases technical and application management workers contribute to this function. The assignment of activities depends on the maturity of the organisation.

IT operations management metrics

IT operations management measures both the effective implementation of defined activities and procedures, as well as execution of process activities. Examples include:
- Successful completion of planned tasks
- The number of exceptions to planned activities and tasks
- Process metrics
- Metrics of maintenance activities
- Metrics related to facility management

IT operations management documentation

IT operations management generates and uses a number of documents, including:
- *Standard Operating Procedures (SOP)* – A series of documents providing detailed instructions and activity schedules for each IT operations management team, department or group.
- *Operations logs* – Each activity that is performed as part of IT operations must be registered for a variety of reasons, in order to:
  - Confirm successful completion of specific tasks or activities
  - Confirm that an IT service was provided as agreed
  - Provide a basis for problem management to research the underlying cause of incidents
  - Provide a basis for reports about performance of IT operations teams and departments
- *Shift schedules and reports* – Documents that display the exact activities that must be performed during a shift; there is also a list showing all dependencies and the sequence of activities. There may be more than one operational schedule because each team may be provided with a version for its own systems.

4.5 Service desk

A service desk is a **functional unit** with a number of personnel members who deal with a variety of service events. Requests may come in through phone calls, the internet or as automatically reported infrastructure events.

The service desk is a very important part of the organisation's IT department. It should be the prime contact point for IT users, and it processes all incidents and service requests. Often the personnel use software tools to record and manage events.

Justification and the role of a service desk

Many organisations consider a service desk as the best resource for first-line support of IT problems. A service desk can provide the following advantages:
- Improved customer service, improved customer perception of the service and increased customer satisfaction
- Increased accessibility due to a single point of contact, communication and information
- Customer and user requests are resolved better and faster
- Improved cooperation and communication
- An improved focus on service and a proactive service approach
- Reduced negative business impact
- Improved infrastructure management and control
- Improved use of resources for IT support, and increased business personnel productivity
- More meaningful management information for decision support
- A good entry position for IT personnel

Service desk objectives

The principal purpose of the service desk is to restore the "normal service" for users as soon as possible. This could entail resolving a technical error, fulfilling a service request or answering a question.

Organisational structure of a service desk

There are all sorts of ways to structure a service desk. The solution will vary for each organisation. The most important options are:
- Local service desk
- Centralised service desk
- Virtual service desk
- Follow the sun – "24/7" service
- Specialised service desk groups

These options are elaborated further below. In practice, an organisation will implement a structure that combines a number of these options in order to satisfy the needs of the business.

The **local service desk** is located at or physically close to the users it is supporting. Because of this, communications are often much smoother and the visible presence is attractive for some users. However, a local service desk is expensive and may be inefficient if the amount of service events does not really justify a service desk.

There may be a few sound reasons for maintaining a local service desk:
• Linguistic, cultural, and political differences
• Different time zones
• Specialised groups of users
• Existence of adjusted or special services for which specialised knowledge is required
• Status of the users

The number of service desks can be reduced by installing them at one single location (or by reducing the number of local service desks). In that case, the associates are assigned to one or more **centralised service desk** structures. This may be less expensive and more efficient, because fewer associates can deal with the service events (calls), while the level of knowledge of the service desk is bound to increase.

By using technology, specifically the internet, and support tools, it is possible to create the impression of a centralised service desk, whereas the associates are in fact spread out over a number of geographic or structural locations: this is the **virtual service desk**.

Some international organisations like to combine two or more geographically spread out service desks in order to offer a **24/7 service**. In this way, a service desk in Asia, for example, can deal with incoming service events during standard office hours, whereby at the end of that period, a service desk in Europe takes care of any outstanding events. That desk deals with those service events together with its own events and at the end of the day, responsibility is transferred to a service desk in America, which then returns responsibility to the Asian service desk, thus completing the cycle.

It may be attractive for some organisations to create specialised **service desk groups**, so that incidents relating to a specific IT service are routed straight to the specialised group. In this way, incidents can be resolved more promptly.

The **environment** of the service desk must be carefully selected, preferably a location where workstations have adequate space with natural light. A quiet environment with good acoustics is equally important, because the associates should not be bothered by each other's telephone conversations. Ergonomic office furniture is also important.

Figure 4.3 provides a sample representation of a local service desk while Figure 4.4 provides a sample representation of a virtual service desk.

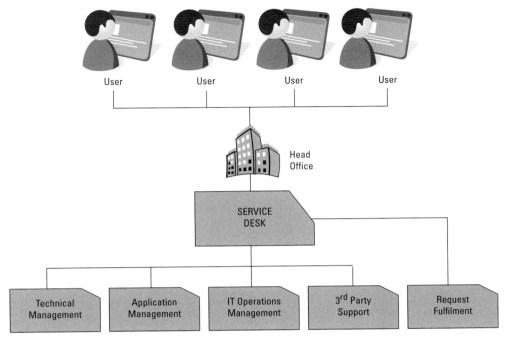

Figure 4.3 Sample local service desk

Source: The Cabinet Office

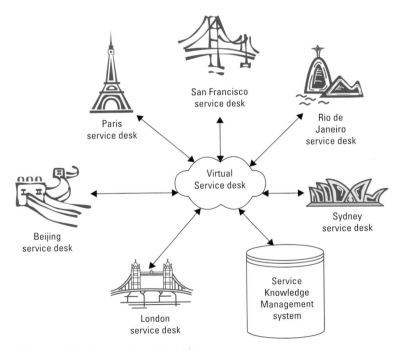

Figure 4.4 Sample virtual service desk

Source: The Cabinet Office

Service desk personnel

It is important to ensure the availability of the correct number of personnel members, so that the service desk can meet the business demands at any time. It is also important to consider all activities executed by the service desk personnel. This includes call handling, monitoring, and updating records, creating documentation, attending meetings, escalation, and reporting. The number of calls can fluctuate significantly each day and from hour to hour. When scheduling, a successful organisation takes both the patterns of business activities (PBA) and business schedules into account. The necessary levels and skills required for service desk personnel are also important. The agreed target resolution times should be balanced against the complexity of the supported systems and "what the business is willing to pay" to determine the required skill level. Most of the time the optimal and most cost-effective approach is first line support through the service desk and IT Operations. In order to increase the effectiveness and efficiency of first-line support, third-line support should "offload" as much as possible of their mundane tasks onto second-line support through documenting, educating, and training, mentoring, and coaching. In turn, the second line support "offloads" their mundane tasks to first-line support by doing the same as per above. The use of knowledge management is a key success factor for this to be successful.

At all times there has to be a good mix of skills present. It is essential that all service desk associates receive sufficient education and training. All new personnel must follow a formal introduction program. The precise content of it will vary with each new employee, subject to the existing expertise and experience.

In order to keep the service desk personnel up-to-date, a program is necessary so that they can be kept informed of new developments, services, and techniques. The timing of these types of activities is essential, because they should not affect the normal tasks. Many service desks organise short training sessions during quiet periods when the associates are handling fewer service events. It is very important that all IT associates realise the importance of the service desk and the people working there. A considerable attrition of associates has a disturbing effect and can lead to an incoherent service. Thus the managers have to engage in efforts to retain the associates.

Regarding super users

Many organisations find it useful to appoint a number of so-called super-users in the user community. They function as contact persons with the IT organisation in general and the service desk in particular.

Organisations can provide the super-users with extra training and use them as communication channels. They can be asked to filter requests and certain problems on behalf of the user community. If an important service or component is down, causing an extra burden for many users, this may lead to many reactions coming in. Super-users do not provide support for the entire IT provision. In many cases, the super-user will offer support only for a specific application, module or business unit.

A super-user often has thorough knowledge of important company processes and knows how services are working in practice. It is very useful to share this with the service desk, so that it can offer better quality services in the future.

Metrics for the service desk
Identifying and defining metrics for the service desk should be based on business goals and objectives as well as the IT-as-a-business-unit goals and objectives. Although this will be discussed in more details in the Continual Service Improvement section, there are three types of metrics to collect. They are service, process, and technology metrics. There are also four primary reasons we measure. The reasons are to direct, to justify, to intervene, and to validate.

Additionally all measurements should follow the SMART approach. SMART stands for specific, measurable, achievable, realistic, and timely (or time-bounded). It is also important to measure against what is important presently; i.e. the critical success factors (CSFs) and the key performance indicators (KPIs). CSFs and KPIs change over time. Service and process-related CSFs and KPIs should be about compliance, performance, quality, and/ or value.

This way, the maturity, efficiency, effectiveness, and opportunities can be assessed, and the service desk activities improved. In order to determine this, further analysis and more detailed metrics are necessary which are researched for a certain period of time. Too often service desk metrics are too narrowly focused on first-level and incident management measures. Service desk metrics must be aligned to the goals and objectives of the organisation. A balanced approach – based on the balanced scorecard – should be used. This way, the service desk would be measuring the following elements: financial, customer, processes, and learning and growth.

Metrics can also be defined as either quantitative (objectives measurements) or qualitative (subjective measurements). Qualitative measurements are often in the form of customer, user, and IT personnel "satisfaction" surveys. These surveys are not restricted to the automated surveys sent by the service management tool; these "mini-surveys" only represent a fraction of the feedback to be collected. Creating a survey involves both science and art. The science resides in selecting the right mix of topics, answer scale, and the audience. The art involves the creation of the questions. There are many other factors in creating surveys but they fall outside the scope of this book. In addition to surveys, focus groups, interviews, meetings, and brainstorming sessions can also be used.

Outsourcing the service desk
The decision to outsource is a strategic one for senior managers, and will be discussed in detail in the domains of Service Strategy and Service Design. Nonetheless, it is important to understand that although the service desk function (or any other function) has been outsourced, they must be integrated in communication, education, training, etc.

Regardless of the reasons for outsourcing or the size of the outsource contract, it is important that the organisation remains responsible for the activities and services provided by the service desk. The organisation is ultimately responsible for the outcome of the decision and must therefore decide which service is going to be offered. If the service desk is being outsourced, the tools must be consistent with the tools being used by the organisation's customer. Outsourcing is frequently seen as a chance to replace obsolescent or inadequate tools; however, serious integration problems often arise between the new and existing tools and processes.

Ideally, the service desk being outsourced must use the same tools and processes to enable a smooth process stream between the service desk and the second and third level support groups.

The SLA targets for incident handling and handling times must be arranged with the customers and between all teams and departments; OLA and underlying contract objectives must be coordinated and in tune with separate support groups, so that they support the SLA targets.

4.6 Technical management

Technical management refers to the **groups, departments, or teams** who offer technical expertise and general management of the IT infrastructure.

The role of technical management
Technical management has a dual role:
- It is the custodian of technical knowledge and expertise in relation to managing the IT infrastructure. In this role, technical management helps ensure that the knowledge required for designing, testing, managing and improving IT services is established, developed, and refined.
- It takes care of the actual resources that are needed to support the IT service management lifecycle. In this role, technical management helps ensure that the resources are trained and implemented effectively, so that it can design, build, transfer, process, and improve the required technology that is needed to provide and support IT services.

By fulfilling these two roles, technical management helps ensure that the organisation is able to access the correct type and level of human resources to manage the technology, and consequently, meet the business goals.

Technical management also drives IT operations while managing the technology operations and providing guidance to IT operations.

Objectives of technical management
Technical management assists in the planning, implementation and maintenance of a stable technical infrastructure to support the organisation's business processes. This is done by:

- Well-designed and cost-effective technical topology
- Using the appropriate technical skills to maintain the technical infrastructure in an optimal condition
- Using technical skills effectively, to diagnose and resolve technical failures quickly

General technical management activities

Technical management is involved in several general activities, such as:

- Starting training programs
- Designing and carrying out training for users, the service desk, and other groups
- Researching and developing resolutions that may help to expand the service portfolio, or may be used to simplify or automate IT operations
- Releases that are often implemented with the assistance of technical management personnel

The technical management organisation

Generally speaking, technical management is not provided by one department or group. One or more technical support teams are needed to provide technical management and support for the IT infrastructure.

IT operations management consists of a number of technological areas. Each area requires a specific set of skills to manage and operate it. Some skills are related to each other, and can be performed by generalists, while others apply specifically to a component, system, or platform.

Technical design and technical maintenance and support

Technical management consists of specialised technical architects, designers, maintenance specialists and support personnel.

Metrics for technical management

Specific metrics for technical management depend largely on which technology is being managed. Some general metrics include:

- Measuring the agreed output
- Process values
- Technological performance
- Mean time between failures (MTBF) of specific equipment
- Maintenance activity measurement
- Training and skill development

Technical management documentation

Among others, technical management documentation consists of:

- Technical documentation (manuals, management and administration manuals, user manuals for CIs)
- Maintenance schedules
- An inventory of skills

4.7 Application management

Application management is responsible for the management of applications during their lifecycle. The application management **function** is executed by a department, group, or team that is involved with management and support of operational applications. Application management also plays an important role in designing, testing and improving applications that are part of IT services.

Application management role

Application management is for applications what technical management is for IT infrastructure. It plays a role in all applications, whether they are purchased or have been internally developed. One of the most important decisions to which they contribute is whether to purchase an application or to develop it internally (discussed in detail in Service Design). When this decision has been made, application management plays a dual role:
- It is the custodian of technical knowledge and expertise for the management of applications
- It provides actual resources for the support of the IT service management lifecycle

Two other roles filled by application management:
- It provides advice to IT operations about the best way to carry out the on-going operational management of applications
- It integrates the Application Management Lifecycle with the IT service management lifecycle

Application management objectives

The objectives of application management are to support the business processes of the organisation by determining functional and management requirements for applications. Another objective is to assist in design and implementation of the applications and to support and improve them.

Application management principles

One of the most important decisions in application management is whether to **develop or purchase** an application which supports the requested functionality. The Chief Technical Officer (CTO), or the IT steering group/committee, makes the ultimate decision, but in doing so, both depend on a number of information sources. If the decision maker wants to have the application developed, they will also have to decide whether to have it developed by personnel or to outsource the development. This is further discussed in detail in Service Design.

Application management lifecycle

The lifecycle that is followed to develop and manage the application goes by many names, such as the Software Lifecycle (SLC™) and the Software Development Lifecycle (SDLC™). These are mostly used by application development teams and their project managers to define their involvement in designing, developing, testing, implementing, and supporting applications. Examples of this approach include Structured Systems Analysis and Design Methodology (SSADM™) and Dynamic Systems Development Method (DSDM™).

Application development and operations are part of the same lifecycle and must be involved through all Service Lifecycle phases, although the degree of involvement depends on the lifecycle phase.

Relations between application management lifecycle and service management lifecycle are:

The application management lifecycle is not an alternative for the service management lifecycle. Applications are part of services and must be managed as such. Nevertheless, applications are a unique mix of technology and functionality and this requires a special focus during each phase of the service management lifecycle.

Each phase of the application management lifecycle has its own specific objectives, activities, deliverables, and dedicated teams. Each phase also has a clear responsibility to ensure that its output corresponds with the specific objectives of the service management lifecycle.

The phases of applications management dealt within the Service Operation book are:
1. Requirements
2. Design
3. Build
4. Deploy
5. Operate
6. Optimise

1. During the first phase, the requirements for a new application are collected, based on the business needs of the organisation. There are six requirement types for an application, whether it is developed in-house, outsourced, or purchased:

Table 4.5 Sample requirements

Functional requirements	What is necessary to support a certain business function?
Management requirements	Concentrate on the need for responsive, available, and secure service, and involve things like deployment, system management, and security
Usability requirements	What are the needs of the user, and how can they be satisfied?
Architecture requirements	Especially if it requires a change in the existing architecture standards
Interface requirements	Where dependencies occur between existing applications or tools and the new application
Service level requirements	Specify how the service is to be delivered, what the quality of the output has to be and other qualitative aspects that are measured by the user or customer

2. The **design phase** will translate the requirements into specifications. Design of the application and the environment or the operational model in which the application is run will also take place during the design phase. Architectural considerations for design and operation are the most important aspects of this phase, because they can affect the structure and content of both the application and the operational model.

3. The **build phase** gets the application and the operational model ready for deployment. Application components are coded and purchased, integrated and tested. Testing is not a separate phase in the lifecycle although it is a separate activity. Testing forms an integral part of the development and roll-out phase, as validation of the activity and output of those phases.

4. The **deployment phase** deploys the operational model and the application. The existing IT environment absorbs the operational model and the application is installed on top of the operational model. This involves the processes of release and deployment management that are described under Service Transition.

5. During the **operate phase** the service organisation uses the application as part of providing services requested by the business. The performance of the application in relation to the total service is measured continually in relation to the service levels and the most important business drivers.

6. The **optimise phase** reviews and analyses the results of the service level performance metrics. Possible improvements are discussed and the necessary developments are initiated. The two main strategies involve maintaining and iteratively improving service levels at lower costs. This can lead to a change in the lifecycle of an application or to its retirement. Good communication with users is important during this phase.

Generic application management activities

Although most application management teams and departments are dedicated to specific applications, they share a number of activities. These include:
- Identifying the knowledge needed to manage and operate applications in the Service Operation phase
- Initiating training programs to develop and refine skills in the appropriate application management resources and to maintain training reports for these resources
- Defining standards for designing new architectures and determining application architectures during Service Strategy processes
- Testing, designing and executing the functionality, performance and controllability of IT services
- Defining event management standards
- Defining, managing, and maintaining attributes and relations of application CIs in the configuration management system

Figure 4.5 provides a sample view of the activities of a generic application management lifecycle model.

Application management organisation

Although application management departments, groups and teams all perform similar functions, each application has its own set of management and operational requirements. Differences may include:

- The purpose of the application
- The functionality of the application
- The platform on which the application is run
- The type or the brand of technology that is used

Application management teams and departments are mostly organised based on the categories of the applications that they support. Examples of typical application management organisation include:

- Financial applications
- HR applications
- Manufacturing support
- Sales support
- Call centre and marketing applications
- Business specific applications
- IT applications
- Web portals

Traditionally, application development and management teams/departments have operated as autonomous units. Each team manages its own environment in its own way and they all have a separate interface to the business. Recent attention for object-oriented and *Service Oriented Architectures* and the growing pressure from business that demands a faster response and improved cooperation has brought these two worlds closer together. This requires a higher involvement of Service Operational personnel in the Service Design phase.

Application management roles and responsibilities

Application management has two roles:

- **The application manager** – supervises and has overall responsibility for management and the decisions that are made
- **The application analyst/architect** – is responsible for requirements that meet the application specifications

Application management metrics

The application management metrics mainly depend on the way in which the applications are managed, but general metrics include:

- Measuring agreed-upon outputs
- Process metrics
- Performance of the application

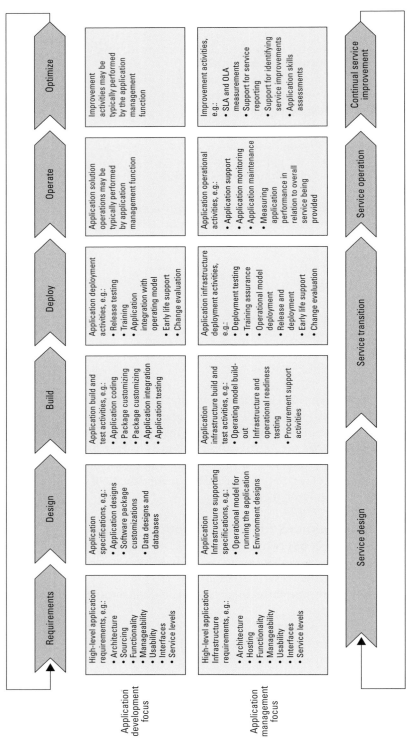

Figure 4.5 Sample application management lifecycle
Source: The Cabinet Office

- Measuring maintenance activities
- Application management teams cooperate closely with application development teams and the correct metrics must be used to measure this
- Training and skill development

4.8 Service Operation roles and responsibilities

The key to effective ITSM is ensuring that there is clear accountability and roles defined to carry out the practice of Service Operation.

IT Operation management roles

The following roles are needed for IT Operations management:
- IT operations manager
- Shift leader
- IT operations analysts
- IT operators

Service desk roles

The following roles are needed for the service desk:
- Service desk manager
  - Manages service desk activities
  - Acts as escalation point for supervisors
  - Takes on wider customer service role
  - Reports to senior managers about any issue that could significantly impact the business
  - Attends Change Advisory Board meetings
  - Overall responsibility for processing incidents and service requests
- Service desk supervisor
  - Ensures that personnel and skill levels are maintained
  - Is responsible for production of management reports
  - Acts as escalation point for difficult calls
- Service desk analysts
  - Deliver first line support by accepting calls and processing the resulting incidents or service requests, using incident and request fulfilment processes
- Super-users
  - Business users who act as liaison points between business and IT

Technical management roles

The following roles are needed for the technical management areas:
- Technical managers/team leaders
  - Responsible for leadership, control and decision-making
- Technical analysts/architects
  - Defining and maintaining knowledge on how systems are related and ensuring that dependencies are understood

- Technical operators
  - Performing day-to-day operational tasks

Application management roles

Application management requires application managers and team leaders. They have overall responsibility for leadership, control, and decision making for the applications team or department.

Application analysts and architects are responsible for matching business requirements to technical specifications.

Event management roles

It is unusual to appoint an "event manager" but it is important that event management procedures are coordinated. The service desk is not typically involved in event management, but if events have been identified as incidents, the service desk will escalate them to the appropriate service operation teams.

Technical and application management play an important role in event management. For example, the teams will perform event management for the systems under their control.

Incident management roles

The **incident manager** is responsible for:
- Driving the effectiveness and efficiency of the incident management process
- Producing management information
- Managing the work of incident support personnel (first tier and second tier)
- Monitoring the effectiveness of incident management and making recommendations for improvement
- Managing major incidents
- Developing and maintaining incident management systems and processes
- Effectively managing incidents using first, second, and third tier support

Request fulfilment roles

Initial service request handling is done by the service desk and incident management personnel. Actual fulfilment will be undertaken by the appropriate service operation team(s) or departments and/or external suppliers.

Problem management roles

One person (or, in larger organisations, a team) should be responsible for problem management. The **problem manager** is responsible for coordinating all problem management activities and is specifically responsible for:
- Liaison with all problem resolution groups to accomplish quick solutions to problems within SLA targets
- Ownership and protection of the Known Error Database
- Formal closure of all problem records

- Liaison with vendors and other parties to ensure compliance with contractual obligations
- Managing, executing, documenting, and planning all (follow-up) activities that relate to major problem reviews

Access management roles

Since access management is the execution of security and availability management, these two areas will be responsible for defining the appropriate roles. Although usually no access manager is appointed by an organisation, it is important there should be one process for managing privileges and access. This process and the related policy are usually defined and maintained by information security management and executed by various service operation functions, such as the service desk, technical management, and application management.

4.9 Service Operation organisation structures

There are several ways to organise Service Operation functions, and each organisation will come to its own decisions based on its size, geography, culture, and business environment.

Organisation by technical specialisation

This organisation type creates departments according to the technology, the skills, and activities necessary to manage that technology. IT operations follow the structure of the technical management and application management departments. As a consequence IT operations are geared to the operational agendas of the technical management and application management departments, and all groups have to be defined during the Service Design phase.

Organisation by activity

This type of organisation structure focuses on the fact that similar activities are performed on all technologies within an organisation. This means that people who perform similar activities, regardless of the technology, are grouped together, although teams may occur within each department that is involved with a specific technology, application, etc.

Organising to manage processes

It is not a good idea to structure the entire organisation according to processes. Processes are used to eliminate the "silo effect" of departments, not to create silos.

In process-based organisations, people are organised in groups or departments that perform or manage a specific process. However, this type of organisation structure should only be used if IT operations management is responsible for more than IT operations. In some organisations IT operations is also responsible for defining the SLA and negotiating the UC.

Process-based departments are only effective if they are capable of coordinating process execution throughout the entire organisation. This means that process-based departments can only be considered if IT operations management can play the role of process owner for specific processes.

Organising IT operation by geography

IT operations can be physically spread out, and in some cases each location must be organised according to its own context. This structure is usually used in the following circumstances, when:
- Data centres are geographically distributed
- Different regions or countries possess different technologies or offer a different range of services
- There are different business models or organisational structures in the different regions; in other words, the business is decentralised according to geography and the each business unit is fairly autonomous
- Legislation differs between country and region
- Different standards apply, per country or region
- There are cultural or language differences between the personnel who are managing IT

Hybrid organisation structures

It is unlikely that IT operations management will be structured using only one type of organisational structure. Most organisations use a technical specialisation combined with some extra activity or process-based departments:
- **Combined functions** – The IT operations, technical management, and application management departments are included in one structure; this sometimes occurs when all groups are co-located in one data centre; in these situations, the data centre manager assumes responsibility for technical, application, and IT production management.
- **Combined technical and application management structure** – Some businesses organise their technical management and application management functions according to systems; this means that every department contains application specialists and IT infrastructure technical specialists who manage services based on a series of systems.

4.10 Teams, roles and positions in ITSM

Organisations divide the various tasks for carrying out processes or activities in many different ways. Tasks can be covered by organisational bodies, such as groups, teams, departments, or divisions. These organisational bodies are then managed in **hierarchical organisations** by a line manager, who has a certain "span of control" and who manages one or more of these bodies. **Flat organisations** have relatively few layers in this hierarchy. Organisations can also divide the tasks more in the spirit of equality, such as, for example, **network organisations**, in which the cooperation between the various bodies is paramount.

Besides hierarchical organisations, which manage through "the line", there are also **project organisations**, which manage primarily by using temporary forms of project cooperation, while **process organisations** are managed primarily by means of an agreed work method. Obviously, these types of management can be combined in innumerable ways. As a result of this, we are seeing a great number of unique organisational configurations in the field.

Organisations can distinguish themselves from other organisations, particularly in respect to the type of organisation they operate. An organisation that is directed toward hierarchy will have personnel primarily of senior line management. A process-oriented organisation will have personnel that are responsible for processes. Depending on the degree to which management is based on processes, the line, or projects, the personnel will consist of a mix of the relevant responsible managers.

When setting up an organisation, positions and roles are also used, in addition to the various groups (teams, departments, divisions). **Roles** are sets of responsibilities, activities, and authorities granted to a person or team. One person or team may have multiple roles; for example, the roles of Configuration Manager and Change Manager may be carried out by a single person. **Positions** (functions) are traditionally recognised as tasks and responsibilities that are assigned to a specific person. A person in a particular position has a clearly defined package of tasks and responsibilities which may include various roles. Positions can also be more broadly defined as a logical concept that refers to the people and automated measures that carry out a clearly defined process, an activity, or a combination of processes or activities.

4.11 Tools used in ITSM

In the performance of tasks in IT service management, innumerable automated support aids can be used: these are referred to as tools. With the help of these tools, management tasks can be automated; for example, monitoring tasks or software distribution tasks. Other tools support the performance of the activities themselves; for example ITIL-compatible single process tools and integrated service management suites. The latter category, in fact, supports the management of several processes.

The fact that the IT field is fundamentally focused on automated facilities (for information processing) has led to a virtual deluge of tools appearing on the market, which have greatly increased the performance capacity of IT organisations.

PART 2: PROCESSES IN THE LIFECYCLE PHASES

5 Service strategy phase

5.1 ITIL Service Strategy

This short section provides a summary of the updates between the 2007 edition and the 2011 edition for the ITIL core book Service Strategy published by TSO.

The concepts within the Service Strategy publication have been clarified, without changing the overall message. The updated publication includes more practical guidance and more examples where relevant.

The newly defined process of strategy management for IT services is responsible for developing and maintaining business and IT strategies, and there are now separate descriptions of business strategy and IT strategy. Financial management has been expanded, and business relationship management and demand management are now covered as processes.

Table 5.1 Summary of updates: ITIL Service Strategy

Area of update	Description
Service strategy processes	The processes have now been clearly named and defined: strategy management for IT services; service portfolio management; financial management for IT services; demand management; and business relationship management. Each process has been described using a standard template.
Business strategy and IT strategy	Business strategy and IT strategy are two different things. ITIL Service Strategy now describes these separately and explains the relationship between the two: business strategy defines IT strategy, and IT strategy supports business strategy.
Strategy assessment, generation and execution	More detailed guidance has been included on how an organisation should go about assessing, generating, and executing its IT strategy, giving practical examples of how to proceed.
Value creation	Greater clarification is provided around how services add and realise value. New text has been included to describe how value is created and how to differentiate between value added and value realised. A new table provides examples of utility and warranty.
Customers	It is now clearer how customers differ from users and consumers; how internal and external customers are differentiated; how business units and other IT departments as customers differ; and how IT performs its role as an external service provider.
Customer and service assets	Definitions of customer asset and service asset have been clarified, with an explanation around why these concepts are important and how they are used – including aligning service assets with customer outcomes. A new series of diagrams demonstrates the relationships between business outcomes, customer assets, service assets, constraints, and service management.

Area of update	Description
Strategy management for IT services	The newly defined process of strategy management for IT services is responsible for developing and maintaining business and IT strategies.
Financial management for IT services	The financial management for IT services process has been expanded to include some of the key elements included in the earlier ITIL publications which had been excluded in the 2007 edition of Service Strategy – such as accounting, budgeting and charging.
Business relationship management	Business relationship management is now covered as a process as well as a role. The differentiation between business relationship management for a Type I, II, and III service provider is better explained and clarified.
Governance	There is now more detail on governance, including a fuller definition of what governance means, the difference between governance and management, a governance framework, and how service management relates to governance.
Cloud computing	Some coverage has been added on how IT service management is impacted by the prevalence of cloud computing, and a new appendix has been added specifically covering service strategy and the cloud: characteristics, types, types of service, and components of cloud architecture.
Types of service management implementation	Coverage has been added regarding the types of service management implementation: even keel, trouble, growth, and radical change.
Organisation	Some discussion on functions has been added and a logical organisation structure for service management has been included, with supporting diagrams.

5.2   ITIL Service Strategy

This chapter sets out the processes and activities on which effective service strategy depends. These comprise both lifecycle processes and those almost wholly contained within service strategy. Each is described in detail, setting out the key elements of that process or activity.

The processes and activities specifically addressed in this chapter are:
- Strategy management for IT services
- Service portfolio management
- Financial management for IT services
- Demand management
- Business relationship management

Most of these processes are used throughout the service lifecycle, but are addressed in *ITIL Service Strategy* since they are central to effective service strategy.

5.3   Strategy management for IT services

This section describes a process for strategy management for an enterprise and shows how it is applied to managing a strategy for IT services. Although senior IT executives will participate in this level of strategy management, most IT organisations use this process to manage a service strategy which forms part of the overall enterprise strategy.

Purpose and objectives

Strategy management for IT services is the process of defining and maintaining an organisation's perspective, position, plans, and patterns with regard to its services and the management of those services. The purpose of a service strategy is to articulate how a service provider will enable an organisation to achieve its business outcomes; it establishes the criteria and mechanisms to decide which services will be best suited to meet the business outcomes and the most effective and efficient way to manage these services.

The objectives of strategy management for IT services are to:
- Analyse the internal and external environments of the service provider, to identify opportunities benefiting the organisation
- Identify (potential) constraints preventing the achievement of business outcomes, the delivery or the management of services; to identify how to remove or reduce effects of the constraints
- Agree the service provider's perspective and review regularly for continued relevance. This will clarify the service provider's vision and mission statements
- Establish the position of the service provider relative to its customers and other service providers. This includes mapping services to market spaces, and maintaining a competitive advantage
- Produce and maintain strategy planning documents ensuring all stakeholders have up-to-date documents. These documents include the strategy for IT, service management, and for each service
- Ensure that strategic plans have been translated into tactical and operational plans for each organisational unit involved with delivering the strategy
- Manage changes to the strategies and related documents to keep pace with changes to the internal and external environments

Scope

Strategy management is the responsibility of the executives of an organisation. It enables them to set the objectives of the organisation, to specify how the organisation will meet those objectives and to prioritise investments required to meet them. An organisation's strategy is not limited to a single document or department. The overall strategy of an organisation will be broken down into a strategy for each unit of the business.

Key message
A service strategy is a subset of the overall strategy for the organisation. In the case of an IT organisation, the IT strategy will encompass the IT service strategy.

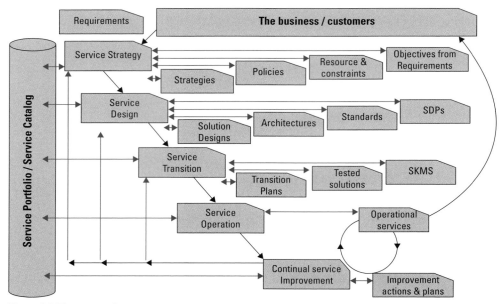

Figure 5.1 The scope of strategy management

Source: The Cabinet Office

Note on strategy for services

Strategy management for IT services is intended for managing the strategy of a service provider. It will include a specification of the type of services it will deliver, the customers of those services and the overall business outcomes to be achieved when the service provider executes the strategy.

The strategy of an individual service is defined during the service portfolio management process and documented in the service portfolio. This will include a description of the specific business outcomes that the service will support, and also define how the service will be delivered.

It is important to note, furthermore, that a service strategy is not the same as an ITSM strategy – which is really a tactical plan. The difference can be summed up as follows:

- **Service strategy** – The strategy that a service provider will follow to define and execute services that meet a customer's business objectives. For an IT service provider the service strategy is a subset of the IT strategy
- **Service management (ITSM) strategy** – The plan for identifying, implementing, and executing the processes used to manage services identified in a service strategy. In an IT service provider, the ITSM strategy will be a subset of the service strategy

Value to the business

The strategy of an organisation articulates its objectives, and defines how it will meet those objectives and how it will know it has met those objectives. Without a strategy the organisation will only be able to react to demands placed by various stakeholders, with little ability to assess each demand and how they will impact the organisation. In these cases the actions of the organisations tend to be led by whoever is making the loudest demands, rather than by what is best for the organisation. Strategy becomes a function of organisational politics and self-interest, rather than the overall achievement of its objectives.

A well-defined and managed strategy ensures that the resources and capabilities of the organisation are aligned to achieving its business outcomes, and that investments match the organisation's intended development and growth.

Strategy management ensures that all stakeholders are represented in deciding the appropriate direction for the organisation and that they all agree on its objectives and the means whereby resources, capabilities, and investment are prioritised. Strategy management also ensures that the resources, capabilities, and investments are appropriately managed to achieve the strategy.

For a service provider, strategy management for IT services ensures that it has the appropriate set of services in its service portfolio, that all of its services have a clear purpose, and that everyone in the service provider organisation knows their role in achieving that purpose. Strategy management for IT services further encourages appropriate levels of investment, which will result in one or more of the following:

- Cost savings, since investments and expenditure are matched to achievement of validated business objectives, rather than unsubstantiated demands
- Increased levels of investment for key projects or service improvements
- Shifting investment priorities

The service provider will be able to de-focus attention from one service, and re-focus on another, ensuring that their efforts and budget are spent on the areas with the highest level of business impact.

For the customer of the service provider, strategy management for IT services enables them to articulate clearly their business priorities in a way that is understandable to the service provider. The service provider is then able to make a decision about how to respond to the customer. In some cases, the customer demand represents a departure from the service provider's strategy.

The service provider will use strategy management for IT services to make a decision about whether to change their strategy, or whether to turn down the business. Where the service provider is an internal IT organisation the second option is not always possible, and in these cases they will use strategy management for IT services to work with the business units to make them aware of the impact of their demand on the current strategy. The business executives will be able to work with IT either to change the existing strategy, or to decline the opportunity.

In other cases, customer demands do not change the service provider's strategy, but will require it to change its priorities. Strategy management for IT services enables the service provider to determine the best way to change its priorities and balance its resources, capabilities, and investments.

Process activities, methods, and techniques
The process for strategy management is illustrated in the following figure.

Strategic assessment
The strategic assessment analyses both the internal environment (the service provider's own organisation) and the external environment (the world with which the service provider's organisation interacts), and then arrives at a set of objectives which will be used to define the actual strategy.

Strategic assessment: Analyse the internal environment
- Existing services
- Financial analysis
- Human resources
- Operations
- Relationship with the business units
- Resources and capabilities
- Existing project

Strategic assessment: Analyse the external environment
- Industry and market analysis
- Customers
- Suppliers
- Partners
- Competitors
- Legislation and regulation
- Political
- Socio-economic
- Technology

Strategic assessment: Define market spaces
In summary, market spaces define opportunities where a service provider can deliver value to its customer(s). They identify opportunities by matching service archetypes with customer assets.

In strategy management, this step results in documentation of all current market spaces and any potential new market spaces that were identified from the internal and external analysis.

Strategic assessment: Identify strategic industry factors
For every market space there are critical factors that determine the success or failure of a service strategy. In business literature these factors are called strategic industry factors (Amit and Schoemaker, 1993). These are influenced by customer needs,

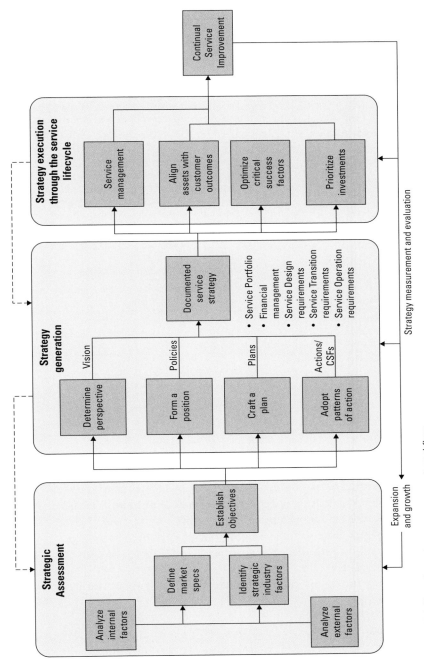

Figure 5.2 Sample strategy management workflow
Source: The Cabinet Office

Table 5.2 Questions to assess existing services as differentiators

Which of our services or service varieties are the most distinctive?
 	
Are there services that the business or customer cannot easily substitute?
	Are there barriers preventing other service providers from offering the same services?
	  Barriers to entry could be the service provider's knowledge of the customer's business or the broadness of service offerings.
	How expensive would it be to switch to another service provider?
	  The service provider might have lower cost structures because of specialisation or service sourcing.
	Do we offer a unique and particular attribute?
	  These could include product knowledge, regulatory compliance, technical capabilities, or global presence.

Which of our services are the most profitable?	The value could be defined as higher profits or lower expenses, or socially related. *For non-profit organisations, are there services that allow the organisation to perform its mission better?* Substitute "profit" with "benefits realised".
Which of our customers and stakeholders are the most satisfied?	The answer will centre on services demonstrating high quality, low cost, unique to a specific customer's requirements *It may be a combination of the three.*
Which customers, channels, or purchase occasions are the most profitable?	The value could be defined as higher profits or lower expenses, or socially related.
Which of our activities in our value chain or value network are the most different and effective?	Activities perceived by the business as a core competency, and therefore will ensure that the service provider is seen as strategic.

business trends, competition, regulatory environment, suppliers, standards, industry best practices, and technologies.

Strategic industry factors have the following general characteristics:
• They are defined in terms of capabilities and resources
• They are proven to be key determinants of success by industry leaders
• They are defined by market space levels, not peculiar to any one firm
• They are the basis for competition among rivals
• They change over time, so they are dynamic – not static
• They usually require significant investments and time to develop

Strategic industry factors by themselves are altered or influenced by one or more of the following factors:
• Customers
• Competitors
• Partners
• Suppliers
• Regulators

Strategic assessment: Establish objectives
The objectives defined as an output of the strategic assessment are the results the service provider expects to achieve by pursuing a strategy. Once the objectives have been defined, the service provider will need to define how it will achieve the anticipated results. This is the strategy (or strategies).

Clear objectives facilitate consistent decision-making, minimising later conflicts. They set forth priorities and serve as standards.

The set of guidelines frequently used to ensure defining meaningful objectives is contained in the "SMART" acronym, which was introduced in Chapter 4.

The following are some additional guidelines to bear in mind when setting objectives:
- Don't have too many
- Use primary and secondary objectives
- Keep them simple
- Avoid ambiguity
- Be positive, but state the negative

Strategy generation
Strategy generation: Evaluation and selection
Once the assessment has been completed and the service provider has defined the objectives of the strategy, it is possible to generate the actual strategy in terms of the "four Ps"; perspective, position, plans and patterns.

Determine perspective
The perspective of a service provider defines its overall direction, values, beliefs and purpose; and, at a high level, how it intends to achieve this. The most common form of perspective statements is vision and mission statements. The vision statement articulates what it is the service provider aims to achieve.

Form a position
The strategic position defines how the service provider will be differentiated from other service providers in the industry. For example, positioning could be based on the type or range of services offered, or providing services at the lowest cost.

Craft a plan
A strategic plan identifies how the organisation will achieve its objectives, vision, and position. The plan is a deliberate course of action towards strategic objectives and describes how the organisation will move from one point to another within a specific scenario. Planning horizons are typically longer term, although lengths may vary across organisations, industries, and strategic context.

Adopt patterns of action
A pattern of action is how an organisation works. Formal hierarchies show one view of the organisation, but the interactions between these hierarchies, the exchange of

information, the handover of units of work, and the exchange of money all contribute to a network of activity that gets things done.

Patterns of action work in two ways. On the one hand, the strategy defines patterns that executives believe will be efficient and effective means of achieving objectives. Patterns are also defined in the formal interactions between service provider personnel and their customers. On the other hand, patterns of action are a way of dealing with the dynamic nature of organisations. As the organisation and its environment change, so the strategy needs to be adapted and strengthened

Strategy execution
Tactical plans describe what approaches and methods will be used to achieve the strategy. If a strategy answers the question "where are we going?" then tactics answer the question "how will we get there?"

Other service management processes
For a service provider, no strategy can be executed without being able to manage the services that they will be providing. Service management processes enable the service provider to achieve alignment between the services and the desired outcomes on an on-going basis. Without service management processes the very best the service provider can do is to react promptly to customers, but will often not be able to follow through to deliver high-quality services over time.

Align assets with customer outcomes
Strategy execution relies on the ability of the service provider to know what service assets they have, where they are located, and how they are deployed.

Optimise critical success factors
The term "critical success factor" refers to any aspect of a strategy, process, project, or initiative that needs to be present in order for it to succeed. Critical success factors could be specific skills, tools, circumstances, finances, executive support or the completion of another activity or project.

Prioritise investments
Each new service or project will require funding. Prioritise Strategic investments are prioritised based on customer needs.

Measurement and evaluation
This stage of strategy management is performed by a number of different areas, including:
• Customers and users
• Service management processes
• Continual service improvement
• The organisation's executives

Service providers should be aware that in many cases they will not be able to measure something that is important to the customer. In these cases what is important is that the customer takes responsibility for performing the measurement, and the service provider will agree to an appropriate response to any exceptions.

Measurement and evaluation: Continual service improvement
CSI activities measure and evaluate the achievement of strategy over time. Firstly, CSI activities identify areas that are not performing to expectation, and therefore threaten the achievement of the strategy. Secondly, CSI activities set the baseline for the next round of strategy assessments. Since the organisation exists in (and is itself) a continuously changing environment, the strategy needs to be continually assessed and revised.

Measurement and evaluation: Expansion and growth
As the organisation achieves its existing strategy, it gets better at being able to deliver services to its existing market spaces.

Strategy management for internal IT service providers
Internal IT organisations often make the mistake of thinking that they do not play a strategic role in the organisation, and that they should confine their activities to tactical planning and execution. However, IT is a strategic part of most businesses, and it is important that the IT organisation strategy is closely aligned and measured with the business strategy.

Strategic assessment for internal service providers
Strategic assessment is similar to the strategy management process described above but it defines its environment more specifically. The purpose of the strategic assessment is to determine the IT organisation's current situation.

The internal environment that should be assessed by IT organisations includes:
- The organisation's business strategy
- Existing services
- Existing technologies
- IT service management
- Human resources
- Relationship with the business units

The external environment that should be assessed by IT organisations specifically includes:
- Other organisations
- Industry IT spending rates
- Vendor strategies and product roadmaps
- Partners
- Technology trends
- Customers
- Standards or regulatory requirements for IT

- Operations
- The relationship between application development and operations

Information management
- Information about the external environment
- Results of assessments of the internal environment
- Information about customer needs and satisfaction levels, current service capabilities and performance levels
- Strategy management for IT services documentation
- The service portfolio
- Financial management
- Business relationship management
- Demand management
- Continual service improvement

Interfaces
Like all processes, the strategy management for IT services process has relationships with all other processes. However, some of the most visible relationships include but are not limited to the following:
- Provides the guidelines and framework within which the service portfolio will be defined and managed
- Provides input to financial management to indicate types of returns required and to prioritise investments
- Identifies any policies that must be taken into account when designing services
- Enables service transition to prioritise and evaluate the services that are built, to ensure that they meet the original intent and strategic requirements of the services
- Knowledge management enables strategic planners to understand the existing environment, its history and its dynamics, and to make informed decisions about the future
- Operational tools and processes must ensure that they have been aligned to the strategic objectives and desired business outcomes
- Continual service improvement will help to evaluate whether the strategy has been executed effectively, and whether it has met its objectives

Triggers
Here are some of the triggers that may start the whole, or part of the, strategy management for IT services process.
- Annual planning cycles
- New business opportunity
- Changes to internal or external environments
- Mergers or acquisitions

Inputs
Here are some of the inputs required by the strategy management for IT services process.
- Existing plans
- Research on aspects of the environment by specialised research organisations

- Vendor strategies and product roadmaps
- Customer interviews and strategic plans
- Service portfolio to indicate the current and planned future service commitments
- Service reporting to indicate the effectiveness of the strategy
- Audit reports that indicate compliance with (or deviation from) the organisation's strategy

Outputs

Here are some of the outputs produced by the strategy management for IT services process.

- Strategic plans
- Tactical plans that identify how the strategy will be executed
- Strategy review schedules and documentation
- Mission and vision statements
- Policies regarding how the plans should be executed, services designed, transitioned, operated, and improved
- Strategic requirements for new services

Critical success factors

The critical success factors, which change over time, for the strategy management for IT services process may include (but are not limited to) the following.

- Access to structured information about the internal and external environments
- Identification and elimination of constraints for the service provider to meet business outcomes, deliver, and manage services
- A clear understanding of their perspective, positions, patterns and plans
- The ability to produce, store, maintain and communicate strategy planning documents
- The ability to translate strategic plans into tactical and operational plans

Metrics

The performance of the strategy management for IT services process can be measured according to the following factors:

- Documented evidence exists for every market space
- Every finding or recommendation is based on validated information
- Forecasts and findings from external research are validated
- The number of corrective actions taken to remove constraints is tracked, and the result of those actions on the achievement of strategic objectives
- Vision and mission statements have been defined and communication to all personnel
- Each service in the service portfolio has a statement about which business outcomes it meets, and is measured in terms of these outcomes
- Stakeholders can provide an overview of the content of the strategy documents relevant to their business unit
- All documents are under document control and changes to the documents have been made through the appropriate change control measures
- Deviation from activities and patterns is identified in the strategy

Challenges

Here are some of the potential challenges faced by the strategy management for IT services process.

- Strategy management for IT services is conducted at the wrong level in the organisation
- Lack of accurate information about the external environment
- Lack of support by stakeholders
- Lack of the appropriate tools or a lack of understanding of how to use the tools and techniques
- Lack of the appropriate document control mechanisms and procedures
- Difficulty in matching the operational targets

Risks

Here are some of the potential risks faced by the strategy management for IT services process.

- A flawed governance model
- Short-term priorities override the directives of the strategy
- Making strategic decisions when there is missing and/or un-validated information about the internal or external environments
- Choosing the wrong strategy
- Strategies are seen as an exercise that happens once a year and that has no bearing on what happens for the rest of the year

5.4 Service portfolio management

A service portfolio describes a provider's services in terms of business value. It articulates business needs and the provider's response to those needs. By definition, business value terms correspond to marketing terms, providing a means for comparing service competitiveness across alternative providers. By acting as the basis of a decision framework, a service portfolio either clarifies or helps to clarify the following strategic questions:

- Why should a customer buy these services?
- Why should they buy these services from us?
- What are the pricing or chargeback models?
- What are our strengths and weaknesses, priorities and risks?
- How should our resources and capabilities be allocated?

The service portfolio is the complete set of services that is managed by a service provider. The service portfolio is used to manage the entire lifecycle of all services. It includes three categories of service: service pipeline (proposed or in development), service catalogue (live or available for deployment) and retired services. The service portfolio represents the investment made in an organisation's services, and also articulates the value that services help it to realise.

Service portfolio management is responsible for managing the service portfolio. It is therefore also the process that is responsible for defining which services will be entered into the service portfolio and how those services are tracked and progressed through their lifecycle. In other words, service portfolio management acts as a gatekeeper for the service provider, ensuring that they only provide services that contribute to strategic objectives and meet the agreed business outcomes.

Purpose and objectives

The purpose of service portfolio management is to ensure that the service provider has the right mix of services to balance the investment in IT with the ability to meet business outcomes. It tracks the investment in services throughout their lifecycle. It ensures that services are clearly defined and linked to the achievement of business outcomes.

The objectives of service portfolio management are to:
* Provide a process and mechanisms to enable an organisation to investigate and decide on which services to provide
* Maintain the definitive portfolio of services provided
* Provide a mechanism for the organisation to evaluate how services enable them to achieve their strategy
* Control which services are offered, under what conditions and at what level of investment
* Track the investment in services throughout their lifecycle
* Analyse which services are no longer viable and when they should be retired

Scope

The scope of service portfolio management is all services a service provider plans to deliver, those currently delivered and those that have been withdrawn from service. The primary concern of service portfolio management is whether the service provider is able to generate value from the services.

Value to the business

Service portfolio management enables the business to make sound decisions about investments. Customers are able to make decisions about whether the service is a good or bad investment, and evaluate potential additional opportunities. It is a tool for innovation for the organisation.

The service provider is viewed as a steward of service assets that are seen as critical or vital to the customer's success.

Policies, principles, and basic concepts

The service portfolio is the complete set of services that is managed by a service provider. The service portfolio also identifies those services in a conceptual stage, namely all services the organisation would provide if it had unlimited resources, capabilities and funding.

The service portfolio represents all the resources presently engaged or being released in various stages of the service lifecycle. Each stage requires resources for completion of projects, initiatives, and contracts. This is a very important governance aspect of service portfolio management.

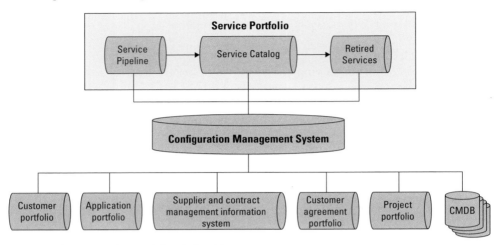

Figure 5.3 Sample service portfolio relationships
Source: The Cabinet Office

Service pipeline

The service pipeline is a database or structured document listing all services that are under consideration or development, but are not yet available to customers. It also includes any major investment opportunities. The service pipeline provides a business view of possible future services and is part of the service portfolio that is not normally published to customers.

The service pipeline represents the service provider's growth and strategic outlook for the future and reflects the general business health of the provider.

Service catalogue

The service catalogue is a database or structured document with information about all live IT services, including those available for deployment. The service catalogue is the only part of the service portfolio published to customers, and is used to support the sale and delivery of IT services. The service catalogue includes information about deliverables, prices, contact points, ordering and request processes.

Items can enter the service catalogue only after due diligence has been performed on related costs and risks. Only operational services or the services chartered to be operational can be found in the service catalogue, and resources are engaged to fully support active services.

In addition, the service catalogue serves as a service order and demand channelling mechanism. It defines and communicates the policies, guidelines, and accountability required for the service provider to deliver and support services to its customers.

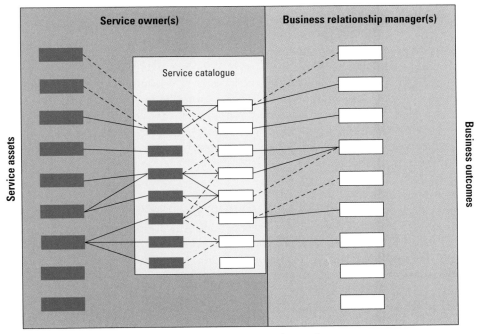

Figure 5.4 The service catalogue and linkages between services and outcomes

Source: The Cabinet Office

The above figure illustrates the linkages between the following:

- The boxes on the left are service assets used by the service provider to provide services. These could be servers, databases, applications, network devices etc.
- Services in the service catalogue. There are two layers of services shown in Figure 5.4. The layer on the left shows supporting services, which are usually not seen by the customer directly (contained in a view of the service catalogue called the technical or supporting service catalogue). One example is application hosting (unless it is a Type III service provider offering application hosting services). The second layer of services is customer-facing services. An example is point of sales.
- The boxes on the right are business outcomes, which the business achieves when it uses these services. An example is the ability to make sales and provide receipts to customers

Retired services

Some services in the service portfolio are phased out or retired. There is a decision to be made by each organisation, following a service review, on when to move a service from catalogue to retired. This is necessary because such services may cost a lot more to support and may disrupt economies of scale and scope.

Service portfolio management will define a policy for the length of time that a service will remain in the service portfolio. This could be expressed in time, or how many alternatives are available in the service catalogue.

Retiring services is managed through service transition.

Configuration management system

The configuration management system is a set of tools and databases that are used to manage an IT service provider's configuration data. The configuration management system also includes information about incidents, problems, known errors, changes and releases, and may contain data about employees, suppliers, locations, business units, customers and users. The configuration management system includes tools for collecting, storing, managing, updating, and presenting data about all configuration items and their relationships.

Application portfolio

The application portfolio is a database or structured document used to manage applications throughout their lifecycle. The application portfolio contains key attributes of all applications. The application portfolio is sometimes implemented as part of the service portfolio or, if this does not yet exist, as part of the service knowledge management system.

Customer portfolio

The customer portfolio is a database or structured document used to record all customers of the IT service provider. The customer portfolio is the business relationship manager's view of the customers who receive services from the IT service provider.

Customer agreement portfolio

The customer agreement portfolio is a database or structured document used to manage service contracts or agreements between an IT service provider and its customers. Each IT service delivered to a customer should have a contract or other agreement that is listed in the customer agreement portfolio.

Project portfolio

The project portfolio is a database or structured document used to manage projects that have been chartered. The project portfolio is used to coordinate projects; ensuring objectives are met within time and cost and to specification. The project portfolio also ensures that projects are not duplicated, that they stay within the agreed scope, and that resources are available for each project. The project portfolio is the tool used to manage single projects as well as large-scale programmes, consisting of multiple projects.

Charter: A document authorising the project and stating its scope, terms and references

Service models

Service portfolio management uses service models to analyse the impact of new services or changes to existing services. If a service model does not exist for a service in the pipeline, service portfolio management will ensure that one is defined.

Market spaces and service growth

Market spaces are helpful to service portfolio management to evaluate the impact of a proposed new service or change to an existing service, since they clarify the opportunity that is being served.

Aligning service assets, services and business outcomes

Service portfolio management plays an important role in achieving this since the service portfolio and configuration management system (CMS) documents the relationship between business outcomes, services, and service assets.

Service portfolio management through the service lifecycle

Service strategy

Although service portfolio management is a process within service strategy, it also plays an important part in every stage in the service lifecycle.

Service design

In service design, service portfolio management ensures that design work is prioritised according to business needs, and that there is a clear understanding of how the service will be measured by the business.

Service portfolio management also provides input to the teams involved in building the services. This will ensure that the teams remain focused on the objectives, outcomes, and priorities of each service. It will also work with the PMO or project manager to monitor the build process, to ensure that the services are built on time, to specification and to budget.

Service transition

Service transition builds and tests the services that will be placed into the service catalogue. The service portfolio provides guidance to service transition in building, testing and evaluating the service. Change management authorisation is necessary to move a service into the service catalogue.

Service operation

Service operation delivers the service in the service catalogue part of the service portfolio. Service portfolio management provides them with an understanding of the services and how and why they need to be delivered.

Continual service improvement

Continual service improvement evaluates whether the services in the portfolio met the stated objectives; and, if not, identifies ways in which the situation can be rectified.

Continual service improvement also evaluates the business cases and objectives to ensure that they are still valid, and therefore that service portfolio management continues to prioritise services appropriately.

Process activities, methods, and techniques

Service portfolio management consists of four main phases of activity, illustrated in the following figure.
- Define
- Analyse
- Approve
- Charter

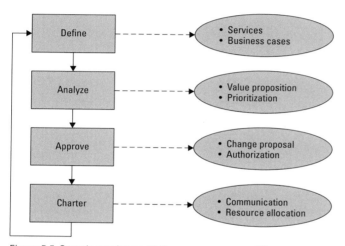

Figure 5.5 Sample service portfolio management workflow
Source: The Cabinet Office

Process initiation

New services and changes to existing services can be initiated from a number of sources, and in a number of different forms. Changes to plans or the identification of a service improvement plan will often trigger this activity.

There are four sub-activities within the process initiation activity.
1. Strategy management for it services
2. Business relationship management
3. Continual service improvement
4. Other service management processes

Define

This activity is about defining desired business outcomes, opportunities, utility and warranty requirements and the services themselves.

There are nine sub-activities within the define activity.
1. Strategy
2. Request from business
3. Service improvement opportunities and plans
4. Service suggestion
5. Existing service.
6. Service, customers, business outcomes (new services)
7. Service model (new services)
8. Impact on service portfolio (existing services)
9. Impact on service model (existing services)

Analyse
The analysis of new or modified services moving between phases of the lifecycle is performed by linking the service to the service strategy.

There are four activities within the analyse activity.

1. Service portfolio review

2. Analyse investments, value and priorities
   Once the services have been analysed, executives need to decide which services will take priority. Services will be classified in one of three strategic categories:
   • Run the business
   • Grow the business
   • Transform the business

   Each of above is further classified according to the type of budget made available for this category of service. These categories are:
   • Venture
   • Growth
   • Discretionary
   • Non-discretionary
   • Core

3. Articulate value proposition

4. Is the service or change feasible?
   The decisions about how services will be progressed through the service portfolio management process fall into six categories:
   • Retain/build
   • Replace
   • Rationalise
   • Refactor
   • Renew
   • Retire

Approve: change proposal

Once a new or modified service is deemed feasible it will need to be submitted through the change management process[1] for a detailed assessment and for final authorisation.

At this point, not all details of the new or modified service have been defined. Service portfolio management will submit a change proposal. This allows the design teams to spend money and prioritise resources even though a final decision regarding the change has yet to be made.

The change proposal will allow change management to coordinate the activities of all resources required to investigate the customer requirements and infrastructure requirements; and also ensure that these activities are prioritised in relation to other authorised changes already being built, tested, and implemented by the same resources.

The change proposal should include:
*   A high-level description of the new or changed service, including business outcomes to be supported, and utility and warranty to be provided
*   Full business case including risks, issues and alternatives, as well as budget and financial expectations
*   Expected implementation schedule

There are two activities within the approve activity.
1. Approve: change management authorisation
2. Approve: is the change proposal authorised?

Service charter

The service charter ensures that all stakeholders, development, testing, and deployment personnel have a common understanding of the cost, timelines, deliverables, and who is involved. The implication of using the term "charter" is that the changes will be managed using a project management approach.

There are six activities within the service charter activity.
1. Communicate with stakeholders
2. Service design and transition processes
3. Track progress and update service portfolio
4. Is the service successful?
5. Retiring services
6. Refreshing the portfolio

Information management
*   The service portfolio, consisting of a service pipeline, service catalogue and retired services
*   The project portfolio

---

1   More on this in the change management process section in Chapter 7.

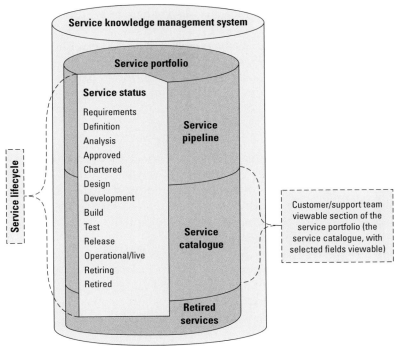

Figure 5.6 Sample contents of the service portfolio

Source: The Cabinet Office

- The application portfolio
- The customer portfolio
- The customer agreement portfolio
- Service models
- The service strategy
- The configuration management system

Interfaces

Like all processes, the service portfolio management process has relationships with all other processes. However, some of the most visible relationships include but are not limited to the following:
- Determines which services will be placed into the service catalogue, while service catalogue management performs all the activities required for this to be done
- **Strategy management for IT services** – To define the overall strategy of services, and the objectives for investments
- **Financial management for IT services** – To provide information and tools to enable service portfolio management to perform return on investment calculations
- **Demand management** – To provide information about the patterns of business activity
- Business relationship management initiates requests and obtains business information and requirements

- **Service level management** – To ensure that services are able to achieve the levels of performance defined
- **Capacity management and availability management** – To ensure that the capacity and availability requirements of chartered services are designed and built
- **IT service continuity management** – To identify the business impact of risks associated with delivering the service, and designs counter-measures and recovery plans
- **Information security management** – To ensure that the confidentiality, integrity and availability objectives are met
- **The supplier management** process – To indicate that a suppler will no longer be able to supply services or that a supplier relationship is at risk
- **Change management** – To evaluates the resources required to introduce new services or changes to existing services,
- **Service asset and configuration management** – To provide the tools, information and data upon which the service portfolio is based
- **Service validation and testing** – To ensures that the anticipated functionality and returns of each service can be achieved
- **Knowledge management** – To enable IT managers and architects to make informed decisions about the best service options
- **Continual service improvement** – To provide feedback about the actual use and return of services against their anticipated use and return

Triggers
Here are some of the triggers that may start the whole, or part of the, service portfolio management process.
- A new strategy has been devised, or an existing strategy is being changed
- Business relationship management receives a request for a new service or a change to an existing service
- Service improvement opportunities from CSI
- Feedback from design, build and transition teams
- Service level management reviews
- Financial management for IT services indicates that a service costs significantly more or less than anticipated

Inputs
Here are some of the inputs required by the service portfolio management process.
- Strategy plans
- Service improvement opportunities
- Financial reports
- Requests, suggestions or complaints from the business
- Project updates for services in the charter stage of the process

Outputs
Here are some of the outputs produced by the service portfolio management process.
- An up-to-date service portfolio
- Service charters

- Reports on the status of new or changed services
- Reports on the investment made in services in the service portfolio, and the returns on that investment
- Change proposals
- Identified strategic risks

Critical success factors

The critical success factors, which change over time, for the service portfolio management process may include but are not limited to the following.

- The existence of a formal process to investigate and decide which services to provide
- A model to analyse the potential return on investment and acceptable level of risk for new services or changes to existing services
- The ability to document each service provided, together with the business need it meets and the business outcome it supports
- A formal process to review whether services are enabling the organisation to achieve its strategy
- The ability to change services in response to changes in the internal and external environments – where appropriate
- Tools that enable the service provider to track the investment in services throughout their lifecycle
- A formal process exists to evaluate the viability of services, and to retire them when they are no longer viable

Metrics

The performance of the service portfolio management process can be measured according to the following factors:

- The service portfolio management process is audited and reviewed annually and meets its objectives
- Every service has a documented statement of the initial investment made in the service
- Accounting records are produced periodically showing the on-going investment in each service. The return on investment is calculated
- Customer surveys indicate a high level of satisfaction with the value they are receiving
- Each service has documented risks associated with it. Mitigation or counter-measures have been taken, where risk is acceptable
- A service portfolio is used for deciding which services to offer. All services are documented in the service portfolio
- Services are linked to at least one business outcome
- Regular and structured feedback shows the performance of each service and its ability to meet stated business outcomes
- Every change to an environment has a corresponding entry to service portfolio management
- All changed business objectives and outcomes continue to be met by the services in the service portfolio

- Customer surveys show continued high levels of satisfaction
- The investment in each service is quantified in the service portfolio
- Investment in each service is periodically reported from the initial investment

Challenges

Here are some of the potential challenges faced by the service portfolio management process.

- Lack of access to customer business information
- Absence of…
  - a formal project management approach
  - a project portfolio
  - a customer portfolio
  - a customer agreement portfolio
- A service portfolio that only focuses on the service provider aspects of services
- The lack of a formal change management process

Risks

Here are some of the potential risks faced by the service portfolio management process.

- Making a decision to offer services without validated or complete information
- Offering services without defining how they will be measured

5.5 Financial management for IT services

Financial management is a complex process that all organisations use as a basis for conducting business. It is usually owned by a senior executive and managed by a financial management function. Financial management enables the organisation to manage its resources, and to ensure that these resources are being used to achieve the organisation's objectives

The IT organisation, along with all other departments in the organisation, is involved in the organisation's financial management process. They apply the organisation's financial management procedures and practices to ensure that they are aligned with the organisation's objectives and financial policies. In doing so, these departments often create their own financial management processes.

In this section, the text will therefore use the term financial management as follows:

- Financial management – This refers to the generic use of the term
- Enterprise financial management – This refers specifically to the process as it is used by the "corporate" financial department
- Financial management for IT services – This refers to the way in which the IT service provider has applied the process

Financial management for IT services is the process responsible for managing an IT service provider's budgeting, accounting and charging requirements. It is also the process that is used to quantify the value that IT services contribute to the business.

More than any other process, financial management enables an IT service provider to play a strategic role in the business. It helps to quantify IT"s value and contributions, and quantifies the business opportunities that IT services enable.

Financial management as a strategic tool is equally applicable to all three service provider types.

Purpose and objectives

The purpose of financial management for IT services is to secure the appropriate level of funding to design, develop, and deliver services that meet the strategy of the organisation. Financial management for IT services identifies the balance between the cost and quality of service and maintains the balance of supply and demand between the service provider and its customers.

The objectives of financial management for IT services include:
- Defining and maintaining a framework to identify, manage and communicate the cost of providing services
- Evaluating the financial impact of new or changed strategies on the service provider
- Securing funding to manage the provision of services
- Facilitating good stewardship of service and customer assets
- Understanding the relationship between expenses and income
- Managing and reporting expenditure on service provision
- Executing the financial policies and practices in the provision of services
- Accounting for money spent on the creation, delivery and support of services
- Forecasting the financial requirements for the organisation
- Where appropriate, defining a framework to recover the costs of service provision

Scope

Financial management is normally a well-established and well-understood part of any organisation. Professional accountants manage dedicated finance departments, which set financial policies, budgeting procedures, financial reporting standards, accounting practices and revenue generation or cost recovery rules.

Financial management consists of three main processes:
- Budgeting – This is the process of predicting and controlling the income and expenditure of money within the organisation. Budgeting consists of a periodic negotiation cycle to set budgets and the monthly monitoring of the current budgets
- Accounting – This is the process that enables the IT organisation to account fully for the way its money is spent. It usually involves accounting systems, including ledgers, charts of accounts, journals etc.
- Charging – This is the process required to bill customers for the services supplied to them. This requires sound IT accounting practices and systems

The table below (5.3) shows there are two distinct cycles associated with accounting, budgeting and charging:

- A planning cycle (annual), where cost projections and workload forecasting form a basis for cost calculations and price setting
- An operational cycle (monthly or quarterly) where costs are monitored and checked against budgets, bills are issued and revenue collected

Table 5.3 Budgeting, IT accounting and charging cycles

	BUDGETING	IT ACCOUNTING	CHARGING
Planning (annual)	Agree overall expenditures	Establish standard unit costs for each IT resource	Establish pricing policy and publish price list
Operational (monthly)	Take actions to manage budget exceptions or changed costs	Monitor expenditure by cost centre	Compile and issue bills

Value to the business

Much like their business counterparts, IT organisations are increasingly using financial management to assist in the pursuit of:

- Enhanced decision-making
- Speed of change
- Service portfolio management
- Financial compliance and control
- Operational control
- Value capture and creation

Specific benefits to the business include:

- The ability to conduct business in a financially responsible manner and to comply with regulatory and legislative requirements and generally accepted accounting principles
- Accurate planning and forecasting of the budget needed to cover the cost of service
- An understanding of the cost of IT to each business unit
- Better matching of IT services to business outcomes
- The ability to make sound business decisions regarding the use of and investment in IT

Policies, principles, and basic concepts

Enterprise financial management policies

The enterprise financial management policies provide a framework within which IT must work to manage all financial aspects of its services and organisation.

Funding

Funding is the sourcing and allocation of money for a specific purpose or project. Funding comes from two sources, external and internal.

Funding models help to define how and when the IT service provider will be funded. Each model uses the same financial data, adapted to the organisational culture and enterprise financial management policies.

Table 5.4 The three funding models

Rolling plan funding	A plan for a fixed number of months, years or other cycles. At the end of the first cycle, the plan is simply extended by one more cycle. This allows the service provider to adjust funding requirements as necessary and also to obtain funding more readily. This is a popular type of planning and funding for specific projects, not the on-going provision of all IT services
Trigger-based funding	A plan to provide funding when a specific situation or event occurs. For example, the change management process would be a trigger to this planning process
Zero-based funding	A plan to provide funding for the actual costs to deliver the IT services only. The service provider is allowed to spend up to an agreed budget amount, or get special approval to spend over the amount, and at the end of the financial period the money is recovered from the other business units through cost transfers.

Compliance

Compliance relates to the ability to demonstrate that proper and consistent accounting methods and/or practices are being employed. It is important that enterprise financial management policies clearly outline what legislative and other regulatory requirements apply to the service provider and customer's organisation.

Process activities, methods, and techniques

Major inputs
- Regulatory requirements
- Enterprise financial management policies
- Service management processes
- Each service management process provides financial information about how money is spent, what services are
- Service, contract, customer, application and project portfolios
- Service knowledge management system

Accounting

Accounting is the process responsible for identifying the actual costs of delivering IT services, comparing these with budgeted costs, and managing variance from the budget. Accounting is also responsible for tracking any income earned by services.

Cost model

A cost model is a framework which allows the service provider to determine the costs of providing services and ensure that they are allocated correctly. Cost models enable the service provider to understand, for example, the impact of proposed changes to the current service. An organisation may use any of the following examples of cost models.
- Cost by IT organisation
- Cost by service

- Cost by customer
- Cost by location
- Hybrid cost models

Accounting: cost centres and cost units
Cost centres and cost units
- In the context of cost models and accounting systems, a cost centre is anything to which a cost can be allocated.
- A cost unit is the lowest level category to which costs will be allocated. They are (usually) easily measured and communicated in customer terms.

Cost types and cost elements
Cost types are the highest level of category to which costs are assigned in budgeting and accounting – for example, hardware, software, people, consulting services and facilities.

Cost elements are the sub-categories to which costs are assigned in budgeting and accounting. Cost elements are sub-categories of cost types. For example, a cost type of "people" could have cost elements of payroll, personnel benefits, expenses, training, overtime etc. In general, cost elements are the same as budget line items where the purpose of the model is simple recovery of costs.

Accounting: Cost classification
There are six major classifications, grouped in three pairs of options. A special type of cost classification (depreciation) is also discussed. The definitions for each term may be found in the glossary at the end of this publication.
- Capital item or operational cost
- Direct cost vs. indirect cost
- Fixed cost vs. variable cost
- Depreciation

Allocation of costs[2]
This is a complex area of accountancy, and a qualified professional will need to ensure that the appropriate methods are chosen and properly used. However, accountants will need the assistance of IT professionals to provide input to these methods, and so this publication provides a very brief definition of four of the most commonly used allocation methods:
- Activity-based costing (ABC)
- Utilisation-based allocation
- Agreed basis for allocation
- Indirect cost rate

---

2   It is beyond the scope of this publication to further explain this topic

Accounting: chart of accounts

The chart of accounts is a list of all the accounts that are used to record income and expenses.

Accounting: analysis and reporting

Amongst many other objectives, the analysis and reporting activity is used to generate an organisation-wide understanding of the income, expenses, and investments of the service provider. This activity, through the reporting aspects, communicates the cost of services to all stakeholders.

Accounting: action plans

Action plans, normally short term, aim at restoring the organisation to its planned path within a specified period, usually a month or a quarter. Action plans may assist stakeholders in agreeing to change the original plan and its targets.

Budgeting

Budgeting is the activity of predicting and controlling the spending of money. Budgeting consists of a periodic negotiation cycle to set future budgets (usually annual) and the routine monitoring and adjusting of current budgets.

Most managers are familiar with the activity of producing and approving an annual budget, and then reviewing the budget regularly to ensure that the targets are being met. What many fail to appreciate, however, is the importance of budgeting as a business tool.

There are five sub-activities within the budgeting activity.
- Budgeting: analysis of previous budget
- Budgeting: assessment of plans
- Budgeting: specification of changes to funding and spending
- Budgeting: cost and income estimation
- Budgeting: creating the budget(s)

Charging

Charging is the activity whereby payment is required for services delivered. For internal service providers charging is optional, and many organisations choose to treat their IT service provider as a cost centre. In this situation charging is often referred to as "chargeback" since the costs of the service provider are simply re-allocated back to other business units by the central financial function, using an internal charging method.

Unless the IT service organisation has the support of the whole organisation in introducing charging, it will fail. It has to be simple, fair, and realistic.

There are three sub-activities within the charging activity.

Charging: charging policies
There are two possible charging policies in determining how charging will work and both are defined by enterprise financial management.
- The first policy decision is whether or not to charge
- The second policy decision is the level of cost recovery[3] that needs to be achieved using one of the options below.
  - Cost recovery or break-even
  - Recovery with an additional margin
  - Cross-subsidisation
  - Notional charging

Charging: decide chargeable items
A chargeable item assists the customer in understanding exactly what they are charged. It also helps to set and then manage expectations about the level of service that will be received.

Charging: pricing
The decision regarding how much to charge depends on two things:
- The chargeable item itself
- The expected value of the service sale and trends of consumption

Several options exist for deciding how much to charge. Options include:
- Cost
- Cost plus
- Going rate
- Market price
- Fixed price
- Tiered subscription
- Differential charging

Billing
Billing is a sub-process of charging. There are three main options for billing.
- No billing
- Informational billing (notional charging)
- Billing and collection (real charging)

Information management
- Financial management systems, such as accounting, budgeting and charging systems
- Financial management policies, legislation and regulations
- Financial reporting structures, templates, reports, and spread sheets
- The organisation's chart of accounts
- The service knowledge management system

---

3   It is beyond the scope of this publication to further explain this topic

Interfaces

Like all processes, the financial management for IT services process has relationships with all other processes. However, some of the most visible relationships include but are not limited to:

- **All service management processes** – To use financial management to determine the costs and benefits of the process itself
- **Strategy management for IT services** – To work with enterprise financial management to determine the financial objectives for the organisation
- **Service portfolio management** – To provide the service structure which will be used to define cost models, accounting and budgeting systems and the basis for charging
- **Business relationship management** – To provide information about the way in which the business measures the value of services and what they are prepared to pay for services
- **Capacity and availability management** – To provide valuable information about the various options of technology and service performance
- **Change management** – To use financial information in determining the financial impact or requirements of changes
- **Service asset and configuration management** – To document financial data about assets and configuration items
- **Continual service improvement** – To determine whether the return of a proposed improvement is worth the investment required to make the improvement

Figure 5.7 provides a sample view of activities, inputs, outputs, and relationhips required to ensure the success of this process.

Triggers

Here are some of the triggers that may start the whole, or part of the, financial management for IT services process.

- Monthly, quarterly and annual financial reporting cycles
- Audits reports
- Requests for financial information from other service management processes
- Investigation into a new service opportunity
- The introduction of charging for IT services
- A request for change

Inputs

Here are some of the inputs required by the financial management for IT services process.

- Policies, standards and practices defined by legislation, regulators and enterprise financial managers
- Generally Accepted Accounting Practices (GAAP) and local variations
- All data sources where financial information is stored
- The service portfolio

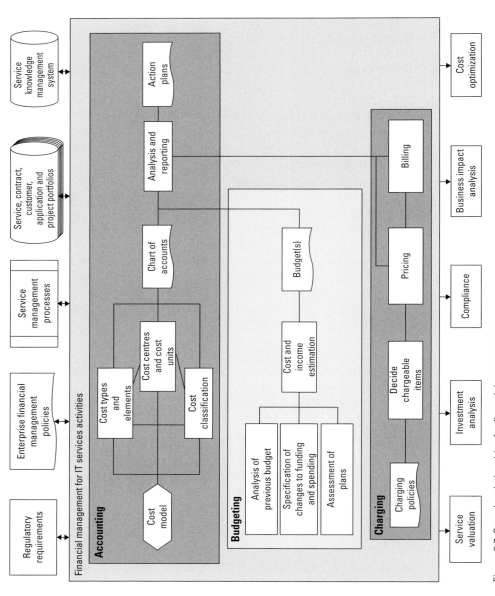

Figure 5.7 Sample relationships for financial management
Source: The Cabinet Office

Outputs

Here are some of the outputs produced by the financial management for IT services process.

- Service valuation
- Service investment analysis
- Compliance
- Cost optimisation
- Business impact analysis (BIA)
- Planning confidence

Critical success factors

The critical success factors, which change over time, for the financial management for IT services process may include but are not limited to the following.

- There is an enterprise-wide framework to identify, manage, and communicate financial information, costs, and associated returns
- Financial management for IT services is a key component of evaluating strategies
- Funding is available to support the provision of services
- Good service asset and configuration management enables stewardship of service- and customer-assets
- The service provider understands the relationship between expenses and income
- Financial reporting to the organisation's stakeholders enables them to make sound decisions
- Ability to account for the money spent on the creation, delivery, and support of services
- Reporting on, and accurately forecasting, the financial requirements

Metrics

The performance of the financial management for IT services process can be measured according to the following factors:

- Enterprise financial management has established standards, policies and charts of accounts
- The financial management for IT services framework specifies how services will be accounted for
- Timely and accurate submission of financial reports
- All strategies have a comprehensive analysis of investment and returns
- Review of strategies indicates financial forecasts were accurate within acceptable margins
- Timely and accurate provision of financial information for service analysis during service portfolio management
- Internal service providers receive the funding required to provide the agreed services
- External service providers are able to sell services at the required levels of profitability
- Funding exists for research and development of new services or improvements initiatives

- Customer and service assets are recorded in the configuration management system
- Regular reports are provided on the costs of services in design, transition, and operation

Challenges

Here are some of the potential challenges faced by the financial management for IT services process.

- Financial reporting and cost models focused on infrastructure and applications cost rather than the cost of services
- Complying with enterprise standards and policies
- Focusing on cost saving rather than cost optimisation
- In the beginning, it may be difficult to find where financial data is located and how it is controlled
- Internal service providers may find it difficult to introduce charging
- External service providers will need to balance the cost of services with the perceived value of those services to ensure the correct pricing models

Risks

Here are some of the potential risks faced by the financial management for IT services process.

- Introducing dedicated financial management processes may be viewed as unnecessary and a waste of money and time
- Not having adequate financial management processes for IT services may expose the organisation to penalties for non-compliance with legislative or regulatory compliance
- Lack of available personnel who understand both the world of the service provider and that of cost accounting

5.6   Demand management

Demand management is the process that seeks to understand, anticipate, and influence customer demand for services and the provision of capacity to meet these demands.

Demand management is a critical aspect of service management. Poorly managed demand is a source of risk for service providers because of uncertainty in demand. Excess capacity generates cost without creating value that provides a basis for cost recovery. Customers are reluctant to pay for idle capacity unless it has value for them.

Purpose and objectives

The purpose of demand management is to understand, anticipate, and influence customer demand for services and to work with capacity management to ensure the service provider has capacity to meet this demand. Demand management works at every stage of the lifecycle to ensure that services are designed, tested, and delivered to support the achievement of business outcomes at the appropriate levels of activity.

This is where the service provider has the opportunity to understand the customer needs and feed these into the service strategies to realise the service potential of the customer and to differentiate the services to the customers.

The objectives of demand management are to:
- Identify and analyse patterns of business activity
- Define and analyse user profiles
- Ensure that services are designed to meet the patterns of business activity
- Work with capacity management to ensure that sufficient resources are available at the right time and place
- Anticipate, prevent, or manage situations where demand for a service exceeds the capacity to deliver it
- Balance the utilisation of resources to meet the fluctuating levels of demand for those services

Scope

The scope of the demand management process is to identify and analyse the patterns of business activity that initiate demand for services, and to identify and analyse how different types of user influence the demand for services.

Demand management activities should include:
- Identifying and analysing patterns of business activity associated with services
- Identifying user profiles and analysing their service usage patterns
- Identifying, agreeing and implementing measures to influence demand together with capacity management

Table 5.5 Comparison of demand management and capacity management

	Demand management	Capacity management
Purpose	Identify, analyse and influence customer demand for services and the capacity to meet this demand	Ensure that current and future capacity requirements of services are provided cost-effectively, and that services are performing at the agreed level
Focus	Anticipating the demand for services based on user profiles and patterns of business activity, and identifying the means to influence that demand to achieve an optimal balance between investment and business outcome achievement	Understanding the current and future requirements for resources and capabilities and ensuring that these are designed, tested and managed to meet the demand on services
Major activities	Identifying patterns of business activity, user profiles, and the resulting demand on services. Anticipating increases or decreases in demand, and identifying strategies for dealing with these. Influencing demand through incentives, penalties or differential charging	Producing a capacity plan to ensure the investment in the appropriate levels of capacity. Ensuring optimal use and performance of resources. Evaluating the impact of new or changed resources and capabilities on existing performance levels

Value to the business

The main value of demand management is to achieve a balance between the cost of a service and the value of the business outcomes it supports. Demand management refines the understanding of how, when and to what level business outcomes, services, resources and capabilities interact. This enables executives to evaluate the real investment required to achieve business outcomes at varying levels of activity.

Policies, principles, and basic concepts

Supply and demand

From a strategic perspective demand management is about matching supply to demand.

Consumption produces demand and production consumes demand in a highly synchronised pattern. Unlike goods, services cannot be manufactured in advance and stocked in a finished goods inventory. The following figure illustrates how tightly coupled demand and capacity management are.

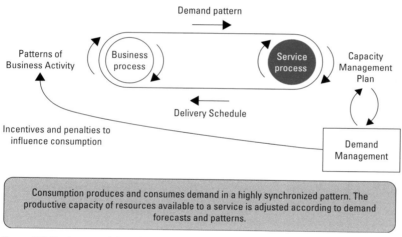

Figure 5.8 Business activity influences patterns of demand for services

Source: The Cabinet Office

Gearing service assets

The balance of supply and demand is achieved by gearing the service assets to meet the dynamic patterns of demand on services.
• Identifying the services through the service portfolio
• Quantifying the patterns of business activity
• Specifying the appropriate architecture to deal with the type and quantity of demand
• Working with capacity and availability planning to ensure the right service assets are available at the right time and perform at the right levels
• Performance management and tuning of service assets to deal with variations in demand

Demand management through the lifecycle

To be fully effective, demand management needs to be active throughout the service lifecycle. The activities of demand management in each stage of the lifecycle will include:

- **Service strategy** – To identify the services and outcomes, and the patterns of business activity that are generated by achieving these outcomes
- **Service design** – To confirm customer requirements regarding availability and performance, and validate that the service assets are designed to meet those requirements
- **Service transition** – Demand management is involved in testing and validating services for forecast utilisation and patterns of business activity
- **Service operation** – Technical, application, and IT operations management functions will monitor service assets and service utilisation level
- **Continual service improvement** – Demand management will work to identify trends in patterns of business activity and to initiate improvements to service or customer-assets or to influence customer behaviours

Process activities, methods, and techniques

Identify sources of demand forecasting

Potential sources of information that can assist demand management to forecast demand include:

- Business plans
- Marketing plans and forecasts
- Production plans
- Sales forecasts
- New product launch plans

Patterns of business activity

Once a pattern of business activity (PBA) has been identified, a PBA profile should be drawn up and details about the PBA documented. The following items need to be documented:

- Classification
- Attributes
- Requirements
- Service asset requirements

User profiles

User profiles (UP) are based on roles and responsibilities within organisations. Pattern matching using PBA and UP ensures a systematic approach to understanding and managing demand from customers. They also require customers to better understand their own business activities and view them as consumers of services and producers of demand.

Activity-based demand management

Business processes are the primary source of demand for services. PBA influences the demand patterns seen by the service providers. It is very important to study the customer's business to identify, analyse, and classify such patterns to provide sufficient basis for capacity management.

Develop differentiated offerings

The analysis of the PBA may reveal that different levels of utility and warranty are needed at different times. Demand management will work with service portfolio management to define the appropriate service packages.

Management of operational demand

This activity works at managing or influencing the demand where live/operational services or resources are being over-utilised.

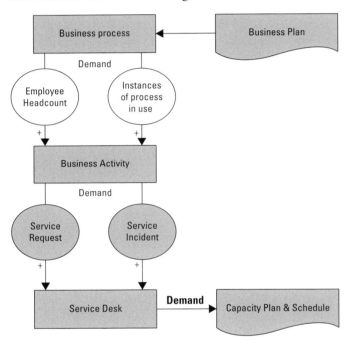

Figure 5.9 Sample activity-based demand management workflow

Source: The Cabinet Office

Information management

- The service portfolio
- The customer portfolio
- The project portfolio
- Minutes of meetings between business relationship managers and customers
- Service level agreements
- The configuration management system

Interfaces

Like all processes, the demand management process has relationships with all other processes. However, some of the most visible relationships include but are not limited to:

- **Strategy management for IT services** – To identify the key business outcomes and business activities
- **Service portfolio management** – To create and evaluate service models, establish and forecast utilisation requirements
- **Financial management for IT services** – To forecast the cost of providing the demand based on forecast patterns of business activity
- **Business relationship management** – As the primary source of information about the business activities of the customer
- **Service level management** – To formalise agreements in which the customer commits to levels of utilisation, and the service provider commits to levels of performance
- **Capacity management** – To define exactly how to match supply and demand in the design and operation of the service
- **Availability management** – To utilise the information about patterns of business activity in determining when service availability is most important
- **IT service continuity management** – To perform the business impact analysis and determine PBA and UP required during a major outage, crisis, or disaster
- **Change management** – To assess the impact of changes on how the business uses services
- **Service asset and configuration management** – To identify the relationship between the demand placed on services and the demand placed on systems and devices
- **Service validation and testing** – To ensure that the service has correctly dealt with patterns of demand, and that measures taken to prevent over-utilisation are effective
- **Event management** – To provide information about actual patterns of service utilisation and validate the anticipated patterns of business activity for a service

Triggers

Here are some of the triggers that may start the whole, or part of the, demand management process.

- A request from a customer for a new service, or change to an existing service
- A new service is being created to meet a strategic initiative
- A service model needs to be defined
- Utilisation rates are causing potential performance issues
- An exception has occurred

Inputs

Here are some of the inputs required by the demand management process.

- Initiative to create a new service, or to change an existing service
- Service models
- Patterns of business activity
- The customer portfolio, service portfolio and customer agreement portfolio

- Charging models
- Chargeable items
- Service improvement opportunities and plans

Outputs

Here are some of the outputs produced by the demand management process.
- User profiles
- Patterns of business activity
- Policies for management of demand
- Policies for addressing higher or lower, real or anticipated, service utilisation
- Documentation of options for differentiated offerings

Critical success factors

The critical success factors, which change over time, for the demand management process may include but are not limited to the following.
- Understand the levels of demand by identifying and analysing the patterns of business activity
- Understand the typical profiles of demand by identifying and analysing the user profiles from different types of user
- Services are designed to meet both the patterns of business activity and the business outcomes
- Working with capacity management to ensure that sufficient resources are available at the right place and right time to meet demand

Metrics

The performance of the demand management process can be measured according to:
- Patterns of business activity...
  - Are defined for each relevant service
  - Have been translated into workload information
- Each documented user profile that exists contains a demand profile for the services used by that type of user
- Demand management activities are routinely included as part of defining the service portfolio
- Capacity plans include details of patterns of business activity and corresponding workloads
- Utilisation monitoring shows balanced workloads
- Capacity plans and service level agreements contain techniques to manage demand

Challenges

Here are some of the potential challenges faced by the demand management process.
- The availability of information about business activities
- Customers might find it difficult to break down individual activities that make sense to the service provider
- Lack of a formal service portfolio management process or service portfolio

Risks

Here are some of the potential risks faced by the demand management process.
- Lack of, or inaccurate, configuration management information
- Not being able to obtain commitments to minimum or maximum utilisation levels

5.7 Business relationship management

Business relationship management (BRM) is the process that enables business relationship managers (BR-Mgr) to provide links between the service provider and customers at the strategic and tactical levels. The primary measure of whether this is being achieved is the level of customer satisfaction.

The role of the business relationship manager often already exists in many organisations to handle various customer-facing activities. The purpose of such role is often used representing IT with one or more customers. In such cases the role is often referred to as an "account manager" or "product manager" although the range of titles used varies greatly. Regardless, this role has matured enough over the last few years that a process is required to support that role.

Purpose and objectives

The purpose of the business relationship management process is two-fold:
- To establish and maintain a business relationship between the service provider and the customer based on understanding the customer and its business needs
- To identify customer needs and ensure that the service provider is able to meet these needs as business needs change over time and between circumstances

The objectives of business relationship management include:
- Ensure that the provider understands the customer's perspective of service
- Ensure high levels of customer satisfaction
- Establish and maintain a constructive relationship between provider and customer
- Identify changes to the customer environment that could potentially impact services
- Identify technology trends that could potentially impact services provided
- Establish and articulate business requirements for new services or changes to existing services
- Ensure that the provider is meeting the business needs of the customer
- Work with customers to ensure that services and service levels are able to deliver value
- Establish formal complaints and escalation processes

Scope

For internal service providers, business relationship management is typically executed between a senior representative from IT and senior managers from the business units. Here the emphasis is on aligning the objectives of the business with the activity of the service provider.

Business relationship management focuses on understanding how services meet customer requirements. To achieve this, the process must focus on understanding and communicating:

- Business outcomes that the customer wants to achieve
- Services presently offered
- How customers use services
- How services are provided, including agreed levels and levels of quality
- Technology trends and the potential impact on current and future needs of the business and services
- Levels of customer satisfaction and improvement initiatives to address the causes of dissatisfaction
- How to optimise services for the future

Other processes are concerned with customer satisfaction, but they focus on the quality of services and on specific actions they can take to meet customer expectations for those services.

A good example is the difference between business relationship management service level management.

Both these processes involve regular interfaces with customers and both are concerned with on-going reviews of service and service quality.

Table 5.6 Differences between business relationship management and service level management

	BUSINESS RELATIONSHIP MANAGEMENT	SERVICE LEVEL MANAGEMENT
Purpose	To establish and maintain a business relationship between the service provider and the customer based on understanding the customer and its business needs. To identify customer needs (utility and warranty) and ensure that the service provider is able to meet these needs.	To negotiate service level agreements (warranty terms) with customers and ensure that all service management processes, operational level agreements and underpinning contracts are appropriate for the agreed service level targets.
Focus	Strategic and tactical – the focus is on the overall relationship between the service provider and their customer, and which services the service provider will deliver to meet customer needs.	Tactical and operational – the focus is on reaching agreement on the level of service that will be delivered for new and existing services, and whether the service provider was able to meet those agreements.
Primary measure	Customer Satisfaction, also an improvement in the customer's intention to better use and pay for the service. Another metric is whether customers are willing to recommend the service to other (potential) customers.	Achieving agreed levels of service (which leads to customer satisfaction).

Value to the business

The value of business relationship management is in the ability of the service provider to articulate and meet the business needs of its customers. Business relationship management creates a forum for on-going, structured communication with its customers. This enables business relationship management to achieve better alignment and integration of services in the future, as well as the ability to achieve the current business outcomes.

Business relationship management and other service management processes

Table 5.7 Business relationship management process activities and other service management processes

SCENARIO	PRIMARY PROCESS BEING EXECUTED	OTHER PROCESSES INVOLVED
Developing high-level customer requirements for a proposed new service	Business relationship management	Service portfolio management
Building a business case for a proposed new service	Business relationship management	Service portfolio management
Confirming customer's detailed functionality requirements for a new service	Design coordination	Business relationship management
Confirming a customer requirement for service availability for a new service	Service level management	Business relationship management Availability management
Establishing patterns of business activity	Demand management	Business relationship management
Evaluating business case for new service request from customer and deciding go/ no go	Service portfolio management	Business relationship management Financial management
Report service performance against service level targets	Service level management	Business relationship management

Policies, principles, and basic concepts

Business relationship management and the business relationship manager

The process of business relationship management is often confused with the business relationship manager (BR-Mgr) role. This is because the role is high profile and many customers identify the process activities with the person playing the role.

The role of the BR-Mgr can also cause confusion about the process. This is because the BR-Mgr often represents other processes when engaged in business relationship management – for example, when obtaining information about customer requirements and business outcomes, they are also providing this input to service portfolio management, demand management and capacity management. Thus, it may seem unclear as to which process the BR-Mgr role is executing.

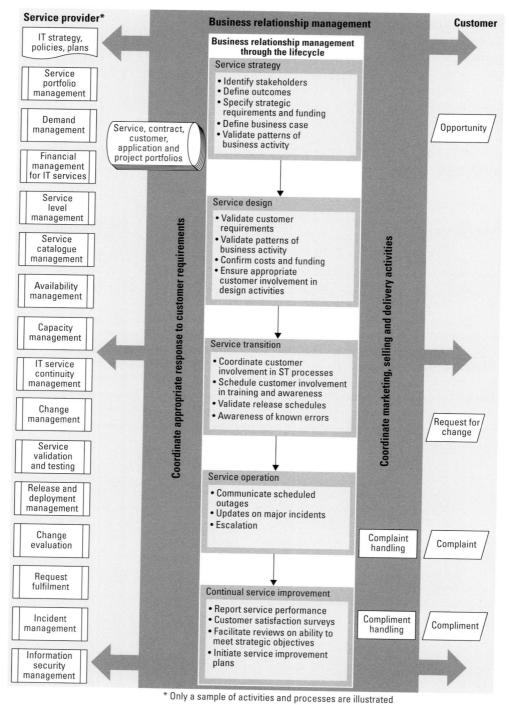

Figure 5.10 Sample business relationship management workflow

Source: The Cabinet Office

Customer portfolio

The customer portfolio is a database or structured document used to record all customers of the IT service provider. The customer portfolio is business relationship management's view of the customers who receive services from the IT service provider.

Customer agreement portfolio

The customer agreement portfolio is a database or structured document used to manage service contracts or agreements between an IT service provider and its customers. Each IT service delivered to a customer should have a contract or other agreement that is listed in the customer agreement portfolio.

Customer satisfaction

Business relationship management measures customer satisfaction and compares service provider performance with customer satisfaction targets and previous scores. Surveys are the most common form of measuring customer satisfaction. Surveys should be easy to complete in a short time. This is different from the customer satisfaction survey performed by many service desks to ensure that incidents were closed and that the service desk analysts were professional in their approach.

Business relationship management should launch an investigation into any significant variations in satisfaction levels so that the reasons are understood. Business relationship management should also trend customer satisfaction metrics, taking care to ensure that similar measurement instruments were used, to ensure consistent metrics. Any issues with customer satisfaction should be investigated and discussed with the customer. Where appropriate, opportunities for improvement should be logged in the CSI register in conjunction with service level management, for later review and prioritisation.

Service requirements

Business relationship management is involved in defining and clarifying requirements for services throughout its lifecycle. The main processes involved here are service portfolio management in service strategy, and design coordination and service level management in service design.

This type of activity is specialised and will require expertise in business analysis. Customers do not always know how to articulate requirements, especially when they have to be translated into the language and format that the service provider can understand and use to design and build the service, and to define metrics to determine success.

In some cases, customers attempt to define requirements that they think will make sense to the service provider. In other cases customers may distrust the service provider, and attempt to dictate a solution rather than requirements – making it difficult for the service provider to understand and deliver the real value.

Business relationship management as facilitator of strategic partnerships

Business relationship management ensures that relevant information about the strategic direction of the customer is communicated to the appropriate people within the service provider organisation. This will enable them to re-assess their own strategy, market spaces, future opportunities, and service portfolio.

This facilitation is valid for internal and external service providers, although the legal and confidentiality issues for external service providers are significantly more complex due to potential conflicts of interest.

Process activities, methods, and techniques

The nature of the business relationship management process

The business relationship management process itself consists of activities in every stage of the service lifecycle, but it is rarely executed as a single end-to-end process. The exact activities that are executed will depend on the situation that has caused the service provider or customer to initiate the process.

The business relationship management process has distinct groups and sequences of activities, even if they are not all performed from beginning to end every time the process is initiated. For example, the process can be initiated in the service design stage of the lifecycle by service level management, without first going through service strategy.

Process initiation

The business relationship management process is initiated either by the customer or by service management processes and functions.

Initiation by customers

Customers communicate with the service provider about their needs, opportunities, and requirements in a number of ways and for many reasons such as:
- An opportunity
- Request for change
- Other requests
- A complaint
  - The service provider needs a formalised way to handle complaints
- Compliments
  - The service provider needs a formalised way to handle compliments

Initiation by the service provider

The service provider can initiate the business relationship management process when they require inputs from customers. The supplier may also initiate the process for the creation of a new service or for making changes to an existing service.

The business relationship management process through the lifecycle

This is the core of the business relationship management process, which enables the service provider's internal process to align, interface, and, where necessary, integrate with the customer's business. The activities in each stage are not always all executed, and they are not always executed in the same sequence.

Service strategy
The main areas that the BRM process will work with in this stage are:
- IT strategy, policies and plans
- Service portfolio management
- Demand management
- Financial management for IT services

Service design
The BRM process will interact with the following service design processes:
- Service level management
- Service catalogue management
- Availability management
- Capacity management
- IT service continuity management

Although it is a methodology and not actually part of the service design phase, the BRM process will have a strong relationship with project management.

Service transition
The BRM process will coordinate customer involvement in the processes active during service transition. They will also ensure that all changes and releases meet the requirements set by the customer.
- Change management
- Knowledge management
- Service testing and validation
- Release and deployment management
- Change evaluation

Service operation
Many organisations feel that once a service has been deployed, the BRM process is no longer required for that service – until a new requirement is raised. This is not true.
- Request fulfilment
- Incident management

Continual service improvement
Processes and activities that BRM interfaces with in this stage of the service lifecycle include:
- Service reporting
- Seven-step improvement process

Information management
- The service portfolio
- The project portfolio
- The application portfolio
- The customer portfolio
- The customer agreement portfolio
- The service catalogue
- Customer satisfaction surveys

Interfaces
Like all processes, the business relationship management process has relationships with all other processes. However, some of the most visible relationships include but are not limited to:
- **Strategy management for IT services** – To identify market spaces with information gleaned from customers
- **Service portfolio management** – To identify more detailed requirements and information about the customer environment required to create service models and assess proposed services
- **Financial management for IT services** – To obtain information about the financial objectives of the customer and helps the service provider to understand what level of funding or pricing the customer is prepared to accept
- **Demand management** – To identify and validate patterns of business and user profiles
- **Service level management** – To use information about customers and service requirements to understand the customer's priorities regarding service performance and deliverables
- **Service catalogue management** – To provide the basis for many discussions, reviews and requests that are initiated through business relationship management
- **Capacity and availability management** – To process, analyse and understand business outcomes and service requirements
- **IT service continuity management** – To provide valuable perspectives and information on business priorities and outcomes during a crisis or a disaster
- **Change management** – To assess the impact and priority of changes
- **Release and deployment management** – To ensure the appropriate level of customer involvement with the release activities as well as with service validation and testing and change evaluation
- **The seven-step improvement process** – To identity, validate, prioritise and communicate improvement opportunities and plans with the customer

Triggers
Here are some of the triggers that may start the whole or part of the business relationship management process.
- A new strategic initiative
- A new service or a change to an existing service has been initiated
- A new opportunity has been identified
- A service has been chartered by service portfolio management

- Customer requests or suggestions
- Customer complaints
- Customer compliments
- A customer meeting has been scheduled
- A customer satisfaction survey has been scheduled

Inputs

Here are some of the inputs required by the business relationship management process.

- Customer requirements
- Customer requests, complaints, escalations, or compliments
- The service strategy
- The customer's strategy
- The service portfolio
- The project portfolio
- Service level agreements
- Requests for change
- Patterns of business activity and user profiles

Outputs

Here are some of the outputs produced by the business relationship management process.

- Stakeholder definitions
- Defined business outcomes
- Agreement to fund (internal) or pay for (external) services
- The customer portfolio
- Service requirements for strategy, design, and transition
- Published results of customer satisfaction surveys
- Schedules of customer activity in various service management process activities
- Schedule of training and awareness events
- Reports on the customer perception of service performance

Critical success factors

The critical success factors, which change over time, for the business relationship management process may include but are not limited to the following.

- The ability to document and understand customer requirements for services, and the business outcomes they wish to achieve
- The ability to measure customer satisfaction levels, and to know what action to take with the results
- The ability to identify changes to the customer environment that could potentially impact the type, level or utilisation of services provided
- The ability to identify technology trends that could potentially impact the type, level or utilisation of services provided
- The ability to establish and articulate business requirements for new services or changes to existing services

- Business relationship management must be able to measure that the service provider is meeting the business needs of the customer
- Formal complaints and escalation processes are available to customers

Metrics

The performance of the business relationship management process can be measured according to the following factors:

- Business outcomes and customer requirements are documented and signed off
- Customer satisfaction levels are consistently high
- Customer satisfaction and customer retention rates are consistently high
- Changes to services and strategy, creating changes to the customer environment result in improved customer satisfaction scores/higher revenues
- Opportunities for leveraging new technologies have been identified with the business and an opportunity's return on investment has been measured
- The service provider is consistently rated above a defined threshold
- Service performance is matched to business outcomes
- The number of complaints and escalations are measured and trended over time and by customer

Challenges

Here are some of the potential challenges faced by the business relationship management process.

- The need to be involved in defining services, and tracking that they are delivered according to the agreed levels of service
- A history of poor service
- Customers not being willing to share requirements, feedback, and opportunities
- Confusion between the role of business relationship manager (BR-Mgr) and the process of business relationship management (BRM)

Risks

Here are some of the potential risks faced by the business relationship management process.

- Confusion about the boundaries with many other processes
- A disconnect between the customer-facing processes and those focusing more on technology

6 Service design phase

6.1 ITIL Service Design

This short section provides a summary of the updates between the 2007 edition and the 2011 edition for the ITIL core book Service Design published by TSO.

Throughout the updated ITIL Service Design publication, there has been particular focus on alignment with ITIL Service Strategy.

A number of concepts and principles have been clarified, most significantly the flow and management of activity throughout the overall service design stage with the addition of the "design coordination" process. Other significant clarifications include the five aspects of service design, the design of the service portfolio, and the terminology related to views of the service catalogue.

Table 6.1 Summary of updates: ITIL Service Design

Area of update	Description
Five aspects of service design	There is now consistency and clarity of references to the five aspects of service design.
Transition of a service from pipeline to catalogue to retired	The descriptions in the 2007 editions of Service Strategy and Service Design were unclear. In the 2011 edition, they have been updated to provide clarity on the definite transition points and the places for policy setting. A new status has been added to make policy setting easier.
Design coordination process	The design coordination process has been added to clarify the flow of activity in the service design lifecycle stage.
Service catalogue terminology	The service catalogue language has been revised with regard to the customer's view of the service catalogue, versus the technical or IT view.

6.2 Introduction

Objective
According to ITIL, the most important objective of Service Design is:

"The design of new or modified services for introduction into the production environment"

Service Design follows Service Strategy in the Service Lifecycle, and deals with the design and development of new or modified services and their related processes. The Service Design processes are used for two distinct purposes.

The first purpose is to design all required aspects of the new or modified service along with the applicable governing IT practices, processes, and policies. This is accomplished through the design coordination process. Service Design creates all the plans to realise the service provider's strategy; facilitates the introduction of these services into supported environments; ensures delivery of the services to the required quality; and ensures customer satisfaction through value creation and cost-effective service provision.

The second purpose is to assist all IT personnel when executing various tasks and activities in Service Strategy, Transition, Operation, and Continual Improvement.

The objectives of Service Design include, but are not limited to:
- To contribute to the business objectives
- To minimise or prevent risks
- To contribute to satisfying the current and future market needs
- To support the development of policies and standards regarding IT services
- To contribute to the quality of IT services
- To assess and improve the effectiveness and efficiency of IT services
- To contribute, where possible, to saving time and money

In order to ensure that the services that are developed meet the customer's expectations, the following actions must be undertaken:
- The new service must be documented from the concept phase of the service portfolio and it must be kept up-to-date throughout the process.
- The service level requirements (SLR) must be clearly defined, documented, signed off and understood by all stakeholders before the service is actually designed.
- Based on the SLRs, the capacity management team can model these requirements within the existing infrastructure to assist in supporting the outputs from the demand management process.
- If it appears that a new infrastructure is needed or more support is desired, then financial management must be involved.
- Before the implementation phase begins, a business impact analysis (BIA) and a risk assessment must be performed. This will provide valuable information for IT Service Continuity Management (ITSCM), availability management and capacity management.
- The service desk must be brought up to speed regarding the new service delivery before the new services are delivered.
- Service Transition can make a plan for the implementation of the service.
- Supplier management must be involved if there are purchases to be made.

A holistic approach should be adopted for all aspects of the service design phase and related areas to ensure the effective and efficient integration between functions and process activities across the entire IT organisation (including all resources and capabilities). By providing a consistent, repeatable and measurable holistic approach, the IT organisation will be better equipped in providing the required end-to-end business-related functionality and quality, thus delivering value to the customers.

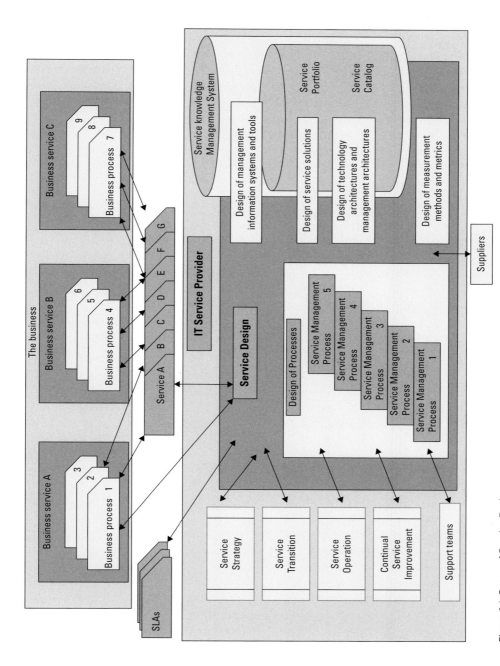

Figure 6.1 Scope of Service Design
Source: The Cabinet Office

To satisfy the changing needs and demands of the business, the design of effective and efficient IT services is a process of balancing among functionality, available resources (human, technical, and financial) and available time. This is a continual process in all phases of the lifecycle of IT services.

The Service Design phase in the lifecycle begins with the demand for new or modified requirements from the customer. Ultimately at the end of the design process, a service solution must be designed that satisfies the requirements before including the service in the transition process. The ultimate output of the design phase is the service design package – more on this later in this chapter. Good preparation and an effective and efficient fusion of *people*, *processes*, *products* (services, technology, and tools) and *partners* – ITIL's four Ps – is necessary if the design plans and projects are to succeed.

Table 6.2 The Four Ps of Service Design

People	Ensure the personnel have the right skills, knowledge, availability, and aptitudes, and display the appropriate attitudes and behaviours
Processes	Review the existing processes to ensure they can support the new or the modified service appropriately
Products	Deploy the appropriate service-assets and customer-assets
Partners	Review the existing agreements to ensure they are appropriately aligned to the new or modified service

Considering the mutual dependence of departments, IT services cannot be designed, transitioned, or implemented in isolation. Everyone in the organisation must be informed of the underlying components and mutual relationships of IT service delivery (and the related involved departments). This process requires a holistic approach, clear communication and the requirement that everyone has access to the correct, most recent and unambiguous IT plans, and is provided with the appropriate information.

Design aspects
In order for the organisation to strive to attain the highest possible quality with a continual "improvement focus" a structured and results-oriented approach is necessary in each of the five separate aspects of design. Results-oriented in this case means aiming "to satisfy the wishes of the customers/users". These five aspects are as follows:
1. Service solutions for new or changed services
2. The management information systems and tools, especially the service portfolio
3. The technology architectures and management architectures
4. The processes required
5. The measurement methods and metrics

The design of service solutions for new or changed services

A structured design approach is necessary in order to produce a new service against agreed costs, functionality, and quality and within the agreed time scale. The process must be iterative and incremental in order to satisfy the customers' changing wishes and requirements. The areas that need to be considered within the design of the service solution should include:

- Analysing the agreed business requirements
- Reviewing the existing IT services and infrastructure and producing alternative service solutions, with a view to reusing, repurpose, recycle existing components
- Designing the service solutions to the new requirements taking into consideration the following items

Table 6.3 List of possible business requirements

All testing requirements	Number of users
Anticipated growth	Operational level agreements
Applications	Priorities
Business continuity requirements	Seamless integration
Business cycles	Security controls
Business impact	Service acceptance criteria
Business outcomes	Service design package
Business process	Service level agreements
Business processes supported	Service level requirements
Core services	Service level targets
Corporate and it governance controls	Service management processes
Criticality	Suppliers
Data	Support requirements
Dependencies	Supporting services
Enterprise and IT policy, strategy, governance, compliance requirements	The service itself
Environments	Timescales
Expected performance	Transaction levels
Functionalities	Underpinning contracts
Information	Utility aspects
Infrastructures	Value proposition
Measuring reporting	Warranty aspects
Monitoring	

- Budgets and expenditure plans for designing, transitioning, operating and improving the service
- Timelines to complete design, develop, build, test and deploy the service
- Reviewing ROI, VOI and TCO (where applicable)

- Agreeing the preferred solution in terms of planned outcomes and target levels for utility and warranty
- Ensuring alignment with all strategies, policies, plans and architectural documents
- Completing the following assessment: organisational readiness, risk analysis, risk mitigation, operational, business capability and maturity, IT capability and maturity
- Alignment of operational level agreements and underpinning contracts with service level requirements

Please note the that list is not exhaustive and is presented in alphabetical order.

The design of the management information systems and tools, especially the service portfolio

The service portfolio is the most critical management information system used to support all processes and describes a provider's services in terms of business value. It articulates business needs and the provider's response to those needs. By definition, business value terms correspond to market terms, providing a means for comparing service competitiveness across alternative providers.

Like good project management practices, no work should start on a new or modified services until the service portfolio management process has chartered the service. Once a strategic decision to charter a service is made, this is the stage in the service lifecycle when service design begins: well, "designing" the service, which will eventually become part of the service catalogue.

The service catalogue is essentially a subset of the overall service portfolio. It is organised into a structured database (or document) with information about all the live IT services, including those available for deployment. The service catalogue is the only part of the service portfolio published to customers, and is used to support the sale and delivery of IT services – more on this topic later in this section.

The service portfolio should contain the information relating to every service and its current status within the organisation. The following is an overview of the service portfolio, highlighting the various phases. It is important to note that the customer has an insight only into the service catalogue. The other sections of the portfolio are not available to the customer.

Important note: The service portfolio is...
...owned and managed by the Service Portfolio Management process
...designed during the Service Design phase (see the service catalogue management process)
...created (built/tested/implemented) during the Service Transition phase

The design of the technology and management architectures

The architecture design activities include preparing the blueprints for the development and deployment of an IT infrastructure, the applications, and data (according to the needs of the business). It should be noted that during this design aspect, the provision of quality, high value services is possible only by the personnel, the processes, and the partners that are involved in this production aspect.

The term "architecture" is used in various contexts with different meaning. In the context of ITIL, architecture is described as: *"the fundamental organisation of a system, embodied in its components, their relationships to each other and to the environment, and the principles guiding its design and evolution."*

In the above description, the term "system" is used in its most general meaning, referring to *"a collection of components organised to accomplish a specific function or set of functions."*

Therefore a system can range from the whole organisation, to a business function, all the way to an information system. Each system in its own right has its own architecture made up of the following:
- Components of the system
- The relationships between them (such as control interfaces and data exchanges)
- The relationships between the system and its environment (political, organisational, technological, etc.)
- Design principles that inform, guide, and constrain its structure and operation

ITIL describes this architecture design as follows:

"Architecture design is the development and maintenance of IT policy, strategies, architectures, designs, documents, plans, and processes for deployment, implementation, and improvement of appropriate IT services and solutions throughout the organisation."

Designing the relevant service-related architecture is not simple, and varying – sometimes conflicting – needs must be taken into account. In any case, it must be ensured that:
- It satisfies the needs of the business, its products and services
- A proper balance is found among innovation, risks and costs
- It conforms to relevant frameworks, strategies, policies, etc.
- There is coordination among the designers, planners, strategists, etc.

Every enterprise is a complex system of functions, processes, structures, and information sources. The architecture of the enterprise must offer insights into how these matters connect with each other in order to achieve the enterprise objectives. The enterprise architecture is, in its own right, equally large, and complex.

There are various frameworks for the development of enterprise architectures. The enterprise architecture must include the following elements:

- **Service Architecture** – translates the applications, infrastructure, organisation and support activities into services to the business
- **Application Architecture** – ensures the development of blueprints for the development of individual applications
- **Information Architecture** – describes how the information sources are managed and distributed
- **IT Infrastructure Architecture** – describes the structure, function and geographic distribution of hardware and software
- **Product Architecture** – describes the particular proprietary products and industry standards that the enterprise uses to implement the infrastructure in conformance with the IT infrastructure architecture principles
- **Management Architecture** – consisting of the management tools used to manage the products, processes, environments etc.
- **Environment Architecture** – describes all of the aspects, types and levels of the environment controls

In addition to a technical component (applications, system software, information and data, infrastructure and environment systems), a management architecture must also be developed. In this regard, there are five elements that must be taken into consideration, namely: the business sector/industry (needs, requirements), personnel, processes, tools, and technology (IT products that are used in providing the services). It is important that the technology is not the primary focus, but rather the wishes and requirements of the customer.

Within the framework described earlier, it is possible to identify (at least) three architectural roles. These could all report to a senior "enterprise architect" in the organisation:

Business/organisational architect – this role is concerned with…
- The business models, the business processes and the organisational design
- The structural and functional components of the organisation and their relationship
- How the business functions and activities of the organisation are distributed among them
- The governance of the organisation and the roles and responsibilities required

Service architect – this role is concerned with…
- The service, the data and the application architectures
- The logical architectures supporting the business
- The relationships between logical architectures

Note: Often, the applications architect and information/data architect are separate roles

IT infrastructure architect – this role is concerned with…
- The physical technology model
- The infrastructure components and their relationships
- The choices for technologies, interfaces and protocols
- The selection of products to implement the infrastructure

The design of the processes required

Working with defined processes is the basis of ITIL. By defining what the activities are and what the input and output are, it is possible to work more efficiently and effectively, and especially in a more customer-oriented way. By assessing these processes, the organisation can enhance its efficiency and effectiveness even further. The next step is to establish norms and standards. In this way the organisation can link the quality requirements with the output. This approach corresponds with Deming's *Plan-Do–Check–Act* Management Cycle.

Every process must have a process owner who is responsible for the process and for its improvement. Service Design offers the process owner support in the design process by standardising terms and templates and ensuring that processes are consistent and are integrated.

ITIL describes a process as follows:

"A process is a structured set of activities designed to achieve a specific goal. A process makes defined outputs out of one or more inputs. A process includes all roles, responsibilities; resources and management controls that are needed to deliver reliable output and can possibly define policy, standards, guidelines, activities, procedures, and work instructions, if necessary."

A process consists of the implementation of activities and the monitoring of that implementation. Process control is defined further as:

"Process control consists of the planning and regulation of a process, with the purpose of executing that process in an efficient, effective, and consistent manner."

Designing roles – the authority matrix

RACI model

When designing a service or a process, it is imperative that all the roles are clearly defined. High-performing organisations have the ability to make the right decisions quickly and execute them effectively. One of the elements for this high performance is the use of and compliance to processes.

A key characteristic of a process is that all related activities need not necessarily be limited to one specific organisational unit. This means that an activity within a process may be performed by all groups or by one group only.

A popular authority matrix is the RACI[1] model. The RACI model provides a compact, concise, easy method of defining and communicating who does what in each process and it enables decisions to be made with pace and confidence. The RACI model defines the following four major roles.

Table 6.4 RACI definitions

Responsible	The person or people responsible for correct execution – for getting the job done.
Accountable	The person who has ownership of quality and the end result; only one person can be accountable for each task
Consulted	The people who are consulted and whose opinions are sought. They have involvement through input of knowledge and information
Informed	The people who are kept up to date on progress; they receive information about process execution and quality

Although the above mentions that only one person may be accountable for a task, it is highly recommended that the same person is accountable for all tasks within a process. This role is often called the process owner.

It is acceptable for a person to be assigned a combination of roles within a process or even for an activity. A person might be responsible for one activity, consulted on a second, and kept informed for a third activity. Additionally, a person may have a combination of roles for one activity such as – not all combinations are shown.
- Accountable and consulted
- Accountable and informed
- Responsible and consulted
- Consulted and informed
- No role at all

The authority matrix can be used for both processes and services. By creating authority matrices for all defined services and processes, an organisation is then able to review and update the job description for the various functions, thus ensuring that some roles are not overburded with too many tasks or underutilised with too few tasks.

By aligning the job descriptions to the authority matrices it becomes easier to properly identify which key goal areas, critical success factors, and key performance indicators are to be selected for the upcoming business cycle.

The design of measurement methods and metrics

In order to lead and manage the development process effectively, regular assessments must be performed. The selected assessment system must be synchronised with the capacity and maturity of the processes that are assessed. Care should be taken as it will affect the behaviour of delivering the service. Immature processes are not capable

---

1   The reason for using RACI in ITIL is to align with the COBIT framework.

of supporting refined assessments. There are four elements that can be investigated, namely **progress**, **fulfilment**, **effectiveness,** and **efficiency** of the process. As the processes develop over time, the units of measure also must develop. Therefore, the emphasis in mature processes is more on the assessment of efficiency and effectiveness.

When assessing how well a service or process is doing, an organisation should be looking at the following elements: compliance, performance, quality, and value. In turn, this will enable the organisation to define why it is measuring the above. The reasons to measure are to direct, to justify, to intervene, and to validate. Additional information can be found in the chapter on Continual Service Improvement.

Value of Service Design
Good Service Design offers the following benefits:
- Improved synchronisation of services with the needs of the business
- Improved quality of service delivery
- Improved consistency of the service
- Improved effectiveness of performance
- More simplified decision-making
- Improved IT administration
- Simpler implementation of new or modified services
- More effective service management and IT processes
- Lower Total Cost of Ownership (TCO)

The subsequent design activities
Once the desired service solution has been designed, then the subsequent activities must also be completed in the service design stage before the solution passes into the service transition stage.

Evaluation of alternative solutions
If external supplier services and solutions are involved, additional evaluations may be necessary.
- Selecting a set of suppliers and completing a tendering process
- Evaluation and review of supplier responses and selection of the preferred supplier(s) and their proposed solution(s)
- Evaluation and costing of the alternative designs

Procurement of the preferred solution
Where external suppliers are involved in the preferred solution, the organisation must
- Complete all necessary checks on the preferred supplier
- Finalise the terms and conditions of any new contracts
- Procure the selected solution

Developing the service solution
The development phase consists of translating the service design into a plan. Depending on the scope and scale of the new or modified service, a program, or project approach may be required. Regardless of the method used, the plan/project/

program will be responsible for delivering one or more components of the service. This may include:
- Business needs/requirements
- The strategy for the development and/or acquisition of the solution
- The timescales involved
- The resources required, funding, architectures, applications, information, and personnel. Regarding the latter, the plan will cover knowledge transfer, skills, aptitudes, attitudes, behaviours and organisational culture
- The development of all constituent components of the service, including management mechanisms, such as measurement, monitoring and reporting
- All test plans

Good project management practices should be used to ensure that conflict is avoided and that the compatible components are developed from the various different development activities.

Design constraints and opportunities

Although designers are free to design services, it must be understood that they are dependent on internal resources (including available financial resources) and external circumstances (e.g. the impact of ISO, SOX, and CobiT). In addition, the design process offers opportunities to enhance the effectiveness and efficiency of IT facilities through the use of a Service Oriented Architecture (SOA) approach, considering the resulting decrease in time for delivering service solutions to the business.

It is important that the services are kept up-to-date in the service catalogue (part of the service portfolio and the CMS). In general, this will position the organisation to link IT facilities with the objectives (business service management). This will allow them to predict the impact of technology on the business and vice versa.

Business service management (BSM) enables the organisation to:
- Synchronise IT facilities with the business objectives
- Set the priorities of IT activities based on their impact on the business
- Increase productivity and profitability
- Support corporate governance
- Enhance competitive advantages
- Increase the quality of service delivery and customer satisfaction

6.3 Basic concepts

Service Design models

Which model should be used for the development of IT services largely depends on the model that is chosen for the delivery of IT services. Before a new design model is adopted, an overview of the available IT capacities and equipment should be made. This overview should focus on the following elements:

- Business drivers and demands
- The requirements and goals of the new service
- The scope and capability of the current service provider
- The scope and capability of current external service providers
- The maturity of the organisations and their processes
- The culture of the organisations
- IT infrastructure, applications, data, services, and other components
- The level of corporate and IT governance
- Available budget and resources
- Personnel levels and available skills

Insights into the above issues will help determine what the opportunities for the organisation are and whether they are in a position to take the next step of providing new or changed services. The manner in which the next step is taken should be based on the business drivers and on the capabilities of the IT organisation (and its partners).

Delivery options for IT services
The gap (between the current and the desired situation) does not necessarily have to be bridged by the organisation itself. There are various strategies that can be considered for outsourcing some or all of the services, each with advantages and disadvantages. The most common of these are summarised in Table 6.5 below.

The choice of one of the above delivery strategies depends on the specific situation in which the organisation finds itself. Various issues play a role in the decision. The organisation's available internal capacities and needs and the personnel (culture) have a significant impact on the delivery strategy. Whichever strategy is chosen, it is always essential to assess and review the performances in order to remain ultimately able to satisfy the changing demands of the market.

Design– and development options for IT services
In order to make the appropriate decision regarding the design and delivery of IT services, it is crucial to understand the current lifecycle stages, methods, and approaches for service development. Insights into the following aspects of lifecycle approaches for service development are essential:
- The structure (milestones)
- Activities (work flows, tasks)
- Primary models associated with the chosen method giving various perspectives (process–, data–, event–, and users' perspectives)

Rapid Application Development
It is necessary to understand the differences between object-oriented and structured system development and the basic principles of Rapid Application Development (RAD) in order to recognise how the choice of a software solution changes the structure of the lifecycle approach.

Table 6.5 IT services delivery strategies

Delivery strategy	Characteristics	Advantages	Disadvantages
In-sourcing	Internal capacity is used for the design, development, maintenance, execution, and/or offer of support for the service.	– Direct control – Freedom of choice – Rapid prototyping of leading-edge services – Familiar policies and processes – Company-specific knowledge	– Scale limitations – Cost/time to market for services readily available outside – Dependent on internal resources, skills/competencies
Outsourcing	Engaging an external organisation for the design, development, maintenance, execution, and/or offering of support of the service.	– Economies of scale – Purchased expertise – Focus on company core competencies – Test drive/trial of new services	– Less direct control – Exit barriers – Solvency risk of suppliers – Unknown supplier skills and competencies – More challenging business process integration – Increased governance
Co-sourcing or multi-sourcing	Often a combination of insourcing and outsourcing, using a number of organisations. Generally involves external organisations working together in designing, developing, transitioning, maintaining, operating, and/or support a portion of a service.	– Time to market – Leveraged expertise – Control – Use of specialised providers	– Project complexity – Intellectual property and copyright protection – Culture clash between companies
Business process outsourcing (BPO)	An external organisation takes over a business process, or part of one, at a cheaper location, e.g. a call centre.	– Single point of responsibility – "One-stop shop" – Access to specialist skills – Risk transferred to the outsourcer – Low-cost location	– Culture clash between companies – Loss of business knowledge – Loss of relationship with the business
Application service provision	Computer-based services are offered to the customer over a network.	– Access to expensive and complex solutions – Low-cost location – Support and upgrades included – Security and ITSCM options included	– Culture clash between companies – Access to facilities only, not knowledge – Often usage-based charging models
Knowledge process outsourcing (KPO)	This goes one step further than BPO, and rather than offering knowledge of a (part of a) process, knowledge of an entire work area is offered.	– Access to specialist skills, knowledge and expertise – Low-cost location – Significant cost savings	– Culture clash between companies – Loss of internal expertise – Loss of relationship with the business

Delivery strategy	Characteristics	Advantages	Disadvantages
The Cloud	Cloud service providers offer specific pre-defined services, usually on-demand. These services can be offered internally, but generally refer to outsourced service provision.	– Services are easily defined – Sourcing is straightforward – Mapping between the service and business outcome is relatively straightforward – Greater customer control of the service	– Internal clouds are still complex – Focus could mask the relationship between IT activities and business outcomes – Difficulty coordinating insourced offerings with external cloud services – Security of information business continuity management
Multi-vendor sourcing	This type of sourcing involves sourcing different sources from different vendors, often representing different sourcing options from the above.	– Less risk in that the organisation is not tied to a single vendor – Leverage of specialised skills in different organisations ensures a more complete support model	– Difficulty in coordinating activities and services from different vendors – Requires a very clear understanding of the overall value chain and each vendor's role
Partnership	Formal arrangements between two or more organisations to work together on strategic initiatives that leverage critical expertise or market opportunities.	– Time to market – Market expansion/entrance – Competitive response – Leveraged expertise – Trust, alignment and mutual benefit – "Risk and reward" agreements	– Project complexity – Intellectual property and copyright protection – Culture clash between companies

Traditional development approaches are based on the principle that the requirements of the customer/client can be determined at the beginning of the lifecycle and that the development costs can be kept under control by managing the changes. RAD approaches begin with the notion that change is inevitable and that discouraging change simply indicates passivity concerning the market. The RAD approach is an incremental and iterative development approach.

The incremental approach implies that a service is designed bit by bit. Parts are developed separately and are delivered piecemeal. Each piece is supported by one of the business functions and together they support the whole. The big advantage in this approach is its shorter delivery time. The development of each part, however, requires that all phases of the lifecycle are continued.

The iterative approach implies that the lifecycle is repeated many times through the design. Prototypes of the entire process are used in order to understand the customer-specific requirements better, after which the design is adapted to it.

A combination of the two approaches is possible. An organisation can begin by specifying the requirements for the entire service, followed by an incremental design and the development of the application.

RAD approaches, such as the Unified Process and the Dynamic Systems Development Method (DSDM), are a response to the customer's demand to keep costs low during the development project. Thus DSDM involves the user in the development process of developing a software system that satisfies the expectations (demands) that can be adjusted, for on–time delivery within the allotted budget.

RAD approaches not only provide substantial savings in time, they also reduce development and implementation risks. Although they might be more difficult to manage than conventional approaches and involve more requirements regarding the skills and experience of the personnel, they make a positive contribution to the implementation and overall acceptance in the organisation. They also support developers to anticipate changing organisation demands more quickly, so that they can modify the design. Contrary to traditional approaches, the RAD teams are smaller and are made up of generalists. In addition, it is easier to make critical decisions during the process.

Commercial off the shelf solutions
Many organisations choose standard software solutions to satisfy needs and demands. A framework is needed for the selection, modification and implementation of packages of this kind, and it is especially important to know at the outset what requirements are set at management and operational levels. It is equally important concerning purchasing, to have an understanding of the advantages and disadvantages of such packages.

Besides defining the functional requirements, it is also crucial to determine the requirements concerning the product, the supplier, and the integration of the service package.

6.4 Processes and other activities

Processes
In this section is a description of Service Design processes and activities that are responsible for the delivery of important information for the design of a new or changed service solution. A results-oriented, structured approach, together with consideration of the five design aspects, guarantees service delivery of the highest quality and consistency in the organisation as a whole.

All of the design activities in this phase of the lifecycle stem from the needs and demands of the customer and are a reflection of the strategy, planning, and policy produced by the Service Strategy. Each phase of the lifecycle is input for the following phase of the lifecycle. Service Strategy provides important input into the Service

Design, which in turn provides input for the Transition phase. Therefore it is, in fact, the backbone of the Service Lifecycle.

In order to develop effective and efficient services that satisfy the customers' needs, it is essential that the output from the other areas and processes is included in the Service Design process. The seven tightly connected processes in the Service Design phase are:
- Design coordination
- Service catalogue management
- Service level management
- Capacity management
- Availability management
- IT service continuity management
- Information security management
- Supplier management

Design coordination
The design coordination process ensures the goals and objectives of the service design stage are met by providing and maintaining a single point of coordination and control for all activities and processes within this stage of the service lifecycle. Only well-coordinated action will enable a service provider to create comprehensive and appropriate designs that will support the achievement of the required business outcomes.

Service Catalogue Management (SCM)
Service catalogue management is an important component of the service portfolio. The two comprise the backbone of the Service Lifecycle by providing information to every other phase. Although the overall portfolio is produced as a component of the Service Strategy, it needs the cooperation of all of the successive phases. At the moment that a service is ready for use, the Service Design produces the specifications that can be included in the service catalogue. Whereas the ultimate goal of service portfolio management is the development and maintenance of a service portfolio that includes accurate details of all services, whether operational, in development or retired, and the business processes they support, the service catalogue management goal is the development and maintenance of a service catalogue that includes accurate details of all services from the chartered status to the operational – thus, the portion of the portfolio that is usually visible to the customer.

Service Level Management (SLM)
Service level management represents the IT service provider to the customer, and the customer internally to the IT service provider. The purpose of this process is to take responsibility for ensuring that the levels of IT service delivery are achieved, both for existing services and for future services in accordance with the agreed targets. SLM includes the planning, coordinating, providing, agreeing, monitoring and reporting of service level agreements (SLAs), including the revision of attained service delivery, to ensure that the quality satisfies, and where possible, exceeds, the

agreed requirements. An SLA is a written established agreement between a service provider and a customer that records the goals and responsibilities of both parties. This process supports service catalogue management by providing information and trends regarding customer satisfaction.

Capacity management

Capacity management is the central point for all designs regarding IT performance and capacity issues. The purpose of capacity management is to ensure that the capacity corresponds to both the existing and future needs of the customer (recorded in a capacity plan). The engine behind the process of capacity management is the requirements that the customer poses and that are recorded in the SLA.

Synchronisation between capacity management, the service portfolio and SLM within the lifecycle of Service Design is essential. Thus capacity management provides information on existing and future resources through which the organisation can decide which components will be renewed, and when and how that will be done. For its part, capacity management must also have a view regarding the plans of the organisation as outlined in the IT Service Strategy.

Availability management

The availability and reliability of IT services have a direct influence on customer satisfaction and the reputation of the service provider. Availability management is, therefore, essential and must be involved at an early stage in the lifecycle, just as is the case with capacity management. Availability management includes the entire process of designing, implementing, assessing, managing, and improving IT services and the components included therein. The purpose of this process is to ensure that the availability level of both new and modified services corresponds with the levels as agreed with the customer. In order to achieve this availability management can implement both proactive and reactive activities that include monitoring and reporting of the availability metrics. It must also maintain the availability management information system, which includes all of the necessary information, and this forms the basis of the availability plan.

IT Service Continuity Management (ITSCM)

IT service continuity management plays a valuable role in the support of the process of business continuity planning. This process can be applied by organisations as a means of focusing attention on continuity and recovery requirements, and to justify the decision to implement a business continuity plan. The ultimate purpose of ITSCM is to support business continuity by ensuring that the required IT facilities can be restored within the agreed time. The process focuses on occurrences that can be considered as disasters (calamities). The focus in the first instance is solely on IT-related matters that support the business processes. Less significant events will be handled through the incident management process.

Information security management

Information security management ensures that the information security policy satisfies the organisation's overall security policy and the requirements originating from corporate governance.

Security is not really a step in the lifecycle. Information security is a continual process and is an integral component of all of the services. This process supports the awareness of the entire organisation concerning service delivery. Information security management must understand the entire playing field of IT and business security so that it is in a position to manage existing and future security aspects of the business. The information security management system (ISMS) serves as the basis for a cost-effective development of an information security program that supports the business objectives.

Supplier management

The process of supplier management draws attention to all of the suppliers and contracts in order to support the delivery of services to the customer. The purpose is to guarantee a constant level of quality for the right price. All activities in this process stem from the suppliers strategy and the policy originating with the Service Strategy. In order to achieve consistency and effectiveness during the implementation of the policy, a suppliers and contracts database must be established which includes suppliers and contracts as well as the execution of the supported services. All of this should be done with an eye towards valuable, high-quality IT service delivery. The supplier management process must be "in sync" with the demands of the organisation as well as the requirements of information security management and ITSCM.

Figure 6.2 below provides a holistic picture of service design: the big picture, so to speak.

Activities

In addition to the seven processes mentioned earlier, three activities can be differentiated in the Service Design process. They are:
- Development of requirements
- Data– and information management
- The management of applications

Development of requirements

Type of requirements

ITIL makes the following assumption.
- The analysis of the existing and required business processes results in functional requirements that fall under IT services
- The IT services consist of service-assets and customer-assets
- The service-assets and the customer-assets are made up of resources and capabilities

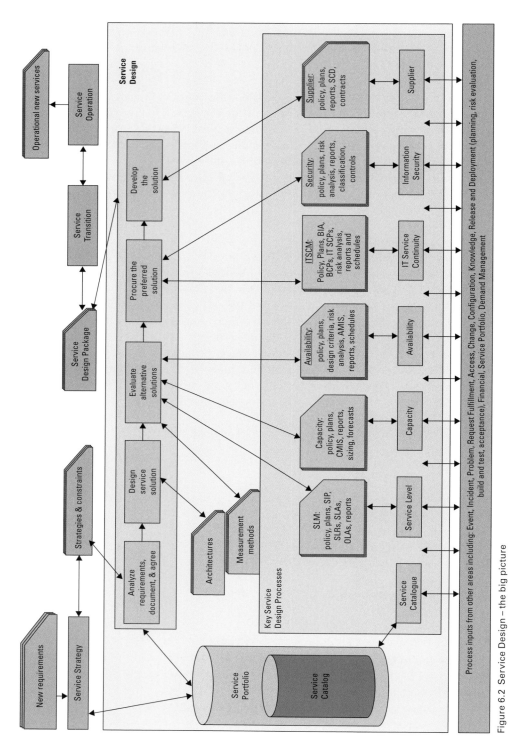

Figure 6.2 Service Design – the big picture
Source: The Cabinet Office

- Resources are made up of money, applications, infrastructures, information and people
- Capabilities include management, organisation, architecture, knowledge and people
- People possess the right skills, knowledge, and aptitudes, and display the appropriate attitudes, behaviours and culture

There are three types of requirements for each service, namely:
- **Functional requirements** – These describe matters for which a service could be done and that can be expressed as a task or function of which a component must be carried out. Various models can be considered for specifying the functional requirements, such as:
  - System context diagram
  - Use case model

- **Management and operational requirements** – These define the non-functional requirements of the IT service. The requirements serve as a basis for the first systems, the estimation of costs and support for the viability of the proposed service. Requirements from the management and execution can relate to a large number of quality aspects:
  - Manageability
  - Efficiency
  - Availability and reliability
  - Capacity and performance
  - Security
  - Installation
  - Continuity
  - Controllability
  - Maintainability
  - Operability
  - Measurability
  - Ability to report

- **Usability requirements** – Ensure that the services satisfy the expectations of the users in terms of ease of use and user-friendliness. In order to achieve this, the following must be done:
  - Develop performance standards for evaluations
  - Define test scenarios

Just as with management and operational requirements, usability requirements can be adopted to test applications for compliance with the usability requirements.

Requirement investigation
There are various investigation techniques for arriving at clearer requirements. Considering that customers are often unsure about the requirements, the support of a developer is sometimes necessary. This person must be aware of the fact that

people may see him/her as "someone from the IT department", which dictates the requirements. A certain amount of care is therefore called for. Possible investigation methods are:
- Interviews
- Workshops
- Observation
- Protocol analysis
- Shadowing
- Scenario analysis
- Prototyping

Problems in the development of requirements
There are various problems that can occur in developing requirements:
- Lack of relevance to the objectives of the service
- Lack of clarity or ambiguity in the wording
- Duplication between requirements
- Conflicts between requirements
- Uncertainty on the part of users
- Inconsistent levels of detail

In order to face these and other problems, it is important to appoint participants. Three groups need to be involved in the establishment of requirements:
- The customer
- The users' community
- The service development team

Documenting requirements
The requirements document is the core of the process. This document contains every individual requirement in a standard template. The requirements that eventually come from the users must also be included. Every requirement must be SMART (Specific, Measurable, Achievable/Appropriate, Realistic/Relevant and Timely/Time-bound) formulated. In addition, they should be checked to make sure they are clear, unambiguous, and reasonable, synchronised with the customer's objectives, and not in conflict with any of the other requirements.

The result can then be recorded in the requirements catalogue. This should be a component of the requirements portfolio in the overall service portfolio. The users' requirements should be included here and labelled with an identification number, the source, the owner, the priority (e.g. according to the MoSCoW-approach: must have, should have, could have, won't have), description, involved business process, and so on.

The requirements analysis is an iterative process. In other words, the requirements change during the course of the development process of the service. It is therefore also important that the users are involved throughout the entire process.

Data and information management

Data is one of the most critical matters that must be kept under control in order to develop, deliver, and support effective IT services. Factors for successful data management include:

- The users have access to the information that they need for their work
- Information is shared in the organisation
- The quality of the information is maintained at an acceptable level
- Legal aspects in the areas of privacy, security, and confidentiality are taken into account

If data assets are not effectively managed, there is a risk that people will collect information and data that are not necessary; emphasis will be placed on outdated information; a lot of information is no longer accessible; and information is made accessible to those who are not authorised to have it.

Scope

There are four management areas in the field of data and information management:

- **Management of data sources** – The sources should be clear and responsibilities must be entrusted to the right person. This process is also known as data administration. This activity includes the following responsibilities:
  - Define the need for information
  - A data inventory and an enterprise data model must be developed
  - Identify shortages and ambiguities
  - Maintain a catalogue
  - Assess the costs and the rewards of the organisation data
- **Management of data and information technology** – This area relates to the management of IT and includes matters such as the design of databases and database management. This is covered in the chapter on Service Operation.
- **Management of information processes** – The data lifecycle (process of creating, collecting, accessing, modifying, storing, deleting, and archiving of data) must be controlled. This often occurs in conjunction with the management of applications process.
- **Management of data standards and policy** – The organisation must formulate standards and policy for data management as a component of the IT strategy.

Data management and the Service Lifecycle

In order to understand the use of data in business processes, it is recommended that a lifecycle approach is followed that looks into subjects such as:

- What data do we have at this time and how are they classified?
- What data should be collected through the business processes?
- How will the data be stored and maintained?
- How are the data accessed and by whom?
- How are the data disposed of and by whom?
- How is the data quality protected?
- How can the data be made more accessible and available?

Data has an important connotation, not only for organisations for which the provision of data is a core business; consider, for example, a press bureau such as Reuters. Data is increasingly viewed as a common property with a value that can be placed in financial terms. Various opportunities for this exist:

- **Valuing data by its availability** – This approach looks at which business processes would not be possible if a certain portion of the data were not available, and what this would cost the organisation.
- **Valuing lost data** – This approach examines the cost of having to replace data if it were lost or destroyed.
- **Valuing data by considering the data lifecycle** – This approach focuses on issues such as how data is created; how it is made available; and how it is archived; the lifecycle differs (and thus, so do the costs) depending on the demand, or if these steps can be performed by an internal or external party.

Classifying data

Data can be classified on three levels:

- **Operational data** – This data is necessary for the continued functioning of the organisation and is the least specific.
- **Tactical data** – This is data that is needed for line– or higher management; among other things, this refers to quarterly data, distilled from management information systems.
- **Strategic data** – Refers to the long-term trends compared with external (market) information.

Data owner

Responsibilities of the data owner include:

- Determining who can create, revise, read and delete data
- Consent given regarding the way in which data are stored for modification
- Approves level of security
- Agreeing business description and a purpose

Data integrity

In defining IT services, it is important that management and operational data requirements be considered. Specifically in the following areas:

- Restoration of lost data
- Controlled access to data
- Implementation of policy on archiving of data
- Periodic monitoring of data integrity

Management of applications

An application is defined by ITIL as:

> *"An application is a software program(s) with specific functions that offer direct support to the execution of business processes and/or procedures."*

Applications, along with data and infrastructure, comprise the technical component of IT services. It is crucial that the applications that are provided correspond with the requirements of the customer. Organisations often expend a great deal of time on the functional requirements of the new service, while too little time is spent on the design of the management and operational (non-functional) requirements of the service. That means that when the service is performed, it completely caters to the functional requirements, but not to the expectations of the business and the customer in the area of quality and performance.

Two alternative approaches are necessary to implement the management of application, namely:

- **Service Development Lifecycle** – (SDLC) is a systematic approach for supporting the development of an IT service. This consists of the following steps:
  - Feasibility study
  - Analysis
  - Design
  - Testing
  - Implementation
  - Evaluation
  - Maintenance
- **Application maintenance** – This approach looks globally at all of the services in order to ensure a continuing process of managing and maintaining the applications. All applications are described consistently in the application portfolio, which is synchronised with the customers' requirements.

Application frameworks
The application framework includes all management and operational aspects and provides solutions for all of the management and operational requirements for an application.

Architecture-related activities must be planned and managed separately from the individual system-based software projects. Application designers must concentrate on one application, while application framework developers focus on more than one application and on the opportunities.

A method which is often employed is to distinguish between different types of applications. For example, not every application can be used on a Microsoft Windows™ platform, coupled with a UNIX™ server in which HTML, Java-applets and JavaBeans must be used. The different application types can be viewed as an application family. Every application in the same family is based on the same application framework.

In this concept the first step of the application design phase is the identification of the right framework. As the application framework matures, various decisions can be made. If it is not mature then the right strategy is to collect and analyse the requirements that do not fit with the existing framework. Based on the application requirements, new requirements can be defined for the application framework, after which the framework can be modified so that it satisfies all of the requirements.

CASE™ tools

An aspect of overall alignment is the need to align applications with their underlying support structures. Development environments traditionally have their own Computer Assisted/Aided Software Engineering tools (CASE) that, for example, offer the means to specify requirements draw design diagrams or generate applications. They are also a location for storage and for managing the elements that are created.

Application development

After the design phase, the application must be further developed. Both the application and the environment must be prepared for the launch. The application development phase includes the following issues:

- Consistent coding conventions
- Independent structural guidelines for applications
- Business-ready testing
- Management checklist for the building phase
- Organisation of the team roles for the structure

Important outputs of application development include:

- Scripts for starting and stopping an application
- Scripts for monitoring both hardware– and software configurations
- Specifications of the unit of measure that can be obtained from the application
- SLA objectives and requirements
- Operational requirements and documentation
- Support requirements

6.5 Design coordination

Introduction

The purpose of the design coordination process is to ensure the goals and objectives of the service design stage are met by providing and maintaining a single point of coordination and control for all activities and processes within this stage of the service lifecycle.

The **objectives** of design coordination are:

- Ensure the consistent design of appropriate new or changed services, their capabilities, and their resources to meet current and evolving business outcomes and requirements
- Coordinate all design activities across programs, projects, changes, and support teams (internal and external) as well as schedules, resources, and (possibly) conflicts
- Produce service design packages (SDPs) based on service charters and change requests

- Ensure that appropriate service designs and/or SDPs are produced and that they are handed over to service transition as agreed
- Manage the quality criteria, requirements and handover points from service strategy to service design and then to service transition
- Ensure that all service models, solutions, and designs conform to all strategic, architectural, governance, and other corporate requirements
- Improve the effectiveness and efficiency of service design activities and processes
- Ensure that all parties involved adopt a common framework of standard, reusable design practices in the form of activities, processes and supporting systems
- Monitor and improve the performance of the service design lifecycle stage

Scope
The scope of the design coordination process includes all design activity, particularly all new or changed service solutions that are being designed for transition into (or out of, in the case of a service retirement) the live environment.

Not every design activity requires the same level of rigour to ensure success, so a significant number of design efforts will require little or no individual attention from the design coordination process. Some design efforts could be:
- Part of a program and/or of a project
- Handled through the change process
- Extensive and complex
- Simple and swift

Each organisation should define the criteria that will be used to determine the level of rigour or attention to be applied in design coordination for each design. Whatever perspective is adopted by an organisation, the end result of the design coordination process should result in more successful changes. A successful change delivers the required business outcomes with minimal disruption or other negative impacts on business operations, at the right level of quality, on time and on budget.

Value for the business
The main value of the design coordination process to the business is the production of a set of consistent quality solution designs and SDPs that will provide the desired business outcomes.

Through the work of design coordination organisations can:
- Achieve the intended business value at acceptable risk and cost levels
- Minimise rework and unplanned labour costs during later service lifecycle stages
- Support the achievement of higher customer and user satisfaction
- Ensure that all services conform to a consistent architecture, allowing seamless integration
- Provide improved focus on service value and business outcomes
- Develop improved efficiency and effectiveness of all design activities and processes
- Achieve greater agility and better quality in the design of service solutions, within projects and major changes

Activities, methods, and techniques

Design coordination activities fall into two categories: overall lifecycle stage activities and individual design activities.

Overall lifecycle stage activities should include:
• Define and maintain policies and methods
• Plan design resources and capabilities
• Coordinate design activities
• Manage design risks and issues
• Improve service design.

Individual design activities should include:
• Plan individual designs
• Coordinate individual designs
• Monitor individual designs
• Review designs and ensure handover of SDPs

The following work occurs during the service design stage and should be coordinated by the design coordination process:
• Requirements collection, analysis and engineering to ensure that
  ○ Business requirements, service provider, and technical requirements are clearly documented and agreed
  ○ They all support the business requirements correctly
• Design of all appropriate aspects of the service solutions
• Review, revision, and maintenance of all processes involved in service design, including designs, plans, architectures, policies, and documentation
• Production and maintenance of IT policies and design documents
• Review and revision of all design documents for completeness and adherence to standards
• Planning for the deployment and implementation of IT strategies using "roadmaps", programs, and project plans
• Risk assessment and management of all design processes and deliverables
• Ensuring alignment with all corporate and IT strategies and policies
• Production of service designs and/or SDP for new or changed services

Information management
The key information generated by the design coordination process is included in the SDP, which contains everything necessary to take the service through all other stages of the service lifecycle. The SDP may consist of multiple documents which should be included in the overall service knowledge management system (SKMS), and described by information in the CMS.

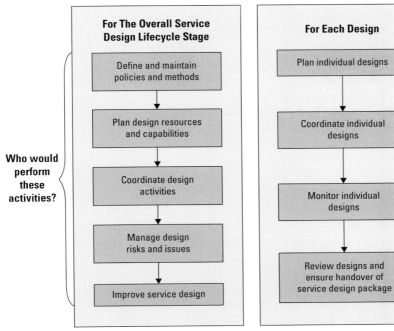

Figure 6.3 Sample design coordination activities

Source: The Cabinet Office

Interfaces

Like all processes, the design coordination process has relationships with all other processes. However, some of the most visible relationships include but are not limited to the following.

The principal interfaces to the adjacent stages of the lifecycle are:

- **Service strategy** – using information contained within the IT strategy and service portfolio
- **Service transition** – with the handover of the design of service solutions within the SDP

The design coordination process also interfaces with all processes directly involved with the planning, designing, and transitioning of services.

- **Service portfolio management** – Provides the service charter and all associated documentation such as business requirements, requirements for service utility and warranty, risks, and priorities.
- **Change management**
  Design coordination and change management:
  ○ Collaboratively defined policies and consistent practices
  Design coordination provides:
  ○ Status information on design milestones relating to changes

Change management provides:
○ Change requests
○ Details of authorised changes
○ Authorisation at defined points
○ Feedback on areas for improvement for design coordination (through the post-implementation reviews)

- **Financial management for IT services** – Provides details of the value proposition for the new or changed service as well as budgets available.
- **Business relationship management** – Provides intelligence and information regarding the business's required outcomes, customer needs and priorities, and serves as the interface with the customer at a strategic level.
- **Transition planning and support**
  ○ Design coordination provides the SDP to the service transition stage
  ○ Transition planning and support carries out the overall planning and coordination for the service transition stage, in the same way that design coordination does for service design.
  ○ **Strategy management for IT services** – Provides information about the current and evolving service strategy to ensure that design guidelines and documentation remain aligned with the strategy over time.
  ○ **Release and deployment management** – Manages the planning and execution of individual authorised changes, releases, and deployments. Planning and design for release and deployment is carried out during service design
  ○ **Service validation and testing** – Plans and executes tests to ensure that the service matches its design specification and will meet the needs of the business.
  ○ **Change evaluation** – Determines the performance of a service change. This includes evaluation of the service design to ensure it is able to meet the intended requirements.
  ○ **Service level management** – Responsible for defining and agreeing the service level requirements for new or changed services, which must be done in a consistent manner according to practices developed cooperatively with design coordination.
  ○ **Availability, capacity, IT service continuity and information security management processes** – Each of these processes is actively involved in service design and must perform these design activities consistently, according to practices developed cooperatively with design coordination.
  ○ **Supplier management** –Ensures the contributions of suppliers to design activities are properly managed. This process will then build these practices into supplier contracts and agreements as appropriate and then manage the performance of the suppliers during service design.

Triggers

Here are some of the triggers that may start the whole, or part of the, design coordination process.

- The triggers for the design coordination process are changes in the business requirements and services, and therefore the main triggers are requests for change (RFCs) and the creation of new programs and projects. Another major trigger for the review of design coordination activities would be the revision of the overall IT strategy.

Inputs
Here are some of the inputs required by the design coordination process.
- Service charters for new or significantly changed services
- Change requests from any stages of the service lifecycle
- Change records and authorised changes
- Business information on their current and future requirements
- Business impact analysis
- Governance requirements
- Corporate, legal and regulatory policies and requirements
- The enterprise architecture
- The IT strategy, including constraints and resource limitations
- The program and project schedules
- The service portfolio
- The service catalogue
- The schedule of changes
- The configuration management system
- Feedback from all other processes
- Management systems
- Measurement and metrics methods
- Processes

Outputs
Here are some of the outputs produced by the design coordination process.
- Comprehensive and consistent set of service designs and SDP
- A revised enterprise architecture
- Revised management systems
- Revised measurement and metrics methods
- Revised processes
- Updated service portfolio
- Updated service catalogue
- Updated change records

Critical success factors
The critical success factors, which change over time, for the design coordination process may include but are not limited to the following.
- Accurate and consistent SDP
- Managing conflicting demands for shared resources
- New and changed services meet customer expectations

Metrics
The performance of the design coordination process can be measured according to:
- Reduction in the number of subsequent revisions of the content of SDP

- Percentage reduction in the re-work required for new or changed service solutions in subsequent lifecycle stages
- Increased satisfaction with the service design activities, within project and change personnel
- Reduced number of issues caused by conflict for service design resources
- Percentage increase in the number of successful new and changed services in terms of outcomes, quality, cost and timeliness
- Improved effectiveness and efficiency in the service design processes, activities and supporting systems
- Reduced number and percentage of emergency change requests submitted by projects
- Percentage increase in the number of transitioned services that consistently achieve the agreed service level targets.

Challenges

Here are some of the potential challenges faced by the design coordination process.

- Maintaining high quality designs and SDPs consistently across all areas of the business, services and infrastructure
- Ensuring that sufficient time and resources are devoted to design coordination activities and that the roles and responsibilities of the process are assigned to the appropriate individuals and/or groups to ensure completion
- Developing common design practices that produce the desired high-quality designs without introducing unnecessary bureaucracy

Risks

Here are some of the potential risks faced by the design coordination process.

- Potential lack of skills and knowledge
- Reluctance of the business to be involved
- Poor direction and strategy
- Lack of information on business priorities and impacts
- Poorly defined requirements and desired outcomes
- Reluctance of project managers to communicate and get involved
- Poor communication
- Lack of involvement from all relevant stakeholders
- Insufficient interaction with and input from other lifecycle stages
- Trying to save time and money during the design stage

6.6 Service Catalogue Management

Introduction

The purpose of service catalogue management (SCM) is to provide a single source of consistent information on all of the agreed services, and ensure that it is widely available to those who are approved to access it.

The purpose of service catalogue management is the development and upkeep of a service catalogue that contains all accurate details, the status, possible interactions, and mutual dependencies of all current services and those being prepared to run operationally.

Value for the business
The service catalogue is the central resource of information on the IT services delivered by the service provider organisation. This ensures that all areas of the business can view an accurate, consistent picture of the IT services, their details, and their status. It contains a customer-facing view of the IT services in use, how they are intended to be used, the business processes they enable, and the level of quality of service the customer can expect for each service.

Basic concepts
Over the years, the IT infrastructures of organisations grow at a rapid pace and there may not be a clear picture of the services offered by the organisation and whom they are offered to. To get a clearer picture, a service portfolio is developed (with a service catalogue as part of it), and maintained. The development of the service portfolio is a component of the Service Strategy phase. The portfolio needs subsequent support from the other phases in the lifecycle.

It is important to make a clear distinction between the portfolio and the catalogue:
• **Service portfolio** – The portfolio contains information about each service and its status. As a result, the portfolio describes the entire process, starting with the customer requirements for the development, building, and execution of the service. The service portfolio represents all active and inactive services in the various phases of the lifecycle.
• **Service catalogue** – The catalogue is a subset of the service portfolio and consists only of active and approved services (at retail level) in service operation. The catalogue divides services into components. It contains policies, guidelines and responsibilities, as well as prices, service level arrangements and delivery conditions. The customer gets to review the largest part of the service catalogue.

The following offers some practical guidance regarding the movement of services within the lifecycle stages. This includes "moving" a service from the pipeline to the catalogue and to the retired section.

○ **Each particular version** – Should be in one and only one section of the portfolio at a time
○ **Newer versions of a service** – May be in the pipeline while the current version is in the catalogue or in the catalogue while an older version is in the retired services.
○ **Live versions of a service** – May be in the in the catalogue while an older version is in the retired section
○ **Clear and unambiguous policies** – Organisations should define what conditions are required for a service to move from pipeline to catalogue and from catalogue to retired

○ **In the service pipeline** – From the "requirements" status to the "approved" status (in the strategy phase)
○ **In the service catalogue** – When a service achieves the "chartered" status in the live environment

Many organisations integrate and maintain the portfolio and catalogue as a part of their CMS. By defining every service, a configuration item (CI) must be defined and, when possible, incorporated into a hierarchy, the organisation can relate the incidents and requests for change to the services in question. It is for this reason that changes in both portfolio and catalogue must be part of the change management process.

The service catalogue can also be used for a business impact analysis (BIA) as part of its service continuity management (ITSCM), or as a starting point for the re-distribution of the workload as part of capacity management. These benefits justify the investment (in time and money) involved in preparing a catalogue and making it worthwhile.

There is no correct or suggested number of views an organisation should project. The number of views projected will depend upon the audiences to be addressed and the uses to which the catalogue will be put. The following tables represent a service catalogue with two views and one with three.

Table 6.6 A service catalogue with two views

View	Definition
Business/ customer	This contains details of all the IT services delivered to the customers (customer-facing services), together with relationships to the business units and the business processes that rely on the IT services. This is the customer view of the service catalogue. In other words, this is the service catalogue for the business to see and use.
Technical/ supporting	This contains details of all the supporting IT services, together with relationships to the customer-facing services they underpin and the components, CI and other supporting services necessary to support the provision of the service to the customers.

Table 6.7 A service catalogue with three views

View	Definition
Wholesale customer	This contains details of all the IT services delivered to wholesale customers (customer-facing services), together with relationships to the customers they support
Retail customer	This contains details of all the IT services delivered to retail customers (customer-facing services), together with relationships to the customers they support
Supporting services	This contains details of all the supporting IT services, together with relationships to the customer-facing services they underpin and the components, CI and other supporting services necessary to support the provision of the service to the customers

Activities, methods, and techniques

The service catalogue is the only resource which contains constant information about all operational services of the service provider. The catalogue should be accessible to every authorised person. Activities in this process include:

* Agreeing and documenting a service definition with all relevant parties
* Interfacing with service portfolio management to agree the contents of the service portfolio and service catalogue
* Producing and maintaining an accurate service catalogue and its contents in conjunction with the service portfolio
* Interfacing with the business and IT service continuity management on the dependencies of business units and their business processes with the supporting IT services, contained within the business service catalogue
* Interfacing with support teams, service providers and configuration management on interfaces and dependencies between IT services and the supporting services, components and CI contained within the *technical/supporting services view* of the service catalogue
* Interfacing with business relationship management and service level management to ensure that the information is aligned to the business and business process

Information management

The key information for this process is contained within the service catalogue. The service portfolio management, the business relationship management, and/ or the service level management processes are the main sources of information for the service catalogue. The service catalogue is considered a configuration item and thus falls under the scope of the change management process. Change management is discussed later in this book. There are many different approaches to managing service catalogue information including:

* Intranet solutions built by the service provider organisation leveraging technology already in place
* Commercially available solutions designed for service catalogue management
* Solutions that are part of a more comprehensive service management suite

The personnel of the organisation will be entitled to view and use portions or the entire service catalogue based on their job description and their user profile. The user profiles are defined in the service strategy phase; they are designed using the security management process and are primarily used by the access management process. This shows that good cooperation and coordination of activities between phases and functions.

Interfaces

Like all processes, the service catalogue management process has relationships with all other processes. However, some of the most visible relationships include but are not limited to:

* **Service portfolio management** –Determines which services will be chartered and therefore move forward for eventual inclusion in the service catalogue, as well as

defining critical information regarding each service or potential service, including any agreed service packages and service options
- **Business relationship management** –Ensures that the relationship between the service and the customer(s) who require it is clearly defined in terms of how the service supports the customer(s) needs
- **Service asset and configuration management** – Works collaboratively to ensure that information in the CMS and in the service catalogue are appropriately linked together to provide a consistent, accurate and comprehensive view of the interfaces and dependencies between services, customers, business processes and service assets, and CI
- **Service level management** – Negotiates specific levels of service warranty to be delivered which will be reflected in the service catalogue.
- **Demand management** – determines how services will be composed into service packages for provisioning and assists service catalogue management in ensuring that these packages are appropriately represented in the service catalogue

Triggers

Here are some of the triggers that may start the whole, or part of the, service catalogue management process.
- The triggers for the service catalogue management process are changes in the business requirements and services, and therefore one of the main triggers is RFCs and the change management process. This will include new services, changes to existing services or services being retired.

Inputs

Here are some of the inputs required by the service catalogue management process.
- Business information from the organisation's business and IT strategy plans and financial plans etc.
- Business impact analysis
- Service portfolio
- CMS
- Feedback from other processes

Outputs

Here are some of the outputs produced by the service catalogue management process.
- Documentation and agreement of a "definition of the service"
- Updates to the service portfolio
- Updated to the service catalogue

Critical success factors

The critical success factors, which change over time, for the service catalogue management process may include but are not limited to the following.
- Accurate service catalogue
- Business users' awareness of the services being provided
- IT personnel awareness of the technology supporting the services

Metrics

The performance of the service catalogue management can be measured according to:

- The number of services recorded and maintained within the service catalogue as a percentage of those being delivered and transitioned in the live environment
- The number of differences discovered between the information from the service catalogue and reality
- Percentage increase in the completeness of the business service catalogue, Compared with the operational services
- Percentage increase in the completeness of the technical/supporting services view of the service catalogue, compared with the IT components in support of the services
- Access of the service desk to information in support of the services, expressed by the percentage of incidents without the appropriate service-related information

Challenges

Here are some of the potential challenges faced by the service catalogue management process.

- Maintaining an accurate service catalogue as part of a service portfolio, incorporating all catalogue views as part of an overall CMS and SKMS

Risks

Here are some of the potential risks faced by the service catalogue management process.

- Inaccurate information in the catalogue and it not being under change management control
- Poor acceptance of the service catalogue and its use in the operational processes
- Inaccuracy of the information supplied by the business, IT and service portfolio
- Tools and resources needed to keep the information up-to-date
- Poor access to accurate change management information and processes
- Circumvention of the use of the service portfolio and service catalogue
- Information too detailed to maintain accurately or at too high level to be of any value

6.7 Service Level Management

Introduction

The purpose of the service level management (SLM) process is to ensure that an agreed level of IT service is provided for all current IT services, and that future services are delivered to agreed achievable targets.

The **objectives** are:

- Defining, documenting, agreeing, monitoring, measuring, reporting and executing a review of the service level

- Delivering and improving the relation and communication with the business and the customers
- Ensuring that specific and measurable targets are being developed
- Monitoring and improving customer satisfaction with the quality of service being delivered
- Ensuring that the IT and the customers have a clear and unambiguous expectation of the level of service to be delivered
- Ensuring that proactive measures to improve levels of service delivered are implemented wherever it is cost-justifiable to do so

Scope
SLM represents the IT service provider to the business, and the business to the IT service provider. There is regular bi-directional contact, whereby both the present service and the future service are discussed. SLM has to manage the expectations of both parties (both internal and external). In addition, SLM assures the quality of service delivered meets the expectations.

The SLM process should include the following items:
- Development of business relationships
- Development and management of Operational Level Agreements (OLAs)
- Reviewing underpinning supplier contracts
- Proactive prevention of service failures, reduction of service risks and improvement in service quality
- Reporting and managing all services and review of SLA breaches and weaknesses

Value for the business
SLM provides a consistent interface to the business for all service related issues. It provides the business with the agreed service targets and the required management information to ensure that those targets have been met. Where targets are breached, SLM should provide feedback on the cause of the breach and details of the actions being taken to prevent the breach recurring.

The service level management process entails planning, coordinating, drafting, agreeing, monitoring and reporting on Service Level Agreements (SLAs), and the on-going review of service achievements to ensure that the required and cost-justifiable service quality is maintained and gradually improved. The SLA is a written agreement between a service provider and its customers defining service targets and responsibilities of both parties.

On the other hand, an OLA is an agreement between an IT service provider and another part of the same organisation that assists with the provision of services.

Activities, methods, and techniques

The activities of service level management are:

- **Design of SLA Frameworks** – SLM has to design the most appropriate SLA structure, so that all services and all customers are covered in a manner best suited to organisational needs. There are a number of options including the following:
- **Service-based SLA** – an SLA covers one service for all customers of that service; an SLA can be established for e-mail services or for supplying certain telephone facilities, for example. This framework can cause difficulties if the specific requirements of one customer vary for the same service.
- **Customer-based** SLA – an agreement with a customer containing all services they use; the customer often prefers this SLA because all of their requirements are captured in one single document
- **Multi-level** SLA – a combination having for example the following structure:
  - Corporate level, covering all generic SLM matters
  - Customer level, covering all SLM issues which are relevant to a specific group of customers or business units
  - Service level, covering all subjects that are relevant to a specific service relating to a specific customer
  - The multi-level SLA keeps the SLA to a manageable size and reduces the need for frequent updates.
- **Determining, documenting and agreeing on the requirements for new services and production of Service Level Requirements (SLRs)** – Once the service catalogue is produced and the SLA structure determined, the first SLR needs to be drafted; at this stage, both customer and the other departments should be involved, in order to prevent the situation where the customer is faced with a "fait accompli" at a later stage and in order to find out how realistic the arrangements are.
- **Monitoring the performance with regard to the SLA and reporting the outcome** – Everything that is incorporated into the SLA must be measurable; otherwise disputes may arise, which may eventually result in confidence loss of faith; for example, the service provider can measure incident response time; report regularly regarding the results and use these reports for discussion with the customer; it is also recommended that all complaints and compliments are recorded and then discussed these with the relevant parties.
- **Improving customer satisfaction** – Besides the "hard" monitoring listed, customer satisfaction with the service provision should be taken into account; this can be done by using questionnaires, for example.
- **Review and revise underpinning agreements** – The IT service provider is dependent to some extent on their own internal technical services (or external partners and suppliers); in order to meet the SLA targets, the underpinning agreements with internal departments (OLA) must support the SLA as must the contracts with external parties; the agreements must at all times be up-to-date and incorporated into the change management and configuration management processes.
- **Produce service reports** – Communication is a core activity in service management and requires adequate reporting. Reporting mechanisms should be specified and agreed, and reports should be delivered at regular intervals. Service reports are input to service review meetings. The reports should contain accurate information

from all areas and processes that is integrated into a comprehensive report on service performance, measured against agreed business targets.

- **Reviewing and improving services** – Consult regularly with the customer to evaluate the services and identify possible improvements in the service provision; focus on those improvement items that yield the greatest benefit to the business; report regularly on the progress of the improvements and incorporate them in the Service Improvement Plan (SIP).
- **Review and revise SLA** – All agreements should be subject to change and configuration management and reviewed periodically, to make sure that changes to the service infrastructure haven't invalidated the agreements.
- **Developing contacts and relations** – SLM has to instil confidence in the business; by using the service catalogue, SLM can start working proactively. The catalogue supplies information with which the relation between services and the business units and the business processes which are dependent on these services, can be better understood. In order to do this thoroughly, SLM can carry out the following activities among others:
  - Consulting and informing stakeholders, customers and managers
  - Maintaining accurate information in the service portfolio and service catalogue
  - Adopting a flexible and responsive attitude towards customer needs
  - Developing a full understanding of the business and customer
  - Undertaking customer satisfaction surveys

Information management
- Provides key information on all operational services, their expected targets and the service achievements and breaches for all operational services
- Provides information on the quality of IT service provided to the customer, and information on the customer's expectation and perception of that quality of service

Interfaces
Like all processes, the service level management process has relationships with all other processes. However, some of the most visible relationships include but are not limited to:

- **Business relationship management** – Ensures that the service provider has a full understanding of the needs and priorities of the business and that customers are appropriately involved/represented in the work of service level management
- **Service catalogue management** – Provides accurate information about services and their interfaces and dependencies to support determining the SLA framework, identifying customers/business units that need to be engaged by SLM and to assist SLM in communicating with customers regarding services provided
- **Incident management** – Provides critical data to SLM to demonstrate performance against many SLA targets, as well as operates with the fulfilment of SLA targets as a CSF. SLM negotiates support-related targets such as target restoration times and then the fulfilment of those targets is embedded into the operation of the incident management process

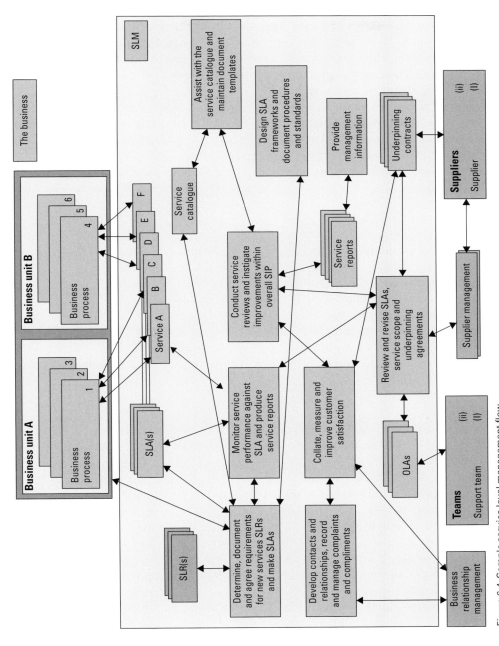

Figure 6.4 Sample service level management flow
Source: The Cabinet Office

- **Supplier management** – Works collaboratively with SLM to define, negotiate, document, and agree terms of service with suppliers. Also manages the performance of suppliers and contracts against these terms of service to ensure related SLA targets are met
- **Availability, capacity, IT service continuity and information security management** – These processes contribute to SLM by helping to define service level targets that relate to their area of responsibility and to validate that the targets are realistic. Once targets are agreed, the day-to-day operation of each process ensures achievements match targets
- **Financial management for IT services** – Works with SLM to validate the predicted cost of delivering the service levels required by the customer to inform their decision-making process and to ensure that actual costs are compared to predicted costs as part of overall management of the cost effectiveness of service
- **Design coordination** – Responsible for ensuring that the overall activities of service design are completed successfully. SLM develops agreed SLR and their associated targets

Triggers

Here are some of the triggers that may start the whole, or part of the, service level management process.

- Changes in the service portfolio,
- New or changed agreements, SLR, SLA, OLA, or contracts
- Service review meetings and actions
- Service breaches or threatened breaches
- Compliments and complaints
- Periodic activities such as reviewing, reporting and customer satisfaction surveys
- Changes in strategy or policy

Inputs

Here are some of the inputs required by the service level management process.

- Business information arising from the organisation's business strategy, plans and financial plans
- Business requirements
- Service portfolio and service catalogue
- Change information
- Configuration Management System

Outputs

Here are some of the outputs produced by the service level management process.

- Service reports
- Service Improvement Plan (SIP)
- Service Quality Plan (SQP)
- Standard document templates
- SLA, SLR and OLA
- Service review meeting minutes

Critical success factors

The critical success factors, which change over time, for the service level management process may include but are not limited to the following.

- Manage the overall quality of IT services required both in the number and level of services provided and managed
- Deliver the service as previously agreed at affordable costs
- Manage the interface with the business and users

Metrics

The performance of the service level management can be measured according to:

- Objective:
  - Number or percentage of service targets being met
  - Number and severity of service breaches
  - Number of services with up-to-date SLA
  - Number of services with timely reports and active service reviews

- Subjective:
  - Improvements in customer satisfaction

Challenges

Here are some of the potential challenges faced by the service level management process.

- Identifying suitable customer representatives with whom to negotiate
- No previous experience with service level management
- Personnel at different levels within the customer community may have different objectives and perceptions

Risks

Here are some of the potential risks faced by the service level management process.

- A lack of accurate input, involvement and commitment from the business and customers
- Lack of appropriate tools and resources required to agree, document, monitor, report and review agreements and service levels
- The process becomes too bureaucratic
- Access to and support of appropriate and up-to-date CMS and SKMS
- Bypassing the process
- Measurements are too difficult to measure and improve, so are not recorded
- Inappropriate business and customer contacts and relationships are developed
- High customer expectations and low perception
- Poor and/or inappropriate communication with the business and customers

6.8 Capacity Management

Introduction

The purpose of capacity management is to ensure that cost-justifiable IT capacity in all areas of IT always exists and is matched to the current and future agreed needs of the business in timely manner.

Capacity management is supported initially in Service Strategy where the decisions and analysis of business requirements and customer outcomes influence the development of Patterns of Business Activity (PBA), Lines of Service (LOS), and Service Level Packages (SLPs). This provides the predictive and on-going capacity indicators needed to align capacity to demand.

The **objectives** of capacity management are:
- Creating and maintaining an up-to-date capacity plan that reflects the current and future needs of the customer
- Internal and external consulting on services in terms of capacity and performance
- Ensuring that the services provided comply with the defined objectives by managing both the performance and the capacity of services
- Contributing to diagnosis of performance and capacity-related incidents and problems
- Investigating the impact of all changes to the capacity plan
- Taking proactive measures to improve performance

Scope

The capacity management process should be the focal point for all IT performance and capacity issues. Network and server support or operation management may take on the majority of day-to-day operational duties, but will provide performance information to the capacity management process. In addition, capacity management also considers space planning and environmental systems capacity. It may also have a task in certain human resource aspects but only where a lack of human resources could result in a breach of OLA or SLA. However, Human Resource Management (HRM) is the main responsibility of line management though the personnel of a service desk could use identical capacity management techniques.

The drivers behind this process are the customer requirements as laid down in the SLA. Because capacity management understands the total IT and customer environment, it is able to comply with current *and* future capacity and performance requirements in a cost-effective manner. Managing large IT infrastructures is a difficult and demanding task, in particular if the IT capacity and required financial investments are growing. Planning is vital to realise economies of scale, for instance, when buying components.

Capacity management should have input to the service portfolio and procurement process to ensure that the best deals with IT service providers are negotiated. Capacity management provides the necessary information on current and planned resource utilisation of individual components to enable organisations to decide with confidence:

- Which components to upgrade
- When to upgrade
- How much the upgrade will cost

Capacity management has a close two-way relationship with Service Strategy since the latter is based on the organisation plans, which in turn are derived from the strategy. In other words, it must understand the short, medium, and long-term plans of the organisation in order to function properly.

Other processes are less effective as well if they do not receive input from capacity management. For example, what is the effect of a change (change management) on the available capacity or are the agreed service level requirements of a new service achievable (SLM)? Thorough capacity management is able to predict events (and their impact) before they occur.

Value for the business
Capacity management is responsible for planning and scheduling IT resources to provide a consistent service level that matches the current and future requirements of the customer. Capacity management delivers a capacity plan in consultation with the customer. The plan specifies the IT and financial resources that are necessary to support the business, including a cost justification of expenditure.

The capacity management process involves balancing cost against resources needed and balancing supply against demand.

Capacity management processes and planning must be involved in every phase of the Service Lifecycle, from strategy and design through transition and operation to continual service improvement.

Activities, methods, and techniques
The capacity management process consists of:
- **Proactive activities**, such as:
  - Pre-empting performance issues
  - Producing trends of the current component utilisation and estimating the future requirements
  - Modelling and trending the predicted changes in IT services and identifying the changes that need to be made to services
  - Ensuring that upgrades are budgeted, planned and implemented
  - Actively seeking to improve service performance wherever it is cost-justifiable
  - Producing and maintaining a capacity plan
  - Tuning (optimising) the performance of services and components

- **Reactive activities**, such as:
  - ○ Monitoring, measuring, reporting and reviewing
  - ○ Responding to all capacity-related "threshold" events and instigating corrective action
  - ○ Reacting to and assisting with specific performance issues

The more proactive the capacity management process, the lesser the need for reactive activities.

Capacity management is an extremely technical, complex, and demanding process that comprises three sub-processes.

Business capacity management
There are two facets to this sub-process. The first supports the design coordination process by:
- Assist with agreeing service level requirements
- Design, procure, or amend service configuration
- Verify service level agreements
- Support service level agreement negotiation
- Control and implementation

The second aspects support the service operation phase by:
- Translates business needs and plans into requirements for service and IT infrastructure
- Ensures that the future business requirements for IT services are quantified, designed, planned and implemented in a timely fashion
- Trend, forecast, model or predict future requirements

Service capacity management
- Focuses on the management, control, and prediction of the end-to-end performance, capacity, usage, and workloads live of IT services
- Ensures that the performance of all services is monitored and measured
- Ensures that the collected data is recorded, analysed and reported
- Instigates proactive and reactive action
- Uses automated thresholds to manage all operational services
- Ensures threatened or breached service targets are rapidly identified and apply cost-effective actions to reduce or avoid their (potential) impact

Component capacity management
- Focuses on the management, control and prediction of the performance, utilisation, and capacity of individual IT technology components
- Ensures that the performance of all components is monitored and measured
- Ensures that the collected data is recorded, analysed and reported
- Instigates proactive and reactive action
- Uses automated thresholds to manage all operational components
- Ensures threatened or breached components targets are rapidly identified and applies cost-effective actions to reduce or avoid their (potential) impact

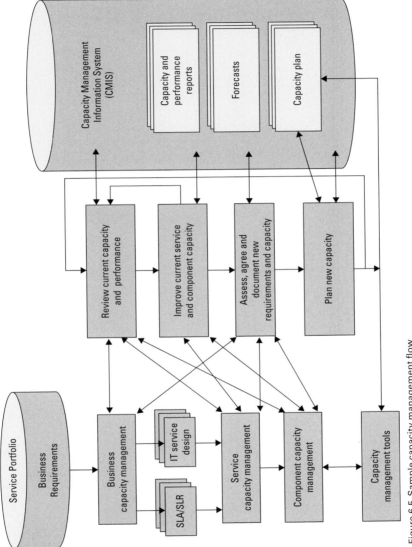

Figure 6.5 Sample capacity management flow
Source: The Cabinet Office

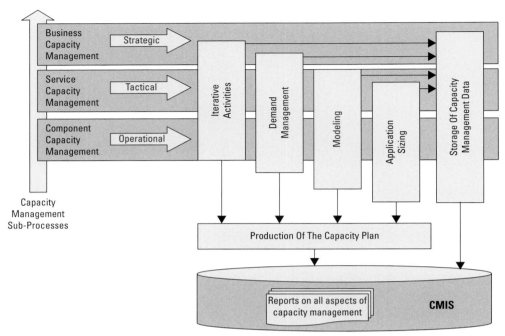

Figure 6.6 Sample capacity management sub-processes workflow

Source: The Cabinet Office

Supporting activities of capacity management

Some activities must be executed repeatedly (proactively or reactively). They provide basic information and triggers for other activities and processes in capacity management. These activities include:

- Tuning and optimisation
- Utilisation monitoring
- Response time monitoring
- Analysis
- Implementation
- Exploitation of new technology
- Designing resilience

Capacity management also includes:

- Threshold management and control
- Demand management
- Predicting "the behaviour" of IT services by using modelling methods such as:
  ○ Baseline model
  ○ Trend analysis
  ○ Analytical model
  ○ Simulation model
  ○ Application sizing, estimating the requirements for resources to support proposed changes

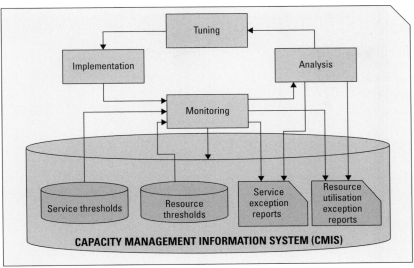

Figure 6.7 Sample iterative activities in capacity management

Source: The Cabinet Office

Design-related activities

The three sub-processes of capacity management benefit from researching new technology and in designing resilience into services and infrastructure.

- Exploitation of new technology
- Understanding new techniques and new technology and how they can be used to support the business and innovate
- Designing resilience
- Identification and improvement of the resilience within the IT infrastructure or any subset of it, wherever it is cost-justified
- Provision of spare capacity and spare components can act as resilience or fail-over in failure situations.
- Incorporating resilience into service design is much more effective and efficient than trying to add it at a later date, once a service has become operational

Information management

The capacity management process should maintain a capacity management information system (CMIS) that contains all of the measurements and information required to complete the capacity management process and provide the appropriate information to the business on the level of IT service provided. This information, covering services, components and supporting services, provides the basis for regular, ad hoc and exception capacity reporting and the identification of trends within the data for the instigation of improvement activities. These activities and the information contained within the CMIS provide the basis for developing the content of the capacity plan.

The aim of the CMIS is to provide the relevant capacity and performance information to produce reports and support the capacity management process. These reports provide valuable information to many IT and service management processes.
- Component-based reports
- Service-based reports
- Exception reports
- Predictive and forecast reports

Capacity management information system (CMIS)
- The CMIS is a set of tools, data, and information that is used to support capacity management and is the cornerstone of a successful capacity management process. The information is stored and analysed by all the sub-processes of capacity management.
- The CMIS is a federated repository that holds a number of different types of data, including business, service, resource, financial, and utilisation from all areas of technology. It is part of the service knowledge management system (SKMS).
- The CMIS can be utilised to record and store selected data and information required to support key activities such as report generation, statistical analysis, and capacity forecasting and planning. The CMIS should be the main repository for the recording of:
  - IT capacity metrics
  - Measurements
  - Targets
  - Documents
  - The capacity plan
  - Capacity measurements
  - Achievement reports
  - Design criteria
  - Action plans
  - Testing schedules

Capacity plan
In order to provide structure and focus to a wide range of initiatives that may need to be undertaken to improve capacity, a capacity plan should be formulated and maintained. It is recommended that the capacity plan is considered complementary to the availability plan and financial plan, and that publication is aligned with the availability and business budgeting cycle. The capacity plan should have
- Goals and objectives
- Deliverables
- People
- Processes
- Products / technology / tools
- Capacity management techniques
- Actual levels of capacity versus agreed levels of capacity
- Activities being progressed to address shortfalls
- Details of changing capacity requirements for existing IT services

- Details of the capacity requirements for forthcoming new IT services
- Upcoming technology trends

Interfaces

Like all processes, the capacity management process has relationships with all other processes. However, some of the most visible relationships include but are not limited to:

- **Availability management** – To determine the resources needed to meet current and future agreed availability target
- **Service level management** – To determine capacity targets, to investigate and resolve capacity-related issues.
- **ITSCM** – To assists with the assessment of business impact and risk and determining the capacity needed to support risk reduction measures and recovery options
- **Incident and problem management** – To assist with incident resolution, problem investigation and justification for addressing capacity-related issues
- **Demand management** – To anticipate the demand for services based on user profiles and patterns of business activity, and identify ways to influence customer behaviours

Triggers

Here are some of the triggers that may start the whole, or part of the, capacity management process.

- New and changed services requiring additional capacity
- Service breaches, capacity or performance events, warnings and alerts
- Exception reports
- Request from SLM to assist with explanation of achievements for capacity and/or performance targets
- Periodic review and revision of
- Current capacity and performance
- Forecasts, reports, and plans
- Periodic trending and modelling
- Business and IT plans and strategies
- Designs and strategies
- SLA, OLA, contracts, and any other agreements

Inputs

Here are some of the inputs required by the capacity management process.

- Business information
- Service and IT information
- Component performance and capacity information
- Service performance issue information
- Service information
- Financial information
- Change information
- Performance information
- CMS
- Workload information

Outputs
Here are some of the outputs produced by the capacity management process.
- Capacity management information system (CMIS)
- Capacity plan
- Service performance information and reports
- Workload analysis and reports
- Ad hoc capacity and performance reports
- Forecasts and predictive reports
- Thresholds, alerts and events
- Improvement actions

Critical success factors
The critical success factors, which change over time, for the capacity management process may include but are not limited to the following.
- Accuracy of business predictions
- Knowledge of current and future technologies
- Ability to demonstrate cost effectiveness
- Ability to plan and implement the appropriate IT capacity to meet business needs

Metrics
The performance of the capacity management process can be measured according to:
- Reduction in the business disruption caused by a lack of adequate IT capacity
- Accurate forecasts of planned expenditure
- Percentage accuracy of forecasts of business trends
- Percentage reduction in lost business due to inadequate capacity
- Production of workload forecasts on time
- Increased ability to monitor performance and throughput of services and components
- Timely justification and implementation of new technology
- Reduction in use of old technology
- Reduction in Incidents and Problems related to inadequate capacity

Challenges
Here are some of the potential challenges faced by the capacity management process
- Persuading the business to provide information on its strategic business plans, to enable the IT service provider organisation to provide effective business capacity management
- Combining all of the component capacity management data into an integrated set of information that can be analysed in a consistent manner
- Difficulty in sifting and analysis the huge amount of data gathered by capacity management

Risks
Here are some of the potential risks faced by the capacity management process
- A lack of...
  - Commitment from the business to the capacity management process

- ○ Appropriate information from the business on future plans and strategies
- ○ Senior management commitment
- ○ Resources and/or budget for the capacity management process
- Capacity management sub-processes conducted in isolation there is a lack of appropriate and accurate business information
- The processes become too bureaucratic or manually intensive
- Too much focus on one of the sub-processes to the detriment of the others
- The reports and information too bulky or too technical

6.9 Availability Management

Introduction
The purpose of availability management is to ensure that the level of service availability delivered in all services is matched to or exceeds the current and future agreed needs of the business, in a cost effective manner.

Its **objectives** are:
- Creating and maintaining an up-to-date availability plan that reflects the current and future needs of the customer
- Advising on availability-related issues
- Guiding the customer and IT service provider
- Ensuring that availability results meet or exceed the defined requirements
- Providing assistance in diagnosis and resolution of availability-related incidents and problems
- Assessing the impact of changes have on the availability plan and the performance and capacity of the services and resources
- Taking proactive measures to improve availability

Scope
Availability management includes designing, implementing, measuring, managing, and improving IT services and the components availability. It must understand the service and component availability requirements from the business perspective in terms of the:
- Current business processes (their operation and requirements)
- Future business plans and requirements
- Service targets and the current service operation and delivery
- IT infrastructure, data, applications and the environment (including performance)
- Business impacts and priorities in relation to the services and their usage

By understanding these issues, availability management is able to ensure that all services and components are designed and delivered in order to meet their targets in terms of agreed business need. Availability management should be applied to all operational services, new, modified, and supporting services. It covers all service aspects that have an impact on availability, such as training, competencies, procedures, and tools.

Value for the business

The availability and reliability of IT services has a direct impact on customer satisfaction and company reputation. Availability management is vital. It should therefore be included (just like capacity management) in all stages of the Service Lifecycle.

Activities, methods, and techniques

The main activities of availability management are:

- Determining the availability requirements of the business
- Determining the Vital Business Functions (VBFs)
- Determining the impact of failing components
- Defining the targets for availability, reliability and maintainability of the IT components
- Monitoring and analysing IT components
- Establishing measures and reporting of availability, reliability, and maintainability that reflect the business user and IT support organisation perspectives
- Investigating the underlying reasons for unacceptable availability
- Creating and maintaining an availability plan

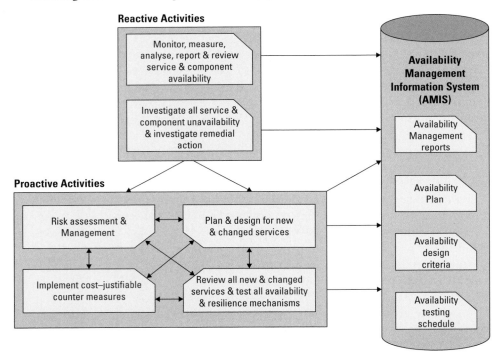

Figure 6.8 Sample availability management workflow

Source: The Cabinet Office

Availability management monitors, measures, analyses and reports on the following aspects:

- **Availability** – the service, component or CI ability to perform its agreed function when required
- **Reliability** – the length of time a service, component or CI can perform its agreed function without interruption
- **Maintainability** – how quickly and effectively a service, component or CI can be restored to normal working after a failure
- **Serviceability** – the ability of an external IT service provider to meet the terms of their contract

Measuring is extremely important. It can be done from three perspectives:

- **Business perspective** – looks at IT availability in terms of its contribution to or impact on the Vital Business Functions that drive the business operation
- **User perspective** – views the availability of IT services as a combination of three factors: frequency, duration and scope of impact (how many users or organisation parts are affected), and also response times
- **The IT service provider's perspective** – considers IT service and component availability in regard to availability, reliability and maintainability

Availability management must ensure that all services meet their agreed targets. New or changed services must be designed in such a way that they will meet their agreed targets. To achieve this, availability management can perform reactive and proactive activities:

- **Reactive activities** – are executed in the operational phase of the lifecycle:
  - Monitoring, measuring, analysing and reporting the availability of services and components
  - Unavailability analysis
  - The expanded incident lifecycle
  - Service Failure Analysis (SFA)
- **Proactive activities** – must be executed in both the design and the CSI phases of the lifecycle:
  - Identifying Vital Business Functions
  - Designing for availability
  - Component Failure Impact Analysis (CFIA)
  - Single Point of Failure (SPOF) analysis
  - Fault Tree Analysis (FTA)
  - Modelling
  - Risk analysis and management
  - Availability testing schedule
  - Planned and preventive maintenance
  - Production of the Projected Service Availability (PSA) document
  - Continual review and improvement

Leading principles

Effective availability management consists of both reactive and proactive activities. Do not lose sight of the following things:

- The availability of services is one of the most important aspects to satisfy customers.
- In the event of failures, an effective response can still result in high customer satisfaction.
- Improving availability is possible only by understanding how the services support the customer's operations.
- Availability can only be managed as well as the weakest link in the chain.
- It is not just a reactive process, but also – and particularly – proactive.
- It is wiser and more cost-effective to build in the right availability level from the start, i.e. in the design of new services.

Starting points for availability management

Figure 6.9 illustrates a number of starting points for availability management. The unavailability of services can be reduced by aiming to reduce each of the phases distinguished in the extended incident lifecycle.

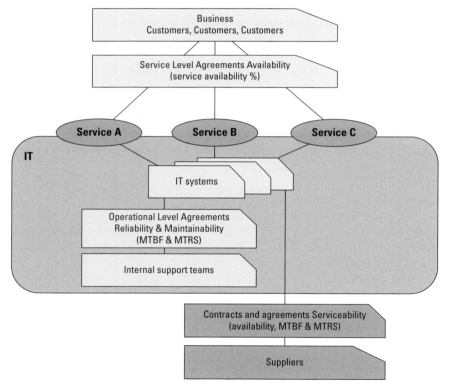

Figure 6.9 Sample of availability terms and measurements

Source: The Cabinet Office

Services must be restored quickly when they are unavailable to users. The **Mean Time to Restore Service (MTRS)** is the time within which a function (service, system, or component) is restored to operational use after a failure. The MTRS depends on a number of factors, such as:
• Configuration of service assets
• MTRS of individual components
• Competencies of support personnel
• Available resources
• Policy plans
• Procedures
• Redundancy

Analysis of the MTRS in relation to each factor is useful to improve the performance and design of services.

The MTRS can be reduced through management for each of its composite components. Reducing the duration of the following factors limits the unavailability time of a service:
• **Incident detection** – the time between occurrence of an incident and its being detected
• **Incident diagnosis** – the time at which diagnosis to determine the underlying cause has been completed
• **Incident repair** – the time at which the failure has been repaired/fixed
• **Incident recovery** – the time at which component recovery has been completed
• **Incident restoration** – the time at which normal business service is resumed

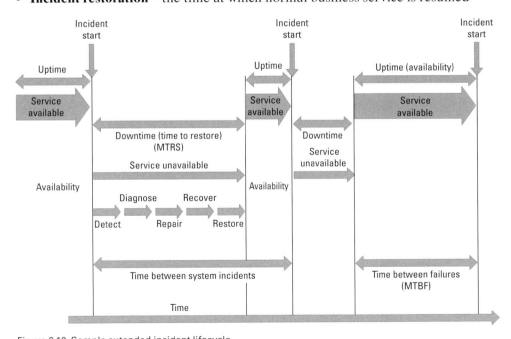

Figure 6.10 Sample extended incident lifecycle

Source: The Cabinet Office

Other metrics for measuring availability include:
- **Mean Time Between Failures (MTBF)** – The average time that a CI or service can perform its agreed function without interruption.
- **Mean Time Between Service Incidents (MTBSI)** – The mean time from when a system or service fails, until it next fails.
- **Mean Time To Repair (MTTR)** – The average time taken to repair a CI or service after a failure. MTTR is measured from when the CI or service fails until it is repaired. MTTR does not include the time required to recover or restore.

Redundancy
Redundancy is a way of increasing reliability and sustainability of systems. ITIL defines the following redundancy types:
- **Active redundancy** – This type is used to support essential services that absolutely cannot be interrupted. The productive capacity of redundancy assets is always available. With active redundancy all redundant units are operating simultaneously. An example would be a set of "mirrored" disks in a server computer.
- **Passive redundancy** – The use of redundant assets that are left inoperative until the event of a failure (reactive). For example stand-by servers or clustered systems.

ITIL also uses the following differentiation to explain redundancy types:
- **Diverse redundancy (heterogeneous redundancy)** – Redundancy through various types of service assets that share the same capabilities (spreading the risk). This type is used when the cause of the failure is difficult to predict. For example, use of different storage media, programming languages, or development teams.
- **Homogeneous redundancy** – Refers to using extra capacity of the same type of service assets. With this type there is a high certainty about the causes of failure. For example use of two identical processors.

The active and passive redundancy types can be used individually or in combination with the homogeneous and heterogeneous types. For example: redundancy that is both active and homogeneous has a low tolerance of failure and a high certainty about the causes of failure.

The following approaches improve the accessibility of services:
- **Various channels** – the demand is led through various types of access channel; this means it is resistant to the failure of a single channel (active diverse redundancy)
- **Closed network** – multiple access gates increase the network's capacity (homogeneous redundancy)
- **Loose link** – interfaces are based on public infrastructure, open source technologies and omnipresent access options, such as mobile phones and browsers; it offers users access to the service via multiple channels and in multiple sites; security developments are making this method increasingly accessible

Information management and the availability management information system
Availability management must maintain an information system. The Availability Management Information System (AMIS) contains all of the measures and

information required to complete the availability management process. It also provides the business with the right information on the level of the service to be delivered in terms of components and supporting services.

The information system constitutes the basis for the availability plan. The availability plan is not the same as an availability management implementation plan, while it can initially be developed jointly with the implementation plan. Availability management changes all the time, which is why the availability plan must contain the following elements:
- Current levels of availability compared against the agreed levels (from the customer's perspective)
- Actions taken to resolve shortcomings in availability
- Details of changed availability requirements for existing and future services
- A forward looking schedule for Service Failure Analysis (SFA) assignments
- Regular review of the SFA assignments
- Benefits and opportunities of planned upgrades

The plan should complement the capacity plan and the financial plan and have a medium term perspective, covering for instance a period of two or three years. The first six months should be covered in more detail. The plan should be updated with minor revisions every quarter, and major revisions occurring every six months.

Information management
The availability management process should maintain an AMIS that contains all of the measurements and information required to complete the availability management process and provide the appropriate information to the business on the level of IT service provided. This information, covering services, components and supporting services, provides the basis for regular, ad hoc and exception availability reporting and the identification of trends within the data for the instigation of improvement activities. These activities and the information contained within the AMIS provide the basis for developing the content of the availability plan.

Availability management information system (AMIS)
The AMIS is a set of tools, data, and information that is used to support availability management and is the cornerstone of a successful availability management process. The information is stored and analysed by all the activities of availability management.

The AMIS is a federated repository that holds a number of different types of data, including business, service, resource, financial, and utilisation from all areas of technology. It is part of the service knowledge management system (SKMS).

The AMIS can be utilised to record and store selected data and information required to support key activities such as report generation, statistical analysis, and availability forecasting and planning. The AMIS should be the main repository for the recording of
- IT availability metrics
- Measurements

- Targets
- Documents
- The availability plan
- Availability measurements
- Achievement reports
- SFA assignment reports
- Design criteria
- Action plans
- Testing schedules

Availability plan

In order to provide structure and focus to a wide range of initiatives that may need to be undertaken to improve availability, an availability plan should be formulated and maintained. It is recommended that the availability plan is considered complementary to the capacity plan and financial plan, and that publication is aligned with the capacity and business budgeting cycle. The availability plan should have:

- Goals and objectives
- Deliverables
- People
- Processes
- Products / technology / tools
- Availability management techniques
- Actual levels of availability versus agreed levels of availability
- Activities being progressed to address shortfalls
- Details of changing availability requirements for existing IT services
- Details of the availability requirements for forthcoming new IT services
- A forward-looking schedule for the planned SFA assignments
- Periodic and regular reviews of SFA assignments
- Upcoming technology trends

Interfaces

Like all processes, the availability management process has relationships with all other processes. However, some of the most visible relationships include but are not limited to:

- **Service level management** – To determine availability targets, to investigate and resolve availability-related issues.
- **ITSCM** – To assist with the assessment of business impact and risk and determining the availability needed to support risk reduction measures and recovery options. Availability focuses on normal business operation and ITSCM focuses on the extraordinary interruption of service.
- **Incident and problem management** – To assist with incident resolution, problem investigation and justification for addressing availability-related issues
- **Demand management** – To anticipate the demand for services based on user profiles and patterns of business activity, and identify ways to influence customer behaviours
- **Capacity management** – To support resilience and overall service availability

- **Change management** – To assist with the creation of the projected service outage report (PSO)
- **Information security management (ISM)** – To define the security measures and policies to include in the design for availability and in the design for recovery. If the data is unavailable, the service is unavailable.
- **Access management** – To provide the methods for appropriately granting and revoking access

Triggers

Here are some of the triggers that may start the whole, or part of the, availability management process.

- New or changed...
  - Business needs
  - Services
  - Targets within agreements, such as SLR, SLA, OLA or contracts
- Service or component breaches, availability events and alerts, including threshold events, exception reports
- Periodic review and revision of...
  - Availability management forecasts, reports and plans
  - Business and IT plans and strategies
  - Designs and strategies
- Recognition/notification of a change of risk or impact for a business process, VBF, a service, or component
- Request from SLM to assist with explanation of achievements for availability targets

Inputs

Here are some of the inputs required by the availability management process.

- Business information
- Business impact information
- Reports and registers
- Service information
- Service information
- Financial information
- Change and release information
- Service asset and configuration management
- Service targets
- Component information
- Technology information
- Past performance
- Unavailability and failure information
- Planning information

Outputs

Here are some of the outputs produced by the availability management process.

- The Availability Management Information System (AMIS)
- The availability plan

- Availability and recovery design criteria
- Reports on the availability, reliability and maintainability of services
- Component availability, reliability and maintainability reports of achievements against targets
- Updated risk register
- Monitoring, management and reporting
- Availability management test schedule
- Planned and preventive maintenance schedule
- Projected Service Outage (PSO)
- Revised risk assessment reviews and reports and an updated risk register
- Contributions for the PSO to be created by change in collaboration with release and deployment management
- Details of the proactive availability techniques and measures
- Improvement actions for inclusion within the service improvement plan

Critical success factors
The critical success factors, which change over time, for the availability management process may include but are not limited to the following.
- Managing the availability and reliability of IT services
- Availability of IT infrastructure (as agreed in the SLA) provided at optimal costs
- Satisfying business needs for access to IT services

Metrics
The performance of the availability management process can be measured according to:
- Percentage reduction in the unavailability of services and components
- Percentage increase in the of reliability of services and components
- Percentage improvement in overall end-to-end availability of service
- Percentage reduction of the cost of unavailability
- Percentage increase in customer satisfaction

Challenges
Here are some of the potential challenges faced by the availability management process.
- Persuading the business to provide information on its strategic business plans, to enable the IT service provider organisation to provide effective availability management
- Combining all of the component availability management data into an integrated set of information that can be analysed in a consistent manner
- Difficulty in sifting and analysing the huge amount of data gathered by availability management
- Determining the components making up the end-to-end service
- Computing end-to-end availability

Risks

Here are some of the potential risks faced by the availability management process
- A lack of…
  - ○ Commitment from the business to the availability management process
  - ○ Appropriate information from the business on future plans and strategies
  - ○ Senior management commitment
  - ○ Resources and/or budget for the availability management process
- Availability management activities, methods, and techniques conducted in isolation – there is a lack of appropriate and accurate business information
- The processes become too bureaucratic or manually intensive
- Too much focus on component/system versus end-to-end service availability
- The reports and information are too bulky or too technical

6.10 IT Service Continuity Management

Introduction

The purpose of IT Service Continuity Management (ITSCM) is to support the overall business continuity process by ensuring that the required IT technical and service facilities (including computer systems, networks, applications, data repositories, telecommunications, environment, technical support, and service desk etc.) can be resumed within required and agreed business timescales.

Objectives include:
- Maintaining a set of continuity plans and recovery plans
- Performing regular Business Impact Analysis (BIA)
- Conducting regular risk estimates and management exercises
- Provide advice and guidance to all other areas of the business and IT on all continuity and recovery-related issues
- Ensuring that the appropriate continuity and recovery mechanisms are put in place to meet or exceed the agreed business continuity targets
- Assessing the impact of all changes on the continuity and recovery plans
- Implementing proactive measures to improve the availability of services (where cost-justifiable to do so)
- Negotiating agreements with IT service providers in relation to the required recovery capability to support continuity plans

Scope

ITSCM focuses on those events that the business considers a disaster. The incident management process handles less significant events. ITSCM primarily considers the IT assets and configurations that support the business processes. If it is necessary to move to an alternative work environment as a result of a disaster, the process also covers office spaces, personnel accommodation and telephone facilities, for example.

ITSCM does not usually directly cover longer-term risks such as those from changes in business direction. While these can have a huge impact, there is generally enough time to identify them and take action. Minor technical problems, such as non-critical disk failures, are not covered by this process – they are handled by incident management. ITSCM does cover:

- Agreements on ITSCM's scope
- A business impact analysis to quantify the impact of disasters
- Risk Analysis (RA) – risk identification and risk assessment to identify potential threats to continuity and the likelihood of the threats becoming reality
- Creating an overall ITSCM strategy that must be integrated into the business continuity management strategy
- Creating continuity plans
- Testing the plans
- On-going operation and maintenance of the plans

Value for the business
ITSCM has a valuable role in supporting the business continuity planning process. Organisations often use it to create awareness of continuity and recovery requirements and justify their decision to implement the process of business continuity planning (including plans).

Activities, methods, and techniques
ITSCM is a cyclic process. It keeps the developed service continuity plans and recovery plans in line with the business continuity plans as these are updated.

The process consists of four phases:
- **Initiation** – This phase covers the entire organisation and includes the following activities:
  - Defining the policy
  - Specifying terms of reference and scope
  - Allocating resources (people, resources and funds)
  - Defining the project organisation and control structure
  - Agree project and quality plans

- **Requirements and strategy** – Determining the business requirements for ITSCM is vital when investigating how well an organisation can survive a disaster. This phase includes *requirements* and *strategy*. The *requirements* involve undertaking a business impact analysis and risk analysis:
  - *Requirement 1*: Business Impact Analysis – (BIA) – Its purpose is to quantify the impact caused by the loss of services. If the impact can be determined in detail, it is called "hard impact" – e.g. financial losses. "Soft impact" is less easily determined. It represents, for instance, the impact on public relations, morale, and health. The BIA identifies the most important services for the organisation and as such provides important input for the strategy. Among other things, the analysis identifies:
    - The type of damage or loss (e.g. income, reputation)
    - How the damage could escalate

- The required competencies, facilities and services to continue important processes
- The timeframe within which partial (the most vital processes) and full recovery must occur
- Determination of recovery periods for every individual service
- Generally speaking, more preventive measures need to be taken with regards to those processes and services with earlier and higher impacts. Greater emphasis should be placed on continuity and recovery measures for those where the impact is lower and takes longer to develop.
  ○ *Requirement 2*: Risk estimate – There are various risk analysis and management methods. Risk analysis is an assessment of risks that may give rise to service disruption or security violation. Risk management identifies the response and cost-justifiable counter-measures that can be taken. A standard method like Management of Risk (M_o_R) can be used to investigate and manage the risks. This method consists of:
    - M_o_R principles
    - M_o_R approach (organisation approach)
    - M_o_R processes (identification, assessment, planning, implementation)
    - M_o_R embedding and review
    - Communication (up-to-date and adequate information provision)
  ○ *Strategy 1*: Risk response measures – Measures to reduce risks must be implemented in combination with availability management since failure reduction has an impact on service availability. Measures may include: fault tolerant systems, good IT security controls, and offsite storage.
  ○ *Strategy 2*: ITSCM recovery options – The continuity strategy is a balance between the cost of risk reduction measures and recovery options to support the recovery of critical business processes within agreed timescales. A number of recovery options are possible:
    - *Manual workarounds*: temporary manual solution for a limited period of time
    - *Reciprocal arrangements*: support agreements between parties with similar infrastructures (not used often these days)
    - *Gradual recovery (or cold standby):* method that makes basic facilities such as accommodation and computer space available at limited costs within several days
    - *Intermediate recovery (warm standby):* recovery within two to three days, generally based on a prepared facility that is often shared with several other parties
    - *Fast recovery (hot standby):* recovery within 24 hours that focuses on the main services, involving e.g. shadow sites that can be operational very quickly and with very low data loss
    - *Immediate recovery (also hot standby):* option for the immediate recovery of mainly business-critical services with the aid of mirroring techniques, dual sites, and other redundancy solutions; no data loss involved

- **Implementation** – The ITSCM plans can be created once the strategy is approved. You should remember, however, that the organisation structure (leadership and decision-making processes) changes in the event of a disaster recovery process. Set this up around a senior manager generally in charge, with a coordinator below them and the recovery teams below that. Test the plans in full, e.g. using the following test types:

- ○ Walkthrough tests
- ○ Full tests
- ○ Partial test (e.g. a single service or server)
- ○ Scenario test (testing for specific responses/scenarios)

- **On-going operation** – This phase includes:
  - ○ Education, awareness and training of personnel
  - ○ Review
  - ○ Testing
  - ○ Change management (ensures that all changes have been assessed for their potential impact)
  - ○ Ultimate test (invocation)

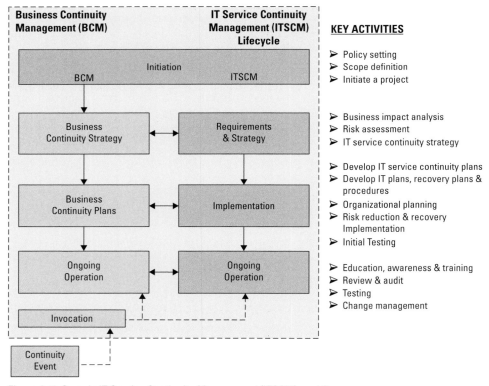

Figure 6.11 Sample IT Service Continuity Management (ITSCM) workflow

Source: The Cabinet Office

Information management

All of the information that is required to maintain the ITSCM plans is recorded. The plan is aligned with the BCM (Business Continuity Management) information. At the very least, it should contain information about:

- The most recent version of the BCM strategy and business impact analysis
- Risks within a risk register including, risk assessment and possible responses to these
- Executed and planned tests
- Details of the ITSCM and related plans
- Existing recovery facilities, suppliers, partners and agreements
- Details on backup and restore processes
- Information from the latest version of the BIA
- Comprehensive information on risk within a risk register, including risk assessment and risk responses
- The latest version of the BCM strategy and business continuity plans
- Details of all...
  - Completed tests and a schedule of all planned tests
  - ITSCM plans and their contents
  - Other plans associated with ITSCM plans
  - Existing recovery facilities, recovery suppliers and partners, recovery agreements and contracts, spare and alternative equipment
  - Backup and recovery processes, schedules, systems and media and their respective locations
- Additional technical plans to create, incorporate and test
  - Emergency response plan
  - Damage assessment plan
  - Salvage plan
  - Vital records plan
  - Crisis management and public relations plan
  - Accommodation and services plan
  - Security plan
  - Personnel plan
  - Communication plan
  - Finance and administration plan

Each critical business area is responsible for the development of a plan detailing the individuals who will be in the recovery teams and the tasks to be undertaken on invocation of recovery arrangements.

Interfaces

Like all processes, the IT service continuity management process has relationships with all other processes. However, some of the most visible relationships include but are not limited to:

- **Change management** – To assess changes against ITSCM plans and activities. The plan itself must be under change management control.

- **Incident and problem management** – Incidents can evolve into major incidents or disasters
- **Availability management** – To coordinate risk assessment and implementing risk responses
- **Service level management** – Recovery requirements will be agreed and documented in the SLA
- **Capacity management** – To ensure that there are sufficient resources to enable recovery onto replacement computers following a disaster
- **Service asset and configuration management** – The CMS documents the components that make up the infrastructure and the relationship between the components
- **Information security management** – A major security breach could be considered a disaster, include security aspects so when conducting BIA and risk assessment

Triggers
Here are some of the triggers that may start the whole, or part of the, IT service continuity management process.
- The occurrence of a major incident that requires assessment for potential invocation of either business or IT continuity plans
- Assessment of changes and attendance at change advisory board meetings
- Lessons learned from previous continuity events and associated recovery activities.
- New or changed…
  - Business needs
  - Services
  - Targets within agreements, such as SLR, SLA, OLA or contracts
- Service or component breaches, availability events and alerts, including threshold events, exception reports
- Periodic review and revision of…
  - Business impact analysis
  - Risk assessment activities
  - Results of continuity and recovery testing
  - Continuity management forecasts, reports and plans
  - Business and IT plans and strategies
  - Designs and strategies
- Recognition/notification of a change of risk or impact for a business process, VBF, a service, or component

Inputs
Here are some of the inputs required by the IT service continuity management process.
- Business information
- A business continuity strategy and a set of business continuity plans
- IT information
- Service information
- Financial information
- Change information

- Service asset and configuration management verification and audit reports
- Business continuity management and availability management testing schedules
- Capacity management information
- IT service continuity plans and test reports from supplier and partners

Outputs

Here are some of the outputs produced by the IT service continuity management process.

- Revised ITSCM policy and strategy
- Business impact analysis exercises and reports
- Risk analysis and management reviews and reports
- A set of ITSCM plans
- Testing schedule
- Test scenarios
- Test reports and reviews

Critical success factors

The critical success factors, which change over time, for the IT service continuity management process may include but are not limited to the following.

- IT services are delivered and can be recovered to meet business objectives
- Awareness throughout the organisation of the business and IT service continuity plans

Metrics

The performance of the IT service continuity management process can be measured according to:

- Increase in…
  - Validated awareness of business impact, needs and requirements throughout IT
  - Successful test results
  - Success of regular audits of the ITSCM plans
- Periodic and regular…
  - Validated communication of the ITSCM objectives and responsibilities
  - Successful validation that all service recovery targets are agreed, achievable
  - Comprehensive testing of ITSCM plans achieved consistently
  - Reviews of all plans
- Validation that IT negotiates and manages all necessary ITSCM contracts with third party
- Overall reduction in the risk and impact of possible failure of IT services

Challenges

Here are some of the potential challenges faced by the IT service continuity management process.

- Provide appropriate plans when there is no BCM process
- Changing the perception that continuity is an IT responsibility, and therefore the business assumes IT services will continue to run under any circumstances.
- Alignment and integration with an existing BCM process

Risks
Here are some of the potential risks faced by the IT service continuity management process.
- A lack of…
  - A BCM process
  - Commitment from the business to ITSCM
  - Appropriate information from the business on future plans and strategies
  - Senior management commitment
  - Resources and/or budget for ITSCM
- Too much focus on technology issues to the detriment of the needs and the priorities of the business and/or IT services
- Risk assessment and management conducted in isolation without input from other service design processes
- Out of date and/or misalignment of ITSCM plans and information with the business and BCM information and plans
- ITSCM activities, methods, and techniques conducted in isolation there is a lack of appropriate and accurate business information
- The processes become too bureaucratic or manually intensive
- The reports and information are too bulky or too technical

6.11 Information Security Management

Introduction
The purpose of information security management is to align IT and business security and ensure that information security is managed effectively in all services and service management activities.

Its **objectives** are:
- Information is available and usable when required (availability)
- Information is available exclusively to authorised persons (confidentiality)
- The information is complete, accurate and protected against unauthorised changes (integrity)
- Transactions and information exchange between companies and partners can be trusted (authenticity and non-repudiation)

Scope
Information security management needs to understand the total IT and business security environment. This means, among other things:
- The current and future business security policy and plans
- Security requirements
- Legal requirements
- Obligations and responsibilities
- Business and IT risks (and their management)

This enables information security management to manage the current and future security aspects of the business cost-effectively. The process should include the following elements:

- Production, maintenance, distribution and enforcement of an information security policy
- Understanding agreed current and future security requirements of the business
- Implementing (and documenting) controls that support the information security policy and manage risks
- Managing IT service providers and contracts concerning access to the system and services
- Management of security breaches and incidents
- Proactive improvement of the security control systems

Value for the business

Information security management ensures that the information security policy complies with the overall business security policy of the organisation and the requirements of corporate governance. It raises internal awareness of the need for security within all services and assets. Executive management is responsible for the organisation's information and is tasked with responding to issues that affect its protection. Boards of directors are expected to make information security an integral part of corporate governance. All IT service provider organisations must therefore ensure that they have a comprehensive information security management policy in place to monitor and enforce the policies.

Basic concepts

The information security management process and framework include:

- Information security policy
- Information Security Management System (ISMS)
- Comprehensive security strategy (related to the business objectives and strategy)
- Effective security organisational structure
- Set of security controls to support the policy
- Risk management
- Monitoring processes
- Communication strategy
- Training and awareness strategy

Activities, methods, and techniques

The key activities within the information security management process are:

- Production and maintenance of an overall information security policy and a set of supporting specific policies
- Communication, implementation and enforcement of the security policies
- Assessment and classification of all information assets and documentation
- Implementation, review, revision and improvement of a set of security controls and risk assessment and responses
- Monitoring and management of all security breaches and major security incidents

- Analysis, reporting, and reduction of the volumes and impact of security breaches and incidents
- Schedule and completion of security reviews, audits, and penetration tests

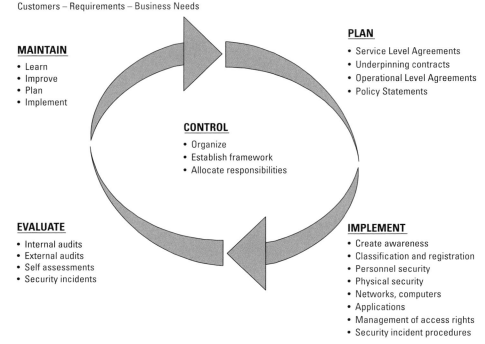

Figure 6.12 Sample IT security management workflow

Source: The Cabinet Office

Information security management system

The Information Security Management System (ISMS) provides the basis for cost-effective development of an information security program that supports the business objectives. Use the four Ps of Personnel, Processes, Products (including technology), and Partners (including service providers) to ensure high levels of security are in place. This system will generally consist of:

- An information security policy and specific security policies
- A security management information system (SMIS)
- A comprehensive security strategy
- An effective security organisational structure
- A set of security controls to support the policy
- The management of security risks
- Monitoring processes to ensure compliance and provide feedback on effectiveness
- Communications strategy and plan for security
- Training and awareness strategy and plan

ISO 27001 is the formal standard against which organisations may seek certification of their ISMS. Figure 6.13 is based on various recommendations, including ISO 27001, and provides insight into the five elements and their objectives.

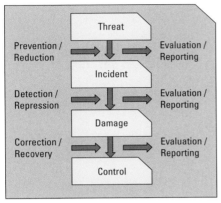

Figure 6.13 Sample framework for managing IT security workflow

Source: The Cabinet Office

Security governance

IT security governance can have six outcomes:
- Strategic alignment:
  - Security requirements driven by enterprise requirements
  - Security solutions fitting enterprise processes
  - Investments aligned with the enterprise strategy and agreed-on risk profile
- Value delivery:
  - A standard set of security practices
  - Properly prioritised efforts to areas with greatest business benefit
  - Institutionalised and commoditised solutions
  - Complete solutions, covering organisation and process as well as technology
  - A culture of continual improvement
- Risk management:
  - Agreed-on risk profile
  - Understanding of risk exposure
  - Awareness of risk management priorities
  - Risk mitigation
  - Risk acceptance/deference
- Performance management:
  - Defined, agreed and meaningful set of metrics
  - Measurement process
  - Independent assurance
- Resource management:
  - Knowledge is captured and available
  - Documented security processes and practices
  - Developed security architecture(s) to efficiently utilise infrastructure resources
  - Business process assurance

The information security manager must understand that security is not merely a step in the lifecycle and that it cannot be solved by technology alone. Information security must be an integral part of all services (and systems) and is an on-going process that needs to be continually managed. Figure 6.14 describes controls that can be used in the process.

The figure shows that a risk may result in a **threat** that in turn causes an **incident**, the consequence of which is damage. Measures of varying nature can be taken between these phases:
- **Preventive measures** – prevent effects (e.g. access management)
- **Reductive measures** – limit effects (e.g. backup and testing)
- **Detective measures** – detect effects (e.g. monitoring)

- **Repressive measures** – suppress effects (e.g. blocking)
- **Corrective measures** – repair effects (e.g. rollback)

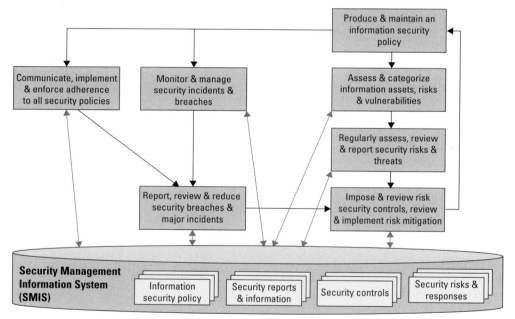

Figure 6.14 Sample security controls for threats and incidents

Source: The Cabinet Office

Information management

All the information required by information security management should be contained within the SMIS. This should include all security controls, risks, breaches, processes, and reports necessary to support and maintain the information security policy and the SMIS. This information should cover all IT services and components, and needs to be integrated and maintained in alignment with all other management information systems, particularly the service portfolio and the CMS. The SMIS will also provide the input to security audits and reviews and to the continual improvement activities so important to all SMISs. The SMIS will also provide invaluable input to the design of new systems and services.

Security management information system (SMIS)

The SMIS is a set of tools, data, and information that is used to support security management and is the cornerstone of a successful security management process. The information is stored and analysed by all the activities of security management.

The SMIS is a federated repository that holds a number of different types of data, including business, service, resource, financial, and user profiles from all areas. It is part of the service knowledge management system (SKMS).

The SMIS can be utilised to record and store selected data and information required to support key activities such as report generation, statistical analysis, and security forecasting and planning. The SMIS should be the main repository for the recording of:
- IT security metrics
- Measurements
- Targets
- Documents
- The security policy
- The security plan
- Security measurements
- Achievement reports
- Design criteria
- Action plans

Interfaces

Like all processes, the information security management process has relationships with all other processes. However, some of the most visible relationships include but are not limited to:
- **Incident and problem management** – Information security management provides support in the decision-making process relating to and the correction of security incidents and problems
- **SLM** – This provides support for the establishment of security requirements and responsibilities and their inclusion in the SLR and SLA
- **Access management** – This performs the actions to grant and revoke access and applies the policies defined by information security management
- **Change management** – Information security management supports change management in determining the possible impact of changes on security
- **IT service continuity management** – To collaborate with ITSCM on the assessment of business impact and risk, and the provision of resilience, fail-over and recovery mechanisms
- **Service asset and configuration management** – To provide accurate asset information to assist with security classifications

- **Availability management** – Data that is unavailable or lacking in integrity compromises the ability of the service to perform its agreed function
- **Capacity management** – For consideration when procuring and/or introducing any new technology or software
- **Financial management for IT services** – To provide adequate funds to finance security requirements
- **Supplier management** – To assist with the joint management of suppliers and the terms and conditions to be included within contracts concerning supplier security responsibilities
- **Legal and human resources issues** – To investigate security issues. ISM should be integrated with these corporate processes and functions

Triggers
Here are some of the triggers that may start the whole, or part of the, information security management process.
- New or changed…
  - Corporate governance guidelines
  - Business security policy
  - Corporate risk management processes and guidelines
  - Business needs
  - Services
  - Targets within agreements, such as SLR, SLA, OLA or contracts
- Service or component security breaches, security events and alerts, including threshold events, exception reports
- Periodic review and revision of…
  - Business and IT plans and strategies
  - Designs and strategies
  - Recognition/notification of a change of risk or impact for a business process, VBF, a service, or component
- Requests from other areas, particularly SLM for assistance with security issues

Inputs
Here are some of the inputs required by the information security management process.
- Business information
- Corporate governance and business security policies and guidelines
- IT information
- Service information
- Risk analysis processes and reports
- Details of security events and breaches
- Change information
- Information from the configuration management system
- Details of partner and service provider access

Outputs

Here are some of the outputs produced by the information security management process.

- Overall information security management policy
- A security management information system (SMIS)
- Revised security risk assessment processes and reports
- Security controls, audits and reports
- Security test schedules and plans
- A set of security classifications
- A set of classified information assets
- Reviews and reports of security breaches and major incidents
- Policies, processes, and procedures for managing partners and suppliers and their access to services and information

Metrics

The performance of the information security management process can be measured according to:

- Percentage decrease in security breaches
- Percentage decrease in the impact of security breaches and incidents
- Percentage increase in SLA conformance to security clauses
- Decrease in the number of non-conformances with the business security policy and process
- Increase in the acceptance and conformance of security procedures
- Increased support and commitment of senior management
- Increased awareness of the security policy and its contents, throughout the organisation

Critical success factors

The critical success factors, which change over time, for the information security management process may include but are not limited to the following.

- Business is protected against *security violations*
- Determination of a clear and agreed policy, integrated with the needs of the business
- Security procedures that are justified, appropriate and supported by senior management
- Effective marketing and education in security requirements
- A mechanism for improvement
- An integral part of IT services, ITSM processes, and business security management
- The availability of services is not compromised by security incidents
- Clear ownership and awareness of the security policies among the customer community

Challenges

Here are some of the potential challenges faced by the information security management process.

- Ensuring there is adequate support from the business, business security and senior management
- Changing the perception that continuity is an IT responsibility, and therefore the business assumes IT services will continue to run under any circumstances.
- Alignment and integration with an existing BCM process

Risks

Here are some of the potential risks faced by the information security management process.

- Risk factors can be both internal and external, including …
  - Widespread use of technology
  - Increasing dependence of the business on it
  - Increasing complexity and interconnectivity of systems
  - Disappearance of the traditional organisational boundaries
  - Increasingly onerous regulatory requirements
  - Increasing requirements for availability and robustness
  - Growing potential for misuse and abuse of information systems affecting privacy and ethical values
  - External dangers from hackers, malware, extortion, industrial espionage, and leakage of organisational or private data
- A lack of commitment from…
  - The business to the information security management process and procedures
  - The business on future plans and strategies
  - Senior management
  - Resources and/or budget for the information security management process
- Focusing too much on technology issues instead of on the needs and priorities of the business
- Out-of-date and misaligned policies, plans, risks and information to the business and business security
- Security policies add no value to the business

6.12 Supplier Management

Introduction

The purpose of the supplier management process is to manage suppliers and the services they supply, to provide seamless quality of IT service to the business, ensuring value for money.

Objectives are:

- Obtain value for money from suppliers and contracts
- Ensure that underpinning contracts and agreements with suppliers are aligned to business needs
- Manage relationships with suppliers and their performance
- Negotiate and agree contracts with suppliers

- Maintain a supplier policy and a supporting supplier and contract management information system (SCMIS)

Scope

The supplier management process includes the management of all suppliers and contracts needed to support the provision of IT services to the business. The greater the contribution of a supplier, the more effort the service provider must put in managing the (relationship with the) supplier, and the more they should be involved with the development and implementation of the strategy. The smaller the supplier's value contribution, the more likely it is that the relationship will be managed mainly at an operational level. The process should include the following aspects:

- Implementation and enforcement of the supplier policy
- Maintenance of a supplier and contract management information system (SCMIS)
- Categorising of suppliers and contracts and risk assessment
- Evaluation of contracts and suppliers
- Developing, negotiating, and agreement of contracts
- Revising, renewing, and terminating contracts

Value for the business

One of the most important goals of supplier management is to get value for money from supplier and contracts and to ensure that all targets in underpinning contracts and agreements are aligned to business needs and agreed targets within the SLA. This ensures the delivery of end-to-end seamless, quality IT services that are aligned to the business expectation. The supplier management process should align with all corporate requirements and the requirements of all other IT and service management processes, particularly information security management and ITSCM.

Basic concepts

All activities in this process should be driven by a supplier strategy and the policy from Service Strategy. A supplier and contract management information system (SCMIS) is created to achieve consistency and effectiveness in implementing policy. Ideally, the SCMIS would be an integrated element of CMS or SKMS. The SCMIS should contain all details regarding suppliers and contracts, together with details about the type of service or product, and any information and relationship to other configuration items.

The data stored here will provide important information for activities and procedures such as:

- Categorising of suppliers
- Maintenance of supplier and contract database
- Evaluation and set-up of new suppliers and contracts
- Establishing new suppliers
- Supplier and contract management and performance
- Renewed and terminated contracts

Activities, methods, and techniques

For external suppliers, it is recommended to draw up a formal contract with clearly defined, agreed upon, and documented responsibilities and goals. This contract is managed during its entire lifecycle.

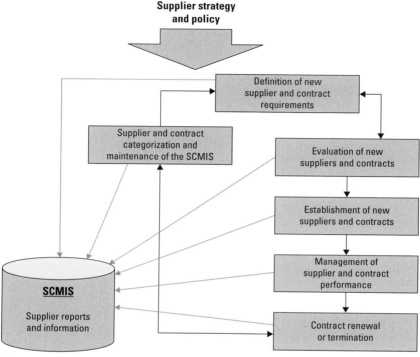

Figure 6.15 Sample supplier management workflow

Source: The Cabinet Office

These phases are:
- **Definition of new supplier and contract requirements:**
  - ○ Identification of business need and preparation of the business case
  - ○ Produce a statement of requirement (SoR) and/or invitation to tender (ITT)
  - ○ Ensure conformance to strategy/policy
- **Evaluation of new suppliers and contracts:**
  - ○ Identify method of purchase or procurement
  - ○ Establish evaluation criteria – for example, services, capability, quality, and cost
  - ○ Evaluate alternative options
  - ○ Select
  - ○ Negotiate contracts, targets and the terms and conditions, including responsibilities, closure, renewal, extension, dispute, and transfer
  - ○ Agree and award the contract
- **Supplier and contract categorisation and maintenance of the SCMIS:**
  - ○ Assessment or reassessment of the supplier and contract
  - ○ Ensure changes progressed through service transition

- o Categorisation of the supplier
- o Update of SCMIS
- o On-going maintenance of the SCMIS
- **Establishment of new suppliers and contracts:**
  - o Set up contract within the SCMIS and any other associated corporate systems
  - o Transition of service
  - o Establish contacts and relationships
- **Manage the supplier and contract performance**
  - o Management and control of the operation and delivery of service
  - o Monitor and report
  - o Review and improve
  - o Management of supplier and relationship
  - o Periodically review service scope against business need, targets, and agreements
  - o Plan for possible closure/renewal/extension
- **Contract renewal or termination**
  - o Review
  - o Renegotiate, renew, terminate and/or transfer
  - o Transition to new supplier or to internal resources

Supplier categorisation:
- **Strategic** – For significant "partnering" relationships that involve senior managers sharing confidential strategic information to facilitate long-term plans. These relationships would probably require involvement of service strategy and service design resources
  - o A network service provider supplying worldwide networks service and their support
- **Tactical** – For relationships involving significant commercial activity and business interaction
  - o A hardware maintenance organisation
  - o A facilities maintenance organisation
- **Operational** – For suppliers of operational products or services
- An internet hosting service provider
  - o Supplying hosting space for a low-usage
  - o Low-impact website
  - o Internally used it service
- **Commodity** – For suppliers providing low-value and/or readily available products and services
  - o Paper or printer cartridge suppliers
  - o Office supplies

Information management

All the information required by supplier management should be contained within the SCMIS. This should include all information relating to suppliers and contracts, as well as all the information relating to the operation of the supporting services provided by suppliers. Information relating to these supporting services should also be contained within the service portfolio, together with the relationships to all other services and components. This information should be integrated and maintained in alignment with all other IT management information systems, particularly the service portfolio, and the SKMS.

Interfaces

Like all processes, the supplier management process has relationships with all other processes. However, some of the most visible relationships include but are not limited to:

- **Service portfolio management** – Ensures that the service portfolio accurately depicts all supporting systems and details
- **Financial management for IT services** – Funds supplier management requirements and contracts, provides financial advice, and guidance on purchase and procurement
- **SLM** – Assists in determining goals, requirements and responsibilities
- **ITSCM** – Works with supplier management with regard to the management of continuity service suppliers
- **Information security management** – Manages suppliers and their access to services
- **Change management** – Supplier contracts and agreements are subject to change management procedures. Involvement of suppliers should be assessed and reflected in planning for changes

Triggers

Here are some of the triggers that may start the whole, or part of the, supplier management process.

- New or changed…
  - Corporate governance guidelines
  - Business and IT strategies, policies or plans
  - Business needs
  - Services
  - Requirements within agreements, such as SLR, SLA, OLA or contracts
- Periodic review and revision of
  - Designs and strategies
  - Supplier management policies, reports and plans
- Requests from other areas, particularly SLM and information security management, for assistance with supplier issues
- Requirements for new contracts, contract renewal or contract termination
- Re-categorisation of suppliers and/or contracts

Inputs

Here are some of the inputs required by the supplier management process.

- Business information
  - Supplier and contracts strategy
  - Supplier plans and strategies
  - Supplier contracts, agreements and targets
  - Supplier and contract performance information
- IT information
  - Performance issues
- Financial information

- Service information
  - CMS

Outputs

Here are some of the outputs produced by the supplier management process.
- SCMIS
- Supplier and contract performance information and reports
- Supplier and contract review meeting minutes
- Supplier SIPs
- Supplier survey reports

Critical success factors

The critical success factors, which change over time, for the supplier management process may include but are not limited to the following.
- Business protected from poor supplier performance or disruption
- Supporting services and their targets align with business needs and targets
- Availability of services is not compromised by supplier performance
- Clear ownership and awareness of supplier and contractual issues

Metrics

The performance of the supplier management can be measured according to:
- Increase in the number of…
  - Suppliers meeting the targets within the contract
  - Service and contractual reviews held with suppliers
  - Supplier and contractual targets aligned with SLA and SLR targets
  - Suppliers with nominated supplier managers
  - Contracts with nominated contract managers
- Reduction in the number of
  - Service breaches caused by suppliers
  - Threatened service breaches caused by suppliers
  - Breaches of contractual targets

Challenges

Here are some of the potential challenges faced by the supplier management process
- Constantly changing business and IT needs
- Existing imperfect contracts
- Legacy issues, especially with services recently outsourced
- Insufficient expertise retained within the organisation
- Being tied into long-term contracts
- Disputes over charges
- Interference by either party in the running of the other's operation
- Being caught in a daily fire-fighting mode, losing the proactive approach
- Poor communication
- Personality conflicts and/or cultural conflicts
- One party using the contract to the detriment of the other party

Risks
Here are some of the potential risks faced by the supplier management process
- Lack of...
  - Commitment from the business to the supplier management process and procedures
  - Commitment from senior management to the supplier management process and procedures
  - Appropriate information on future business and IT policies, plans and strategies
  - Resources and/or budget for the supplier management process
  - Clarity and integration by supplier with service management processes, policies and procedures of the service provider
- Legacy of badly written and agreed contracts
- Suppliers fail or are incapable of meeting the terms and conditions of the contract
- Misaligned culture between provider and supplier
- Uncooperative/unwilling suppliers in supporting the supplier management process
- Suppliers are taken over and relationships, personnel and contracts are changed
- Excessive and bureaucratic demands
- Targets and service levels within contracts that are impossible to meet
- Poor corporate financial processes

6.13 Organisation

Roles and responsibilities
Well performing organisations can quickly and accurately make the right decisions and execute them successfully. In order to achieve this, it is crucial that the roles and responsibilities are clearly defined. This is also an essential issue in the Service Design process. One of the possible models that can be helpful in this regard is the RACI model. RACI is an acronym for the four most important roles:
- **Responsible** – the person who is responsible for completing the task
- **Accountable** – just one person who is accountable for each task
- **Consulted** – people who give advice
- **Informed** – people who must be kept "in the loop" regarding the progress of the project

In establishing a RACI system, the following steps are necessary:
- Identify activities and processes
- Identify and define functional roles
- Conduct meetings and delegate the RACI codes
- Identify gaps and potential overlaps
- Distribute the chart and build in feedback
- Ensure that the allocations are followed

Skills

Despite the fact that every position brings with it specific skills and competencies (see "Roles" below), the responsible person must:

- Be aware of the business priorities and objectives
- Be aware of the role that IT plays
- Possess customer service skills
- Be aware of what IT can provide to the customer
- Have the competencies and knowledge that are needed in order to perform the function well
- Have the ability to use, understand and interpret the best practice policies and procedures to ensure adherence

Roles

In this section is a description of the roles and responsibilities of the most important positions in the Service Design process. Depending on the size of an organisation these roles can be combined. The most important roles are:

- **The process owner** is responsible for ensuring that the process is implemented as agreed and that the established objectives will therefore be achieved. Tasks are:
  - Documenting and recording the process
  - Defining the KPIs and if necessary revising them
  - Improving the effectiveness and efficiency of the process
  - Providing input to the Service Improvement Plan
  - Reviewing the process, the roles and responsibilities
- **The service design manager** is responsible for the overall coordination and inputting of the service designs. Tasks include:
  - Ensure that the Service Strategy corresponds with the design process and that the designs satisfy the established requirements
  - Design the functional aspects of the services
  - Produce and maintain the design documentation
  - Assess the effectiveness and efficiency of the design process
- **The service catalogue manager** is responsible for the production and maintenance of the service catalogue. In addition, the service catalogue manager must:
  - Ensure that the services are recorded in the service catalogue
  - Ensure that the information that has been included is up-to-date and is consistent with the information in the service portfolio
  - Ensure that the catalogue is secure and that there are backups
- **The service level manager** has as their most important responsibilities to:
  - Have an insight into the changing demands of the customer and the market
  - Ensure that the customers' existing and future requirements have been identified
  - Negotiate and make agreements on the delivery of services
  - Assist in the production and maintenance of an accurate services portfolio
  - Ensure that the objectives that have been ratified in underlying contracts are synchronised with the SLA
- **The availability manager** is responsible for:
  - Ensuring that the existing services are available as agreed
  - Assisting in investigating and diagnosing all incidents and problems

    ○ Contributing to the design of the IT infrastructure
    ○ Proactively improving the availability of services
- **The security manager** has as their most important tasks to:
    ○ Design and maintain the information security policy
    ○ Communicate with the involved parties on matters pertaining to the security policy
    ○ Assist in the business impact analysis
    ○ Perform risk analyses and risk management together with availability management and ITSCM

In addition, there are still the following responsible positions to recognise in this process:
- IT planner
- IT designer/architect
- Service continuity manager
- Capacity manager
- Supplier manager

6.14 Methods, techniques and tools

Technological considerations

It is extremely important that someone ensures that the tools to be used support the processes and not the other way around. There are various tools and techniques that can be used for supporting the service and component designs. They not only make the hardware and software designs possible, but also enable the development of environment designs, process designs and data designs. The great variety of tools and techniques offer the following benefits:
- Attainment of speed in the design process
- Adherence to standards
- The development of prototypes and models
- Take into account diverse scenarios (what if…?)

The design process can be simplified by making use of tools that give a graphic image of the service and its components: from the business processes to the service and the SLA, through the infrastructure, environment, data and applications, processes, OLA (operational level agreements), teams, contracts and suppliers. If the tool also contains financial information and is coupled with a "metrics tree", the service can be guarded and managed through all of the phases in its lifecycle.

These tools not only facilitate the design process, they also support all of the phases in the Service Lifecycle, including:
- Management of all levels of the Service Lifecycle
- All aspects of the service and the performances
- Management of costs

- Management of the service portfolio and catalogue
- A CMS and a SKMS

The following generic activities must be performed:
- Ensure that there is a generic lifecycle for IT assets
- Formalise relationships between different types of IT assets
- Define the roles and responsibilities
- Ensure that a study is performed in order to understand the TCO of an IT service

Even more can be added for application assets:
- Define an acquisition strategy for IT assets and analyse how this can be synchronised with both the IT– and the business strategy
- Document the role that the application plays in the provision of IT services
- Determine standards for the use of various approaches to the design of applications

For data/information assets still more can be added:
- Ensure that data designs are made in the light of:
- The importance of standardisation
- The need for qualitatively valuable data
- The value of data to the organisation

For IT infrastructure assets more can be added:
- Establish standards for the acquisition and management of IT– and environmental infrastructure (electricity, space, middleware, database systems etc.)
- Determine activities for the optimum use of the IT infrastructure assets
- Specify the need for tools and describe how they would be used

For skills assets more can be added:
- Formalise how competencies could be considered as assets in the organisation
- Ensure that the competencies are documented

In order to establish interfaces and dependencies the following can be added:
- Formalise the interfaces that the acquisition and management of IT assets have with functions and processes outside the IT sphere
- Formalise quality control in the acquisition and management of IT assets

Service management tools
Tools help ensure that Service Design processes can function effectively. They enhance efficiency and provide valuable management information on the identification of possible weak points. The long-term benefit is that the use of tools serves to reduce costs and increase productivity, in the interest of improving the quality of IT service delivery. In addition, the use of tools makes possible the centralisation of essential processes, as well as the automation and integration of "core" service management processes.

Considerations in the evaluation of service management tools include:
• Data structure, data handling and integration
• Conformity with international standards
• Flexibility in implementation, use, and sharing of data
• Support in the monitoring of service levels

The tool serves to support the process rather than the other way around. If possible, it is recommended that a completely integrated tool is acquired, that supports the many service management processes. If this is not possible, then interfaces among the various tools should be taken into consideration. During the selection process it is advisable to employ a Statement of Requirements (SoR). The requirements should be considered using the MoSCoW analysis:
• **M** – must have this
• **S** – should have this
• **C** – could have this
• **W** – won't have this now, but would like in the future

The tool must be flexible so that it can support individual access rights. It is necessary to determine who has access to the data and with what objective. In addition, it must be decided as to which platform the tool can work on. During the first consideration it is wise to look into the credit-worthiness of the supplier and find out if they offer support (training) for a few months or years. In this process it is important to realise that a solution almost never satisfies 100 percent of the requirements. The 80/20 rule is perhaps more realistic in this framework. In other words, the tool is likely to satisfy closer to 80 percent of the established requirements.

6.15 Implementation considerations

In this section the implementation considerations for Service Design are addressed. In addition, the interfaces of Service Design with the other phases of the Service Lifecycle will be discussed.

Business impact analysis

The Business Impact Analysis (BIA) is a valuable source of information for establishing the customer's needs, and the impact and the risk of a service. The BIA is an essential element in the business continuity process and dictates the strategy to be followed for risk reduction and recovery after a catastrophe. The BIA consists of two parts: on the one hand is the investigation of the impact of the loss of a business process or function; on the other hand is the stopping of the effect of that loss.

The BIA must be conducted in order to support the definition of the business continuity strategy, and makes it possible to better understand the function and the importance of the service. In this way the organisation can determine, among other things:
• What the critical services are
• What an acceptable time is for the service to be unavailable

- What an acceptable level of unavailability of the service is
- What the costs of the loss of the service are
- What the critical business and service periods are?

Implementation of Service Design

The process, policy, and architecture for the design of IT services, as described in this book, must be documented and used in order to design and implement appropriate IT services. In principle, it is recommended that all of the processes are implemented at the same time since all of the processes are related to each other and often are also dependent on each other. What is ultimately needed is an integrated set of processes that IT services can manage and oversee throughout the entire lifecycle. Since organisations can rarely implement everything at once, the process for which there is the greatest need should be the first to be done, realising that all processes are interlinked. In addition, this also depends on the maturity of the organisation's IT service management. The implementation priorities must correspond with the objectives of the Service Improvement Program (SIP). If, for example, availability of IT services is an important point, then the organisation must focus on those processes that will improve availability; in this case, incident management, problem management, change management and availability management. Various other processes, such as capacity management, security management and continuity management also influence availability, as illustrated by the intertwining of the ITIL processes.

It is important that a structured project management method be used during the implementation phase. The CSI model is a good example of such a method. The success of the Service Design and the success of the improvement of the Service Design processes must be assessed. The results must then be analysed and reported. If it does not satisfy the requirements, then an adjustment is probably needed. During the entire process assessments must be made. One of the possible methods is the Balanced Scorecard, which was developed by Robert Kaplan and David Norton as a method for measuring business activities in terms of its strategy and vision, and with which a good image of the organisation's performance can be sketched.

Prerequisites

There are various prerequisites for new or revised processes. They are often requirements of other processes. For example, before Service Level Management (SLM) can design the Service Level Agreement (SLA) a business service catalogue and a *technical/supporting services view* of the service catalogue are necessary. Problem management depends on a mature incident management process. These things are much bigger than just ITSM: availability and capacity management need information about the business plan. There are more of these examples which need to be considered first before high process maturity can be achieved.

Critical success factors

Management support

Support from higher and middle management is necessary for all IT service management activities and processes. It is crucial for obtaining sufficient financing and resources. Senior management must also offer visible support during the launch of new Service Design initiatives.

Middle management must also provide the necessary support and actions.

Business support
It is also important that Service Design is supported by the business units. This works well if the Service Design personnel involve the business in all their activities, and are open about what is and isn't feasible in terms of meeting business requirements.

Regular communication with the business is crucial to building a good relationship and to ensuring support; Service Design will be better placed to understand the needs and concerns of the business. Additionally, the business can provide feedback on the efforts of Service Design to satisfy the business needs.

Hiring and retaining personnel
The correct number of personnel with the correct skills is critical for successful Service Design. Consider the following challenges:
- Projects for new services often clearly specify what the new skills must be, but may underestimate how many personnel are needed and how skills can be retained.
- There may be a lack of personnel with solid knowledge of service management; having good technicians is important, but there must also be a certain number of people who have knowledge of both technological and service problems.
- Because personnel with both technological and service knowledge are fairly rare, they are often specially trained; it is important to retain them by offering a clear career path and solid compensation.
- Personnel are often assigned new tasks too quickly, while they are still extremely busy with their current workloads. Successful service management projects may require a short term investment in temporary workers.

Service management training
Good training and awareness can provide great advantages. In addition to increasing expertise, they can generate enthusiasm in people. Service Design personnel must be aware of the consequences of their actions for the organisation. A "service management culture" must be created. Service management will only be successful if the people are focused on overall service management objectives.

Appropriate tools
Many service management processes and activities cannot be effectively executed without proper support tools. Senior management must ensure that financing for such tools is included in annual budgets, and must support acquisition, implementation, and maintenance.

Test validity
The quality level will improve considerably if solid and complete testing of new components and releases is planned as part of the service design in a timely manner.

Also, the documentation should be planned as well and included in the service design package.

Measuring and reporting

Clear agreements are necessary regarding the way in which things are measured and reported; all personnel will have clear targets to aim for, and IT and business managers will be able to evaluate quickly and simply whether progress is being made and which areas deserve extra attention.

Challenges

Here are some of the potential challenges faced by the Service Design phase.
- The need for synchronisation of existing architecture, strategy, and policy
- The use of various technologies and applications
- Unclear or changing customer requirements
- Lack of awareness and knowledge of service delivery
- Resistance to working systematically
- Inefficient use of resources

In order to overcome the challenges, consideration may be given to the following matters:
- Insights into the customer's requirements and priorities
- Adequate communication with involved parties, but equally, be a "listening ear"
- Involve all the required people in the design process
- Ensure the involvement of management and personnel

Risks

Here are some of the potential risks faced by the Service Design phase.
- If the level of maturity in one of the processes is low, it is impossible to reach a high level of maturity in other processes
- Business requirements are not clear for the IT personnel
- Too little time is allotted for Service Design
- Synchronisation among infrastructure, customer, and partners is not good, which means the requirements cannot be satisfied
- The Service Design phase is not clear or on the whole is not available

Interfaces with other phases in the lifecycle

Like all other phases and all processes, the Service Design phase has relationships with all other phases and processes. However, some of the most visible relationships include but are not limited to:
- All activities in the Service Design phase originate from the customer's needs and requirements, and are then also a reflection of the strategy, plans, and policy produced by the first phase of the lifecycle: the Services Strategy.
- The Service Design phase in the lifecycle begins with the new or changed requirements of the customer. Ultimately, by the end of the design process, a service solution must be designed which satisfies those requirements before they begin the transition process together with the service package. In the transition

phase, the service will be evaluated, structured, tested and deployment will take place after which the implementation will be transferred to Service Operation.

The output from every phase is input for the next phase in the lifecycle. Thus Service Strategy provides important input to Service Design, which in turn, provides input to the transition phase.

The service portfolio provides information to every process in every phase of the lifecycle. In this respect it is in fact the backbone of the Service Lifecycle. The service portfolio must be a component of the service knowledge management system and be included as a document in the configuration management system. This will be described in greater detail in the following section, "Service Transition".

7 Service transition phase

7.1 Service Transition

This short section provides a summary of the updates between the 2007 edition and the 2011 edition for the ITIL core book Service Transition published by TSO.

The structure, content, and relationships of the CMS and the SKMS have been clarified to help the reader to understand these key concepts.

There is new content explaining how a change proposal should be used. The evaluation process has been renamed "change evaluation" and the purpose and scope have been modified to help clarify when and how this process should be used.

The service asset and configuration management process has additional content relating to asset management, and there are improvements in the flow and integration of a number of processes, including change management, release and deployment management, and change evaluation.

Table 7.1 Summary of changes: ITIL Service Transition

Area of update	Description
Change management	Top-level flowchart and section headings have been modified so that they are consistent with each other.
Change process model	The name "change model" is now used consistently. Previously the description used the term "change process model" but many places in Service Transition and the other publications used "change model".
Change proposal	More detail has been added to help clarify how and when a change proposal should be used.
Configuration record, configuration item (CI), CMS, SKMS	Many people were confused by the descriptions of a configuration record, CI, CMS and SKMS in the 2007 edition of Service Transition and wanted a clear and unambiguous explanation of these concepts.
Evaluation	The process name has been changed to "change evaluation" and the purpose and scope have been clarified to show that this process is used for evaluating changes only.
Release and deployment management	Some sections have been reordered and a high-level process diagram has been provided showing how it all fits together.
Service asset and configuration management	Text has been added to explain the service asset management aspects better.

7.2 Introduction

This chapter explains how the specifications from Service Design can be effectively converted to a new or changed service.

Objectives

The **goals** of Service Transition include:
- Supporting the change process of the business (customer)
- Reducing variations in the performance and known errors of the new/changed service
- Ensuring the service meets the requirements of the service specifications

The **objectives** of Service Transition include:
- The necessary means to realise, plan, and manage the new service
- Ensuring the minimum impact for the services which are already in production
- Improving customer satisfaction and stimulate the proper use of the service and mutual technology

Scope

ITIL defines the **scope** of Service Transition as follows:

> *"Service Transition includes the management and coordination of the processes, systems and functions required for the packaging, building, testing, and deployment of a release into production, and establish the service specified in the customer and stakeholder requirements."*

A Service Transition generally comprises the following steps:
- Planning and preparation
- Building and testing
- Any pilots
- Planning and preparation of the deployment
- Deployment and transition
- Review and closing of Service Transition

Although change management, service asset and configuration management and knowledge management support all phases of the Service Lifecycle, the ITIL Service Transition book covers these. Release and deployment management, service validation and testing, and change evaluation are included in the scope of Service Transition.

Value for the business

An effective Service Transition ensures that the new or changed services are better aligned with the customer's business operation. Specifically:
- The capacity of the business to react quickly and adequately to changes in the market
- Changes in the business as a result of takeovers, contracting, etc. are well managed
- More successful changes and releases for the business

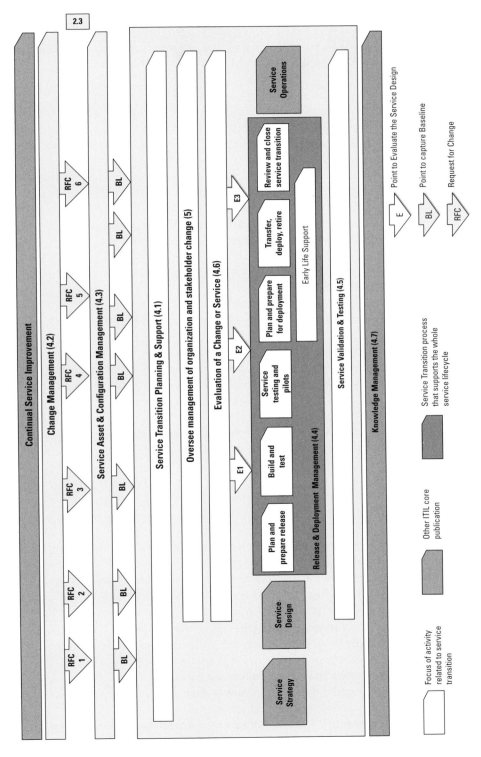

Figure 7.1 The scope of Service Transition
Source: The Cabinet Office

- Better compliance of business and governing rules
- Less deviation between planned budgets and the actual costs
- Better insight into the possible risks during and after the input of a service
- Higher productivity of customer personnel

Optimisation

A Service Transition is effective and efficient if the transition delivers what the business requested within the limitations in terms of money and other necessary means. Additionally, it is important that the phase and release plans are coordinated with the business, the service management, and the IT strategy.

That is why it is important to understand the extent to which the results of the transition correspond with the specifications of the Service Design: what are the differences between the actual values and those from the specifications? These can influence aspects such as time, money, quality, and risks.

7.3   Basic concepts

The following policies are important for an effective Service Transition and apply to every organisation. The approach must still be adjusted to the conditions which differ from organisation to organisation:

- **Define and implement guidelines and procedures for Service Transition** – Define and document policies for Service Transition. The management team must approve the policies. The management team must pass the policies on to the organisation, service providers, and partners.
- **Always implement all changes through Service Transition** – All changes in the service portfolio or service catalogue undergo the change management process and the Service Transition phase.
- **Utilise frameworks and standards** – Design Service Transition on generally accepted frameworks, processes, and systems. This promotes cooperation between the parties involved in the Service Transition and ensures that they "speak the same language".
- **Maximise re-use of established processes and systems** – Service Transition processes are aligned with the organisation's processes and related systems to improve efficiency and effectiveness and where new processes are required, they are developed with re-use in mind. Re-use established processes and systems wherever possible.
- **Align service transition plans with the needs of the business** – Align transition plans, and new or changed services to the requirements and needs of the customer organisation.
- **Create relations with stakeholders and maintain these** – During Service Transition, build up a relationship with customer (representatives), users, and suppliers, to map their expectations of the new or changed service.
- **Set up effective "controls"** – Set up suitable control mechanisms for the entire lifecycle to guarantee a smooth transition of service changes and releases.

- **Deliver systems for knowledge transfer and decision support** – Service Transition develops systems and processes for knowledge transfer as necessary for an effective delivery of the service, and in order to make decision-making possible.
- **Plan releases and deployment packages** – Release packages must be clear, traceable, clearly planned, designed, built, tested, delivered, distributed and deployed for everyone involved.
- **Anticipate and manage changes in direction** – Ensure that the personnel are trained in order to see when "direction adjustments" are necessary during the transition.
- **Manage resources proactively** – Deliver (and manage) shared and specialist resources for the different Service Transition activities in order to avoid delays.
- **Ensure the involvement in an early stage in the Service Lifecycle** – Consult stakeholders at an early stage, so that new or changed services are actually delivering what has been agreed.
- **Assure the quality of a new or changed service** – Verify and validate that the proposed changes can deliver the required service requirements.
- **Proactively improve the quality during a Service Transition** – Proactively plan and improve the quality of a new or changed service.

7.4   Processes and other activities

This section explains the processes and activities of a Service Transition:
- Transition planning and support
- Change management
- Service asset and configuration management
- Release and deployment management
- Service validation and testing
- Change evaluation
- Service knowledge management

Some of these processes and activities occur in more than one phase of the Service Lifecycle, but are stated in this section as they are central during the Service Transition.

Transition planning and support
Transition planning and support ensures the planning and coordination of resources in order to realise the specification of the Service Design. Additionally, the process ensures the identification, management, and minimisation of risks which can interrupt the service during the transition phase.

The scope of transition planning consists of:
- Design specifications and requirements of the production department in the transition planning process
- Management of:
  - Planning
  - Support activities

   ○ Transition progress
   ○ Changes
   ○ Issues
   ○ Risks
   ○ Deviations
   ○ Processes
   ○ Supported systems and tools
- Monitoring the Service Transition performance
- Communication with the client, users and stakeholders

The planning and support activities are:
- Set up transition strategy
- Prepare Service Transition
- Planning and coordination of Service Transition
- Support

Change management

The objective of the change management process is to ensure that changes are deployed in a controlled way, evaluated, prioritised, planned, tested, implemented, and documented. There can be different reasons for a change such as: cost reduction, service improvement, failure of the service provision or a changed environment.

> A **change** is the addition, modification, or removal of authorised, planned, or supported service or service component and its associated documentation.

In the change management process it is important to ensure that:
- Standardised methods and procedures are used
- All changes are kept in the configuration management database (CMDB)
- Consideration is given to the risks for the business

Universally the change management activities are comprised of:
- Change planning and management
- Release planning
- Communication
- Change authorisation
- Set up recovery plan
- Reporting
- Impact assessment
- Continual improvement

The specific activities for the management of individual changes are comprised of:
- Create and record the Request for Change (RFC)
- Review the RFC
- Assess and evaluate change
- Authorise change
- Plan updates

- Coordinate change implementation
- Review and close change

Service Asset and Configuration Management (SACM)

SACM manages the service assets in order to support the other service management processes.

The objective is: the definition of service and infrastructure components and the maintenance of accurate configuration records. For this it is important that:
- The integrity of the service assets and configuration items (CI) is protected
- All assets and CI are categorised in configuration management
- The business and service management processes are effectively supported

SACM may cover non-IT assets and CI of work products which support the development of services. The scope of the process also includes assets and CI of other suppliers ("shared assets") in as far as these are important for the service.

The SACM activities are:
- Management and planning
- Configuration identification
- Configuration management (control)
- Status accounting and reporting
- Verification and audits

Release and deployment management

Release and deployment management is aimed at the building, testing and deploying of the services specified in the Service Design, and ensuring that the customer utilises the service effectively.

The objective of release and deployment management is to ensure that:
- There are release and deployment plans
- Release packages (composition) are successfully deployed
- The IT organisation transfers knowledge to the customers
- There is minimal disturbance to the services

The process activities of release and deployment management are mainly comprised of:
- Planning
- Preparation of building, testing, and deployment
- Building and testing
- Service tests and pilots
- Planning and preparation for deployment
- Transfer, deployment or retirement
- Verifing deployment
- Early Life Support (ELS)
- Review and close

Service validation and testing

Service tests deliver an important contribution to the quality of IT service provision. Tests ensure that the new or changed services are "fit for purpose" and "fit for use".

The purpose of service validation and testing is to deliver a service which is of benefit to the customer's business. When not properly tested, additional incidents, problems and costs occur.

The objectives of service validation and testing are to ensure that:
• The release fulfils the expectation of the customer
• The services are "fit for purpose" and "fit for use"
• The specifications (requirements) of the customer and other stakeholders are defined

Service validation and testing are applied during the entire Service Lifecycle and are intended to test the quality of the service (parts). Testing directly supports the release and deployment process. The output from testing is used by the change evaluation process.

The test process activities are not conducted in a fixed order and can be implemented in parallel. In any case they include:
• Validation and test management
• Planning and design test
• Verification of test plan and design
• Preparing the test environment
• Testing
• Evaluation of exit criteria and reports
• Cleaning up and closure

There are many different test techniques and approaches, including: document review, simulation, scenario and laboratory tests, and role plays. The best choice depends on the type of service, the risk profile, the test goal, and the test level.

Change evaluation

Change evaluation is a generic process that is intended to verify whether the performance of "something" is acceptable; for example, whether it has the right price/quality ratio, whether it is continued, whether it is in use, whether it is paid for, and so on.

In the context of Service Transition, the objective of change evaluation is the definition of the performance of a service change. Evaluation delivers important input for continual service improvement (CSI) and future improvement of service development and change management.

The change evaluation process is comprised from the following activities:
• Planning the evaluation
• Evaluation of the predicted performance

- Evaluation of the actual performance
- Risk management

Knowledge management

The purpose of knowledge management is the improvement of the quality of decision-making by ensuring that reliable and secure information is available during the Service Lifecycle.

The objectives of knowledge management include:
- Enabling the service provider to improve the efficiency and quality of the services
- Ensuring that the service provider's personnel have access to adequate information

Knowledge management is used in the entire lifecycle, but is particularly relevant during the Service Transition: A successful transition depends to a large degree on the information available and knowledge of users, service desk, support, and service provider.

Effective sharing of knowledge requires the development and maintenance of a service knowledge management system (SKMS). This system should be available to all information stakeholders and suit all information requirements.

Knowledge management is comprised of the following activities, methods, and techniques:
- Knowledge management strategy
- Knowledge transfer
- Data and information management
- The use of the SKMS

Other activities

Communication is central during every Service Transition: the greater the change, the greater the need for communication of the reasons for the change, the possible advantages, the plans for implementation, and the effects.

Other operational activities of Service Transition such as the management of organisational changes and the management of stakeholders are explained in the Section "Organisation".

7.5 Transition Planning and Support

Introduction

The **goals** for transition planning and support include:
- Planning and coordinating resources in order to ensure that the specifications of the Service Design are realised
- Starting with the transition phase, identify, manage, and limit risks that could interrupt the service

The **objectives** for transition planning and support include:
- Plan and coordinate people and means within the frameworks
- Make sure that everyone applies the same frameworks and standards
- Report service issues
- Provide clear and extensive plans
- Support transition teams and others involved
- Controlled planning of changes
- Report issues, risks and other deviations

Scope
The following activities are included in the scope of transition planning:
- Include design specifications and product requirements in the transition plans
- Manage:
  - Plans
  - Supporting activities
  - Transition progress
  - Changes
  - Issues
  - Risks
  - Deviations
  - Processes
  - Supporting systems and tools
- Monitor Service Transition achievements
- Communicate with customers, users and stakeholders

Value for the business
An integrated approach to planning improves the alignment of transition plans with the customer, service provider, business and change project plans.

Basic concepts
The **Service Design Package (SDP)** contains the following information required by the service transition team:
- Applicable service packages (e.g. core service package, service level package)
- Service specifications
- Service models
- Architectural design required to deliver the new or changed service including constraints
- Definition and design of each release package
- Detailed design of how the components will be assembled and integrated into a release package
- Release and deployment plans
- Service acceptance criteria

In the **release guidelines and policy**, the following subjects are addressed:
- Naming conventions, distinguishing release types, such as: **major release**, **minor release** and **emergency release**

- Roles and responsibilities: many people from different organisations can be involved with a release; it is useful to set up a responsibility matrix for this purpose
- Release frequency, the expected frequency of each type of release
- Approach for accepting and grouping changes in to a release
- How the configuration baseline for the release is captured and verified against the actual release contents e.g. hardware, software, documentation and knowledge
- Entry and exit criteria and authority for acceptance of the release into each service transition stage and into the controlled test, training, disaster recovery and production environments
- The criteria authorisation for leaving *early life support* (ELS) and handover to service operations

Activities, methods, and techniques
The activities for planning and support consist of:
- Set up transition strategy
- Prepare service transition
- Plan and coordinate service transition
- Support

1. Set up transition strategy
The transition strategy defines the overall approach to organising Service Transition and allocating resources. Aspects that may be addressed in the transition strategy are:
- Purpose, goals and objectives
- Context and scope
- Applicable standards, agreements, legal, regulatory and contractual agreements
- Organisations and stakeholders involved in the service transition
- Framework for service transition
- Criteria for success and failure
- People: roles and responsibilities
- Approach including transition model, plans for managing changes, assets, configurations and knowledge; transition estimation; preparation; evaluation; error handling; KPI
- The products (deliverables) that are the result of the transition activities such as transition plans, schedule of milestones, financial requirements

The SDP defines the various phases of the Service Transition. These may consist of: acquiring and testing components, testing service release, Service Operation ready test, rollout, ELS, review, and close service transition.

2. Prepare Service Transition
Preparatory activities consist of:
- Review and acceptance of inputs from other Service Lifecycle phases review and check the input deliverables e.g. SDP, Service Acceptance Criteria (SAC) and evaluation report
- Identifying, raising and scheduling RFC

- Checking the configuration baselines are recorded in configuration management before the start of service transition
- Checking transition readiness

3. Plan and coordinate Service Transition

A **service transition plan** describes the tasks and activities required to release and deploy a release into the test environments and into production including:
- Work environment and infrastructure
- Schedule of milestones
- Activities and tasks to be performed
- Personnel, resource requirements, budgets and timescales at each stage
- Lead times and contingency

Good **integrated planning** and management are essential to deploy a release across distributed environments and locations into production successfully. An **integrated set of transition plans** should be maintained that are linked to lower level plans such as release, build and test plans.

It is *best practice* to manage several releases in a **program**, with each significant deployment run as a **project**.

Implement **quality reviews** for all Service Transition, release, and deployment plans. Questions that might be asked are:
- Are the service transition plans and release plans up-to-date, authorised and are the release dates known?
- Were any risks related to impact on costs, organisation, and technology taken into account?
- Are new configuration items (CI) compatible with each other and with configuration items in the target environment?
- Are the people who need to work with it sufficiently trained?
- Have potential changes in the business environment been taken into account?

4. Transition process support

Service Transition advises and **supports** all stakeholders. The planning and support team will provide insight for the stakeholders regarding Service Transition processes and supporting systems and tools. In addition, the team will perform **management/administration** of changes, work orders, issues, risks, communication, and deployment. The team will also update stakeholders regarding planning and process.

Finally, Service Transition activities are **monitored**: the implementation of activities is compared with the way they were intended (as formulated in the transition plan and model).

Service transition lifecycle stages

The SDP should define the lifecycle stages for the service transition, and the move from one stage to the next should be subject to formal checks. For each stage there will

be exit criteria, entry criteria, and mandatory deliverables. Each criteria or "quality gate" defines a set of standards which must be met before moving on to the next stage. Typical stages in the life of a transition might include:
- Acquire and test new configuration items (CI) and components
- Build and test
- Service release test
- Service operational readiness test
- Deployment
- Early life support
- Review and close service transition.

Information management
The transition planning and support process makes heavy use of the service knowledge management system, to provide access to the full range of information needed for short-, medium- and long-range planning.

Interfaces
Like all processes, the transition planning and support process has relationships with all other processes. However, some of the most visible relationships include but are not limited to:
- **Demand management** – To provide long-term information about likely resource requirements
- **Service portfolio management** process – To engage transition planning and support to provide input to their planning and decision-making. For change proposals to trigger longer-term planning within transition planning and support
- **Business relationship management** – To manage appropriate two-way communication with customers
- **Service design stage** – In the form of a service design package
- **Supplier management** – To during the service transition to ensure that appropriate contracts are in place
- **Service transition phase** – All processes in this phase are coordinated by transition planning and support
- **Pilots, handover, and early life support** – To be coordinated with the service operation functions
- **Various groups within the organisation** – To provide the personnel needed to carry out many aspects of service transition
  - Technical management
  - Application management
  - Project and programme management
  - Customers and end-users

Triggers

Here are some of the triggers that may start the whole, or part of the, transition planning and support process.

Table 7.2 Triggers for transition planning and support process

• For planning a single transition	An authorised change
• Longer-term planning	Receipt of a change proposal from service portfolio management
• Budgeting for future transition requirements	The organisation's budgetary planning cycle

Inputs

Here are some of the inputs required by the transition planning and support process.
- Change proposal
- Authorised change
- Service design package, which includes:
- Release package definition
- Design specification
- Test plans
- Deployment plans
- Service acceptance criteria (SAC)

Outputs

Here are some of the outputs produced by the transition planning and support process.
- Transition strategy and budget
- Integrated set of service transition plans

Critical success factors

The critical success factors, which change over time, for the transition planning and support process may include but are not limited to the following.
- Understanding and managing the trade-offs between cost, quality and time
- Effective communication with stakeholders
- Identifying and managing risks of failure and disruption
- Coordinating activities of multiple processes involved in each transition
- Managing conflicting demands for shared resources

Metrics

The performance of the transition planning and support process can be measured according to:
- Increase in…
  - The number of releases implemented that meet the customer's agreed requirements in terms of cost, quality, scope and release schedule
  - Customer and user satisfaction
  - Project and service team satisfaction

- Improved...
  - Service transition success rates
  - Efficiency and effectiveness of the processes and supporting systems
- Reduced...
  - Business disruption
  - Number of issues, risks and delays
  - Variation of actual versus predicted scope, quality, cost and time
  - Time and resource to develop and maintain integrated plans and coordination activities
  - Number of issues caused by conflicting demands for shared resources

Challenges

Here are some of the potential challenges faced by the transition planning and support process.

- Building up the relationships needed to manage and coordinate the many stakeholders
- Coordinating and prioritising many new or changed services concurrently
- Understanding the risks and issues for each project to proactively manage resource planning

Risks

Here are some of the potential risks faced by the transition planning and support process.

- Lack of information from demand management and service portfolio management
- Poor relationships with project and program
- Delays to one transition having a subsequent effect on future transitions, due to resource constraints
- Insufficient information to address conflicts

7.6 Change Management

Introduction

Changes have a proactive or reactive **reason**. Examples of a proactive reason are cost reduction or service improvement. Examples of reactive changes are solving service disruptions or adapting the service to a changing environment.

Changes must be **controlled** adequately, so that:

- Exposure to risks is minimised
- The severity of the impact and service interruption is minimised
- The change is implemented successfully on first attempt

The **purpose** of change management is to:

- Respond to the customer's changing business
- Respond to requests for change (RFC) from the business and IT

The **objective** of the change management process is ensuring that changes are recorded, assessed, authorised, prioritised, planned, tested, implemented and documented and reviewed in a controlled manner.

The change management process must:
- Use standardised methods and procedures
- Ensure all changes are recorded in the CMDB
- Take account of risks for the business

Scope
The ITIL definition of a change is:

"A change is the addition, modification, or removal of authorised, planned, or supported service or service component and its associated documentation."

The scope of service management covers changes to baselined service assets and CI across the whole Service Lifecycle. The section "service asset and configuration management" later in this chapter discusses these issues in greater detail.

Every organisation must define for itself which changes its change management process does and does not cover. For instance, changing a defective hard drive of a PC may not be part of the change management process.

The following figure shows the scope of the change management process as well as the interfaces of the process with the business at the strategic, tactical, and operational levels.

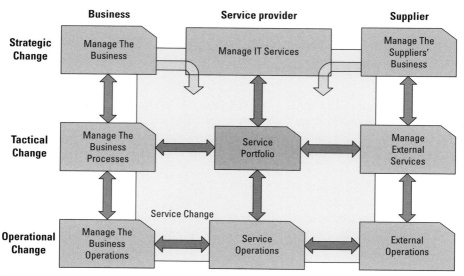

Figure 7.2 The scope of change management

Source: The Cabinet Office

Value for the business

Service and infrastructure changes can have a negative impact on the business through service disruption and delay in identifying business requirements, but change management enables the service providers to add value to the business.

For example:
- Changes relating to financial regulations, such as SOX, or other rules of good governance
- Timely implementation of changes so that the business' deadlines are achieved
- Reducing the number of failed changes, thereby reducing the number of service interruptions
- Prioritising changes and responding adequately to change requests from the customer
- Reducing the mean time to restore services (MTRS)

Thanks to the increased dependency on IT services, and because the underlying information technology has become so complex, significant efficiency benefits can be realised by means of well-structured and planned changes and releases. Some indicators of inadequate change management are:
- Unauthorised changes
- Unplanned downtime
- Implemented changes with little success
- High number of "emergency changes"
- Delayed project implementations

Policies

Policies for supporting change management are:
- Creating a zero tolerance culture in relation to unauthorised changes
- Aligning the change management process with other change processes in the organisation
- Effective prioritisation, e.g. innovative versus preventive versus detective versus corrective changes
- Establishing accountability and responsibilities for changes through the lifecycle
- Establishing a single focal point for changes
- Ensuring integration with other service management processes
- Setting up "change windows", performance and risk assessments, performance measures

Design and planning

The change management process is planned in combination with release and configuration management. This makes it possible to assess the impact of changes on services and releases.

The requirement and design for the change management processes include:
- Requirements relating to relevant laws and regulations
- An approach to eliminate unauthorised changes

- Identification and classification
- Organisation, roles, responsibilities
- Stakeholders
- Grouping and relating changes
- Procedures
- Interfaces with other service management processes

Basic concepts

The terms "change", "change record" and "RFC" are often used inconsistently thus leading to confusion and misunderstanding. ITIL defines them as follows:

> *"Change – The addition, modification or removal of anything that could have an effect on IT services*
> *RFC (request for change) – a formal proposal for a change to be made. It may be recorded on paper or electronically*
> *Change record – A record (in a database, usually as part of an integrated service management suite) containing the details of a change. Each change record documents the lifecycle of a single change. A change record is created for every request for change that is received."*

Emergency change

An **emergency change** is intended to repair a failure (ASAP) in an IT service that has a large negative impact on the business. If this requires permission from the CAB, but the full CAB cannot be convened, it is necessary to identify a smaller group to make emergency decisions: the **Emergency CAB (ECAB)**.

An emergency change, too, must be tested and documented to the greatest possible extent.

Change models and workflows

A change model is a way of predefining the steps that should be taken to handle a particular type of change in an agreed way. This helps ensuring that changes of all types are handled in a predefined path and to predefined timescales.

The change model includes:
- Steps
- Chronological order of the steps
- Responsibilities
- Timescales and thresholds for completion
- Escalation procedures

Change proposals

Change proposals are submitted to change management before chartering new or changed services in order to ensure that potential conflicts for resources or other issues are identified. Authorisation of the change proposal does not authorise implementation of the change but simply allows the service to be chartered so that service design activity can begin.

A change proposal is used to communicate a high-level description of the change. This change proposal is normally created by the service portfolio management process.

Standard changes (pre-authorised)

A standard change is a change to a service or other configuration item for which the approach is pre-authorised by change management, and this approach follows an accepted and established procedure. The following are characteristics of standard changes.

- The tasks are well known, documented, and proven to work
- The change authority may the submitter's immediate manager
- The budget approval usually lies with the submitter's immediate manager
- The risk is usually minimal, well understood, and accepted
- They may be used as workarounds by the incident management process
- They may be used to fulfil service requests by the request fulfilment process
- They may be automated to handle events by the event management process

Remediation planning

No change should be approved without having an answer to the following question: "what will we do if the change is unsuccessful"? An organisation must always ensure that a *fall-back option* is available.

Remediation is a set of actions taken to recover after a failed change or release. Remediation may include back-out, invocation of service continuity plans, or other actions designed to enable the business process to continue.

Change implementation plans should include milestones and other triggers for invoking and implementing remediation in order to ensure that there is sufficient time in the agreed change window for back-out or other remediation when necessary.

Change advisory board (CAB)

This is a consultation body that meets at fixed intervals to assess changes and help change management prioritise the changes. It may include representatives from all key stakeholders and departments, including:

- Customers
- End users
- Application developers
- System administrators
- Experts
- Service desk representatives
- Production
- Service provider representatives

The CAB must have a number of standard agenda items, including:

- Unauthorised changes
- Authorised changes not handled by the CAB
- RFC that must be reviewed by the CAB members

- On-going or closed changes
- Assessment of implemented changes

Emergency change advisory board (ECAB)
This is a consultation body that meets when the need for an emergency change arises. These are situations where there may not be time to convene the full CAB. Even in an emergency, it is necessary to identify a smaller organisation with authority to make emergency decisions. The ECAB assists the change manager in assessing that the emergency is real. Specific emergency change models should be built to ensure all appropriate steps are taken, including documentation.

Activities, methods, and techniques
Overall the change management activities include:
- Change planning and control
- Change and release scheduling
- Communications
- Change decision making and authorisation
- Ensuring there are remediation plans
- Measurement and control
- Management reporting
- Understanding impact
- Continual improvement

The specific activities to manage individual changes are discussed in subsequent sections:
- Create and record RFC
- Review the RFC and change proposal
- Assess and evaluate the change
- Authorise the change
- Plan updates
- Coordinate change implementation
- Review and close change

This section outlines the aspects followed within a "normal" change. The general principles set out apply to all changes and the "normal" change procedure is modified accordingly, to deal with standard and emergency changes for example.

1. Create and record
The change is raised by a request from the initiator – the individual or organisational group that requires the change. For example, this may be a business unit that requires additional facilities, or problem management personnel instigating an error resolution from many other sources.

All RFC are registered and it must be possible to identify them via a unique identification number.

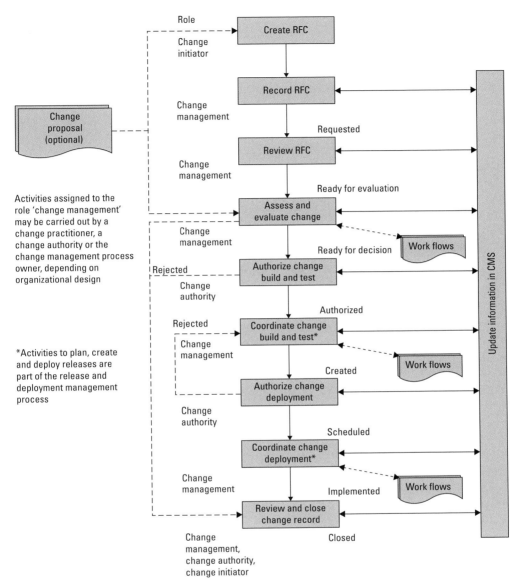

Figure 7.3 Sample process workflow of a regular change

Source: The Cabinet Office

The scope and impact of the eventual change determine how much information is required for the change.

2. Review the RFC

After registration, the stakeholders verify whether the RFC is: totally impractical, repeats of earlier RFC, accepted, rejected, or still under consideration, incomplete submissions e.g. inadequate description, without necessary budgetary approval. Such requests are rejected and returned to the initiator with details of the reason for the rejection. The initiator should have a right of appeal against rejection.

3. Assess and evaluate changes

This step starts with **categorising** the change. The issue of risk must be considered prior to the authorisation of any change. The **likelihood** that the risk will occur and its possible **impact** determine the **risk category** of the change. In practice, a risk categorisation matrix is generally used for this purpose.

After the change has been categorised, it is **evaluated**. Based on the impact, risk assessment, potential benefits, and costs of the change, t**he change authority (whoever has the relevant authority to approve the change, according to internal policy and organisation)** determine whether the change is supported or not.

The following questions must be answered for all changes. Without this information, the impact assessment cannot be completed, and the balance of risk and benefit to the live service will not be understood. The **seven Rs of change management** represent a good starting point for impact analysis:
- Who raised the change? (**R**aised)
- What is the reason for the change? (**R**eason)
- What is the return required from the change? (**R**eturn)
- What are the change's risks? (**R**isk)
- What resources does it require? (**R**esources)
- Who are responsible for build, testing, and implementation? (**R**esponsible)
- Which relationships exist between this and other changes? (**R**elationship)

Determine the change's **priority** to establish the order in which the changes put forward must be considered. Priority is derived from the agreed impact and urgency. **Impact** is based on the beneficial change to the business that will result or on the degree of damage and cost to the business if it fails. **Urgency** indicates how long implementation can be delayed.

Examples of priority codes are:
- **Low priority** – a change is desirable but can wait until a suitable opportunity occurs
- **Medium priority** – no huge urgency or high impact, but the change must not be delayed until a later time; the change advisory board gives this change average priority when allocating resources
- **High priority** – this change represents a serious failure for a number of users or an annoying failure for a large group of users, or it is related to other urgent issues; the change advisory board gives this change top priority in its next meeting
- **Immediate priority** – causing significant loss of revenue or the ability to deliver important public services; immediate action is required

4. Change planning and scheduling

Change management schedules the changes on the change calendar: the **Schedule of Change** (SC). The SC contains the details for all approved changes and their planning e.g. implementation dates.

Changes can be bundled into a release. In consultation with the relevant IT departments, the CAB may set up fixed times to implement changes – moments where services will be hindered as little as possible by changes. A recovery plan must be prepared in case a change implementation is unsuccessful.

5. Authorise the change

Formal authorisation from a change authority is required for every change. This may be a role, person, or group of people. The level at which approval is required depends on the change type. An example is shown in the following figure.

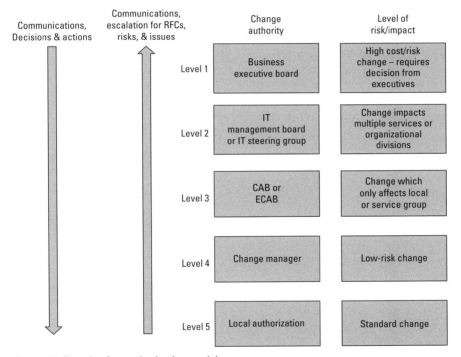

Figure 7.4 Sample of an authorisation model

Source: The Cabinet Office

6. Coordinate change implementation

Authorised RFC should be passed on to the relevant technical groups for building of the changes. Building and creating a release are issues discussed in the section on "Release and deployment management".

You should **test** the changes, the remediation, and the implementation method for the changes thoroughly. Section "service validation and testing" discusses testing in detail.

7. Review and close change record

Implemented changes – perhaps with the exception of standard changes – are evaluated after some time. The CAB then determines whether further follow-up is required. The CAB pays attention to the following matters:
- Did the change realise its intended purpose?
- Are all the stakeholders satisfied with the outcome?
- Did any side-effects occur?
- Were the estimated costs and effort exceeded?

If the change is successful, it can be closed. The outcome should be included in the **Post Implementation Review (PIR)**: the change evaluation. If the change is unsuccessful, change management or the CAB decides what should be done. A new or modified RFC may result.

Information management
- All change requests must be associated with services and other CI. This means they must be included within the CMS
- Correlate changes with incidents and to review the history of changes to any CI as part of incident or problem management
- Change management must have access to the CMS and to information and documents within the SKMS in order to plan and manage changes, to identify stakeholders in any change, and to predict the potential impact of changes

Interfaces
Like all processes, the change management process has relationships with all other processes. However, some of the most visible relationships include but are not limited to:
- **Transition planning and support** – To ensure that there is a coordinated overall approach to managing service transitions
- **IT change processes** – To define clear boundaries, dependencies, and rules
  - Release and deployment management
  - Program and project management
  - Supplier management
- **Change evaluation** – To deliver the change evaluation report be to change management in time for the CAB (or other change authority) to use it to assist in their decision-making
- **Business change processes** – To ensure that change issues, aims, impacts and developments are exchanged and cascaded throughout the organisation where applicable
  - Business program management
  - Business project management
  - Business change management

- **Service portfolio management** – To submit change proposals before chartering new or changed services, in order to identify potential conflicts for resources or other issues
- **Service portfolio management** – To assess whether a service should move to another section of the service portfolio
- **All service management processes**
  - To implement process improvements
  - To participate with impact assessment and implementation of service changes
  - To assess the impact of a change on the policies, plans, or initiatives, of that process
- **Service asset and configuration management**
  - To provide reliable, quick and easy access to accurate configuration information
  - To enable stakeholders and personnel to assess the impact of proposed changes and to track change work flow.
  - To identify related CI that will be affected by the change
- **Problem management** – To implement workarounds and to fix known errors

Triggers

Table 7.3 (overleaf) lists some of the triggers that may start the whole, or part of the, change management process.

Inputs

Here are some of the inputs required by the change management process.
- Policy and strategy for change and release
- Request for change
- Change proposal
- Plans – change, transition, release, test, evaluation, and remediation
- Current change schedule and PSO
- Evaluation reports and interim evaluation reports
- Current assets or configuration items
- As-planned configuration baseline
- Test results, test report, and evaluation report

Outputs

Here are some of the outputs produced by the change management process.
- Rejected and cancelled RFCs
- Authorised changes
- Authorised change proposals
- Change to the service or infrastructure resulting from authorised changes
- New, changed, or disposed configuration items
- Revised change schedule
- Revised PSO
- Authorised change plans
- Change decisions and actions
- Change documents and records
- Change management reports

Table 7.3 Triggers for Change Management

Strategic changes	Change to one or more services
Legal/regulatory change	Service catalogue
Organisational change	Service package
Policy and standards change	Service definition and characteristics
Change after analysing business, customer and user activity patterns	Release package
Addition of new service to the market space	Capacity and resource requirements
Updates to the service portfolio, customer portfolio or customer agreement portfolio	Service level requirements
Change of sourcing model	Warranties
Technology innovation	Utilities
	Cost of utilisation
Operational change	Service assets
Standard changes as defined by the request fulfilment process	Acceptance criteria
Implementation of corrective and preventative changes	Predicted quality of service
	Predicted performance
Changes to deliver continual improvement	Predicted value
Some strategy and service changes will be initiated by CSI	Organisational design
	Stakeholder and communications plans
	Physical change in the environment
	Measurement system
	Plans from capacity, ITSCM, change, transition, test, and release and deployment
	Decommission/retire services
	Procedures, manuals, service desk scripts

Critical success factors

The critical success factors, which change over time, for the change management process may include but are not limited to the following.

- Responding to business and IT requests for change that will align the services with the business needs while maximising value
- Optimising overall business risk
- Ensuring that all changes to configuration items are well managed and recorded in the configuration management system

Metrics

The performance of the change management process can be measured according to:

- Increase in...
  - ○ The percentage of changes that meet the customer's agreed requirements
  - ○ Accuracy of predictions for time, quality, cost, risk, resource, and commercial impact
- Reduction in the...
  - ○ Backlog of change requests
  - ○ Number of disruptions to services, defects and re-work caused by inaccurate specification, poor or incomplete impact assessment
  - ○ Percentage of changes that are categorised as emergency changes
  - ○ Number of unauthorised changes identified
  - ○ Number of incidents attributed to changes

Challenges

Here are some of the potential challenges faced by the change management process.

- Ensuring that every change is recorded and managed
- Ensuring there is active and visible sponsorship from executives and senior management
- Changing the perception that the process bureaucratic and time-wasting, so it will not be valued
- Migrating from operational change control to a true change management process involved early enough in the service lifecycle, includes assessment of benefits and costs, and helps to plan and manage changes
- Agreeing and documenting the many levels of change authority and communicating effectively between these change authorities

Risks

Here are some of the potential risks faced by the change management process.

- Lack of commitment to the change management process...
  - ○ By the business / business sponsorship
  - ○ By IT management / it management sponsorship
  - ○ By IT personnel
- Lack of clarity on interaction with...
  - ○ Other service management processes
  - ○ Project management or service design activities
- Implementation of changes without the use of change management
- Change assessment being reduced to box ticking
- Introduction of delays to change implementation without adding sufficient value
- Excessively bureaucratic change management processes that introduce excessive delay to required changes.
- Insufficient...
  - ○ Time for proper assessment and pressure to expedite decisions
  - ○ Time for implementation of changes, trying to fit too many changes into change window
  - ○ Resources for assessment, planning, and implementation

7.7 Service Asset and Configuration Management

Introduction
The purpose of service asset and configuration management (SACM) is to provide a logical model of the IT infrastructure. In this model the IT services are related to the different IT components needed to supply these services.

The **objective** is: to define service and infrastructure components and maintain accurate configuration records. In this context it is important that:
- The integrity of the service assets and Configuration Items (CI) are protected
- All assets and CI are located in configuration management system
- The operational and service management processes are supported effectively

Scope
All assets that are used during the Service Lifecycle fall within the scope of asset management. The process offers a complete overview of all assets, and shows who is responsible for the control and maintenance of these assets.

Configuration management ensures that all components (CI) that form part of the service or product are identified, **baselined** (the configuration) and maintained. It ensures that releases into controlled environments and operational use are on the basis of formal approvals. The process also provides a logical model of all services, assets, the physical infrastructure, and the mutual relations.

SACM also relates to non-IT assets and CI, such as work products used to develop the services and configurations items required to support the service that are not formally classified as assets. The scope of the process also includes assets and CI of other suppliers ("shared assets"), to the extent that they are relevant to the service.

Value for the business
SACM increases the visibility and performance of the service, release, or environment. Among other things this results in:
- Better forecasting and planning of changes
- Changes and releases to be assessed, planned and successfully delivered
- Incidents and problems to be resolved within the service level targets
- Better adherence to standards, legal and regulatory obligations (less non-conformances)
- Ability to identify the costs for a service

Policies
The first step is to develop and maintain the SACM policies that set the objectives, scope and principles and critical success factors for what is to be achieved by the process. There are significant costs and resource implications to implementing SACM and therefore strategic decisions need to be made about the priorities to be addressed. Many IT service providers focus initially on the basic IT assets (hardware

and software) and services that are business-critical or covered by legal and regulatory compliance e.g. SOX, software licensing.

Starting points

The policies describe the starting points for the development and control of assets and CI, for instance:

- The costs of SACM are proportionate to the potential risks to the service if SACM were not implemented
- The need to provide specifications for "corporate governance"
- The need to guarantee the agreements in the SLA and other contracts
- The specifications for available, reliable and cost-effective services
- The specifications for performance criteria
- The transition from reactive maintenance to proactive control
- The requirement to maintain adequate asset and configuration information for stakeholders

Basic concepts

Service assets, configuration items, configuration records, the CMS and the SKMS
It is important to distinguish between service assets, configuration items and configuration records, as these concepts are often confused.

> **Service asset**
> A service asset is any resource or capability that could contribute to the delivery of a service.
>
> Examples of service assets include resources such as:
> - **Funds** – in the form of budgets to run, grow and/or transform the business
> - **Applications** – commercial-off-the-shelf, developed internally, purchased from vendors
> - **Infrastructure** –hardware systems or components with a unique identifier
> - **Information** – All platforms and all file formats used by the organisation

Examples of service assets include capabilities the ability and the (delegated) authority of management team to make decisions, the ability of the organisation to respond to situations, the ability of the processes to be as effective and as efficient as possible, and the knowledge of the IT personnel.

Note that people are a type of resource in the form of staff numbers and their availability at a given time. People are also a capability type in the form of their skills (technical and soft), knowledge, experience, and aptitudes. It is important to remember that the performance of people is influenced by many factors such as attitudes, behaviours, and cultures of the organisation.

Note: service assets and customer assets are essentially defined the same way. The primary difference is that *service assets* are used by the service provider while *customer assets* are used by the customers (within the business).

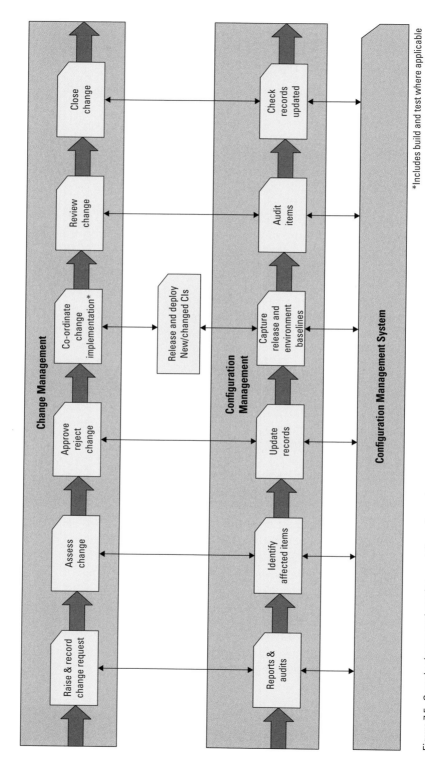

Figure 7.5   Sample change and service asset & configuration management workflow
Source: The Cabinet Office

Configuration item
A configuration item (CI) is a service asset that needs to be managed in order to deliver an IT service. Every CI is under the control of the change management process. Note that a change considered as a "pre-approved standard change" is part of the change management process even if it does not have to be submitted to the CAB.

Configuration record
A configuration record is stored in a CMDB and managed with a CMS. The CI record contains a set of attributes and relationships about a CI – either parent-child or peer-to-peer. It is important to note that a CI is not stored in a CMDB; the configuration records in the CMDB describe the CI.

The configuration management database (CMDB)
The CMDB is a set of tools and databases that are used to manage data and information about configuration items. The CMDB is a federated and logical model where multiple individual databases are linked together.

The configuration management system (CMS)
The CMS is a set of the tools, files, and databases that are used to manage the data, information, and knowledge used by the service provider to run itself and support the business. The SACM process is responsible for managing the CMS. the SACM process owns some items in the CMS but others – items such as incident, problem, known error, change, release databases, the management information systems of the service design processes (to name but a few) – will be owned and managed by respective processes.

The service knowledge management system (SKMS)
The service knowledge management system (SKMS) is a set of the tools, files, and databases delivered and supported by the service provider to manage the data, information, and knowledge used by the business to accomplish their outcomes. The SACM process is *not* responsible for managing the SKMS. As with the CMS, various items will be owned and managed by various processes. The knowledge management process is responsible for managing the SKMS.

The CMS and the SKMS generally consists of four logical layers:

Table 7.4 Logical layers of CMS and SKMS

Presentation layer (top layer)	To provide different "views" of the three previous layers to the service provider and to the business
Knowledge layer	To process the information into meaningful reports and queries for analysis purposes
Information layer	To collate, structure, and integrate the data into meaningful information
Data layer (bottom layer)	To collect the data and information from different sources in different file formats

The configuration model

Service asset and configuration management delivers a model of the services, assets, service-assets, customer-assets, and the infrastructure by recording the relationships between configuration items. Configuration models are used to:

- Assess the impact and cause of incidents and problems
- Assess the impact of proposed changes
- Plan and design new or changed services
- Plan technology refresh and software upgrades
- Plan releases
- Optimise asset utilisation and costs

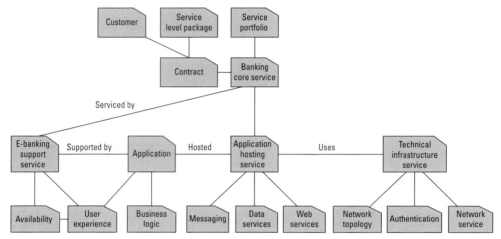

Figure 7.6 Sample logical configuration model

Source: The Cabinet Office

CI types

There are many types of CI, such as:

- Service lifecycle CI
- Service CI
- Organisational CI
- Internal CI
- External CI
- Interface CI

Where possible, automated tools (such as discovery, inventory and audit tools) are used to populate and maintain the CMDB, CMS and SKMS. This minimises the opportunity for error and saves costs.

Libraries and stores

ITIL defines various libraries to support the CMDB, the CMS, and the SKMS. The libraries will of course be referenced in the CMDB in the form of CI records. They are also considered part of the CMS or the SKMS.

Table 7.5 Libraries and stores

Definition	Example	
A **secure media library** is a collection of software, electronic or document CI of a known type and status.	Definitive Media Library (DML)	This is a secure store where the definitive, authorised (approved) versions of all media CI are stored and protected.
A **secure hardware store** is a secure location (storage space) where IT assets are stored.	Definitive spares	These are areas set aside for secure storage of definitive hardware spares.

Configuration baseline

A *configuration baseline* is a configuration of a service, or part of a service, that has been formally reviewed, agreed, and signed off. It serves as the basis for further activities, which can only be changed through formal change procedures. Configuration baselines are included in the CMS. A baseline is also used to:

- Mark a milestone in the lifecycle of a service
- Build a service component from a defined set of inputs
- Change or rebuild a specific version at a later stage
- Assemble all relevant components in readiness for a change or release
- Fall-back to a previous known state in the case of issues during or after a change

Snapshot

A *snapshot* (moment in time) is the most recent status of a CI or environment. A snapshot is stored in the CMS and is kept as a read-only historical record. A snapshot can be used to assist:

- Problem management in analysing the situation at the time incidents occurred
- Security management in facilitating system restore for security scanning software

Activities, methods, and techniques

The basic SACM process activities consist of:

- Management and planning
- Configuration identification
- Configuration control
- Status accounting and reporting
- Verification and audit

1. Management and planning

The management team and configuration management decide what level of configuration management is needed and how this level will be achieved. This is documented in a **configuration management plan**. Contents of a configuration management plan include:

- Context and objective
- Scope
- Requirements
- Applicable policies and standards

- Organisation for configuration management including roles and responsibilities
- SACM systems and tools
- Selection and application of processes and procedures to implement SACM activities including configuration identification, version management, build management, etc.
- Reference implementation plan
- Relationship management and interface controls e.g. with financial asset management, with projects, with development and customers, etc.
- Relationship management and control of service providers and sub-contractors

2. Configuration identification
Configuration identification focuses on determining and maintaining the naming and version numbering of assets and CI, the mutual relations and the relevant attributes. The most important activities of configuration identification are:
- Defining and documenting criteria for the selection of CI and the components within them
- Selecting the CI on the basis of the defined criteria
- Giving all CI unique numbers for identification purposes
- Specifying the attributes of each CI
- Indicating when each CI will be placed under configuration management
- Identifying the "owner" of each CI

Create a **configuration structure** for each IT service. This structure shows the relations and hierarchy between CI for a certain service. The configuration structure has a top-down approach. The highest level is the service in question. The lowest CI level is determined by:
- The available information
- The necessary level of control
- The necessary resources required to maintain that CI level

It is only useful to include a certain CI if it supports the other service management processes.

Document **naming conventions** and apply them in the identification of CI, documents and changes, but also, for instance, in basic configurations, releases, and compilations.

Each CI must be uniquely identifiable by means of a version number, as there may be several versions of the same CI; for example different versions of software. During the planning of the naming conventions, allow for future growth. The names must also be short but meaningful, and correspond with the existing conventions as much as possible.

Provide all physical CI, such as hardware, with **labels**, so that they are easy to identify. The labels must be easy to read and accessible, so that a user can pass the information on the label on to the service desk. Labels with a barcode are very efficient for physical audits of the CI. During such audits it is checked whether the CI in the organisation correspond with those within the CMS.

With the aid of **attributes** information is stored that is relevant for the CI in question. Note that different CI types require different attributes. This is one of the reasons why there are many CMDBs. A common attribute must be identified and used to link the various CI types found in various CMDBs. A relationship attribute is one such way to accomplish this. The following is a list of *potential* attributes.

Table 7.6 Potential CI attributes

CI unique identifier (number/label or barcode)	Related software
CI type	Historical data (verification or audit trail)
Name	Relationship type
Description	Applicable agreements (SLA, OLA, UC)
Version	Purchase date
Location	Acceptance date
Licence details (type, expiry date)	Current status
Owner	Planned status
Status	Purchase value
Supplier/source	Residual value after depreciation
Related documents	Comments

The characteristics of a CI or CI type are often recorded in **configuration documentation**.

Table 7.7 is a *sample* RACI table (*Responsible, Accountable, Consulted, and Informed*) that shows different documentation types of service CI and indicates who takes responsibility for the documents in the different phases of the Service Lifecycle.

Relationships describe how CI work together to provide a service. The CMDB maintains these relations to demonstrate the interdependencies between CI, for instance:

- A CI **is part of** another CI – a software module is part of an application (parent-child relation)
- A CI **is connected to** – a workstation is connected to the LAN
- A CI **uses** another CI – a business application uses a database
- A CI **is installed on** another CI – word processor is installed on a PC

Relationships are also the mechanism for associating RFC, incidents, problems, known errors, and releases to CI. Relations can be 1-to-1, 1-to-many and many-to-1. Configuration items are classed by means of a **classification**, for instance: service, hardware, software documentation, personnel.

Table 7.7 RACI table for configuration documentation in the lifecycle

Service Lifecycle State	Examples of Service Lifecycle Assets and CI impacted	Service Strategy	Service Design	Service Transition	Service Operations	CSI
Service Strategy	Portfolios – service contract, customer Service Strategy requirements Service Lifecycle Model	A	C	C	R	C
Service Design	Service Package (including SLA) Service Design Package e.g. Service Model, Contract, Supplier's service management plan, Process interface definition, Customer Engagement plan Release Policy Release Package definition	I	A	C	R	C
Service Transition	Service Transition model Test plan Controlled environments Build/Installation plan Build specification Release plan Deployment plan CMS SKMS Release Package Release baseline Release documentation Test report	I	C	A	R	C
Service Operations	Service Operations model Service Support model Service Desk User assets User documentation Operations documentation Support documentation	I	C	C	A/R	R
Continual Service Improvement	CSI model Service improvement plan Service reporting process	A/C	A/C	A/C	R	A

3. Configuration control

Configuration control ensures that the CI is adequately managed. No CI can be added, modified, replaced, or removed without following the agreed procedure. Establish guidelines and procedures for, among others:

- License management
- Change management
- Version management

- Access control
- Build control
- Promotion
- Deployment
- Installation
- Baseline configurations integrity management

4. Status accounting and reporting

The lifecycle of a component is classified into different stages and the stages that different types of CI go through must be properly documented. For instance, a release goes through the following stages: registered, accepted, installed, and withdrawn.

Status reports give an insight into the current and historical data of each CI and the status changes that have occurred.

Different types of **service asset and configuration reports** are needed for configuration management. The reports may relate to individuals CI, but also to a complete service. Such reports may consist of:

- A list of CI and their baseline
- Details on the current status and change history
- A list of unauthorised CI detected
- Reports on the unauthorised use of hardware and software

5. Verification and audit

SACM conducts verifications and audits to ensure that:

- There are no discrepancies between the documented baselines and the actual business environment to which they refer
- CI physically exist in the organisation or DML and spares stores, the functional and operational characteristics of CI can be verified and checks can be made that records in the CMDB match the physical infrastructure
- Release and configuration documentation is present before the release is rolled out

Table 7.8 Verification and audit

Verification	Regular (on-going) activity responsible for ensuring that information in the CMDB is accurate and that all configuration items have been identified and recorded in the CMDB
Audit	Periodical formal inspection to check whether a standard or set of guidelines is being followed, that records are accurate, or that efficiency and effectiveness targets are being met. An audit may be carried out by internal or external groups

Document all exceptions resulting from the verifications and audits and report them. Corrective actions (CI that need to be added, changed, or deleted) are handled via the change management process.

Verification or audits are conducted at the following times:
- Shortly after changes to the CMS
- Before and after changes to IT services or infrastructure
- At random and planned intervals
- Before a release to ensure the environment is as expected
- In response to the detection of unauthorised CI
- Following recovery from disasters

Audit tools can perform checks at regular intervals, for instance weekly. For example a desktop audit tool compares the configuration of an individual's desktop against the "master" configuration that was installed.

Information management
- Backup copies of the CMS should be taken regularly and stored securely. It is advisable for one copy to be kept at a remote location for use in the event of a disaster
- The CMS contains information on backup copies of CI. It will also contain historical records of CI and CI versions that are archived, and possibly also of deleted CI or CI versions
- Typically, the CMS should contain records only for items that are physically available or could be easily created using procedures known to, and under the control of, service asset and configuration management
- The CMS includes pointers to knowledge and information assets that are stored in the SKMS, and it is important to maintain these links and to verify their validity as part of regular audits
- SACM is responsible for the maintenance of many knowledge and information assets within the SKMS, and these must be maintained with the same level of control as the CMS

Interfaces
By being the single process for managing configuration data and information for IT service management, SACM supports and interfaces with every other service management process and activity to some degree. However, some of the most visible relationships include but are not limited to:
- **Change management** – Identifying the impact of proposed changes
- **Financial management for IT services** – To capture key financial information such as cost, depreciation methods, owner and user, maintenance and repair costs
- **ITSCM** – For increased awareness of the assets on which the business services depend, control of key spares and software
- **Incident and problem management** – To provide and maintain key diagnostic information
- **Availability management** – To assist in the detection of points of failure
- **Change and release and deployment management** – To benefit from a single coordinated planning approach
- **Configuration control is synonymous with change control** – Understanding and capturing updates to the infrastructure and services

- SACM also has close relationships with some business processes, especially fixed asset management and procurement

Triggers

Here are some of the triggers that may start the whole, or part of the, service asset and configuration management process.

- Updates from change management
- Updates from release and deployment management
- Purchase orders
- Acquisitions
- Service requests

Inputs

Here are some of the inputs required by the service asset and configuration management process.

- Designs, plans and configurations from service design packages
- Requests for change and work orders from change management
- Actual configuration information collected by tools and audits
- Information in the organisation's fixed asset register

Outputs

Here are some of the outputs produced by the service asset and configuration management process.

- New and updated configuration records
- Updated asset information for use in updating the fixed asset register
- Information about attributes and relationships of configuration items
- Configuration snapshots and baselines
- Status reports and other consolidated configuration information
- Audit reports

Critical success factors

The critical success factors, which change over time, for the service asset and configuration management process may include but are not limited to the following.

- Accounting for, managing and protecting the integrity of CI throughout the service lifecycle
- Supporting efficient and effective service management processes by providing accurate configuration information at the right time
- Establishing and maintaining an accurate and complete configuration management system (CMS)

Metrics

The performance of the service asset and configuration management process can be measured according to:

- Improved accuracy regarding the assets utilised by each customer or business unit
- Increase in re-use and redistribution of under-utilised resources and assets
- Reduction in the use of unauthorised service- and customer-assets

- Reduced number of exceptions reported during configuration audits
- Reduction in time and cost of diagnosing and resolving incidents and problems
- Improved ratio of used licences against paid-for licences
- Reduction in risks due to early identification of unauthorised change
- Improved audit compliance
- Shorter audits as quality configuration information is easily accessible

Challenges
Here are some of the potential challenges faced by the service asset and configuration management process
- Persuading technical support personnel to adopt a checking in/out policy
- Attracting and justifying funding for SACM
- An attitude of "just collecting data because it is possible to do"
- Lack of commitment and support from management

Risks
Here are some of the potential risks faced by the service asset and configuration management process
- The temptation to focus on technology rather than service and business needs
- Degradation of the accuracy of configuration information over time
- Setting the scope too wide
- Setting the scope too narrow
- The CMS becomes out of date due to the movement of hardware assets by non-authorised personnel

7.8   Release and Deployment Management

Introduction
ITIL defines release and deployment management as follows:

> *"Release and deployment management aims to build, test, and deliver the capability to provide the services specified by service design and that will accomplish the stakeholders' requirements and deliver the intended objectives."*

The purpose of release and deployment management is the deployment of releases into production, and the establishment of effective use of the service in order to deliver value to the customer and to be able to hand over to service operations.

The **objective** of release and deployment management is to ensure that:
- Release and deployment plans are in place
- Release packages (compilation) are deployed successfully
- Knowledge transfer to the customers takes place
- There is minimum disruption to the services

Scope

The processes, systems, and functions for packaging, building, testing, and deployment of a release into production and establishment of the service specified in the service design package before final handover to service operations.

Value for the business

Effective release and deployment management contributes to the business because:
- Changes are realised faster, cheaper and with fewer risks, and the operational objectives are supported better
- The implementation approach is more consistent and the traceability requirements (e.g. audits, legislation etc.) are complied with more closely

Basic concepts

> A **release** is a set of new or changed configuration items that are tested and will be implemented into production together.
>
> A **release unit** is the portion of the service or infrastructure that is included in the release, in accordance with the organisation's release policy and guidelines. Releases are documented in the CMS for the support of the release and deployment process.

It is important to determine the correct level of the release. For a business critical application it may make sense to include the complete application in the release unit, but for a website it may only have to be the HTML page that is changed.

Releases can be classified into the following **release categories**:
- **Major releases** – Important deployment of new hardware and software with, in most cases, a considerable expansion of the functionality (V1.0, 2.0, etc.)
- **Minor releases** – These usually contain a number of smaller improvements; some of these improvements were previously implemented as quick fixes but are now included integrally within a release (V1.1, V1.2, etc.)
- **Emergency releases** – Usually implemented as a temporary solution for a problem or known error (V1.1.1, V1.1.2, etc.)

In the **release design** different considerations apply in respect of the way in which the release is deployed. The most frequently occurring options for the rollout of releases are:
- **Big bang versus phased** – A big bang release deploys the new or changed service for all the users at the same time. A phased deployment deploys the release for part of the user base at a time.
- **Push and pull** – With a push approach the service component is deployment from the "centre" to the target locations. With a pull approach the new release is made available to the users from a central location from which they download to their location at a time they choose.
- **Automated or manual** – Releases can, to a large extent, be automated; e.g. the use of installation software.

The release and deployment teams must have a good understanding of the relevant IT architecture involved in a release and deployment process. This understanding is essential to determine the sequence in which the activities are implemented and for mapping out all the interdependencies.

A **release package** is a single release unit or a structured set of release units. In the case of a new or a changed service all the elements of which the service consists – the infrastructure, hardware, software, applications, documentation, knowledge, etc. – must be taken into account.

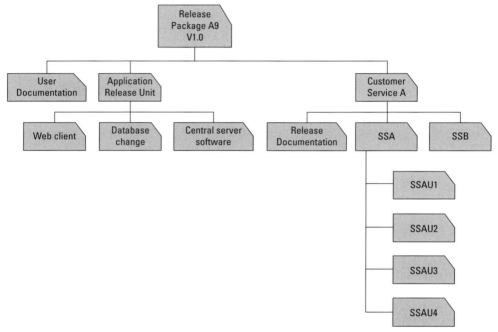

Figure 7.7 Sample of a release package

Source: The Cabinet Office

Release and deployment models

Release and deployment models define:

- Release structure
- The exit and entry criteria
- Controlled environments for builds and tests
- The roles and responsibilities for each CI
- The release promotion and configuration baseline model
- Template release and deployment schedules
- Supporting systems, tools and procedures for documenting activities

Activities, methods, and techniques

There are four phases to release and deployment management:

Table 7.9 The four phases to release and deployment management

Release and deployment planning	Plans for creating and deploying the release are created
Release build and test	The release package is built, tested and checked into the DML
Deployment	The release package in the DML is deployed to the live environment
Review and close	Experience and feedback are captured, performance targets and achievements are reviewed and lessons are learned

1. Release and deployment planning

Prior to a deployment into production different plans are formulated. The type and number depends on the size and complexity of the environment and the changed or new service. Release and deployment plans form part of the overall Service Transition plan. Change management will approve or reject the plans.

The plans will include the following:
- Scope and content of the release
- Risk assessment and risk profile for the release
- Organisations and stakeholders affected by the release
- Stakeholders that may authorise the change request for each stage of the release
- Team responsible for the release
- Deployment schedule for the release
  - Approach to working with stakeholders and deployment groups to determine:
    - Delivery and deployment strategy
    - Resources for the release build, test and deployment, and for early life support
    - Amount of change that can be absorbed.

The following (sub) plans are relevant for release and deployment:
- **Pass/fail criteria** – Service Transition is responsible for planning the pass/fail situations for every phase of the release and deployment.
- **Building and test plans** – Building and test plans are needed that describe the approach to the building, testing, and maintenance of the pre-production environment; different environments are needed for each test type: for unit testing, service release testing and integration testing.
  - Developing build plans from the SDP, design specifications and environment configuration requirements
  - Establishing the logistics, lead times and build times to set up the environments
  - Defining a configuration baseline for the build environment, to ensure that each build is carried out in a known environment
  - Testing the build and related procedures
  - Scheduling the build and test activities

    ○ Assigning resources, roles and responsibilities to perform key activities
    ○ Defining and agreeing the build exit and entry criteria

Controlled environments
Various controlled environments will need to be built or made available for the different types and levels of testing as well as to support other transition activities such as training

Planning release packaging and build
Planning the release packaging and build activities includes developing mechanisms, plans, or procedures

Preparations for release build and test
Before authorising the release build and test stage, the service design, and the release design must be validated against the requirement for the new or changed service offering. Record, track and measure any risks and issues against the services, service assets and CIs within the service package, SDP or release package.

Deployment planning
There are many planning considerations. Planners should be able to answer the following questions.
- What needs to be deployed?
- Who are the users?
- Are there location dependencies?
- Where are the users?
- Who else needs to be prepared well in advance?
- When does the deployment need to be completed?
- Why is the deployment happening?
- What are the critical success factors and exit criteria?
- What is the current capability of the service provider?

Logistics and delivery planning
Once the overall deployment approach is understood, develop the logistics and delivery plans.

Planning of pilots
A pilot can be used to establish the viability of most, if not all, aspects of the service.

Financial/commercial planning
Specifically checked before the deployment, and activities should be added to the deployment plans where necessary.

2. Release build and test
During the release build and test stage, the common services, and infrastructure need to be managed carefully, since they can significantly affect the build and test of a technology-enabled service and its underlying technology infrastructure.

Release and build documentation
Procedures, templates, and guidance should be used to enable the release team to take service assets and products from internal and external suppliers and build an integrated release package efficiently and effectively.

Acquire and test input configuration items and components
Configuration items and components are acquired from projects, suppliers, partners, and development groups. Historical information should be consulted when repetitive releases of same or similar CI are performed. There should be documented procedures and templates (models) for purchasing, distributing, installing, moving, and controlling assets and components.

Release packaging
Build management procedures, methodologies, tools and checklists should be applied to ensure that the release package is built in a standard, controlled, and reproducible way in line with the solution design defined in the service design package.

Build and manage the test environments
Effective build and test environment management is essential to ensure that the builds and tests are executed in a repeatable and manageable manner. Preparation of the test environments includes building, changing, or enhancing the test environments ready to receive the release.

Service testing and pilots
The testing activities are coordinated through test management. Testing aims to build confidence in the service capability prior to final acceptance during pilot or early life support. It will be based on the test strategy and model for the service being changed.

Service rehearsals
A service rehearsal (sometimes referred to as "model office" or a "table top") is a simulation of as much of the service as possible in an extensive and widely participatory practice session. A service rehearsal takes place just before deployment of the service but not too early or too close to the live date.

Pilots
A pilot sets out to detect if any elements of the service do not deliver as required and to identify gaps/issues in service management that put the service and/or the customer's business and assets at risk. As far as possible it should check that the utilities are fit for purpose and the warranties are fit for use.

3. Deployment

Plan and prepare for deployment
The planning and preparation activities prepare the group for deployment. This is an opportunity to prepare the organisation and people for organisational change.

During the actual deployment stage the detailed implementation plan is developed. This includes assigning individuals to specific activities.

Assess readiness of target group
The assessment of the deployment should be conducted early and periodically. The results of this assessment are provided as part of the detailed implementation plans for the target deployment group.

Develop plans
This activity includes assigning specific resources to perform deployment and early life support activities. Identify and assess risks specific to this deployment group by using the service model to identify business and service-critical assets that have the highest risk of causing disruption.

Perform transfer, deployment, and retirement
The following activities provide an example of the different aspects that will be performed in the order specified on the deployment plan.

Change/transfer financial assets
Changes and transfers of financial assets need to be completed as part of deployment.

Transfer/transition business and organisation
The transfer of a business unit, service or service unit will involve changing the organisation. When the change includes a transfer of service provider such as outsourcing, insourcing, or changing outsourcing providers, consider the following organisational elements: organisational change, quick wins, and communication.

Deploy processes and materials
Deploy or publish the processes and materials ready for people involved in the business and service organisation change. The materials may include policies, processes, procedures, manuals, overviews, training products, organisational change products, etc. Training people to use new processes and procedures can take time.

Deploy service management capability
This activity involves the deployment of the new or changed processes, systems, and tools to the service provider teams responsible for service management activities. Ensure personnel involved are competent and confident in operating, maintaining, and managing the service in accordance with the service model.

Transfer service
Transferring a service will also involve organisational change described earlier in this section.

Deploy service
This activity performs the deployment of the service release and carries out the activities to distribute and install the service, supporting services, applications, data, information, infrastructure, and facilities.

Decommissioning and service retirement
Some specific aspects need to be considered for decommissioning and retiring services and service assets. Procedures for retiring, transferring, or redeploying service assets should consider security, licensing, environmental, or other contractual requirements.

Remove redundant assets
Identify and remove redundant assets, thereby potentially saving licence fees, liberating capacity, and preventing accidental use.

Verify deployment
It is important to verify that users, service operation functions, other personnel, and stakeholders are capable of using or operating the service.

Remediate/back out release
The most common form of remediation is to back out the release, restoring all hardware, software, and data to the previous baseline. Alternative forms of remediation include implementing normal changes or emergency changes to resolve problems, or invoking IT service continuity plans to provide the service.

Early life support
Early life support (ELS) provides the opportunity to transition the new or changed service to service operation in a controlled manner and establish the new service capability and resources. Formal handover of the new or changed service to the service operation functions happens in two stages. At the beginning of early life support there should be a formal notification that the service is now in live use. At the end of early life support there should be a formal notification that all SLAs are now being enforced and the service is fully operational.

4. Review and close
In the review of a deployment, check whether:
- The knowledge transfer and training were adequate
- All user experiences have been documented
- All fixes and changes are complete and all problems, known errors and workarounds have been documented
- The quality criteria have been complied with
- The service is ready for transition from ELS into production

Also check whether there are issues that have to be passed on to CSI. The deployment is completed when the support is transferred to Operations. Finally, change management will conduct a Post Implementation Review (PIR).

To finalise the Service Transition as a whole a formal change evaluation must be performed that is tailored to with the scale and scope of the change.

Information management

Throughout the release and deployment management process, appropriate records will be created and maintained. As configuration items are successfully deployed, the CMS will be updated with information such as:
- New, changed, or removed configuration items
- Relationships between requirements and test cases
- New, changed, or removed locations and users
- Status updates
- Change in ownership of assets
- Licence holding

Other data and information will also be captured and recorded within the broader service knowledge management system. This could include:
- Release packages in the DML
- Installation/build plans
- Logistics and delivery plans
- Validation and test plans, evidence and reports
- Deployment information, deployment history, who was involved, timings, etc.
- Training records
- Access rules and levels
- Known errors

As part of the deployment clean-up activities it is important to delete or archive redundant records related to the previous service or products.

Interfaces

Like all processes, the release and deployment management process has relationships with all other processes. However, some of the most visible relationships include but are not limited to the following.

Design coordination
- The design coordination process creates the service design package that defines the new service, including all aspects of how it should be created
- Plans and packages should be developed and documented during the service design stage, and design coordination will ensure that these are documented in the SDP

Transition planning and support
- Provides the framework for release and deployment management to operate in, and transition plans provide the context for release and deployment plans

Change management
- Provides the authorisation for the work
- Release and deployment management provides the execution of many changes

- Release and deployment plans are a significant part of the change schedule
- Deployment review is often combined with the review and closure of the change

Service asset and configuration management
- Release and deployment management depends on data and information in the CMS, and provides many updates to the CMS. It is important that these updates are coordinated and managed properly as otherwise the data will not be kept up to date.

Service validation and testing
- To ensure that testing is carried out when necessary
- To ensure that builds are available when required by service validation and testing

Triggers
Here are some of the triggers that may start the whole, or part of the, release and deployment management process.
- Starts with receipt of an authorised change to plan, build, and test a production-ready release package. Deployment starts with receipt of an authorised change to deploy a release package to a target deployment group or environment

Inputs
Here are some of the inputs required by the release and deployment management process.
- Authorised change
- Service design package
- IT service continuity plan and related business continuity plan
- Service management and operations plans and standards
- Technology and procurement standards and catalogues
- Acquired service assets and components and their documentation
- Build models and plans
- Environment requirements and specifications for build, test, release, training, disaster recovery, pilot and deployment
- Release policy and release design from service design
- Release and deployment models including template plans
- Exit and entry criteria for each stage of release and deployment management

Outputs
Here are some of the outputs produced by the release and deployment management process.
- New, changed or retired services
- Release and deployment plan
- Updates to change management for the release and deployment activities
- Service notification
- Notification to service catalogue management to update the service catalogue with the relevant information about the new or changed service
- New tested service capability and environments

- New or changed service management documentation
- SLA, underpinning OLA, and contracts
- New or changed service reports
- Tested continuity plans
- Complete and accurate configuration item list with an audit trail for the CI in the release package and also the new or changed service and infrastructure configurations
- Updated service capacity plan aligned to the relevant business plans
- Base-lined release package – checked in to DML and ready for future deployments
- Service transition report

Critical success factors

The critical success factors, which change over time, for the release and deployment management process may include but are not limited to the following.
- Defining and agreeing release plans with customers and stakeholders
- Ensuring integrity of a release package and its constituent components throughout the transition activities
- Ensuring that the new or changed service is capable of delivering the agreed utility and warranty
- Ensuring that there is appropriate knowledge transfer

Metrics

The performance of the release and deployment management process can be measured according to:
- Increased…
  - Number and percentage of releases that make use of a common framework of standards, re-usable processes and supporting documentation
  - Number and percentage of releases that meet customer expectations for cost, time and quality
  - Score in surveys of customer, user, and service operation function satisfaction with release and deployment management
  - Customer and user satisfaction with the services delivered
- Reduced…
  - Number of CMS and DML audit failures related to releases
  - Number of deployments from sources other than the DML
  - Number of incidents due to incorrect components being deployed
  - Variance from service performance required by customers
  - Number of incidents against the service
  - Customer dissatisfaction
  - Resources and costs to diagnose and fix incidents and problems in deployment and live use
  - Number of incidents categorised as "user knowledge"

Challenges

Here are some of the potential challenges faced by the release and deployment management process

- Developing standard performance measures and measurement methods across projects and suppliers
- Dealing with projects and suppliers where estimated delivery dates are inaccurate and there are delays in scheduling service transition activities
- Understanding the different stakeholder perspectives that underpin effective risk management for the change impact assessment and test activities
- Building a thorough understanding of risks that have impacted or may impact successful service transition of services and releases
- Encouraging a risk management culture where people share information and take a pragmatic and measured approach to risk

Risks

Here are some of the potential risks faced by the release and deployment management process.

- Poorly defined scope and understanding of dependencies in earlier lifecycle stages
- Using personnel who are not dedicated to release and deployment management activities
- Failing to use the release and deployment management process to manage service retirement
- Lack of…
  - Integration with the appropriate financial cycles and activities
  - Integration with the appropriate corporate governance, regulatory controls, and requirements regarding licensing and security
  - Operational support
  - Consideration for all capabilities and resources
  - Consideration for people, process, products and partner aspects
- Not managing or addressing organisational and stakeholder change:
- Poor commitment and decision-making
- Failure to obtain appropriate authorisation at the right time
- Indecision or late decision-making
- Inadequate or inaccurate information
- Health and safety compromised
- Time allowed for release and deployment management
- Not managing suppliers/sourcing/partnering relationships during transition:
- Inadequate "back-out" or "contingency" plan if sourcing/partnering fails

7.9   Service Validation and Testing

Introduction

Testing of services is an important contribution to the quality of IT service provision. Testing ensures that new (or changed) services are **fit for** purpose and **fit for use**.

Fit for purpose means that the service does what the customer expects of it, so that the service supports the business. "Fit for use" addresses such aspects as availability, continuity, capacity and security of the service.

Insufficient attention to testing may result in: increase of incidents, issues, and errors, extra service desk phone calls with questions regarding the functioning of the service, higher costs, and a service that is improperly used.

The purpose of service validation and testing is to provide a service that adds value to the customers and their business.

The **objective** of service validation and testing is to make sure that:
- The release delivers the expected outcomes and value for the customers within projected costs, capacity and constraints
- Services are fit for purpose and fit for use
- Specifications (requirements) by customer and other stakeholders are met

Scope
Service validation and testing is applied during the entire Service Lifecycle, and is aimed at testing the quality of service (units), and intended to verify whether the service provider has sufficient capacity and resources in order to provide a service or service release successfully.

Testing is also particularly supportive of the release and deployment processes. In addition, the change evaluation process will be using test results.

Value for the business
Service interruptions may be damaging to business operations of the service provider and customers who are recipients of the services. They may result in damage to reputation, financial loss and even (fatal) accidents. For example, the role of IT in hospitals, the automotive or aerospace industries can mean injury or death if service delivery fails.

Basic concepts

The **service model** describes the structure and dynamics of a service provided by Service Operation. The structure consists of core and supporting services and service assets needed. When a new (or changed) service is designed, developed, and built, these service assets are tested in relation to design specifications and requirements. Activities, flow of resources, coordination, and interactions describe the dynamics.

Policies for service validation and testing are:
- Service quality policies
- Risk policies
- Reusability policies
- Service transition policies

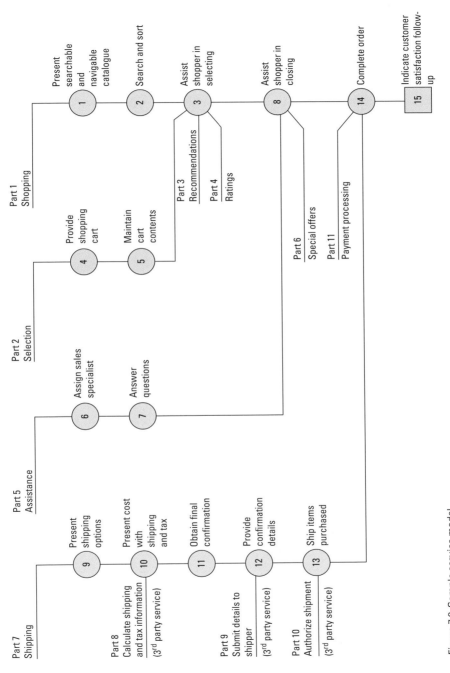

Figure 7.8 Sample service model
Source: The Cabinet Office

- Release policies
- Mandatory integral testing
- Involving all stakeholders in testing
- Change management policies

The **test strategy** defines the overall testing approach and the allocation of required resources. This strategy might be applicable to the entire organisation, a collection of services or an individual service. All test strategies are developed in collaboration with the stakeholders. Attention is paid to objectives, scope, standards, test processes, test metrics, test approach, requirements and "deliverables".

A **test model** consists of a test plan, what is to be tested and test scripts which indicate the method by which each element must be tested. In order to ensure that the process can be repeated, test models must be structured in such a way that:
- The specification or design criteria being tested can be traced
- Test activities, evaluation and reports can be audited
- Test elements can be maintained and changed

Whether or not testing is effective will be determined, in part, by the degree to which the service meets requirements. These requirements, in turn, are based on the perspectives of those who use, provide, deploy, or manage the service. The Service Design package therefore defines entry and exit criteria for all **test perspectives**.

There are very many different **test techniques** and **test approaches**. The technique and approach depends on the service type, risk profile, test goal and test level. Examples include: document review, modelling, simulation, scenario testing, role play and laboratory testing, live pilot.

Design considerations that are important for testing relate to finances (is the budget big enough?), documentation (is everything available, and in the correct format?), composition (build), testability (think of resources, time and facilities), traceability (traceable to specifications), when and where testing is to take place, and remediation (is there a backup plan?).

Also remember to take management and maintenance of test data into account in the design. This concerns the separation of test and live data, regulations with respect to data security, backing up of test data, and so on.

In addition to all kinds of functional and non-functional **test types**, role playing is also possible based on perspective (target group):
- **Service requirements testing** "fit for purpose" (service provider, users and customer) – does the service meet the specifications determined?
- **Service level testing** (service level managers, operation managers and customer) – this concerns testing whether the new service meets the service levels determined
- **Service assurance testing** "fit for use" (customer) – to verify availability, capacity, continuity and security

- **Usability testing** (end users and maintainers) – to verify user-friendliness and usability for groups such as visually impaired users
- **Contract and regulation testing** (service providers) – this could be for service providers who must (contractually) comply with ISO/IEC 20000 and industries that must comply with very specific regulations such as the (UK) Ministry of Defence and the pharmaceutical industry
- **Service management testing** (service provider) – ISO/IEC 20000 could be used for this; ISO/IEC 20000 indicates the minimum requirements that processes must meet
- **Operational testing** (system, services) – these could be stress tests, security and recoverability
- **Regression testing** – being able to repeat earlier (successful) tests in order to compare new results with the previous ones

Activities, methods, and techniques

The activities below are not necessarily performed in this order; they might also take place parallel to each other. The following activities can be distinguished:

- Validation and test management
- Planning and design
- Verification test plan and design
- Prepare test environment
- Testing
- Evaluate exit criteria and report
- Clean up and closure

The following figure schematically displays the testing process.

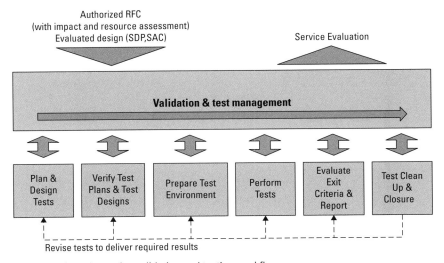

Figure 7.9 Sample service validation and testing workflow

Source: The Cabinet Office

1. Validation and test management

Test management consists of planning and managing (control), and reporting on the activities taking place during all test phases of the Service Transition. This includes the following activities:
- Planning of resources, and what is being tested at what time
- Managing incidents, problems, errors, deviations, issues, risks (including during the discovery in the transition phase)
- Collecting test metrics; analyse, report and manage

2. Planning and design

Test planning and design activities take place early in the Service Lifecycle and relate to the following:
- Resources such as hardware, network, number of personnel members, capacity, ability and finances
- Business/customer resources required
- Supporting services
- Schedule of milestones and delivery and acceptance

3. Verification of Test Plan and Design

Test plans and designs are verified to make sure that everything (including scripts) is complete, and that test models sufficiently take into account the risk profile of the service in question and all possible interfaces.

4. Preparation test environment

Prepare the test environment and make a baseline configuration of the test environment.

5. Testing

The tests are executed using manual or automated testing techniques and procedures. Testers register all results. If a test fails, the reason is documented. Proceed with the test as closely as possible according to test plans and scripts. Document the cause of the failure.

6. Evaluate exit criteria and report

The actual results are compared with projected results (exit criteria). Test results can be interpreted in terms of "pass/fail" (approval or not), any risks the tested object may contain for service provider or customer, or in terms of costs required to reach the projected goal.

Collect the test results and recapitulate for the report. Examples of exit criteria are:
- The tested service complies with quality requirements
- The service and supporting it infrastructure will enable the end user to perform all functions as defined
- Configuration baselines are captured into the CMS

7. Clean up and closure
Make sure that the test environment is cleaned up. Review the test approach and identify improvements.

Information management
Testing benefits greatly by reuse, and for this reason it is advisable to create a library of relevant tests and ensure that it is up-to-date. Also record the way in which these tests should be executed and implemented.

No matter how well a test is designed, without good **test data**, the test is useless. Therefore, take the upkeep of test data seriously. For this purpose, it is important that:
- Test data is separated from live data
- Data protection regulations are taken into account
- Backup and recovery procedures are in place

Interfaces
Testing is **triggered** by the planned test activity in a release plan, test plan, or plan for quality assurance.

Inputs to the test and validation processes are:
- The service package and Service Level Package (SLP)
- Interface definitions by the service provider
- Service Design package
- Release and deployment plans
- Acceptance criteria and RFC

Outputs of the test and validation process are:
- Configuration baselines of the test environment
- Testing carried out
- Results from the tests
- Analysis of results
- Test incidents, problems, and error records
- Improvement ideas (for CSI)
- Updated data
- Information and knowledge for the knowledge management system

Tests support all release and deployment steps in the Service Transition process. In addition, testing is **related** to Service Design, CSI, Service Operation, and Service Strategy.

Metrics
The effectiveness of testing from a **customer perspective** (external) can be measured by:
- Reduction in the impact of incidents and errors in production that are attributable to a newly transitioned service

- More effective use of resources and involvement from the customer (e.g. user acceptance tests)
- A better understanding by all stakeholders of the roles and responsibilities that relate to the new or changed service

Service provider related (internal)
The test process must be executed as effectively and efficiently as possible. Potential measures to achieve this are:
- Decreased effort and costs in setting up the test environment
- Decrease in effort required to discover errors and decrease in the number of "repeated errors"
- Reuse of test data
- Decrease in the percentage of incidents related to errors discovered during testing
- Number of known errors documented during prior test phases

Implementation
The greatest **challenge** still lies in the fact that testing is not taken seriously enough by many organisations. As a result, there is often a lack of funding.

Critical success factors are:
- Issues are identified in an early stage of the lifecycle
- Quality is built into every phase of the lifecycle, for example by using the 'V' model
- Reusable test models are designed, and testing provides the proof that all configurations have been built and implemented according to client requirements

Risks are:
- Unclear expectations and objectives, lack of understanding that testing is a critical process in relation to quality of service provision
- Lack of resources

Information management
Testing benefits greatly from re-use. To this end it is sensible to create and maintain a library of relevant tests and an updated and maintained data set for applying and performing tests.

Test data: However well a test has been designed, it relies on the relevance of the data used to run it. This clearly applies to software testing, but equivalent concerns relate to the environments within which hardware, documentation etc. is tested

Test environments
Test environments must be actively maintained and protected.
- Consequential updating of the test data
- A new separate set of data or a new test environment, since the original is still required for other services
- Redundancy of the test data or environment

- Acceptance that a lower level of testing is taking place since the test data/environment cannot be updated to deliver equivalent test coverage for the changed service

Maintenance
Maintenance of test data should be an active exercise and should address relevant issues including:
- Separation from any live data, and steps to ensure that it cannot be mistaken for live data when being used, and vice versa
- Data protection regulations
- Backup of test data, and restoration to a known baseline for enabling repeatable testing

Interfaces
Like all processes, the service validation and testing process has relationships with all other processes. However, some of the most visible relationships include but are not limited to:
- Testing supports all of the **release and deployment management** steps within service transition
- **Release and deployment management** is responsible for ensuring that appropriate testing takes place
- The output of service validation and testing is a key input to **change evaluation**, and must be provided at an appropriate time and in a suitable format to enable changes to be evaluated in time for change management decision-making
- The **test strategy** will ensure that the testing process works with all stages of the lifecycle
- Working with **design coordination** to ensure that designs are inherently testable and providing positive support in achieving this
- Working closely with **CSI** to feed failure information and improvement ideas resulting from testing exercises.
- **Service operation** will use maintenance tests to ensure the continued efficacy of services
- **Service strategy** should accommodate testing in terms of adequate funding, resource, profile, etc.

Triggers
Here are some of the triggers that may start the whole, or part of the, service validation and testing process.
- The trigger for testing is a scheduled activity on a release plan, test plan, or quality assurance plan.

Inputs
Here are some of the inputs required by the service validation and testing process.
- The service design package; this defines the agreed requirements of the service, expressed in terms of the service model and service operation plan. It includes:
  - The service charter

   ○ Service provider interface definitions
   ○ Operation models
   ○ Capacity/resource model and plan
   ○ Financial/economic/cost models (with TCO, TCU)
   ○ Service management model
   ○ Test conditions and expected results
   ○ Design and interface specifications
   ○ Release and deployment plans
   ○ Acceptance criteria
- RFC

Outputs

Here are some of the outputs produced by the service validation and testing process.
- The direct output from testing is the report delivered to change evaluation
- Configuration baseline of the testing environment
   ○ Testing carried out
   ○ Results from those tests
   ○ Analysis of the results
- Other outputs include:
   ○ Updated data, information and knowledge to be added to the service knowledge management system
   ○ Test incidents, problems and error records
   ○ Entries in the CSI register to address potential improvements in any area that impacts on testing
   ○ Third-party relationships, suppliers of equipment or services, partners, users and customers or other stakeholders

Critical success factors

The critical success factors, which change over time, for the service validation and testing process may include but are not limited to the following.
- Understanding the different stakeholder perspectives that underpin effective risk management for the change impact assessment and test activities
- Building a thorough understanding of risks that have impacted or may impact successful service transition of services and releases
- Encouraging a risk management culture where people share information and take a pragmatic and measured approach to risk
- Providing evidence that the service assets and configurations have been built and implemented correctly in addition to the service delivering what the customer needs
- Developing re-usable test models
- Achieving a balance between cost of testing and effectiveness of testing

Metrics

The performance of the service validation and testing process can be measured according to:
- Roles and responsibilities for...
   ○ Impact assessment and test activities have been agreed and documented

○ Customers, users and service provider personnel have been agreed and documented
- Increase in...
  ○ The percentage of impact assessments and test activities where the documented roles have been correctly involved
  ○ The number of risks identified in service design or early in service transition compared to those detected during or after testing
  ○ Ratio of errors detected in service design compared to service transition, and of errors detected in service transition compared to service operation
  ○ Percentage of service acceptance criteria that have been tested for new and changed services
- Reduction in...
  ○ The impact of incidents and errors for newly transitioned services
  ○ The variance between test budget and test expenditure
  ○ The cost of fixing errors, due to earlier detection
  ○ The business impact due to delays in testing

Challenges

Here are some of the potential challenges faced by the service validation and testing process.
- Inability to maintain a test environment and test data that matches the live environment
- Insufficient personnel, skills and testing tools to deliver adequate testing coverage
- Projects overrunning and allocated testing time frames being squeezed to restore project go-live dates but at the cost of quality
- Development of standard performance measures and measurement methods across projects and suppliers
- Projects and suppliers estimating delivery dates inaccurately and causing delays in scheduling service transition activities

Risks

Here are some of the potential risks faced by the service validation and testing process.
- Unclear expectations/objectives
- Lack of understanding of the risks, resulting in testing that is not targeted at critical elements which need to be well controlled and therefore tested
- Resource shortages which introduce delays and have an impact on other service transitions

7.10 Change Evaluation

Introduction

ITIL defines the change evaluation process as:

> *"Change evaluation is the process of providing a consistent and standardised means of determining the performance of a service change, its (potential) impacts on business outcomes, on existing and proposed services, and the IT infrastructure. The actual performance of a change is assessed against its predicted performance. Risks and issues related to the change are identified and managed."*

The **objective** of the ITIL change evaluation process is to:
- Appropriately set stakeholder expectations and provide accurate information
- Evaluate the intended and non-intended (as is reasonably practical) effects of a service change
- Provide good quality outputs

Scope

The scope covers the evaluation of new or changed services at regular intervals during the lifecycle of a change as required by the change model or business requirements.

Value for the business

Change evaluation delivers an important piece of input for CSI and the future improvement of service development and change management.

Policies, starting points and basic concepts

The following **policies** apply:
- Service designs or service changes are evaluated before being transitioned
- All deviations between predicted and actual performance are managed by the customer (agent), e.g. acceptance yes/no
- All changes will be assessed as required
- Identify risks and issues related to the service that is being changed
- The customer is involved with change evaluation

The following **starting points** are important in the execution of the process:
- The unintended effects of a change (and its consequences) must be identified
- A service change is evaluated fairly, consistently, openly and objectively

Activities, methods, and techniques

The change evaluation process consists of the following activities:

Create an evaluation plan

When planning an evaluation, the intended and unintended effects of a change are analysed. The intended effects must meet with the acceptance criteria; the unintended effects are often invisible for a long time.

Understand the intended effect of a change

Clearly define the intended effect of the change and the specific measures that should be used to determine effectiveness of that change.

Understanding the unintended effect of a change

With the assistance of stakeholders, identify and define the unintended effect of the change and the specific measures that should be used if they materialise.

Identify the factors for considering the effect of a service change

Identify which of the following factors to include when considering the effect of a service change.

Service provider capability, tolerance, organisational setting, resources, modelling and measurement, people, use, and purpose

Evaluate the predicted performance

Carry out a risk assessment utilising the customer requirements, the predicted performance, and the performance model, then produce an interim evaluation report for the change management process.

Evaluate the actual performance

Before change management makes a decision on whether to authorise each step in a change, change evaluation will evaluate the actual performance.

Perform risk management

At regular intervals during its lifecycle, a proposed service change must assess the existing risks within a service change and the predicted risks following implementation of the change.

Generate an evaluation report

The evaluation report contains the following sections:
- Risk
- Deviations
- A qualification statement (if appropriate)
- A validation statement (if appropriate)
- A recommendation

The following figure shows a sample change evaluation workflow including inputs and outputs.

Information management
- The SKMS provides most of the information required for change evaluation
- All evaluation reports should be checked into, and out of, the CMS
- Softcopy versions of the reports should be stored in the SKMS

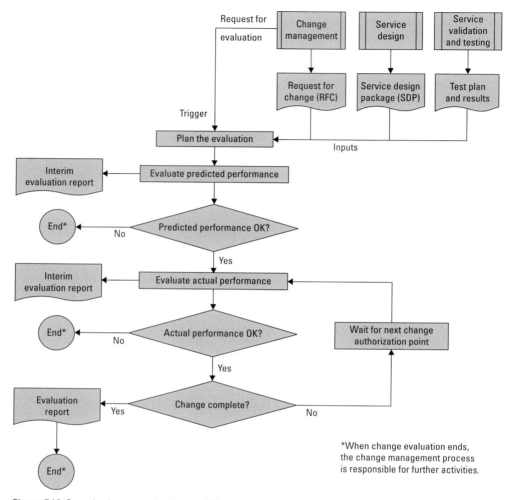

Figure 7.10 Sample change evaluation workflow

Source: The Cabinet Office

Interfaces

Like all processes, the change evaluation process has relationships with all other processes. However, some of the most visible relationships include but are not limited to:

- **Transition planning and support** – To ensure that appropriate resources are available when needed
- **Change management** – To agree on which types of change will be subject to formal evaluation
- Service design – To provide the service design package
- **Service level management** – To ensure a full understanding of the impact of any issues identified, and to obtain use of user or customer resources

- **Business relationship management** – To ensure a full understanding of the impact of any issues identified, and to obtain use of user or customer resources
- **Service validation and testing** – To coordinate activities with this process to ensure that required inputs are available in sufficient time

Triggers

Here is one of the triggers that may start the whole, or part of the, change evaluation process.

- The receipt of a request for change evaluation from change management

Inputs

Here are some of the inputs required by the change evaluation process.

- SDP, including service charter and SAC
- Change proposal
- RFC, change record and detailed change documentation
- Discussions with stakeholders
- Test results and report

Outputs

Here are some of the outputs produced by the change evaluation process.

- Interim evaluation report(s) for change management
- Evaluation report for change management

Critical success factors

The critical success factors, which change over time, for the change evaluation process may include but are not limited to the following.

- Stakeholders have a good understanding of the expected performance of new and changed services
- Change management has good quality evaluations to help them make correct decisions

Metrics

The performance of the change evaluation process can be measured according to:

- Increased…
  - ○ Stakeholder satisfaction with new or changed services as measured in customer surveys
  - ○ Percentage of evaluations delivered by agreed times
  - ○ Change management personnel satisfaction with the change evaluation process as measured in regular surveys.
- Reduced number of…
  - ○ Incidents for new or changed services due to failure to deliver expected utility or warranty
  - ○ Changes that have to be backed out due to unexpected errors or failures
  - ○ Failed changes

Challenges
Here are some of the potential challenges faced by the change evaluation process.
- Developing standard performance measures and measurement methods across projects and suppliers
- Understanding the different stakeholder perspectives
- Understanding, and being able to assess, the balance between managing and taking risks
- Measuring and demonstrating the variation in predictions during and after transition
- Taking a pragmatic and measured approach to risk
- Effectively communicating the organisation's risk appetite and approach to risk management during risk evaluation
- Building a thorough understanding of how risks can impact successful service transition
- Encouraging a culture where people share information

Risks
Here are some of the potential risks faced by the change evaluation process.
- Lack of clear understanding when change evaluation should be used
- Unrealistic expectations of the time required to complete change evaluation
- Personnel with insufficient experience or organisational authority to be able to influence change authorities
- Inaccurately estimating dates for project or supplier delivery

7.11 Knowledge Management

Introduction
The purpose of knowledge management is to improve the quality of the (management's) decision-making process by ensuring that reliable and secure information is available during the Service Lifecycle.

The **objectives** of knowledge management are, among others:
- To support the service provider in order to improve the efficiency and quality of the services
- To ensure that the service provider's personnel have adequate information available

Scope
Knowledge management is used throughout the entire lifecycle. In ITIL version 3 the book on Service Transition explains the basic principles of the process.

Value for the business
Knowledge management is particularly relevant during Service Transition, since relevant and appropriate knowledge is one of the key service elements being transitioned. Specific examples of the application of knowledge management during Service Transition are:

- Training and knowledge transfer, intellectual property, compliance information and standards
- The documentation of errors, workarounds and test information

Basic concepts

Knowledge management is often visualised using the **DIKW** structure: **D**ata-**I**nformation-**K**nowledge-**W**isdom.

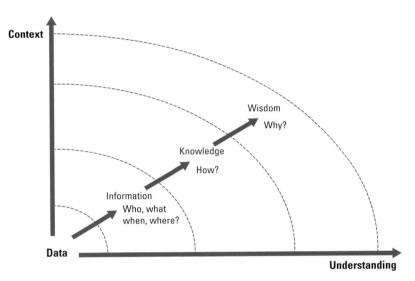

Figure 7.11 The DIKW model

Source: The Cabinet Office

The basis of the **Service Knowledge Management System (SKMS)** is formed by a considerable amount of data in a central repository or CMS and the CMDB: the CMDB feeds the CMS and the CMS provides input for the SKMS and so supports the decision-making process. However, the scope of the SKMS is broader: information is also stored that relates to matters such as:

- The experience and skills of personnel
- Information about peripheral matters such as the behaviour of users and the performance of the organisation
- Requirements and expectations of service providers and partners

Activities, methods, and techniques

Knowledge management consists of the following activities, methods, and techniques:

- Knowledge management strategy
- Knowledge transfer
- Data and information management
- The use of the SKMS

1. Knowledge management strategy

An organisation needs an overall knowledge management strategy. If such a strategy is already in place, the service management knowledge strategy can link into it. Whether there is an existing strategy or not, the strategy must in any case cover the following elements:

- Policies, procedures and methods for knowledge management
- The governance model, forthcoming organisational changes, the definition of roles and responsibilities and the financing
  - The required technology and other resources
  - Performance measures
  - Establishing roles and responsibilities and on-going funding

The knowledge management strategy also focuses specifically on documenting relevant knowledge, and on the data and information that support this knowledge.

2. Knowledge transfer

The transfer of knowledge is a challenging task, requiring, in the first place, an analysis to determine what the knowledge gap is between the department or person in possession of the knowledge and those in need of the knowledge. Based on the outcome of this analysis, a communication (improvement) plan is formulated to facilitate the knowledge transfer.

There are a number of knowledge transfer techniques, such as:

- **Learning styles** – everyone has a different style of learning; the method must therefore be tailored to the target group in question
- **Knowledge visualisation** – this technique uses visual aids such as photos, diagrams, pictures and "storyboards" for knowledge transfer
- **Driving behaviour** – consider, for instance, service desk scripts and compulsory fields in software applications
- **Seminars, "webinars", advertisements** – it is very effective to organise a special event for the launch of a new service
- **Newsletter, newspaper** – regular communication channels such as newsletters or "e-alerts" lend themselves very well to the transfer of knowledge in small steps (incremental instead of "big bang")

3. Information management

Data and information management consists of the following activities:

- **Establishing data and information requirements** – data and information are often collected without a clear idea of how the information will be used; this can be very expensive so it pays to determine the requirements first
- **Definition of information architecture** – to effectively use data, an architecture needs to be created that corresponds with the requirements and the organisation
- **Establishing data and information management procedures** – once the requirements and architecture are known the procedures for the control and support of the knowledge management can be formulated

- **Evaluation and improvement** – as in all processes, evaluation is needed for the purpose of continual improvement

4. Use of the SKMS

Supplying services to customers in different time zones and regions and with different operating hours imposes strenuous requirements on the sharing of knowledge. For this reason the service provider must develop and maintain an SKMS system that is available to all stakeholders and suits all information requirements. An example of such a system can be seen in the following figure (Figure 7.12).

In addition to material for training and knowledge gathering it is useful to:
- Incorporate (IT and business) terminology lists and their translation into the system
- Document the operational processes and where they interface with IT
- Include SLA and other contracts that can change as a result of a Service Transition
- Include known errors, workarounds and process diagrams

Information management

- The SKMS consists of a large number of tools and repositories, either running independently or within a federated model allowing for cross-referencing, thus creating additional value.
- The most important aspect of information management is to understand and document items of data, information, and knowledge that the organisation actually needs.
  - How does it relate to other data, information, and knowledge?
  - Where and how is it stored?
  - Who is responsible for collecting, updating, and maintaining it?
  - What are the legal, regulatory or governance considerations?
  - What are the criteria and/or business rules for availability, storage, archiving, and deletion?
  - What type of access will each stakeholder received?

Interfaces

Like all processes, the knowledge management process has relationships with all other processes. However, some of the most visible relationships include but are not limited to:
- The SKMS can only be truly effective if all personnel, through the execution of all process activities, use it to store and manage data and information. All processes managing their data and information should use knowledge management concepts and activities to manage these.
- The selection of a knowledge management tool will impact the tool selection for all other service management processes, and vice versa.

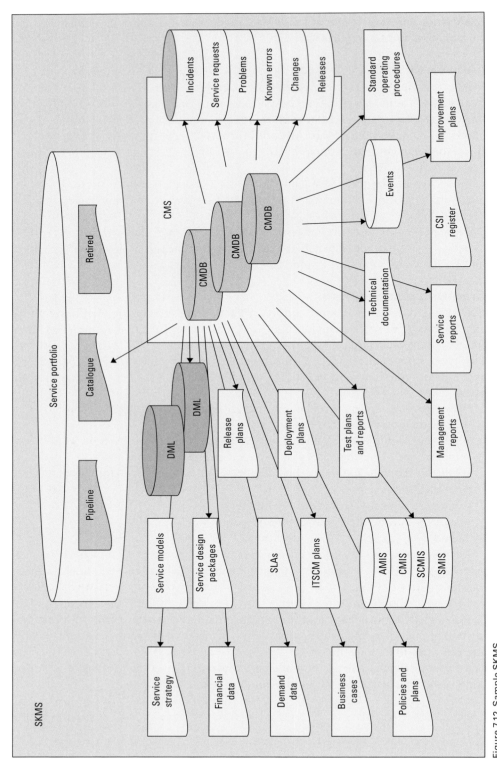

Figure 7.12 Sample SKMS
Source: The Cabinet Office

Triggers

Here are some of the triggers that may start the whole, or part of the, knowledge management process.

- Business relationship management storing the minutes of a customer meeting
- Updates to the service catalogue or service portfolio
- Modification of a service design package
- Creation of a new or updated capacity plan
- Receipt of an updated user manual from a supplier
- Creation of a customer report
- Updates to the CSI register

Inputs

Here are some of the inputs required by the knowledge management process.

- Inputs to knowledge management include all data, information, and knowledge used by the service provider, as well as relevant business data

Outputs

Here are some of the outputs produced by the knowledge management process.

- The knowledge, maintained within the SKMS, that is required to make decisions and to manage the IT services
- Errors detected during a service transition will be made available to the personnel involved with service operation functions

Critical success factors

The critical success factors, which change over time, for the knowledge management process may include but are not limited to the following.

- Availability of information and knowledge that supports management decision-making
- Reduced time and effort required in supporting and maintaining services
- Successful implementation with few knowledge-related errors and early life operation of new and changed services
- Improved management of standards and policies
- Reduced dependency on personnel for knowledge

Metrics

The performance of the knowledge management process can be measured according to:

- Reduced transfer of issues to other people and more resolution at lower personnel levels
- Increased number of times that material is re-used in documentation such as procedures, test design and service desk scripts
- Increased percentage of incidents solved by use of known errors
- Increased percentage of successful service transitions
- Increased number of times that standards and policies in the SKMS have been accessed

- Increased percentage of standards and policies that have been reviewed by the agreed review date
- Increased percentage of SKMS searches that receive a rating of "good" by users, IT personnel and management

Challenges

Here are some of the potential challenges faced by the knowledge management process.

- Justifying the effort needed to create a consistent architecture for managing data, information, and knowledge
- Helping all the stakeholders understand the added value of pursuing a holistic and on-going approach to knowledge management

Risks

Here are some of the potential risks faced by the knowledge management process.

- Focusing on the technology instead of creating value
- Insufficient understanding of the data, information, and knowledge that are needed by the organisation
- Lack of investment in the planning, designing, implementing, and maintenance of the SKMS, including technology and personnel
- Focusing too much on capturing knowledge to the detriment of knowledge transfer and re-use
- Storing and sharing outdated and irrelevant data, information and knowledge
- Lack of support and commitment from stakeholders

7.12 Organisation

On the whole, the activities of a process are not carried out by a single department. The different activities, for example of SACM, are carried out by departments such as service operation, application management, network management, and system management. Therefore, the process activities are related to the different IT departments and their respective personnel. Roles and responsibilities are also defined.

Generic roles

Process owner – The process owner ensures that all process activities are carried out and:

- Is responsible for the process strategy, and assists in the design
- Provides process documentation, guidelines and procedures and their application
- Ensures there are adequate resources

Service owner – The service owner holds the responsibility, toward the customer, for the initiation, transition, and maintenance of a service and:

- Is the contact person and ensures that the service meets the requirements
- Identifies improvement points and provides data and reports for service monitoring
- Is accountable for the delivery of the service to IT Management

Organisational context

The interfaces of other departments and third parties in service transition must be clearly defined and known. Programs, projects, Service Design, and service provider all contribute towards the service transition.

Service transition is actively managed by a **service transition manager**. The service transition manager is responsible for the daily management and control of the Service Transition teams and their activities. An example of a Service Transition organisation is presented in the next figure.

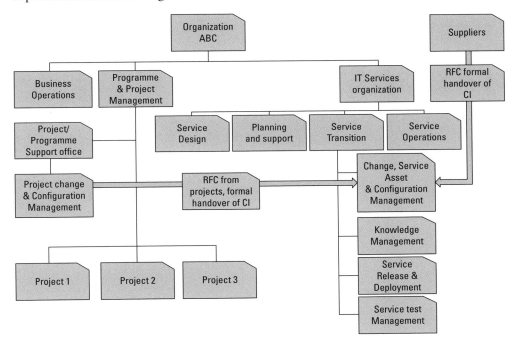

Figure 7.13 Sample service transition organisation

Source: The Cabinet Office

Service transition roles and responsibilities

This section describes a number of roles and responsibilities within service transition, although some roles also fall within other lifecycle phases. Depending on the size of the organisation and the scope of the service which is changed, some of these roles can be carried out by one person.

The responsibilities of the **service asset manager** include:
- Formulating process objectives and implementing the policy, the process standards, plans and procedures
- Indicating the scope and function of the process, which items must be managed and the information that must be established
- Taking care of communication about the process and making it known
- Taking care of resources and training

- Setting up the identification and the naming conventions of assets
- Taking care of the evaluation of the use of tooling
- Setting up interfaces with other processes
- Planning the completion of the asset database
- Making reports
- Assisting with audits and taking care of corrective actions

The responsibilities of the **configuration manager** include:
- Formulating process objectives and implementing the policy, the process standards, plans and procedures
- Evaluating the existing configuration management systems and implementing the new systems
- Indicating the scope and function of the process, which items must be managed and the information that must be established
- Taking care of communication about the process and making it known
- Taking care of resources and training
- Setting up the identification and the naming conventions of CI
- Taking care of the evaluation of the use of tooling
- Setting up interfaces with other processes
- Evaluating existing CMS systems and implementation of new systems
- Planning the filling in of CMS in the CMDBs
- Making reports
- Assisting with audits and taking corrective actions

The **change manager** has responsibilities (some of which can be delegated) including:
- Receiving, logging and prioritising (in collaboration with the initiator) RFCs, or rejecting RFCs based on the criteria
- Preparing and chairing CAB and ECAB meetings
- Deciding who attends which meeting, who receives RFCs, what must be changed, etc.
- Publishing Changes Schedules
- Maintaining change logs
- Closing RFCs
- Reviewing implemented changes
- Making reports

The **Change Advisory Board (CAB)** is an advisory consultation body. The specific roles and responsibilities of the CAB will be explained in Section 7.2.

The responsibilities of the **release packaging and build manager** include:
- Final release configuration
- Building the final release and testing it (prior to independent testing)
- Reporting known faults and workarounds
- Input to the final implementation sign-off

The **deployment manager** is responsible for the following including:
- The final service implementation
- Coordination of all release documentation, release notes, and communication
- Planning of the deployment, in combination with change management, knowledge management and SACM
- Providing guidance during the release process
- Giving feedback concerning the effectiveness of a release
- Recording metrics for deployment to ensure within agreed SLA

ITIL recognises the following roles in the Service Transition phase of the Service Lifecycle, but this falls outside the scope of this book and the ITIL Foundations exams:
- Configuration analyst
- Configuration manager
- CMS manager
- Configuration management team
- Change authority
- Risk evaluation manager
- Service knowledge manager
- Test support
- Early Life Support (ELS)
- Building and test environment management

Organisational change management

Significant change of a service also means a change of the organisation. This can vary from "the transfer of a personnel member to another department" to large changes such as "the manner of working in the organisation". For example: a mail order company no longer sells its products by a printed catalogue but via a website.

The following aspects are important in organisational change management:
- **The emotional change cycle** – One of the biggest causes of failure of changes is not sufficiently considering the way in which the changes affect people. Therefore consider the emotional phases that people can experience before accepting changes. The emotional phases are: shock, avoidance, external blame, self-blame and acceptance.
- **The role of Service Transition in organisational changes** – The management of change is the responsibility of the managers and heads of department involved in this specific change. However, the Service Transition manager or process owner is an important party in the change, and therefore Service Transition plays an important role in organisational changes. Service Transition must:
  - Show awareness of the different cultures at organisational and individual levels
  - Include active participation in the changing of people's attitudes (who are active within the lifecycle)
  - Support individuals in such a way that the implementation of changes is consistently executed
  - Evaluate whether the IT organisation is sufficiently capable

- Guarantee that the change is accepted by the majority in their daily work method
- Take care to ensure that knowledge transfer, training, team building, process improvement and evaluation of personnel are sufficiently competent
- **Planning and implementation of organisational changes** – In the planning and design of changes there is often insufficient consideration for the organisational side and the people. The focus lies on the technical aspect of the change. That is why it is important that the project plans also state the organisational changes caused by the change.
- **Products** – Service Strategy and Service Design result in several work products which support the management of organisational changes during the Service Transition, for example:
  - Stakeholder analysis
  - Organisational and competency assessments
  - Service management process models
  - Guidelines for processes and procedures
  - Communication plan
  - RACI matrix (Responsible, Accountable, Consulted, Informed)
- **Evaluation of readiness for organisational change** – It is good practice to make a checklist to assess if the organisation fulfils the requirements for transition in terms of roles and skills.
- **Monitoring of progress** – Research and surveys must be carried out on a regular basis at different levels in the organisation concerning the effectiveness and the success of a Service Transition program. Use the result of the research to define how much progress is achieved with the transition. It will also indicate to personnel that they are being heard and that their input is important in the transition.
- **Manage organisational changes in sourcing** – the sourcing of IT services is one of the most serious organisational changes. There are many consequences for the personnel which must be considered and carefully prepared, such as:
  - The shock for personnel
  - Changes in the way in which the business and the service provider do business with each other
  - Change of location with all the associated risks
- **Methods and techniques for organisational changes** – Numerous methods, techniques, and best practices exist for management of changes, such as Kotter's "Changes in eight steps" and Rosabeth Moss Kanter's theory about the reasons why people resist change. It is important to make the best possible use of these.

Stakeholder management

Stakeholder management is a crucial success factor in Service Transition. This is why a strategy should be developed in the Service Design phase. Explain:

- Who the stakeholders are
- What their interest are
- What their influence is
- How they are included in the project or program
- What information is shared with them

A stakeholder map is a useful tool to map the different interests of the stakeholders.

Stakeholders	Strategic direction	Financial	Operational changes	Interface with customers	Public safety	Competitive position
Business partner	●	●		●		●
Project teams			●			
Customers		●		●	●	
Press and media						●
Trade unions			●			
Staff	●		●			
Regulatory bodies		●			●	

Figure 7.14 Sample stakeholder matrix

Source: The Cabinet Office

Further, a **stakeholder analysis** assists in finding out what the requirements and interests of the stakeholders are, and what their final influence and power will be during the transition.

Finally, the turnover of stakeholders during the Service Lifecycle must also be considered.

7.13 Methods, technology and tools

Technology plays an important part in the support of Service Transition. It can be divided into two types:

- **IT service management systems**:
  - ○ Enterprise frameworks which offer integration capabilities to integrate and link in the CMDB or other tools
  - ○ System, network and application management tools
  - ○ Service dashboards and reporting tools
- **Specific ITSM technology and tools**:
  - ○ Service knowledge management systems
  - ○ Collaboration tools, content management systems and workflow tools
  - ○ Tools for data mining, data extraction and data transformation
  - ○ Tools for measuring and reporting
  - ○ Test (management) tools
  - ○ Publication tools
  - ○ Release and deployment technology

In addition, specialised tools are available for change management, configuration management and release management, such as:

- Configuration management
- Tools for version control
- Document management systems
- Design tools
- Distribution and installation tools
- Construction and deployment tools

A more elaborate description of the various tools for Service Transition and the underlying processes is beyond the scope of this book.

7.14 Implementation

The implementation of Service Transition in a "greenfield" situation (from zero) is only feasible when establishing a new service provider. Most service providers focus on the improvement of the Service Transition (processes). For the improvement of Service Transition (processes) the following five aspects are also important:

- **Justification** – The benefits of effective Service Transition are not always immediately visible to the customer. Gathering evidence of the damage caused by an ineffective transition phase can justify the establishment or improvement of Service Transition. Take into consideration aspects such as: the costs of failed changes or errors in services in the production environment which could have been avoided if a good test process had been used.
- **Design** – Factors to take into account when designing Service Transition are:
  - Standards and guidelines to which the design must adhere
  - Relationships with other supporting services (human resources management, telecommunications, facilities management), project and program management, customers, end users and other stakeholders
  - Budget and means
- **Introduction** – Experience has taught us that it is unwise to apply the improved or newly implemented (and therefore unproven) Service Transition to current projects. In all likelihood the advantages do not outweigh the disadvantages resulting from the disruption of the project.
- **Cultural aspects** – Even formalising existing procedures will lead to cultural changes in an organisation. Take this into consideration and do not only think of those personnel that are directly involved in the Service Transition, but consider all stakeholders.
- **Risks and advantages** – Do not make any decisions about the introduction or improvement of Service Transition without an insight into the risks and advantages to expect.

Relationships with other lifecycle phases

Even though this book presents Service Transition as a more or less delimited lifecycle phase, this does not mean that it can be viewed on its own. Without the input from Service Design and the output to Service Operation, Service Transition has no purpose.

There is also the input and output of knowledge and experience from and to Service Transition. This flow of knowledge and experience works both ways:
- **Against the flow** – For instance Service Operation shares practical experiences with Service Transition as to how similar services behave in the production environment. Experiences from Service Transition supply input for the assessment of the designs from Service Design.
- **With the flow** – Service Design supplies Service Transition with the knowledge needed to implement a change (for instance the different designs), and Service Transition supplies production experiences (for instance from testing) which could prove to be important for the daily management of the service.

Challenges and critical success factors

For a successful Service Transition, several challenges need to be conquered, such as:
- Taking into account all stakeholders (and their different perspectives) and maintaining relationships which could be important within Service Transition
- The lack of harmonisation and integration of processes and disciplines which influence Service Transition
- Finding the balance between a stable operation environment and being able to respond to changing business requirements in a flexible manner
- Finding the balance between pragmatism and bureaucracy
- Creating an environment in which standardisation and knowledge sharing is stimulated
- Creating a culture in which one is responsive to cooperation and cultural changes
- Ensuring that the quality of services corresponds to the quality of the business
- Finding the balance between "taking risks" and "avoiding risks"; this balance must correspond to that of the business
- The integration with other lifecycle phases, processes and disciplines
- A clear definition of the roles and responsibilities
- Having the correct tools for managing the IT infrastructure
- Developing good quality systems, tools, processes, procedures for Service Transition

Critical success factors

Management support

Support from higher and middle management is necessary for all IT service management activities and processes. It is crucial for obtaining sufficient financing and resources. Senior management must also offer visible support during the launch of new Service Transition initiatives.

Middle management must also provide the necessary support and actions.

Business support

It is also important that Service Transition is supported by the business units. This works well if the Service Transition personnel involve the business in all their activities, and are open about what is and isn't feasible in terms of meeting business requirements.

Regular communication with the business is crucial to building a good relationship and to ensuring support; Service Design will be better placed to understand the needs and concerns of the business. Additionally, the business can provide feedback on the efforts of Service Design to satisfy the business needs.

Hiring and retaining personnel

The correct number of personnel with the correct skills is critical for successful Service Transition. Consider the following challenges:

- Projects for new services often clearly specify what the new skills must be, but may underestimate how many personnel are needed and how skills can be retained.
- There may be a lack of personnel with solid knowledge of service management; having good technicians is important, but there must also be a certain number of people who have knowledge of both technological and service problems.
- Because personnel with both technological and service knowledge are fairly rare, they are often specially trained; it is important to retain them by offering a clear career path and solid compensation.
- Personnel are often assigned new tasks too quickly, while they are still extremely busy with their current workloads. Successful service management projects may require a short term investment in temporary workers.

Service management training

Good training and awareness can provide great advantages. In addition to increasing expertise, they can generate enthusiasm in people. Service transition personnel must be aware of the consequences of their actions for the organisation. A "service management culture" must be created. Service management will only be successful if the people are focused on overall service management objectives.

Appropriate tools

Many service management processes and activities cannot be effectively executed without proper support tools. Senior management must ensure that financing for such tools is included in annual budgets, and must support acquisition, implementation, and maintenance.

Test validity

The quality of IT services provided by Service Operation depends on the quality of systems and components that are delivered in the operational environment.

The quality level will improve considerably if solid and complete testing of new components and releases is performed in a timely manner. Also, the documentation should be independently tested for completeness and quality.

Measuring and reporting

Clear agreements are necessary regarding the way in which things are measured and reported; all personnel will have clear targets to aim for, and IT and business managers will be able to evaluate quickly and simply whether progress is being made and which areas deserve extra attention.

Risks

Potential risks of Service Transition are:

- De-motivation of personnel as a result of changed responsibilities and roles
- Unforeseen expenses
- Resistance to change
- Lack of knowledge sharing
- Poor integration between processes
- Lack of maturity and integration of systems and tools

Finally, there can be circumstances in which Service Transition can have additional risk, for instance as a result of a lack of money or resources, or political problems.

8 Service operation phase

8.1 Service Operation

This short section provides a summary of the updates between the 2007 edition and the 2011 edition for the ITIL core book Service Operation published by TSO.

Process flows have been updated or added for all processes including request fulfilment, access management, and event management.

Key principles – *including guidance around service requests and request models, and proactive problem management* – have been clarified. The publication has been updated to explain how basic events flow into filters and rule engines to produce meaningful event information. The relationship between application management activities versus application development activities is also clarified.

Other improvements include an expanded section on problem analysis techniques, a procedure flow for incident matching, and further guidance for escalating incidents to problem management. In addition, the guidance for managing physical facilities has been expanded.

Table 8.1 Summary of updates: ITIL Service Operation

Area of update	Description
Service request	The concept of a service request has been significantly enhanced to provide a clearer definition, with examples and diagrams to illustrate how service requests link with the services they support. The relationship of service requests to request models and standard changes is also highlighted.
Request model	This concept has been expanded to clarify how each service request should be linked to a request model that documents the steps and tasks, and the roles and responsibilities needed to fulfil requests.
Event filtering and correlation	Additional clarification has been provided to illustrate how basic events flow into filters and rule engines to produce meaningful information.
Normal service operation	A clearer definition for this has now been included and added to the glossary.
Incident matching	A procedure has been added to provide examples of how incidents should initially be matched against known error records before escalation. A detailed procedure flow for matching incidents and escalating to problem management has been added.
Request fulfilment process flow	A new process flow now illustrates a suggested set of activities and steps for the request fulfilment process. This process flow also includes decision points for escalating requests to service transition as change proposals or incident management as incidents.

Area of update	Description
Problem analysis techniques	This section has been expanded to include more techniques for finding root causes. In addition, each technique now indicates the kinds of situations and incidents where it may be advantageous to use the particular technique described.
Problem investigation and analysis	A concept has been added to recreate problems when they are being investigated.
Mainframe and server management	The concept that the activities and procedures for managing mainframes are no different from servers has been added. How these activities might be carried out may differ, but the outcomes and kinds of management task are essentially the same.
Proactive problem management	The concept and description of activities for proactive problem management have been added to the problem management process.
Application management versus application development	The differences between application management and application development are now clarified. A diagram has been added to show the key activities that take place during each stage of the application management lifecycle to demonstrate how application management differs from application development.
Facilities management	This appendix has been greatly enhanced with additional information for managing physical facilities.

8.2   Introduction

Well designed and implemented processes are of little value when the day-to-day fulfilment of these processes is not well organised. Nor are service improvements possible when the day-to-day performance measuring and data gathering activities are not fulfilled systematically during Service Operation.

Objectives

The goals of Service Operation are to coordinate and fulfil activities and processes required to provide and manage services for business users and customers with a specified agreed level. Service Operation is also responsible for management of the technology required to provide and support the services.

Scope

Service Operation is about fulfilling all activities required to provide and support services. These include:
- The services
- The service management processes
- The technology
- The people

Optimising the Service Operation performance

Service Operation can be improved in two ways:
- *Long-term incremental improvement* – This is based on the review of the performances and output of all Service Operation processes, functions and outputs

over time; examples include putting new tools into use or changes in the design process.

- *Short-term on-going improvement of existing situations within the Service Operation processes, functions and technology* – These are small changes that are implemented to change the fundamental significance of a process or technology; examples are tuning, training or personnel transfer.

8.3 Processes and other activities

This section devotes its attention to the following processes, activities, and functions:
- Event management
- Incident management
- Problem management
- Request fulfilment
- Access management
- Monitoring and control (activity)
- IT operations (function)

Additionally, there are other processes that will be executed or supported during Service Operation, but are driven by other phases of the service management lifecycle:
- Change management
- Capacity management
- Availability management
- Financial management
- Knowledge management
- IT Service Continuity Management (ITSCM)
- Service reporting and measurement

Event management
An event is an occurrence that affects the IT infrastructure management or the provision of an IT service. For the most part, events are notifications created by an IT service, configuration item or monitoring tool. For an effective Service Operation, the organisation must know its infrastructure status, and be able to trace deviations of the regular or expected performance. Good monitoring and control systems provide information for this.

Event management surveys all events that occur in the IT infrastructure in order to monitor the regular performance, and which can be automated to trace and escalate unforeseen circumstances.

Event management can be applied to any aspect of service management that must be managed and can be automated.

The most important activities of the event management process are:
- Event occurs
- Event notification
- Event detection
- Event filtering
- Event significance/classification
- Event correlation
- Trigger
- Response selection
- Action assessment
- Close event

There is no standard record for event management; metrics should be set accordingly.

Incident management

The incident management process focuses on restoring failure of service as quickly as possible for customers, so that it has a minimal impact on the business.

Incident management includes any event that interrupts or can interrupt a service; so they also include events reported by customers, either by the service desk or through various tools.

The incident management process consists of the following steps:
- Identifying
- Recording/logging
- Categorising
- Prioritising
- Initial diagnosing
- Escalating
- Investigating and diagnosing
- Resolving and restoring
- Closing

Request fulfilment

Request fulfilment is the process of handling service requests, where a separate process is utilised that initiates the need for a request.

The goals of the request fulfilment process are:
- Offering users a channel where they can request and receive standard services (changes); there must be an agreed approval and qualification process for this
- Providing information to customers about the availability of services and the procedure to obtain them
- Providing the standard services components (such as licences and software media)
- Assisting with general information, complaints or remarks

Request fulfilment consists of the following activities, methods, and techniques:
- Menu selection
- Financial approval
- Other approval
- Fulfilment
- Closure

Problem management

Problem management is responsible for analysing and resolving the causes of incidents. In addition, it develops proactive activities to prevent current and future incidents, using a so-called "known error sub-process" that enables a quicker diagnosis when new incidents happen.

Problem management includes all activities that are needed for a diagnosis of the underlying cause of incidents, and to determine a resolution for those problems. It must also ensure that the resolution is implemented through the appropriate control procedures (i.e. with change management and release management).

Problem management consists of two important processes:
- Reactive problem management
- Proactive problem management

Reactive problem management consists of:
- Detection
- Logging
- Categorising
- Prioritising
- Investigating and diagnosing
- Determining workarounds
- Identifying a known error
- Finding a resolution
- Closing
- Reviewing major problems
- Handling mistakes in the development environment

Proactive problem management consists of:
- Improving the overall availability of IT services
- Improving the overall end user satisfaction with IT services
- Conducting periodic scheduled reviews of incident records to find patterns and trends

Access management

Access management is the process of allowing authorised users access to use a service, while access of unauthorised users is limited. In some organisations this is also known as rights or identity management.

Access management helps ensure that this access is always available at agreed times. This is provided by availability management.

A service request through the service desk can initiate access management.

Access management consists of:
- Requesting access
- Verification
- Assigning rights
- Monitoring of the identity status
- Logging and tracking access
- Removing or restricting rights

8.4 Methods, techniques and tools

The most important requirements for Service Operation are:
- An integrated IT service management technology
- Self-help
- Workflow or process management engine
- An integrated CMS
- Discovery/deployment/licensing technology
- Remote control
- Diagnostic utilities
- Reporting capabilities
- Dashboards
- Integration with business service management

8.5 Event Management

Introduction
ITIL defines an event as follows:

> "An event can be defined as any change of state that has significance for the management of a configuration item (CI) or IT service."

Events are typically notifications created by an IT service, CI, or monitoring tool. To ensure effective Service Operations, an organisation must be aware of the status of its infrastructure and be able to detect deviations from the regular or expected operation. Good monitoring and control systems are required.

The **objective** of event management is to detect events, analyse them, and determine the right management action. It provides the entry point for the execution of many Service Operation processes and activities.

Scope

Event management can be applied to any aspect of service management that requires control and can be automated. For example configuration items, security, software license monitoring and environmental conditions (e.g. detecting fire and smoke).

The difference between monitoring and event management

Monitoring and event management are closely related, but slightly different in nature. Event management is focused on generating and detecting meaningful notifications about the status of the IT infrastructure and services.

Value for the business

Event management generally has indirect value. Some examples of benefit for the business:

- Event management provides mechanisms for early detection of incidents
- Event management makes it possible for some types of automated activity to be monitored by exception
- If event management is integrated into other service management processes, it may detect status changes or exceptions; this allows the right person or team to respond more quickly, thereby improving the process performance
- Event management provides a basis for automated operations; this improves effectiveness and frees up costly human resources for more innovative work

Basic concepts

There are many different event types, such as:

- Events that indicate a normal operation, such as a user logging on to use an application
- Events that indicate an exception, such as a user who is trying to log on to an application with an incorrect password or a PC scan that reveals the installation of unauthorised software
- Events that signify an unusual but not exceptional operation; it may provide an indication that the situation requires a little more supervision For example utilisation of a server's memory reaches within five per cent of its highest acceptable level

Activities, methods, and techniques

The following figure reflects a sample flow for event management. Like all sample flows provided in this book, it is a high level and generic representation and should be used as a reference point rather than an actual event management (process) flowchart.

The main activities of the event management process are described below.

Event occurs

Events occur continuously, but not all of them are detected or registered. It is therefore important that everybody involved in designing, developing, managing and supporting IT services and the IT infrastructure that they run on understands what types of event need to be detected.

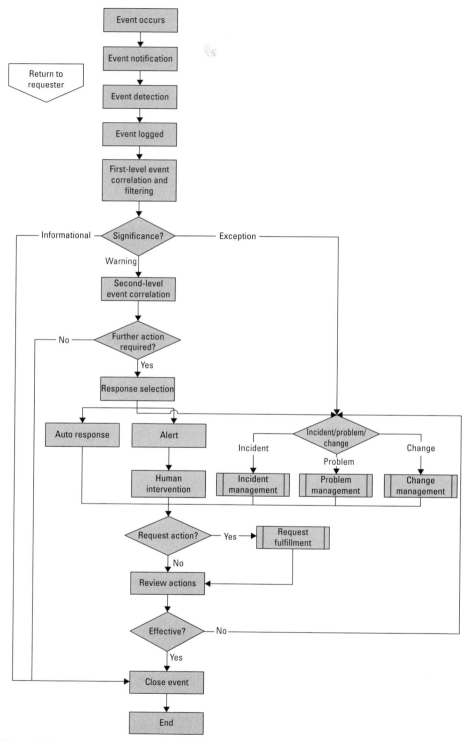

Figure 8.1 Sample event management workflow

Source: The Cabinet Office

Event notification

Many CIs are configured to generate a standard set of events, based on the designer's experience of what is required to operate the CI, with the ability to generate additional types of event by "turning on" the relevant event generation mechanism. For other CI types, some form of "agent" software will have to be installed in order to initiate the monitoring.

The service design process should define which events need to be generated and then specify how this can be done for each type of CI. During service transition, the event generation options would be set and tested.

In many organisations, however, defining which events to generate is done by trial and error. System managers use the standard set of events as a starting point and then tune the CI over time, to include or exclude events as required.

Event detection

Once an event notification has been generated, it will be detected by an agent running on the same system, or transmitted directly to a management tool specifically designed to read and interpret the meaning of the event.

Event logged

There should be a record of the event and any subsequent actions. The event can be logged as an event record in the event management tool or it can simply be left as an entry in the system log of the device or application that generated the event. Whatever the case, there needs to be a standing order for the appropriate operations management personnel to check the logs on a regular basis and clear instructions about how to use each log.

First-level event correlation and filtering

The purpose of first-level event correlation and filtering is to decide whether to communicate the event to a management tool or to ignore it. If ignored, the event will usually be recorded in a log file on the device, but no further action will be taken.

This step may not always require events to be correlated. For some CIs, every event is significant and moves directly into a management tool's correlation engine, even if it is duplicated. Also, it may not have been possible to turn off all unwanted event notifications.

Significance of events

Every organisation will have its own categorisation of the significance of an event, but it is suggested that at least these three broad categories be represented.

Informational

This refers to an event that does not require any action and does not represent an exception. They are typically stored in the system or service log files and kept for a predetermined period. Informational events are typically used to check on the status of a device or service, or to confirm the successful completion of an activity.

Warning
A warning is an event that is generated when a service or device has reached a threshold that indicates a situation must be checked and appropriate actions taken to prevent an exception.

Exception
An exception means that a service or device is currently operating abnormally (as defined by the organisation). Typically, this means that an OLA and SLA have been breached and the business is being impacted. Exceptions could represent a total failure, impaired functionality, or degraded performance. However, an exception does not always represent a failure or abnormal operation.

Second-level event correlation
If an event is a warning, a decision has to be made about exactly what the significance is and what actions need to be taken to deal with it. It is here that the meaning of the event is determined.

Correlation is normally done by a "correlation engine", usually part of a management tool that compares the event with a set of criteria and rules in a prescribed order. These criteria are often called business rules, although they are generally fairly technical.

Further action required?
If the second-level correlation activity recognises an event, a response will be required. There are many different types of responses, each designed specifically for the task it has to initiate.

Response selection
At this point in the process, there are a number of response options available. It is important to note that the response options can be chosen in any combination.
• *Auto response*
• *Alert and human intervention*
• *Incident, problem, or change?*

It is possible that the appropriate response to an event is to open an incident record, link to a problem record, and/or open a change record (ticket).

Review actions
With thousands of events being generated every day, it is not possible formally to review every individual event. However, it is important to check that any significant events or exceptions have been handled appropriately, or to track trends or counts of event types etc.

The review will also be used as input into continual improvement and the evaluation and audit of the event management process.

Close event

Some events will remain open until a certain action takes place, for example an event that is linked to an open incident. However, most events are not "opened" or "closed".

In the case of events that generated an incident, problem, or change, these should be formally closed with a link to the appropriate record from the other process.

Designing for event management

Event management is the basis for monitoring the performance and availability of a service. This is why availability and capacity management must specify and agree on the precise monitoring targets and mechanisms. Various instruments exist for this purpose:

- **Instrumentation** – defines how best to monitor and manage the IT infrastructure and IT services, and creates an appropriate design.
  - Determine:
    - What needs to be monitored?
    - What monitoring type is required (active or passive, performance or output)
    - When the monitoring should generate an event
    - What type of information needs to be communicated?
    - Who is the audience?

  - Mechanisms that need to be designed include:
    - How will events be generated?
    - Does the CI already have event generation?
    - What data will be used to populate the Event Record?
    - Are events generated automatically or does the CI have to be polled?
    - Where will events be logged and stored?

- **Error messages** – important for all components (hardware, software, networks, etc.); design all software applications in such a way that they can support event management, e.g. by means of meaningful error messages or codes that clearly indicate what is going wrong, where and the likely causes
- **Event detection and alert mechanisms** – for a good design, you need the following:
  - Detailed knowledge of the Service Level Requirements of the service that is supported by every CI
  - Information on who will support the CI
  - Knowledge of the normal and abnormal state of affairs for the CI
  - Information that can help determine problems with CI

Information management

- Technical information about the status of components of an IT infrastructure
- The ability to interrogate varied data sources and files formats and compare them to a predefined norm.

- Software agents for event monitoring tools
- Correlation engines detailing rules to determine significance of events and appropriate control actions

The following represent a small list of some key data usually required from each event to be useful in analysis.
- Unique identifier
- Service
- Component
- Type of event
- Date/time
- Parameters in exception
- Value

Interfaces
Like all processes, the event management process has relationships with all other processes. However, some of the most visible relationships include but are not limited to:
- Event management can interface to any process that requires monitoring and control, whether real-time or not, and require some form of intervention following an event or group of events.

Service design
- **Service level management** – For early detection of real or potential service level target breaches to ensure timely corrective action
- **Information security management**– Interface with business applications and/or business processes allowing potentially or real significant and disruptive security-related events to be detected and acted upon.
- **Capacity and availability management** – To define and categorise events, thresholds, and appropriate control action. Event management for improving the performance and availability of services by responding according to design requirements

Service transition
- **Service asset and configuration management** – To use events to determine the current status (within its lifecycle) of any CI in the infrastructure.
- **Knowledge management** – To act as a rich source of information that can be processed for inclusion in the SKMS
- Change management – To identify conditions that may require a response or action

Service operation
- **Incident and problem management** – To assist in the resolution of incidents and problems and to identify the conditions that may require appropriate control action
- **Access management** – To detect unauthorised access attempts and security breaches

Triggers

Here are some of the triggers that may start the whole, or part of the, event management process.

- Exceptions to any level of CI performance defined in the design specifications
- Exceptions to an automated procedure or process
- An exception within a business process monitored by event management
- The completion of an automated task or job
- A status change in a server or database CI
- Access of an application or database by a user or automated procedure or job
- A situation where a device, database, or application etc. has reached a predefined threshold of performance

Inputs

Here are some of the inputs required by the event management process.

- Operational and service level requirements associated with events and their actions
- Thresholds for recognising events, warnings, and alerts
- Event correlation tables, rules, event codes and automated response solutions enabling or supporting event management activities
- Roles and responsibilities for taking appropriate actions
- Operational procedures for identifying, logging, correlating, escalating, and communicating events

Outputs

Here are some of the outputs produced by the event management process.

- Events communicated and escalated to those responsible for further action
- Event logs describing appropriate events details, escalation, and communication activities taken to support further activities
- Events indicating an incident has occurred
- Events indicating a change has occurred
- Events indicating the potential breach to an agreement; SLA, OLA, or UC
- Events indicating status of activities within any process requiring it
- SKMS updated with event information and history

Critical success factors

The critical success factors, which change over time, for the event management process may include but are not limited to the following.

- Detecting all changes of state that have significance for the management of CI and IT services
- Ensuring all events are communicated to the appropriate functions that need to be informed or take further control actions
- Providing the trigger, or entry point, for the execution of many service operation processes and operations management activities
- Provide the means to compare actual operating performance and behaviour against design standards and SLA
- Providing a basis for service assurance, reporting and service improvement

Metrics

The performance of the event management process can be measured according to:

- Number and percentage of…
  - Events compared with the number of incidents
  - Each type of event per service, system or component
  - Events that required human intervention and whether this was performed
  - Incidents without a corresponding event
  - Events that resulted in incidents or changes
  - Events caused by existing problems or known errors
  - Events indicating utility or warranty issues
  - Repeated or duplicated events

Challenges

Here are some of the potential challenges faced by the event management process.

- To obtain funding for the necessary tools and effort needed to install and exploit the benefits of the tools
- Setting the correct level of filtering
- Deploying the necessary monitoring agents across the entire IT infrastructure
- Automated monitoring activities can generate additional network traffic that might impact planned network capacity levels
- Acquiring the necessary skills can be time-consuming and costly
- Deploying event management tools without appropriate event management process in place

Risks

Here are some of the potential risks faced by the event management process.

- Failure to obtain adequate funding
- Ensuring the correct level of filtering
- Failure to maintain momentum in deploying the necessary monitoring agents across the IT infrastructure

8.6 Incident Management

Introduction

The incident management process handles all incidents. These are reported by users (generally via a call to the service desk) or technical personnel, or they are automatically detected and reported by tools to monitor events.

ITIL defines an incident as:

"An incident is an unplanned interruption to an IT service or reduction in the quality of an IT service. Failure of a CI that has not yet affected service is also an incident."

The main **objective** of the incident management process is to resume the regular state of affairs as quickly as possible and minimise the impact on business processes.

Normal service operation is defined as an operational state where services and CIs are performing within their agreed service and operational levels.

Scope

Incident management covers every event that disrupts or might disrupt a service. This means that it includes events reported directly by users, either via the service desk or via various tools.

Incidents can also be reported or logged by technical personnel, which does not necessarily mean that every event is an incident.

While incidents and *service requests* are both reported to the service desk, they are not the same thing. *Service requests* are not service disruptions but user requests for support, delivery, information, advice, or documentation.

Value for the business

The value of incident management includes:

- The possibility to track and solve incidents results in reduced downtime for the business; as a result the service is available for longer
- The possibility to align IT operations with the business priorities; the reason is that incident management is able to identify business priorities and distribute resources dynamically
- The possibility to establish potential improvements for services

Incident management is clearly visible to the business, meaning that its value is easier to demonstrate than for other areas in Service Operations. For this reason, it is one of the first processes to be implemented in service management projects.

Basic concepts

The following elements should be taken into account in incident management:

- **Time limits** – Agree on time limits for all phases and use them as targets in Operational Level Agreements (OLA) and Underpinning Contracts (UC).
- **Incident models** – An incident model is a way to determine the steps that are necessary to execute a process correctly (in this case, the processing of certain incident types); it means that standard incidents will be handled correctly and within the agreed timeframes.
- **Major incidents** – A separate procedure is required for major incidents, with shorter timeframes and higher urgency; agree what a major incident is and map the entire incident priority system.

People sometimes confuse a major incident with a problem. However, an incident always remains an incident. Its impact or priority may increase, but it never becomes a problem. A problem is the underlying cause of one or more incidents and always remains a separate entity.

Activities, methods, and techniques

The incident management process consists of the following steps:
1. Identification
2. Registration
3. Classification
4. Prioritisation
5. Diagnosis
6. Escalation
7. Investigation and diagnosis
8. Resolution and recovery
9. Closing

An incident is not handled until it is known to exist. This is called **incident identification**. From a business perspective, it is generally unacceptable to wait until a user experiences the impact of an incident and contacts the service desk. The organisation must try to monitor all important components, so that failures or potential failures can be detected as early as possible and the incident management process can be initiated. In the perfect situation, incidents are solved before they have an impact on the users.

All incidents must be registered in full, including date and time: **incident registration**. This applies to incidents received via the service desk as well as those that are detected automatically via an event warning system. Register all relevant information relating to the nature of the incident to ensure a complete historical record. If the incident is transferred to other support groups, they will have all of the relevant information at their disposal. You should at least record:
• A unique reference number
• Incident category
• Incident urgency
• Incident priority
• Name/ID of the person and/or group who registered the incident
• Description of symptoms
• Activities undertaken to solve the incident

Use an appropriate **incident classification** coding for registration to record the precise call type. This is important at a later stage when incident types and frequencies are analysed, to establish trends that can be used for problem management, provider management and other ITSM activities.

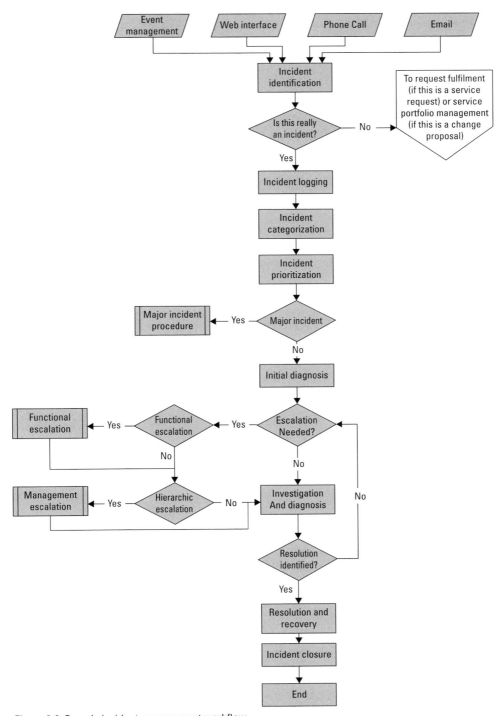

Figure 8.2 Sample incident management workflow

Source: The Cabinet Office

When registering an incident, it is possible that the available data are incomplete, misleading, or incorrect. It is therefore important to check the classification of the incident and update it while concluding a call. An example of a categorised incident is: software, application, finance suite, and purchase order system.

Another important aspect of registering every incident is to allocate the right **priority** code. Support agents and tools use this code to determine how they should handle the incident.

The priority of an incident can usually be determined by establishing its **urgency** (how fast does the business need a solution) and impact. The number of users affected by an incident is often an indication of its **impact**.

When a user reports an incident via the service desk, the service desk agent must try to record the greatest possible number of symptoms of the incident in terms of a first **diagnosis**.

> **Incident matching procedure**
> A procedure for matching incident classification data against that for problems and known errors allows for efficient and quick access to proven resolution actions, thus reducing the time it takes to restore service back to users. This activity also minimises the need for escalation to other support personnel.

The service desk agent also tries to establish what went wrong and how it should be corrected. Diagnostic scripts and *known error* information can be very useful in this context. If possible, the service desk agent solves the incident immediately and closes the incident.

If this is impossible, the incident is *escalated*.

This can be achieved in two ways:
- **Functional escalation** – If it is clear that the service desk cannot solve the incident (quickly enough), it must be escalated immediately for further support; if the organisation has a second line support group and the service desk believes that they can solve the incident, it forwards the incident to the second line; if it is clear that more technical knowledge is required for the incident and the second line support is unable to solve the incident within the agreed timeframe, it must be escalated to the third line support group
- **Hierarchical escalation** – The relevant IT managers must be warned in the event of more serious incidents (e.g. priority 1 incidents); hierarchical escalation is also used if there are inadequate resources to solve the incident. Hierarchical escalation means that the organisation calls upon the management higher up in the chain; senior managers are aware of the incident and can take the required steps, such as allocating additional resources or calling upon suppliers.

When handling an incident, each support group **investigates** what went wrong. It also makes a **diagnosis**. Document all these activities in the incident record to ensure that a complete overview of all activities is available.

In case the user is only looking for information, the service desk must be able to provide the answer quickly and solve the service request via the normal Request Fulfilment process.

If a possible solution has been determined, it must be implemented and tested: Solution and recovery. The following actions can then be taken:
- Ask the user to perform specific operations on his desktop
- The service desk can execute the solution centrally or use remote software to take control of the user's computer and implement a solution
- Ask a supplier to solve the error

Any support group can close an incident. A support group should not return the incident to the service desk otherwise the service desk only becomes an administrative group.

The incident management agent that resolved the incident first checks the incident has been solved and that the users are satisfied with the solution. Then the incident management agent selects the closing classification, updates the incident documentation, determines whether the incident could recur, and decide whether action should be taken to prevent this. The incident can then be formally closed.

It is beyond the scope of this publication to explore exactly how an organisation should set up all its policies and procedures. Suffice to say that updating and closing records or any kind must be properly defined, documented, and agreed, especially when external vendors are involved.

Information management
Most information used in incident management comes from the following sources.
- **Incident management tools**
  - Incident and problem history
  - Incident categories
  - Action taken to resolve incidents
  - Diagnostic scripts which can help first-line analysts to resolve the incident, or at least gather information that will help second- or third-line analysts resolve it faster.
- **Incident records**
  - Unique reference number
  - Incident classification
  - Date and time of recording and any subsequent activities
  - Name and identity of the person recording and updating the incident record
  - Name/organisation/contact details of affected user(s)
  - Description of the incident symptoms

- ○ Details of any actions taken to try to diagnose, resolve or recreate the incident
- ○ Incident category, impact, urgency and priority
- ○ Relationship with other incidents, problems, changes or known errors
- ○ Closure details, including time, category, action taken and identity of person closing the record
- **Service catalogue**
  - ○ Key service delivery objectives, levels and targets
  - ○ Information about the service in user-friendly terms
  - ○ Information that can be used for communicating with customers and users

Incident management also requires access and to the known error databases and to the CMS.

Interfaces
Like all processes, the incident management process has relationships with all other processes. However, some of the most visible relationships include but are not limited to the following.

Service design
- **Service level management** – To define the acceptable levels of service within which incident management works, including:
  - ○ Incident response times
  - ○ Impact definitions
  - ○ Target fix times
  - ○ Service definitions, which are mapped to users
  - ○ Rules for requesting services
  - ○ Expectations for providing feedback to users.
- **Information security management** – Providing security-related incident information by maintaining logs, audit files, and incident records
- **Capacity management** – Incident management provides a trigger for performance monitoring and capacity management assists in developing workarounds for incidents
- **Availability management** – To determine the availability of IT services and investigate improvements to reduce mean time to repair and increase mean time between failures

Service transition
- **Service asset and configuration management** – To provide the data used to identify and progress incidents. Incident management can assist with the verification activity of SACM when working to resolve an incident
- **Change management** – To implement a workaround or resolution using change models. Incident management identifies incidents arising from changes

Service operation
- **Problem management** – To investigate and resolve the underlying cause to prevent or reduce the impact of recurrence. To provide information on problems, known errors, and workarounds

- **Access management** – To records as incidents any detected unauthorised access attempts and security breaches

Triggers

Here are some of the triggers that may start the whole, or part of the, incident management process.

- Web-based incident-logging screen
- Event management tools
- Technical personnel
- Suppliers

Inputs

Here are some of the inputs required by the incident management process.

- Information about CIs and their status
- Information about known errors and their workarounds
- Communication and feedback about incidents and their symptoms
- Communication and feedback about RFCs and releases that have been implemented or planned for implementation
- Communication of events that were triggered from event management
- Operational and service level objectives
- Customer feedback on success of incident resolution activities and overall quality of incident management activities
- Agreed criteria for prioritising and escalating incidents

Outputs

Here are some of the outputs produced by the incident management process.

- Resolved incidents and actions taken to achieve their resolution
- Updated incident management records with accurate incident detail and history
- Updated classification of incidents to be used to support proactive problem management activities
- Raising of problem records for incidents where an underlying cause has not been identified
- Validation that incidents have not recurred for problems that have been resolved
- Feedback on incidents related to changes and releases
- Identification of CI associated with or impacted by incidents
- Satisfaction feedback from customers who have experienced incidents
- Feedback on level and quality of monitoring technologies and event management activities
- Communications about incident and resolution history detail to assist with identification of overall service quality

Critical success factors

The critical success factors, which change over time, for the incident management process may include but are not limited to the following.

- Resolve incidents as quickly as possible minimising impacts to the business
- Maintain quality of IT services
- Maintain user satisfaction with IT services
- Align incident management activities and priorities with those of the business
- Increase visibility and communication of incidents to business and IT support personnel

Metrics

The performance of the incident management process can be measured according to:
- Mean times
  - To repair
  - To restore service
  - Between failures
  - Between service/system incident
- Breakdown of incidents at each stage
- Size of current incident backlog for each IT service
- Percentage of incidents
- Average cost per incident
- Number and percentage of incidents...
  - Closed at "first point of contact"
  - Classified as major
  - Incorrectly assigned
  - Incorrectly categorised
  - Processed per it personnel
  - Related to changes and releases
  - Handled within agreed response
  - Resolved remotely, without the need for a visit

Challenges

Here are some of the potential challenges faced by the incident management process
- The ability to detect incidents as early as possible
- Convincing all IT personnel that all incidents must be logged, and encouraging the use of self-help web-based capabilities
- Availability of information about problems and known errors
- Integration into the CMS to determine relationships between CIs and to refer to the history of CIs
- Integration into the SLM process

Risks

Here are some of the potential risks faced by the incident management process.
- Lack of available or properly trained resources resulting in delays in handling incidents within agreed timescales
- Lack of support tools to raise alerts and prompt progress, causing a backlog in handling incidents

- Inadequate tools or lack of integration between tools, resulting in missing or poor access to data and information sources
- Poorly aligned or non-existent OLA and/or UC

8.7 Request Fulfilment

Introduction

ITIL uses the term "service request" as a general description for the varying requests that users submit to the IT department.

A **service request** is a request from a user for information, advice, a standard change, or access to a service.

For example, a service request can be a request for a password change or the additional installation of a software application on a certain work station. Because these requests occur on a regular basis and involve little risk, it is better that they are handled in a separate process.

Request fulfilment (implementation of requests) processes service requests from the users. The **objectives** of the request fulfilment process are:
- To offer users a channel through which they can request and receive services; to this effect an agreed approval and qualification process must exist
- To provide users and customers with information about available services and the procedure for obtaining these services
- To supply the components of standard services (for instance, licences and software media)
- To assist with general information, complaints or comments

Scope

The process for handling requests depends on the nature of the request. In most cases the process can be divided into a series of activities that need to be completed. Some organisations treat service requests as a special type of incident. However, there is an important difference between an incident and a service request. An incident is usually an unplanned event, whereas a service request tends to be something that can and must be planned.

Value for the business

The value of request fulfilment is the ability to offer fast and effective access to standard services that the business can use to improve the productivity or the quality of the business services and products.

Request fulfilment reduces the amount of "red tape" in requesting and receiving access to existing or new services. This reduces the cost for the supply of these services.

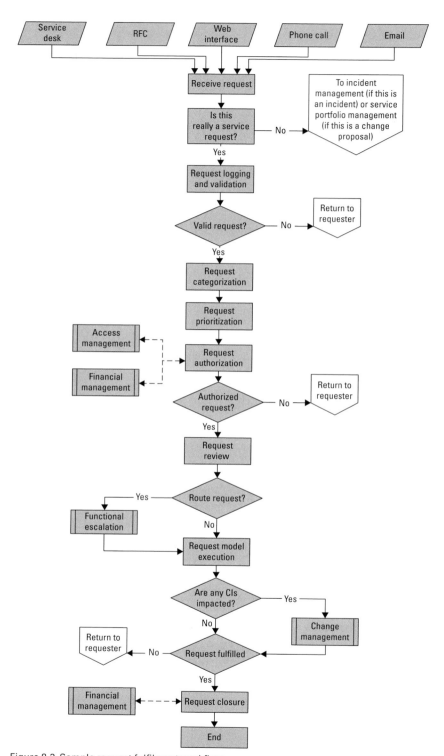

Figure 8.3 Sample request fulfilment workflow

Source: The Cabinet Office

Basic concepts

Many service requests recur on a regular basis. This is why a process flow can be devised in advance, stipulating the phases needed to handle the requests, the individuals or support groups involved, time limits and escalation paths. The service request is usually handled as a standard change.

Request models should be built for the defined types of request. As with incidents, problems and changes, the development of various statuses as requests should be monitored throughout their lifecycle.

Activities, working methods and techniques

Request fulfilment consists of the following activities, methods, and techniques:

- **Menu selection** – by means of request fulfilment, users can submit their own service request via a link to service management tools. In the ideal situation the user will be offered a menu via a web interface, so that they can select and enter the details of a service request
- **Financial approval** – most service requests have financial implications; the cost for handling a request must first be determined. It is possible to agree fixed prices for standard requests and give instant authorisation for these requests; in all other cases the cost must first be estimated, after which the user must give permission
- **Fulfilment** – the actual fulfilment activity depends on the nature of the service request; the service desk can handle simple requests, whereas others must be forwarded to specialised groups or suppliers
- **Closure** – once the service request has been completed the service desk will close off the request

Information management

- Which service is being requested
- Who requested and/or authorised the service
- Which process will be used to fulfil the request
- Who was it assigned to and what action was taken
- All relevant dates and times throughout the request lifecycle
- Closure details
- Request for change
- The service portfolio and the service catalogue
- Security policies

Interfaces

Like all processes, the request fulfilment process has relationships with all other processes. However, some of the most visible relationships include but are not limited to the following.

Service strategy
- **Financial management for IT services** – To identify, if required, the costs for fulfilling requests

Service design
- **Service catalogue management** – To ensure that available requests are well communicated to users

Service transition
- **Release and deployment management** – To create "release models" can be predefined, built and tested but only deployed upon request by those who want the "release"
- **Service asset and configuration management** – To reflect changes that may have been made as part of fulfilment activities
- **Change management** – To correctly log requests that are actually changes and vice versa and to progress RFCs through change management

Service operation
- **Incident management** – To correctly log requests that are actually incidents and vice versa and to progress incidents through incident management. Some organisations will develop separate processes to handles incidents and requests. Other organisations will use the incident process to handle request and simply use a category called "request"
- **Access management** – To ensure that those making requests are authorised to do so in accordance with the information security policy

Triggers
Here are some of the triggers that may start the whole, or part of the, request fulfilment process.
- User calling the service desk
- A user completing a form of self-help web-based input screen

Inputs
Here are some of the inputs required by the request fulfilment process.
- Work requests
- Authorisation forms
- Service requests
- RFCs
- Requests for information

Outputs
Here are some of the outputs produced by the request fulfilment process.
- Authorised/rejected service requests
- Request fulfilment status reports
- Fulfilled service requests
- Incidents
- RFCs/standard changes
- Asset/CI updates
- Updated request records

- Closed service requests
- Cancelled service requests

Critical success factors

The critical success factors, which change over time, for the request fulfilment process may include but are not limited to the following.

- Requests must be fulfilled in an efficient and timely manner that is aligned to agreed service level targets for each type of request
- Only authorised requests should be fulfilled
- User satisfaction must be maintained

Metrics

The performance of the request fulfilment process can be measured according to:

- Percentage of service requests…
  - Completed within agreed target times
  - Fulfilled that were appropriately authorised
  - At each stage of their lifecycle
  - Closed at "first point of contact"
  - Handled remotely, through automation, or without the need for a visit
- The average cost per type of service request
- The average elapsed time for handling each type of service request
- Level of user satisfaction with the handling of service requests
- The size of current backlog of outstanding service requests

Challenges

Here are some of the potential challenges faced by the request fulfilment process.

- Defining and documenting the type of requests that will be handled within the request fulfilment process
- Establishing self-help front-end capabilities that allow the users to interface successfully with the request fulfilment process
- Establishing agreed and communicated service level targets for each type of request
- Agreeing to the costs for fulfilling requests
- Agreeing which services will be standardised and who can request them
- Ensuring easy accessibility to information about which requests are available to the organisation
- Identifying and documented request models
- Setting and managing user and customer satisfaction

Risks

Here are some of the potential risks faced by the request fulfilment process.

- Poorly defined scope
- Poorly designed or implemented user interfaces
- Badly designed or operated back-end fulfilment processes
- Inadequate monitoring capabilities

8.8 Problem Management

Introduction
ITIL defines a problem as follows:

> *"A problem is the cause of one or more incidents."*

Problem management is responsible for the control of the lifecycle of all problems. The primary **objective** of problem management is to prevent problems and incidents, eliminate repeating incidents, and minimise the impact of incidents that cannot be prevented.

Scope
Problem management comprises all the activities needed to diagnose the underlying cause of incidents and to find a solution for these problems. It must also ensure that the solution is implemented via the correct control procedures, in other words through the use of change management and release management.

Value for the business
Problem management works together with incident management and change management to ensure improvements in the availability and quality of the IT service provision. When incidents are resolved the solution is registered. At a given moment this information is used to accelerate the incident handling and identify permanent solutions. This reduces the number of incidents and the handling time, resulting in shorter disruption times and fewer disruptions to the business critical systems.

Basic concepts
Many problems are unique and need to be handled separately. However, it is possible that some incidents may occur more than once as a result of underlying problems.

ITIL defines a known error as:

> *"A known error is an identified problem (an incident that has a documented root cause) OR a workaround. Known errors are created and managed throughout their lifecycle by problem management. Known errors may also be identified by development or suppliers."*

ITIL defines a workaround as:

> *"Workaround: reducing or eliminating the impact of an incident or problem for which a full resolution is not yet available."*

In addition to creating a Known Error Database (KEDB) for faster diagnoses, the creation of a **problem model** for the handling of future problems may be useful. Such a standard model supports the steps that need to be taken, the responsibilities of people involved and the necessary timescales.

Activities, methods, and techniques

Problem management consists of two important processes:

- **Reactive problem management** – performed by Service Operation
- **Proactive problem management** – initiated by Service Operation, but usually managed by CSI (Continual Service Improvement) (Chapter 9)

Reactive problem management consists of the following activities:

- Identification
- Registration
- Classification
- Prioritisation
- Investigation and diagnosis
- Decide on workarounds
- Identification of known errors
- Resolution
- Conclusion
- Review
- Correction of errors found

Identification of problems is carried out using the following methods:

- The service desk suspects or identifies an unknown cause of one or more incidents. This results in a problem registration. It may also be clear straightaway that an incident was caused by a major problem. In this case a problem registration takes place immediately.
- Analysis of an incident by the technical support group reveals that there is an underlying problem.
- There is automatic tracing of an infrastructural or application error, whereby event or alert tools automatically create an incident registration that highlights the need for a problem registration.
- The supplier reports a problem that needs to be resolved.
- Analysis of incidents takes place as part of corrective problem management. This results in a problem registration so that the underlying cause can be investigated further.

Analyse incident and problem data on a regular basis in order to identify trends. To this effect an efficient and detailed classification of incidents and problems is required, as well as regular reporting of patterns and problem areas.

Irrespective of the identification method, all details of the problem must be registered (**problem registration**), so that a comprehensive historic report is created. The information must be date and time stamped, so that proper control and escalation are possible.

Problems must be classified in the same way as incidents, so that the true nature of the problem can be established quickly and easily. **Problem classification** provides useful management information.

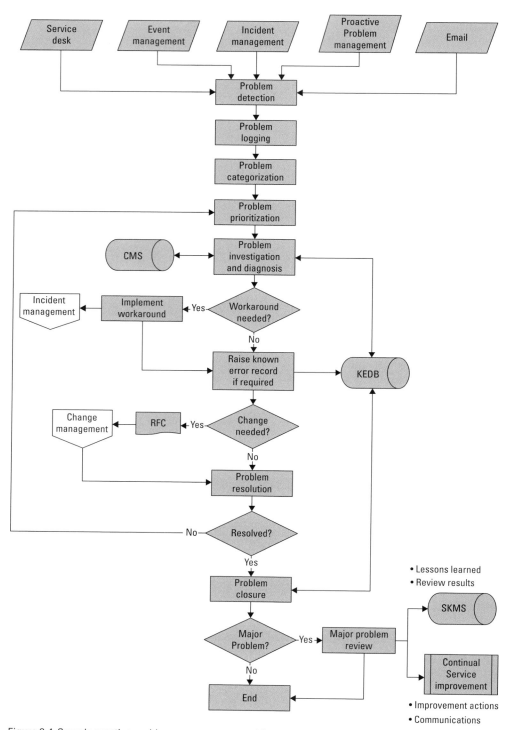

Figure 8.4 Sample reactive problem management workflow

Source: The Cabinet Office

As is the case for incidents, problems must also be given a **priority** in the same manner and for the same reasons. In this context also take into account the frequency and impact of the related incidents and the seriousness of the problems. Examples of such considerations are:

- Can the system be repaired or does it need to be replaced?
- What are the costs?
- How many people, and with what expertise are needed to resolve the problem?
- How much time is needed to resolve the problem?
- How big is the problem?

In order to find the underlying cause of the incident or the series of incidents (the problem) and make a **diagnosis**, an **investigation** must be performed. The speed and nature of this investigation depend on the impact, seriousness, and urgency of the problem. Use the proper level of resources and expertise to find a solution.

Recreating the failure is a valuable means in understanding what has gone wrong and then trying various ways of finding the most appropriate and cost-effective resolution to the problem. It is less disruptive to use a test environment that mirrors the live environment without causing further disruption to users.

Many problem analyses, diagnosis and solution techniques are available, including the following.

Table 8.2 Sample problem analyses, diagnosis and solution techniques

Chronological analysis	Affinity mapping
Pain value analysis	Hypothesis testing
Kepner and Tregoe	Technical observation post
Brainstorming	Ishikawa diagrams
5-Whys	Pareto analysis
Fault isolation	

In some cases a temporary solution, a **workaround**, is possible for incidents that were caused by a problem. It is important, however, that the problem record remains open and that the details about the workaround are included in the problem record.

As soon as the diagnosis has been made (the cause is known) *or* if a workaround has been found, the identified known errors must be listed in a known error report and placed in the known error database. If other incidents and problems occur they can be identified and the service can be resumed more quickly.

As soon as a **solution** has been found it should, ideally, be applied to resolve the problem. In reality, there are preventative measures to make sure that the solution does not cause further problems. If a change in in a CI is needed a *Request for Change* is required that must follow the steps of the change management process.

If the change has been completed and successfully evaluated and the solution has been applied, the problem record can formerly be **closed off**, as can the related incident records that are still outstanding. Remember to check whether the record contains a full description of all the events.

After every **major problem** a **review** must be performed to learn lessons for the future. In particular the review must assess:
• What went well?
• What went wrong?
• What can be done better in future?
• How the same problem can be prevented from recurring
• Whether a third party is responsible and whether any follow-up actions are needed

It is very rare that new applications, systems, or software releases do not contain **errors**. In most cases a priority system is used during testing that removes the most serious errors, but it is possible that minor errors are not corrected.

Information management
The *CMS* contains details on all the components of the IT infrastructure and on the relationship between these components. It is a valuable source for problem diagnosis and for the evaluation of the impact of problems.

The purpose of a **Known Error Database** (KEDB) is to store knowledge about incidents and problems and how they were remedied, so that a quicker diagnosis and solution can be found if further incidents and problems occur.

The known error registration must contain the exact details about the error and the symptoms that occurred, together with the exact details of a workaround or solution that can be implemented to resume the service or resolve the problem.

It may be that there is no business case for a permanent solution for certain problems. For instance, if the problem does not cause serious disruptions, a workaround already exists, and the costs of resolving the problem exceed the advantages of a permanent solution, problem management may decide to tolerate the problem.

Information management
Most information used in problem management comes from the following sources:
• Configuration management system
• Known error database

Interfaces

Like all processes, the problem management process has relationships with all other processes. However, some of the most visible relationships include but are not limited to the following.

Service strategy
- **Financial management for IT services** – To assist in assessing the impact of proposed resolutions or workarounds, as well as pain-value analysis. Problem management provides information about the cost of resolving and preventing problems

Service design
- **Availability management** – To reduce downtime and increase uptime using availability management methods and techniques, and helping in assessing proactive measures
- **Capacity management** – To improve performance issues, to assist problem investigation using capacity management methods and techniques, and helping in assessing proactive measures
- **IT service continuity management** – To act as an entry point into IT SCM to address an unresolved significant problem before it impacts the business
- **Service level management** – To contribute in improving the service levels. SLM provides prioritisation parameters

Service transition
- **Change management** – To ensure that all resolutions or workarounds that require a change to a CI are submitted using an RFC
- **Service asset and configuration management** – To identify faulty CIs and also to determine the impact of problems and resolutions
- **Release and deployment management** – To assist in ensuring that new known errors in the development KEDB are transferred into the problem known error database
- **Knowledge management** – The problem and know error databases are part of the SKMS.

Continual service improvement
- **The seven-step improvement process** – To provide a basis for identifying opportunities for service improvement

Triggers

Here are some of the triggers that may start the whole, or part of the, problem management process.
- Reactive problem management
- One or more incidents
- Release testing
- Notifications from suppliers
- Proactive problem management
- Identification of patterns and trends

- A review of...
  - Operational logs
  - Operational communications
  - Event logs

Inputs
Here are some of the inputs required by the problem management process.
- Incident records
- Incident reports and histories
- Information about CIs and their status
- Communication and feedback about incidents and their symptoms
- Communication and feedback about RFCs and releases
- Communication of events from event management
- Operational and service level targets
- Customer feedback
- Agreed problem prioritisation and escalation criteria
- Risk management reports

Outputs
Here are some of the outputs produced by the problem management process.
- Resolved problems and actions taken to achieve their resolution
- New or updated problem management records
- Request for changes
- Workarounds for incidents
- New or updated known error records
- Problem management reports
- Major problem review action items and reports

Critical success factors
The critical success factors, which change over time, for the problem management process may include but are not limited to the following.
- Minimise the impact to the business of incidents that cannot be prevented
- Maintain quality of IT services through elimination of recurring incidents
- Provide overall quality and professionalism of problem handling activities to maintain business confidence in IT capabilities

Metrics
The performance of the problem management process can be measured according to:
- The number of known errors properly added to the KEDB
- Number and percentage of
  - Incidents closed by "first point of contact"
  - Major problem reviews completed successfully and on time
  - Problems incorrectly assigned
  - Problems incorrectly categorised
  - Outstanding problems and the associated trends
  - Problems resolved/not resolved within service level targets

- Average incident resolution time for incidents linked to problem records
- Average cost per problem

Challenges

Here are some of the potential challenges faced by the problem management process.

- Establishing an effective incident management process and related tools
- Improving the analytical and investigative skills and capabilities of problem management personnel
- Ensuring that problem management personnel are able to use all resources available (CMS and SKMS) to investigate and resolve problems
- Ensuring on-going training of technical personnel in both the business implications of the services they support as well as the technical aspects of their job
- The ability to...
  - Link incident records to problems records
  - Integrate problem management activities with the CMS
  - Have a good working relationship between all four functions; service desk, IT Operations, technical and application management as well as with suppliers

Risks

Here are some of the potential risks faced by the problem management process.

- Lack of available or properly trained resources, resulting in delays in handling incidents within agreed timescales
- Lack of support tools to raise alerts and prompt progress, causing a backlog in handling incidents
- Inadequate tools or lack of integration between tools, resulting in missing or poor access to data and information sources
- Poorly aligned or non-existent OLA and/or UC
- Lack of analytical and investigative skills for problem management personnel

8.9 Access Management

Introduction

Access management grants authorised users the right to use a service, but denies unauthorised users access. Some organisations also call it "rights management" or "identity management".

Scope

Access management ensures that users have access to a service, but it does not guarantee that access is always available at the agreed times. This is handled by availability management.

Access management can be initiated via a number of mechanisms, such as the service desk, by means of a *service request*.

Value for the business
Access management has the following value:
- Controlled access to services enables the organisation to maintain confidentiality of its information more effectively
- Personnel have the right access level to do their jobs properly
- The risk of errors during data entry or the use of a vital service by an unqualified user is lower
- There is the option to withdraw access rights more easily when access may be necessary for compliance (e.g. SOX, HIPAA, and CobiT)

Basic concepts
Access management has the following basic concepts:
- **Access** – refers to the level and scope of the functionality of a service or data that a user is allowed to use
- **Identity** – refers to the information about the persons who the organisation distinguish as individuals; establishes their status in the organisation
- **Rights** (also called privileges) – refers to the actual settings for a user; which service (group) they are allowed to use; typical rights include reading, writing, executing, editing and deleting
- **Services or service groups** – most users have access to multiple services; it is therefore more effective to grant every user or group of users access to an entire series of services that they are allowed to use simultaneously
- **Directory services** – refers to a specific type of tool used to manage access and rights

Activities, methods, and techniques
Access (or limitation of access) can be requested via a number of mechanisms, such as:
- A standard request generated by the human resources department; this generally occurs when someone is hired, promoted or leaves the company
- A Request for Change (RFC)
- An RFC submitted via the request fulfilment process
- Execution of an authorised script or option

Access management consists of the following activities:
- **Verification** – Access management must verify every access request for an IT service from two perspectives:
  - Is the user requesting access truly the person he/she says he/she is?
  - Does the user have a legitimate reason to use the service?
- **Granting rights** – Access management does not decide who gets access to what IT services; it only executes the policy and rules defined by Service Strategy and Service Design.
  - The more groups and roles exist, the greater the chance of a role conflict occurring. In this context, role conflicts refer to a situation in which two specific roles or groups allocated to a user can cause trouble due to conflicting interests. One example is that one role requires access while the other forbids it.

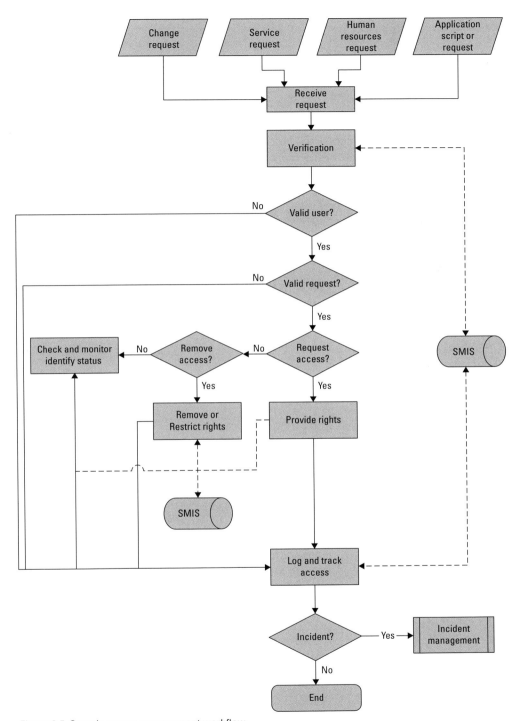

Figure 8.5 Sample access management workflow

Source: The Cabinet Office

- **Monitoring identity status** – User roles may vary over time, with an impact on their service needs; examples of what may change a role are: job changes, promotion, dismissal, retirement, or death.
- **Registering and monitoring access** – Access management does not only respond to requests; it must also ensure that the rights it has granted are used correctly.
  - This is why access monitoring and control must be included in the monitoring activities of all technical and application management functions as well as all Service Operation processes.
- **Revoking or limiting rights** – In addition to granting rights to use a service, access management is also responsible for withdrawing those rights; but it cannot make the actual decision.

Information management
Identity is usually established using some of the following pieces of information:
- Name
- Address
- Contact details
- Physical documentation
- Unique identifier
- Biometric information
- Expiration date

A user identity is provided to anyone with a legitimate requirement to access IT services or organisational information:
- Employees; IT and non-IT
- Contractors
- Vendor personnel
- Customers
- Users, groups, roles and service groups

While each user has an individual identity, and each IT service can be seen as an entity in its own right, it is often helpful to group them together so that they can be managed more easily. Sometimes the terms "user profile", "user template", or "user role" are used to describe this type of grouping.

Interfaces
Like all processes, the access management process has relationships with all other processes. However, some of the most visible relationships include but are not limited to:
- Appropriate controls and rights to services should be assured in accordance with the information security policy

Service strategy
- **Demand management** – To identify the necessary resource levels to handle expected volumes of requests for access
- **Strategy management for IT services** – To determine if access management activities could be more efficient if handled locally rather than centrally

Service design
- **Information security management** – To provide the security and data protection policies and tools needed to execute access management. Human resource management to assist in verifying user identity and the services they are entitled to use
- **Service catalogue management** – To provide methods and means by which users can access the services they are entitled to use
- **IT service continuity management** – To manage access to services in the event of a major business disruption
- **SLM** – To maintain the agreements (SLA, OLA, UC) for access to each service

Service transition
- **Change management** – To control the actual requests for access because any request for access is usually processed as either a standard change or a service request
- **Service asset and configuration management** – To identify data storage and interrogate CIs to determine current access details

Service operation
- **Request fulfilment** – To provide methods and means by which users can request access to the services they are entitled to use

Triggers
Here are some of the triggers that may start the whole, or part of the, access management process.
- An RFC
- A service request
- A request from human resources management
- A request from a manager
- A request from a user

Inputs
Here are some of the inputs required by the access management process.
- Information security policies
- Operational and service level requirements and targets for access management activities
- Authorised requests to grant or terminate access rights

Outputs
Here are some of the outputs produced by the access management process.
- Provision of access to IT services as per information security policies
- Access management records and reports
- Timely communications concerning inappropriate access or abuse of services

Critical success factors

The critical success factors, which change over time, for the access management process may include but are not limited to the following.

- Ensuring that the confidentiality, integrity and availability of services are protected in accordance with the information security policy
- Providing timely communications about improper access or abuse of services on a timely basis
- Providing appropriate access to services on a timely basis that meets business needs

Metrics

The performance of the access management process can be measured according to:

- Number and percentage of…
  - Incidents regarding inappropriate attempts to access a service
  - Incidents requiring a reset of access rights
  - Incidents caused by incorrect access settings
  - Requests for access that were provided within established SLA and OLA
- Number of audit findings regarding users who have changed roles or left the company
- Average duration of access-related incidents

Challenges

Here are some of the potential challenges faced by the access management process.

- Monitoring and reporting on access activity, access-related incidents and problems
- Verifying…
  - The identity of a user
  - The identity of the approving person or body
  - A user qualifies for access to a specific service
- Linking multiple access rights to an individual user
- Determining the status of users at any time
- Managing changes to access requirements for a user
- Restricting access rights to unauthorised users
- Building and maintaining a database of all users and the rights that they have been granted

Risks

Here are some of the potential risks faced by the access management process.

- Lack of appropriate supporting technologies to manage and control access to services
- Controlling access from "back door" sources such as application interfaces and changes to firewall rules for special needs
- Managing and controlling access to services by external third-party suppliers
- Lack of management support for access management activities and controls
- Ensuring that necessary levels of access to services and the necessary management controls are provided without hindering the business

8.10 Implementation

Here are general implementation guidelines for Service Operation.

Managing change in Service Operation

Service Operation personnel must implement changes without negative impact on the stability of offered IT services.

Change triggers

There are many things that can trigger change in the Service Operation environment, including:

- New or to be upgraded hardware or software
- Legislation
- Obsolete components
- Business imperatives
- Process enhancements
- Changes in management or personnel
- Change in service levels
- New services

Change assessment

Involve Service Operation as early as possible in assessment of all changes. This way, operational issues will be handled properly.

Assessing and managing risk in Service Operation

In a number of cases, it is necessary that risk evaluation is conducted swiftly, in order to take appropriate action. This is especially necessary for potential changes or known errors, but also in case of failures, projects, environmental risks, vendors, security risks, and new clients that need support.

Operational personnel in Service Design and Transition

Service Operation personnel should be particularly involved in the early stages of Service Design and Transition. This will ensure that the new services will actually work in practice and that they can be supported by Service Operation personnel.

Planning and implementation of service management technologies

There are several factors that organisations must plan before and during deployment of ITSM support tools, such as:

- Licences
- Deployment
- Capacity checks
- Timing of technology deployment
- The type of introduction – the choice of a big-bang introduction or a phased approach

Next, we will discuss some challenges that Service Operation must overcome.

Lack of engagement with development and project personnel

Historically, there is a separation between Service Operation personnel and personnel involved in the development of new applications or in the execution of projects that deliver new functionality in an operational environment.

This perception is damaging because contemplating Service Operation issues is best done at the beginning of new developments or projects, when there is still time to include these factors in the planning stages.

Service Design and Service Transition describe the steps necessary to include IT production issues in new developments and projects right from the start.

Justifying funding

Often is it difficult to justify expenditure for Service Operation because funds spent are often considered to be "infrastructure" costs.

In reality, many investments in IT service management, especially for Service Operation, can save money and show a positive ROI as well as improving service quality.

Challenges for Service Operation managers

Managers in Service Operation can be faced with the following challenges:

- Service Design has the tendency to focus on one service while Service Operation aims at delivering and supporting all services.
- Service Design will often be conducted in projects while Service Operation focuses on continual management processes and activities that recur.
- The two phases of the lifecycle possess different metrics that encourage Service Design to conclude the project on time, as specified and within the arranged budget. However, it is hard to predict how the service will look, and what will be the costs after roll-out and some initial time in service. If the service does not work as expected, IT operations management will be responsible.
- Ineffective Service Transition may hamper the transition from design to production.

Another series of challenges involves metrics. Each alternative structure will introduce a different combination of items that can be easy or difficult to measure.

A third set of challenges concerns the use of virtual teams. Traditional, hierarchical management structures are unable to handle the complexity and diversity of most organisations. Knowledge management and mapping authority structures becomes increasingly important as organisations expand and diversify. Service Strategy will expand on this further.

One of the most important challenges facing Service Operation managers is the balance between the many internal and external relationships. There is an increasing use of networks, partnerships, and shared services models. A Service Operation manager must invest in relation management knowledge and skills in order to handle the complexity of these challenges.

Critical success factors

Management support
Support from higher and middle management is necessary for all IT service management activities and processes, especially in Service Operation. It is crucial for obtaining sufficient financing and resources. Senior management must also offer visible support during the launch of new Service Operation initiatives.

Middle management must also provide the necessary support and actions.

Business support
It is also important that Service Operation is supported by the business units. This works better if the Service Operation personnel involve the business in all their activities, and are open about successes and failures.

Regular communication with the business is crucial to building a good relationship and to ensuring support; Service Operation will be better placed to understand the aspirations and concerns of the business. Additionally, the business can provide feedback on the efforts of Service Operation to satisfy the business needs.

Hiring and retaining personnel
The correct number of personnel with the correct skills is critical for successful Service Operation. Consider the following challenges:
- Projects for new services often clearly specify what the new skills must be, but may underestimate how many personnel are needed and how skills can be retained.
- There may be a lack of personnel with solid knowledge of service management; having good technicians is important, but there must also be a certain number of people who have knowledge of both technological and service problems.
- Because personnel with both technological and service knowledge are fairly rare, they are often specially trained; it is important to retain them by offering a clear career path and solid compensation.
- Personnel are often assigned new tasks too quickly, while they are still extremely busy with their current workloads. Successful service management projects may require a short term investment in temporary workers.

Service management training
Good training and awareness can provide great advantages. In addition to increasing expertise, they can generate enthusiasm in people. Service Operation personnel must be aware of the consequences of their actions for the organisation. A "service management culture" must be created. Service management will only be successful if the people are focused on overall service management objectives.

Appropriate tools

Many service management processes and activities cannot be effectively executed without proper support tools. Senior management must ensure that financing for such tools is included in annual budgets, and must support acquisition, implementation, and maintenance.

Test validity

The quality of IT services provided by Service Operation depends on the quality of systems and components that are delivered in the operational environment.

The quality level will improve considerably if solid and complete testing of new components and releases is performed in a timely manner. Also, the documentation should be independently tested for completeness and quality.

Measuring and reporting

Clear agreements are necessary regarding the way in which things are measured and reported; all personnel will have clear targets to aim for, and IT and business managers will be able to evaluate quickly and simply whether progress is being made and which areas deserve extra attention.

Risks

Consider the following risks:

- **Service loss** – The greatest risk run by Service Operation is the loss of essential IT services with adverse impact on personnel, customers, and finances. In extreme cases, loss may occur to life and health, when IT services are used for essential health and security purposes.
- **Risks to successful Service Operation**:
  - Insufficient financing and resources
  - Loss of momentum
  - Loss of important personnel
  - Resistance to change
  - Lack of management support
  - If the design fails to meet the requirements, successful implementation will never deliver the required results; this will require new design
  - In some organisations, service management is viewed with suspicion by both IT and the business. The advantages of service management must be clear for all stakeholders; this problem can be solved by clear service level management and careful communication during Service Design

9 Continual service improvement phase

9.1 Continual Service Improvement

This short section provides a summary of the updates between the 2007 edition and the 2011 edition for the ITIL core book Continual Service Improvement published by TSO.

The seven-step improvement process and its relationship with the Plan-Do-Check-Act cycle (Deming Cycle) and knowledge management have been clarified. The continual service improvement (CSI) model has been re-named the CSI approach, and the concept of a CSI register has been introduced as a place to record details of all improvement initiatives within an organisation.

Minor changes have been made throughout the publication to clarify the meaning and to improve readability. Particular emphasis has been placed on documenting the interfaces between CSI and other lifecycle stages.

Table 9.1 Summary of updates: ITIL Continual Service Improvement

Area of update	Description
Introduction of the CSI register	The CSI register is where all improvement opportunities are recorded. Each opportunity should be categorised as a small, medium, or large undertaking. An indication of the amount of time it would take to complete the initiative should also be provided, along with the associated benefits. Together, this information will help produce a clear prioritised list of improvement initiatives. A full description of the CSI register is given in Chapter 3, and an example is provided in Appendix C.
Service measurement and service reporting	The treatment of service measurement and service reporting has been clarified. Because all processes have an element of measurement and reporting embedded within them, service measurement and service reporting are not considered to be processes. Therefore, these topics are covered in Chapters 3 and 5, rather than Chapter 4.
Seven-step improvement process	It is now clear that the seven-step process only contains seven steps. Some step names and activities have been amended, but the overall purpose of the process remains unchanged. The interface with the Deming Cycle and with knowledge management has been clarified.
The CSI approach	The CSI model has been re-named the CSI approach, because it is an approach to continual improvement and not a model.

9.2   Introduction

IT must continually align and re-align IT services to the changing business needs by identifying and implementing improvements to IT services that support the business. ITIL places this within the lifecycle phase of **Continual Service Improvement**.

In English there is a difference between *continual* and *continuous*:

Continuous means that the organisation is involved in an activity without interruption; the efforts are constantly at the same level; for example, continuous operation

Continual means a succession of closely placed activities; in this way a sequence of improvement efforts is created: continual improvement

An IT service is created by a number of activities. The quality of these activities and the process which links these activities determine the quality of the eventual service. CSI focuses on the activities and processes to improve the quality of services. To this end, it uses the *Plan-Do-Check-Act* Cycle of Deming (PDCA). This cycle prescribes a consolidation phase for each improvement, to embed the new procedures in the organisation. This implies a repeating pattern of improvement efforts with varying levels of intensity, instead of a single continuing improvement effort which is always on the same level. This is the reason why, in ITIL, the "C" of CSI stands for continual and not continuous.

Measuring and analysing is crucial to CSI; by measuring it is possible to identify which services are profitable and which services can do better. The **CSI improvement process** has a seven step plan. Creating a **Service Improvement Plan** (SIP) is an SLM activity within the CSI scope. The section "Processes and other activities" pursues this matter in more depth. Next we will describe the roles which execute the core activities, followed by the methods, techniques, and technology which assist them. The interfaces between service level management and CSI are dealt with in the last section on interfaces with the other phases and IT service management processes from the ITIL lifecycle. First of all, we will consider the justification of CSI and a number of basic concepts.

Purpose and objectives

The purpose of CSI is for continual improvement of the effectiveness and efficiency of IT services, allowing them to meet the business requirements better. This entails both achieving and surpassing the objectives (**effectiveness**), and obtaining these objectives at the lowest cost possible (**efficiency**). To increase the effectiveness you can, for instance, reduce the number of errors in a process. To make a process more efficient you can eliminate unnecessary activities or automate manual operations.

By measuring and analysing the process results in all Service Lifecycle phases you can determine which results are structurally worse than others. These offer the highest improvement probability.

CSI mainly measures and monitors the following matters:
- **Process compliance** – Does the organisation follow the new or modified service management processes and does it use the new tools?
- **Quality** – Do the various process activities meet their goals?
- **Performance** – How efficient is the process? What are the elapsed times?
- **Business value of a process** – Does the process make a difference? Is it effective? How does the customer rate the process?

The main **objectives** of CSI are:
- To measure and analyse service level achievements by comparing them to the requirements in the Service Level Agreement (SLA)
- To recommend improvements in all phases of the lifecycle
- To introduce activities which will increase the quality, efficiency, effectiveness and customer satisfaction of the services and the IT service management processes
- To operate more cost effective IT services without sacrificing customer satisfaction
- To use suitable quality management methods for improvement activities

Scope
The scope of CSI contains three important areas:
- General quality of the IT management
- Continual tuning of the IT services to the current and future needs of the business
- Continual tuning of the IT service portfolio
- The maturity of the IT processes which make the services possible

9.3   Basic concepts

The CSI register
The CSI register contains important information for the overall service provider. It is an integral part of the service knowledge management system (SKMS).

The CSI register provides both structure and visibility to CSI by ensuring that all improvement initiatives are recorded and benefits realised. The benefits are measured to demonstrate the achievement of the desired outcomes. Proposed benefits should be quantified in terms of key performance indicator (KPI) metrics. This will assist the prioritising of initiatives delivering the most significant and cost-effective incremental benefit to the business.

CSI and Organisational Change
In order to make continual improvement a permanent part of the organisational culture, a change in mentality is often needed. This is one of the most difficult aspects of CSI and, in reality, many CSI programs fail because they do not (or cannot) achieve this cultural change. John P. Kotter, *Professor of Leadership* at the Harvard Business

School, examined over a hundred companies and discovered eight crucial steps needed to successfully change an organisation:

- **Create a sense of urgency** – For instance, answer the question "what if we do nothing?"
- **Form a leading coalition** – A single pioneer cannot change an entire organisation; a small key team is needed with the necessary authority and resources. This team can be expanded as the support grows
- **Create a vision** – A good vision formulates the purpose of CSI, provides direction, motivates, coordinates and formulates goals for the senior management. Make these goals SMART: *Specific, Measurable, Achievable/Appropriate, Realistic/Relevant* and *Timely/Time-bound*. Without a vision, a CSI program will soon become a repository of projects which do not have obvious benefits for the organisation; tailor the vision to the client's requirements
- **Communicate the vision** – Stakeholders must know what the vision is, what its use is for them, and why CSI is needed; to achieve this, put together a communication plan, and demonstrate by example
- **Empower others to act on the vision** – Remove obstacles, give direction by setting clear goals and supply people with the proper resources such as tools and training; create security and self-confidence; only then will they be able to take responsibility for their part in CSI
- **Plan for and create quick wins** – Evaluate per service or process what can be improved rapidly; plan this, execute it and communicate it in order to increase support
- **Consolidate improvements and create more change** – Quick wins convince and motivate; medium term successes offer confidence in the organisation's own improvement capabilities and foresee a set of standard procedures. But in the long run improvement can only be considered a success if people and processes are continually improving themselves
- **Institutionalise the changes**:
  - Hire personnel with experience in best practices in the field of IT management
  - From day one hand out work instructions
  - Clarify what the procedures are
  - Train personnel in IT management
  - Match the goals and reports to changing demands
  - Define clear action points in the minutes
  - Integrate new IT solutions and development projects in existing processes

Combined with good project management, these steps will considerably increase the chances of success.

The PDCA Cycle

A "*big bang*" approach does not usually result in a successful improvement program. That is why the American statistician Dr. W Edwards Deming developed a systematic improvement approach in the 1980s: the ***Plan-Do-Check-Act* Cycle (PDCA)**:

- **Plan** – What needs to happen, who will do what and how?
- **Do** – Execute the planned activities

- **Check** – Check whether the activities yield the desired result
- **Act** – Adjust the plan in accordance to the checks

Next is a consolidation phase to engrain the changes into the organisation. The Cycle is also known as the **Deming Cycle** (Figure 9.1).

Continual quality control and consolidation

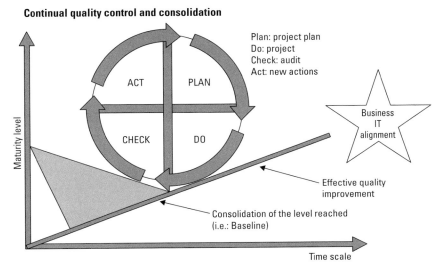

Figure 9.1 Sample PDCA cycle

Source: The Cabinet Office

CSI uses the PDCA Cycle in two areas:
- Implementation of CSI
- Continual improvement of services and processes

Now, we discuss the Cycle for the *implementation of CSI* (Figure 9.2):
- **Plan CSI**:
  - Determine the scope
  - Determine the requirements CSI must meet
  - Set goals, for instance using gap analysis
  - Define action points
  - Determine which checks need to be executed during the check phase
  - Determine the interfaces between CSI and the rest of the lifecycle
  - Determine which process activities need to be introduced
  - Set (management) roles and responsibilities
  - Find out which tools are needed to support and document processes
  - Select the methods and techniques to measure and document the quality and effectiveness of the services and processes
- **Implement CSI (*do*)**:
  - Determine the budget
  - Document roles and responsibilities

○ Determine the CSI policy, plans and procedures, maintain these, communicate about them and train your personnel
○ Supply monitoring, analysis and reporting tools
○ Integrate CSI with Service Strategy, Service Design, Service Transition and Service Operation
- **Monitor, measure, and evaluate CSI (*check*)**:
    ○ Report on the accomplishments with regard to the plans
    ○ Evaluate the documentation
    ○ Perform process assessments and audits
    ○ Formulate proposals for process improvement
- **Adjust CSI (*act*)**:
    ○ Introduce the improvements
    ○ Adjust the policy, procedures, roles, and responsibilities

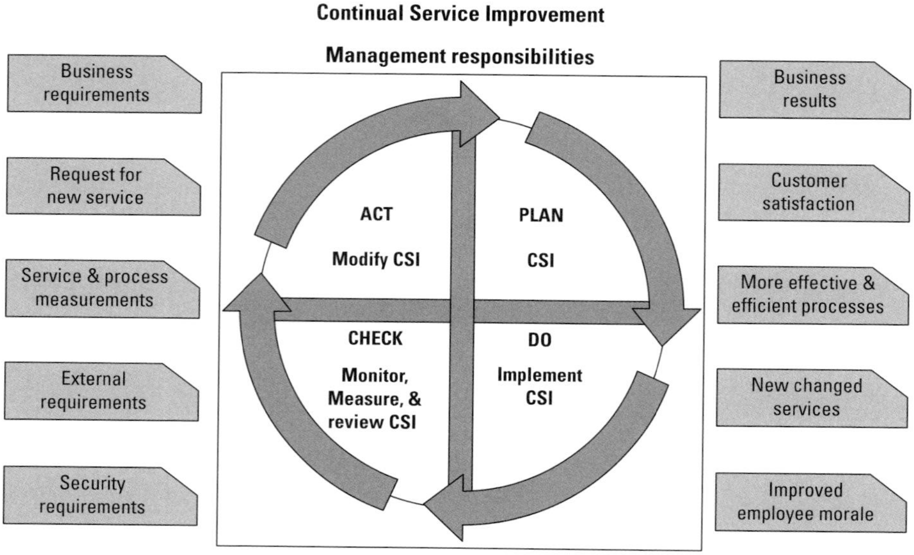

Figure 9.2 Sample PDCA cycle for the improvement of services
Source: The Cabinet Office

During the implementation of CSI all phases play an important part. In the second area where the PDCA Cycle is used – *continual improvement of services and processes* – the focus is mainly on the "check" and "act" phases. There are, however, also activities in the "plan" and "do" phase which are involved:
- Plan improvement initiatives:
    ○ Set goals and check methods
    ○ Perform gap analysis
    ○ Determine action points
- Implement the improvement initiative:
    ○ Eliminate the discrepancies found
    ○ Provide a smooth execution of the process

- Monitor, check, and evaluate services and processes:
  - Compare the checks after the improvement to those before the improvement and to the goals set in the plan phase
  - Determine whether the discrepancies found need to be eliminated
  - Make recommendations for the improvement such as adjusting the service catalogue and the new SLA checks
- Continual improvement of services and processes:
  - Introduce the improvements
  - Determine which discrepancies need to be addressed; this constitutes the input for the plan phase

Metrics, KPI and CSF

An IT service manager needs to know whether their organisation as a whole meets its goals and which processes contribute to this. **Metrics** measures the results of a process or activity by determining whether a certain variable meets its set target. For instance, a metric measures whether the required numbers of incidents are resolved within one hour.

Metrics are mainly interpreted on a strategic and tactical level. They must describe all processes within an organisation. Three types are needed for CSI:

- **Technology metrics** – Measure the performance and availability of components and applications
- **Process metrics** – Measure the performance of service management processes; they stem from **Key Performance Indicators** (**KPIs**), which in turn stem from **Critical Success Factors** (**CSFs**); also see step four of the CSI improvement process: "process data"; these metrics help to determine the improvement opportunities for each process
- **Service metrics** – The results of the end service; these are measured using component metrics

A metric originates from the goal set by an organisation. If the business views IT as a *cost centre* then it will probably want to decrease the costs. If, however, it sees IT as the enabler of the company, then the goal will probably be to develop flexible services which will decrease the *time-to-market*. The measuring system should not focus solely on only one of the three aspects of money, time, and quality, otherwise the remaining two aspects will receive insufficient attention.

For the business mission, a **CSF** is defined as elements essential to achieving the mission. The **KPIs** following on from these CSFs determine the quality, performance, value, and process compliance. They can either be *qualitative* (such as customer satisfaction), or *quantitative* (such as costs of a printer incident).

At the start of the improvement program two to three KPIs per CSF will already supply a great deal of information which will need to be processed. The KPIs can be extended or adjusted later according to new developments. For instance, if the organisation has achieved its goals or when new service management processes are introduced.

Determine if the KPI is suitable by answering these questions:
- Do we achieve our goals if we achieve the KPI?
- Can the KPI be interpreted correctly? Does it help in determining the action needed?
- Who needs the information? When? How often? How fast does the information need to be available?
- Is the KPI stable and accurate or subject to external, uncontrollable influences?
- How easy is it to adjust the KPI to new developments?
- To what extent can the KPI be measured now; under which circumstances?
- Who collects and analyses the measurements? Who is responsible for the improvements resulting from this information?

Data, information, knowledge, and wisdom (DIKW)

Metrics supply quantitative **data**; for instance, that the service desk registers 12,000 incidents each month. CSI transforms this data into qualitative **information**, a received and understood message which stems from processed and grouped data; such as the fact that 18 percent of the incidents reported are related to the organisation's email facility. By combining information with experience, context, interpretation and reflection it becomes **knowledge**; for example, since we know that the organisation is a web store, we can determine the impact of the incidents concerning the email facility.

What it comes down to in CSI is **wisdom**: being able to make the correct assessments and the correct decisions by using the data, information, and knowledge in the best possible way. For example, because we know the impact of the email incidents on the client, we can decide to focus on this service because we want to improve our customer customer. The CSI improvement process focuses on the acquirement of wisdom (see the section "Processes and other activities" and step 6 in the CSI improvement process about service reporting).

Governance

Governance drives organisations and controls them. *Corporate governance* provides a good, honest, transparent, and responsible management of an organisation. *Business governance* results in good company performances. Together they are known as *enterprise governance*.

IT governance is also part of *enterprise governance*. It shapes the processes and structure of an IT organisation and ensures that it achieves its goals. Complying with the new rules, such as the American *Sarbanes-Oxley Act* from 2002 (corporate governance), and constantly performing better at a lower cost (business governance) are both part of IT governance.

These two developments are the main motive for CSI: IT service providers must offer their services from a strategic rather than a tactical perspective. IT departments which only focus on technology will soon become less appealing to their business.

An ITSM standard such as ITIL helps to control an organisation by forging it into a coherent system of roles, responsibilities, processes, policy, and *controls*.

CSI policies and procedures

The CSI policies capture agreements concerning the measuring, reporting, the service levels, the CSFs, the KPIs, and the evaluations. These must be known to the whole organisation. Most organisations assess the process results each month. It is wise to evaluate new services more often.

An IT organisation should implement the following CSI policies:
* All improvement initiatives must go through the change management process
* All functional groups are responsible for CSI activities
* CSI roles and responsibilities are recorded and announced (see section "Organisation")

9.4   Processes and other activities

To improve the services of the IT organisation CSI measures the yield of these services. The main CSI activities are:
* Check:
  * Check the results of the processes
  * Examine customer satisfaction
  * Assess process maturity
  * Check whether the personnel follow the internal guidelines
  * Analyse the measurement data and compare these to the goals set in the SLA
* Report:
  * Propose improvements for all phases in the lifecycle
  * Consider the relevance of existing goals
* Improve:
  * Introduce activities which increase the quality, efficiency, effectiveness, and customer satisfaction of the services
  * Use appropriate quality management methods for improvement activities

Setting directions

The effect of the improvement is greatly determined by the direction in which the improvement takes place.

"Would you tell me, please, which way I ought to go from here?"

"That depends a good deal on where you want to get to," said the Cat.

"I don't much care where –" said Alice.

"Then it doesn't matter which way you go," said the Cat.

"– so long as I get somewhere," Alice added as an explanation.

"Oh, you're sure to do that," said the Cat, "if you only walk long enough."

Source: Lewis Carroll, Alice's Adventures in Wonderland, 1865

Without a vision about the direction of the improvement, an improvement has only a limited value. Because of this, you should determine a vision including its goals before you start with an improvement process.

The organisation must continually assess its current improvement course (CSI goals) on relevance, completeness, and feasibility. The **CSI approach** in Figure 9.3 can provide some support.

This continual cycle consists of six phases:
- **Determine the vision** – IT gets an insight into the goals of its business, and together with the business formulates a vision to tune the IT strategy to the business strategy; together they formulate a mission, goals, and objectives.
- **Record the current situation** – Record the starting point (baseline) of the customer, organisation, people, process, and technology.
- **Determine measurable targets** – Set priorities together with the client based on the vision: what do we improve first, how extensive must the improvement be and when should it be finished?
- **Plan** – Draw up a detailed service improvement plan (SIP) including actions to achieve the desired situation.
- **Check** – Measure whether the objectives have been achieved, and check whether the processes are complied with.
- **Assure** – Embed the changes in order to maintain them.

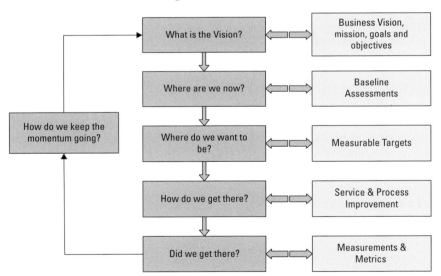

Figure 9.3 Sample CSI approach

Source: The Cabinet Office

Announce this plan to the whole organisation in order to create a consciousness, understanding, enthusiasm, and support. Create a dialogue with the organisation and regularly communicate and report on the actual achievements.

Service measurement

Measuring enables an organisation to analyse and determine the true cause and effect of either positive or negative situations.

IT services have become an integral means for conducting business. This holds true for businesses of all types and sizes, in any industry, whether private or public. Without IT services most organisations would not be able to deliver the products and services in today's marketplace.

Design and develop a service measurement framework.

Setting up a framework is as much an art as a science. Service measurement is not an end in itself but should enable and support improving both services and accountability.

The primary output of a service measurement framework is to provide the ability for making operational, tactical, or strategic decisions.

This can only be accomplished if the organisation selects a combination of measures that provides an accurate, balanced, and unbiased perspective capable of handling change

Different levels of measurement and reporting

Creating a service measurement framework will require the ability to build upon different metrics and measurements.

When developing a service management framework it is important to understand which are the most suitable types of report to create, their target audience and intended usage.

Service management process measurement

There are four major levels to report on. The first (bottom) level contains the activity metrics for a process. The second level contains the KPIs associated with each process. The third level represents the high-level purpose of the process. Finally, the fourth (top) level represents the balanced scorecard for IT or for the organisation.

Creating a measurement framework grid

It is recommended to define the high-level goals and identify the KPIs that will support those goals. KPI categories can be classified as:

Compliance: .... Are we doing it?
Quality: .... How well are we doing it?
Performance: ... How fast or slow are we doing it?
Value: .... Are our efforts making a difference?

Service reporting

Service reporting is the process which is responsible for the generation and supply of reports about the results achieved and the developments in service levels. A reporting approach that focuses equally on the future and the past provides the service provider with the means to market its services and accomplishments directly aligned to the experiences of the business: either positive or negative.

Numerous policies and rules can exist as long as it is clear for each report which policies and rules have been applied. However, all policies and rules form part of the single reporting framework.

Targeted audience(s) and the related business views on what the service delivered are:
• Agreement on what to measure and report
• Agreed definitions of all terms and boundaries
• Basis of all calculations
• Reporting schedules
• Access to reports and medium to be used
• Meetings scheduled to review and discuss reports.

Right content for the right audience

Reports should be presented via the medium of choice such as paper-based copies, online soft copies, web-enabled dynamic HTML, current snapshot whiteboards, or even real-time portal/dashboards.

The targeted audience must receive relevant, unambiguous, and, clear information in a style and language of their choice.

The CSI improvement process

The **CSI improvement process** or seven-step improvement process describes how you should measure and report. The plan phase in CSI yields a **Service Improvement Plan (SIP)**.

If service level management discovers that something can be improved, it will pass this on to CSI. CSI can then formulate activities which will bring about the improvement. For the execution CSI generates a SIP. This turns "improvement" into an IT process with input, activities, output, roles, and reporting.

9.5 CSI Improvement Process

Introduction

The **CSI improvement process** or **seven-step improvement process** describes how to measure and report on services as well as initiating improvement efforts. Improvement takes place according to the PDCA Cycle (Deming's cycle). The most significant output of this phase, other than reports, is the **Service Improvement Plan (SIP)**. The next section will explain how an organisation can set up such a plan.

It is important to note that all improvement initiatives require a business impact analysis, a cost-benefit analysis, and that they must follow the change management process. Whenever possible the benefits anticipated by the improvement effort must be quantified in monetary terms. This is called the return on investment (ROI). However, not all benefits are tangible; some have to do with perception, and preferences, which are two elements of how the customer defines value. This is known as the value on investment (VOI).

Activities, methods, and techniques

CSI is already incorporated in every process, thus everyone is involved in CSI. CSI simply utilises the outputs of the other processes, analyses them and proposes improvement ideas. In some cases it might be possible to recommend *not* improving something as the workaround is good enough for the customer or the solution might be prohibitive in terms of cost, time, and effort. It may also be possible for the service to be scheduled for retirement in the near future.

If someone working in service level management discovers that something could improve, they will turn to CSI. Using CSI methods and techniques, this someone can think up activities to accomplish these improvements. Still using CSI, this someone will create a SIP for execution purposes. This will transform "improvement" into an actual process with input, activities, output, roles, and reports.

CSI will measure and process these measurements in a continual improvement process (Figure 9.4). This will take place in **seven steps from measurement to improvement**:
1. **Identify the strategy for improvement** – What would be the ideal situation? This must follow from the vision (Phase I of the CSI approach) and precede the assessment of the current situation (Phase II of the CSI approach).
2. **Define what you will measure** – This step follows from Phase III of the CSI approach: where do we want to be? By researching what the organisation can and will measure, it will discover new business requirements and new IT options. By using a *gap analysis* CSI can find areas for improvement and plan these (Phase IV of the CSI approach).
3. **Gather data (measure)** – In order to verify whether the organisation has reached its purpose (Phase V of the CSI approach), it must perform measurements. The measurements must follow from its vision, mission, goals, and objectives.
4. **Process data** – The processing of data is also necessary for monitoring purposes. This must happen according to the CSFs and KPIs determined.
5. **Analyse data** – Discrepancies, trends and possible explanations are prepared for presentation to the business. This is also an important part of Phase V of the CSI approach.
6. **Present and use information** – This is where the stakeholder is informed whether their goals have been achieved (still Phase V).
7. **Implement corrective action** – Create improvements, establish a new baseline and start the cycle from the top.

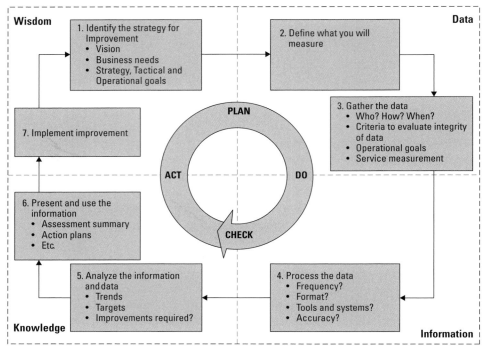

Figure 9.4 Sample CSI 7-step improvement workflow
Source: The Cabinet Office

The cycle is preceded and closed by **identification of vision and goals** *(identify)*. This is where the vision, strategy, tactical and operational goals are charted. This step returns in Phase I of the CSI approach: determine the vision.

Steps 1 and 2 should be the direct result of the strategic, tactical, and operational goals of the organisation. They are iterative: in every step you should question whether you are measuring what you should be measuring and whether the measured values are reliable and useful. Answer these questions together with the business in order to be sure that you will be able to provide it with useful information in Step 6.

If no **baseline** has yet been determined, that measurement must take place first. The first measuring results will be the baseline. Every level should be charted in this process: strategic goals and objectives, tactical process maturity and operational **metrics** and KPIs. In this way, a knowledge spiral develops: the information from Step 6 in the operational level is input for Step 3 (gather data) of the tactical level, and information from the tactical level will provide data to the strategic level (Figure 9.5).

If there is little data available, you must first determine a basic measurement system. Start collecting consistent data, for example by having IT personnel record data in the same way. You can also measure the process maturity of current processes to discover those processes that deviate most from *best practice*. However, this will only show a lack of data; you will not be collecting any new information in this way.

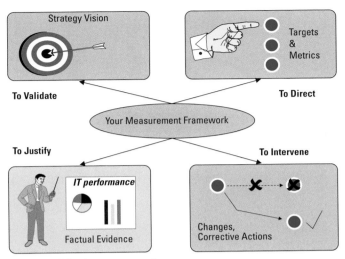

Figure 9.5 Why do we measure?

Source: The Cabinet Office

Never allow "measuring" to become a goal in itself. Before a manager decides what they will be measuring and for how long, they should contemplate why they should measure and how they will put the results to use. This depends on the goal of the manager. The four most common reasons to measure are shown in the table below.

Table 9.2 Four most common reasons to measure

Validate	To test prior decisions
Direct	Set direction to activities in order to reach goals
Justify	Support for the necessity of a certain action
Intervene	Determine a point at which corrective actions or changes in the process are required

In addition, it is important to also determine what we are measuring. We measure to ensure people *comply* with the services and processes based on a defined and adopted standard. We measure to ensure the services and processes *perform* as planned. We measure to ensure the services and processes are delivered at the right level of defined *quality*. Finally, we measure to ensure the services and processes actually make a difference, that is, they deliver *value*.

It is always important to keep sight of these reasons, including when we measure something. Concerning reports, a manager should consider:

"Do we (still) need this"?
"What am I really measuring"?
"How will I retrieve the information"?

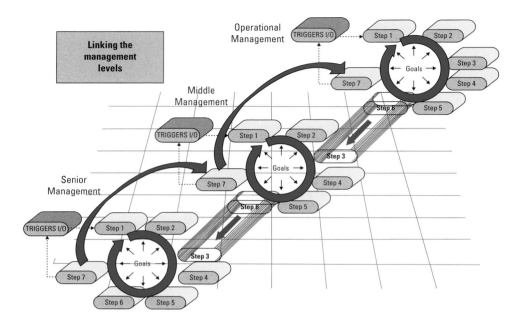

Figure 9.6 Sample knowledge spiral
Source: The Cabinet Office

The above questions are always important and should be regularly asked against all reports. The responsibility for this lies with the owner of every dashboard; they must create useful reports and make sure that the (customer) organisation actually uses them.

If you follow the seven steps of the improvement process, these questions will become a habit. More details about these steps follow below.

Step 1 – Identify the strategy for improvement

In an ideal situation the **service owners** determine what they should measure. For this reason, they will chart the activities that are needed for the service management processes, or to provide services. They then plan which metrics will show whether the services actually provide what was agreed with the business, and the way in which they can measure whether processes are proceeding smoothly.

The final list should reflect the following:
* The four Ps of strategy; perspective, position, plans, and patterns
* The visions, missions, goals and objectives of the business and of the IT organisation

This should result in a number of CSF, as well as *Service Level Targets*. The job descriptions of IT personnel should also be related to this.

You should have discussions with the business and the service providers for this purpose, and use the service portfolio, the service catalogue, and the *service level requirements* (SLRs) as starting points. Prioritise the CSI activities based on the business priorities. In this, also remember about third party services; what portion of these services should you be measuring (and possibly including) in your service reporting in determining whether you are capable or not of providing your service?

Inputs into Step 1:
- Business plans and strategy
- Vision, mission, goals, and objectives of the organisation as a whole, and of the various units
- Legislative requirements
- Governance requirements
- Budgeting and accounting requirements
- Balanced scorecard
- Service level requirements and targets
- Service portfolio and service catalogue
- Service review meetings
- Customer satisfaction surveys
- CSI initiatives already logged in the CSI register
- Service models
- Service design package
- Benchmark and baseline data
- Risk assessments and risk mitigation plans.

The **outputs** from Step 1 are:
- A service improvement strategy
- A prioritised list of improvement
- An updated CSI register

Step 2 – Define what you will measure?
In this step you need to define
- What you should measure based on your improvement strategy
- Define what you can actually measure based on your resources and capabilities
- Carry out a gap analysis between 1. and 2. above
- Negotiate, bargain, discuss with the business if and when you cannot measure what you should be measuring
- Finalise the actual measurement plan

Step 2 is iterative during the rest of the CSI activities. Depending on the goals and objectives to support service improvement activities, an organisation may have to purchase and install new technology to support the gathering and processing of the data and/or hire personnel with the required skills sets.

Effective service measures must concentrate on a few vital, meaningful indicators that are economical, quantitative, and usable for the desired results (business outcomes).

Inventory what you are already measuring, the reports you are producing, their frequency, and their target audience. Determine what is being measured and why. If no one uses it, why measure it in the first place?

More information about CSFs and KPIs can be found under "Basic concepts" in the section about CSI in Chapter 7 ("Metrics and KPIs"). Step 4 in the CSI process, process data, also provides additional information.

Inputs into Step 2: The inputs into Step 1 plus...
• A service improvement strategy
• A prioritised list of improvement
• An updated CSI register
• End-to-end service definition
• Process flows
• Procedures
• Work instructions
• Technical and user manuals for existing tools
• Existing reports

Outputs from Step 2:
• List of what can be measured, including CSFs, KPIs and metrics
• List of required adjustments to resources
• List of required adjustments to capabilities
• List of required new resources

Step 3 – Gather data (measuring)

It seems obvious that gathering data requires having monitoring tools in place. Monitoring could be executed using technology such as application, system, and component monitoring tools such as used in the event management process (documented in service operation) or via a manual process such as free-form text in various event records (sometimes referred to as *tickets*) for incidents, problems, changes, and releases, to name but a very few. The security policy will influence the data gathering, especially from the confidentiality, integrity, and availability perspectives.

Quality is a key objective of monitoring for CSI. Monitoring will therefore focus on the effectiveness and efficiency of a service, process, tool, organisation, or configuration item (CI).

CSI is interested in all types of events such as business as usual, warnings and alerts. Therefore people involved in CSI need to have the right level of access to the appropriate data sources.

It is also important in this activity to look at the data that was collected and ask whether it makes any sense. If it turns out that data collected cannot be used or is unreliable, at least put it to use analysing which data will be needed. For this purpose, repeat steps one and two.

It is important to remember that there are three types of metrics that an organisation will need to collect to support CSI and other process activities:

Table 9.3 Three types of metrics required to support CSI

Technology metrics	These are often associated with component and application-based metrics such as performance, availability etc.
Process metrics	These are captured in the form of CSF, KPI and activity metrics for the service management processes. These metrics can help determine the overall health of a process. KPIs can help answer key questions on quality, performance, value, and compliance in following the process. CSI would use these metrics as input in identifying improvement opportunities for each process.
Service metrics	These are the results of the end-to-end service. Technology metrics are normally used to help compute the service metrics.

When a new service is being designed or an existing one changed, this is a perfect opportunity to ensure that what CSI needs to monitor is designed into the service requirements (see ITIL Service Design).

Business requirements for monitoring will change over time. This is why Service Operation and CSI must design a process that will help the business and IT reach an agreement about what should be monitored and why.

Personnel are collecting data **manually** all the time, therefore they must agree to the following:
• Who is responsible for monitoring and collecting the data?
• What data will be collected?
• Where will the data be collected and stored?
• When and how often will data be collected?
• Why is the data required?
  ○ How will the data be collected?
• Which criteria guarantee the integrity of the data: the correctness, the reliability, and the trustworthiness of the source?

Data gathering consists of the following **activities**:
• Based on the SIP, goals, objectives and business requirements, specify which process activities you must monitor:
  ○ Specify monitoring requirements
  ○ Define requirements for data collection
  ○ Record results
  ○ Apply for approval from the internal IT department
• Determine how and how often you want to collect data
• Determine which tools are required; develop or buy these, or customise existing tools
• Test and install the tool
• Write monitoring procedures and work instructions

- Create a monitoring plan and discuss it; ask for approval from internal and external IT service providers
- Realise availability and capacity planning
- Start monitoring and gathering data
- Organise the data in a logical fashion in a report
- Evaluate data in order to be sure that it is correct and useful

Inputs into Step 3:
- List stating what you should measure
- List stating what you can measure
- List stating what you will be measuring
- Existing SLA
- New business requirements
- Existing monitoring and data capture capability
- Prior trend analyses
- Gap analysis report
- Customer satisfaction studies
- Plans and policies from other processes
- The CSI register and existing service improvement plans (SIPs)
- Previous trend analysis reports
- Customer satisfaction surveys.

Outputs from Step 3:
- Updated availability and capacity plans
- Monitoring procedures
- Identified tools to use
- Monitoring plan
- Input on IT capability
- Collection of data
- Agreement on the integrity of the data.

Step 4 – Process data

Here you will process the raw data from Step 3 into the required format for the target audience. Follow the path from metric via KPI to CSF, right back to the vision if necessary.

Many people unfortunately believe that once the data has been processed by the tool it can be presented and used. Such is not the case. The data must be analysed first. This is the next activity in CSI.

Report-generating technologies have the ability to transform raw data into information and then information into a format that is much easier to analyse. The reporting tools also have the ability to provide end-to-end measuring of a service. This requires the proper tool configuration, the identification, and maintenance of configurations and relationships making up the service.

Key questions that need to be addressed in the processing activity are:

What is the frequency of processing the data?
What format is required for the output?
What tools and systems can be used for processing the data?
How do we evaluate the accuracy of the processed data?

There are two aspects to processing data. One is automated and the other is manual. While both are important and contribute greatly to the measuring process, accuracy is a major differentiator between the two types. On-going communication about the benefits of performing administrative tasks is of utmost importance.

Data processing consists of the following **activities**:
- Define the requirements of the processed data based on strategy, goals, and SLA
- Determine how data is being processed; for new services or processes, it is preferable to select shorter intervals; is this by hour, day, week, or month?
- Determine the data grouping based on the method of analysis and target group; formulate the requirements for tools; develop or buy them; test and install them
- Develop procedures to process data, and train people in the procedures
- Create a monitoring plan and discuss it; ask for approval from internal and external IT service providers
- Update availability and capacity planning
- Start data processing
- Group the data in a logical fashion
- Evaluate data accuracy

Inputs into Step 4:
- Data gathered through monitoring
- Reporting requirements
- SLA, OLA, and UC
- Service catalogue
- List with metrics, KPIs, CSFs, objectives, and goals
- Reporting frequency
- Reporting templates

Output from Step 4:
- Current availability and capacity planning
- Reports
- Processed, logically grouped data ready for analysis

Step 5 – Analyse data
Without analysis, data is "only" information. It does not provide understanding of areas for improvement. Analysis evaluates whether IT services support the goals and objectives determined.

Data analysis transforms the information into knowledge of the events that are affecting the organisation. More skill and experience is required to perform data analysis than data gathering and processing. Verification against goals and objectives is expected during this activity. This verification validates that objectives are being supported and value is being added. It is not sufficient to simply produce graphs of various types but to also document the observations and conclusions.

What do you actually analyse?

Positive and negative trends
Are the agreed targets with the customer, within IT and, with the suppliers met?
Cause and effect
Intended vs. actual performance

However, key questions still need to be asked, such as:

Is this good?
Is this bad?
Is this expected?

Without analysis the data is merely information. With analysis come improvement opportunities. Throughout CSI, assessment should identify whether targets were achieved and, if so, whether new targets (and therefore new KPIs) need to be defined. If targets were achieved but the perception has not improved, then new targets may need to be set and new measures put in place to ensure that these new targets are being met.

Because of prior discussions about improvement options, IT will make the first move in the dialogue with the business that follows analysis. A good analysis of the information is also to the advantage of the business. This will allow a more accurate determination of whether improvement is required based on strategic, tactical, and operational goals. At this point, information becomes *knowledge*, according to the DIKW model.

Inputs into Step 5:
- Results of the monitored data
- Existing KPI and targets
- Perceptions from customer satisfaction surveys, etc.

Step 6 – Present and use information (service reporting)
The sixth step is to take our knowledge, which is represented in the reports, monitors, action plans, reviews, evaluations and opportunities, and present it to the target audience in a clear, digestible, and timely way. This stage involves presenting the information in a format that is understandable, at the right level, provides value, notes

exceptions to service, identifies benefits that were revealed during the time period, and allows those receiving the information to make strategic, tactical and operational decisions. In other words, present the information in the manner that makes it the most useful for the target audience.

Most organisations create reports and present information to some extent or another; however, it often is not done well. Many organisations simply take the gathered raw data (often straight from the tool) and report it to everyone, without necessarily processing or analysing the data. The report should emphasise and ideally highlight areas where the recipient needs to take action.

The other issue often associated with presenting and using information it that it is overdone. Managers at all levels are bombarded with too many emails, too many meetings, too many reports. The reality is that the managers often don't need this information or, at the very least, not in that format. It is often unclear what role the manager has in making decisions and providing guidance on improvement programmes.

Consider the target audience; make sure that you identify exceptions to the service, benefits that have been revealed, or can be expected. There are usually four distinct audiences; the customers, IT executives/senior managers, internal IT, and the suppliers.
Data gathering occurs at the operational level of an organisation. Format this data into knowledge that all levels can appreciate and gain insight into their needs and expectations.

Here are some of the common problems associated with the presenting and reporting activity:
- Everyone gets the same report
- The format is not what people want
- Lack of an executive
- Reports are not linked to any baseline, or scorecard
- Too much supporting data is provided
- Reports are presented in terms that are not understandable

Inputs include:
- Collated information
- Format details and templates
- Stakeholder contact details

Step 7 – Implement corrective action
An organisation will not be able to implement all of the determined improvement options immediately. For this reason, options should be assigned a **priority** based on the organisational goals and external regulations determined in the Service Strategy.

It is recommended to use the knowledge gained and combine it with previous experience to make informed decisions about optimising, improving, and correcting services. Managers need to identify issues and present solutions.

This stage may include any number of activities such as approval of improvement activities, prioritisation, and submitting a business case, integration with change management, integration with other lifecycle stages, and guidance on how to manage an on-going improvement project successfully, and on checking whether the improvement actually achieved its objective.

CSI identifies many opportunities for improvement, but organisations cannot afford to implement all of them. As discussed earlier, an organisation needs to prioritise improvement activities for its goals, objectives, return on investment (ROI), types of service breaches etc., and document them in the CSI register. Improvement initiatives can also be externally driven by regulatory requirements, changes in competition, or even political decisions.

There are various levels of management in an organisation; when implementing improvements it is important to understand which level to focus their activities on. Managers need to show overall performance and improvement. Directors need to show that quality and performance targets are being met, while risk is being minimised. Overall, senior management need to know what is going on so they can make informed choices and exercise judgement. Each level has its own perspective. Understanding these perspectives is where maximum value of information is leveraged.

Inputs include:
- Knowledge gained from presenting and using the information
- Agreed implementation plans (from Step 6)
- A CSI register for those initiatives that have been initiated from other sources.

Generic process information
The following information is specific to the seven-step process but not necessarily to any particular activity within the process.

Information management
As indicated in the activities above, the information required to understand what needs to be improved by how much, and when comes from many sources. It is important in order to get a full and clear picture to gather and analyse all information.
- The service catalogue
- Service level requirements
- Monitored and reported service level targets
- Service knowledge management system
- Configuration management system
- Process metrics
- Customer satisfactory surveys
- Complaints and compliments
- All data, information, knowledge produced by the process itself

Interfaces

Like all processes, the seven-step improvement process has relationships with all other processes. However, some of the most visible relationships include but are not limited to:

Each step of the CSI lifecycle will be involved in every one of the other lifecycle stages.

Service Strategy
To monitor the progress of, and analyse the results of, strategies, standards, policies, and architectural decisions that have been made and implemented

Service Design
To monitor and gather data and information associated with creating and modifying services and service management processes. To measure the effectiveness and ability to measure CSFs and KPIs defined while gathering business requirements

Service Transition
To develop and test the monitoring procedures and criteria to be used during and after implementation

Service Operation
To actively gather, process, analyse, and present data and information regarding the services in the live environment

Triggers

Many triggers of the process are already documented and discussed within the steps discussed earlier.

Inputs

Many inputs to the process are documented within the steps discussed earlier but examples of key inputs include:
- Service catalogue
- SLRs
- The service review meeting
- Vision and mission statements
- Corporate, divisional, and departmental goals and objectives
- Legislative requirements
- Governance requirements
- Budget cycle
- Customer satisfaction surveys
- The overall IT strategy
- Market expectations
- New technology drivers
- Flexible commercial models

Outputs

Many outputs of the process are already documented and discussed within the steps discussed earlier.

Critical success factors

The critical success factors, used to judge the success of the seven-step improvement process, are actually those of the other lifecycle stages and processes to which they are applied. As a result the examples given here come from other areas.
- All improvement opportunities identified
- The cost of providing services is reduced
- The required business outcomes from IT services are achieved

Metrics

The key performance indicators, used to judge the success of the seven-step improvement process, are actually those of the other lifecycle stages and processes to which they are applied. As a result the examples given here come from other areas.
- Percentage improvement in defects
- Percentage decrease in overall cost of service provision
- Percentage increase in customer satisfaction with the service desk

Figure 9.7 provides a visual representation of the flow from vision to measurements and back.

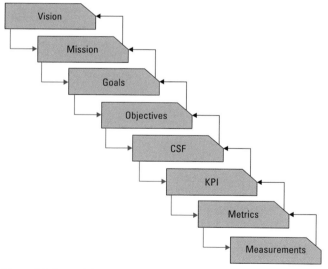

Figure 9.7 From vision to measurements and back

Source: The Cabinet Office

Challenges

Here are some of the potential challenges faced by the seven-step improvement process.

- Getting the required resources to implement and run the process
- Gathering the right level of data and having the tools to manipulate it
- To get the IT organisation to approach CSI in a consistent and structured way
- Get commitment from executives, managers, and IT personnel
- Obtaining sufficient information from the business regarding improvement requirements and cost reductions
- Persuading suppliers to include improvement in their contractual agreements

Risks

Here are some of the potential risks faced by the seven-step improvement process

- Initiatives being taken on randomly and/or in an ad hoc manner
- No formalised approach to CSI
- Insufficient monitoring and analysis in prioritising areas with the greatest need of improvement
- The attitude of "We have always done it this way", "It has always been good enough"
- Inability to "sell" the benefits of a formal approach to improvement
- Lack of, or loss of, ownership/champion
- No clear understanding of business needs and objectives

9.6 Organisation

Process activities are not limited to one part of the organisation. Because of this the process manager must map the defined process roles and activities to existing personnel. Clear definitions of the responsibility and accountability are required, for instance in a **RACI matrix** (*Responsible, Accountable, Consulted, Informed*).

Roles and responsibilities

CSI comprises permanent production roles such as the **service manager**, the **service owner**, the **process owner,** the analysts, as well as temporary project roles such as project managers and project team members.

Table 9.4 provides an overview of the accompanying key activities and roles. Not all roles are full-time. Make a global division and adjust this later on if needed.

Table 9.4 Key activities and the roles to be divided

Key activity	Key role
Gather data from the measurement of service results and service management processes and compare these to the starting point (baseline), goals, SLA and benchmarks; analyse trends	− Service manager − Service owner − IT process owner
Set targets for efficiency improvement and cost effectiveness throughout the entire Service Lifecycle	− Service manager
Set targets for service improvements and use of resources	− Service manager − Service owner − Business process owner
Consider new business and security requirements	− Service manager − business process owner
Create a SIP and implement improvements	− Service manager − Service owner − Process owner
Enable personnel to propose improvements	− Service manager
Measure, report and communicate about improvement initiatives	− Service manager
Revise policy, processes, procedures and plans if needed	− Service manager
Ensure that all approved actions are completed and that they achieve the desired result	− Service manager − Business manager − IT process owner − Business process owner

Table 9.5 provides an overview of the roles, activities, and skills needed for the different steps in the CSI improvement process.

For the ITIL Foundations exam, knowledge is required on the roles printed in bold in Table 9.5. We will discuss these further, except for the role of **service level manager**. The section on "Service Design" describes this role. The section "Other roles" mentions other roles present in CSI.

Service manager
Service manager is a generic term for any manager within the service provider. The term is commonly used to refer to a business relationship manager, a process manager or a senior manager with responsibility for IT services overall. A service manager is often assigned several roles such as business relationship management (BRM), service level management (SLM) and CSI. The service manager often manages the development, implementation, evaluation, and on-going management of new and existing products and services. Additionally, the service manager is responsible for:
• Achieving company strategy and goals
• Benchmarking
• Financial management
• Customer management
• Supplier management

- Full lifecycle management
- Inventory management

Table 9.5 Roles for the CSI process

Step	Roles	Activity types	Skills
1. What should you measure? – What can you measure?	Decision makers, such as the service manager, service owner, service level manager, CSI manager, process owner	– High management level – High variation – Action oriented – Communicative – Focus on future	– Management skills – Communicate – Create and use concepts – Handle complex and uncertain situations – Education and experience
2. What will you measure?	Internal and external service providers who know the possibilities, such as the service manager, service owner, process owner and the process manager	– Intellectual – Investigative – Medium to high variation – Goal oriented – Specialised in business management	– Analyse – Model – Inventive attitude – Education – Program
3. Gather data (measure)	Personnel who supply services in the Service Transition and Service Operation life cycle phases, such as the service desk personnel on a daily basis	– Standardised – Routine (low variation) – Automated – Clerical level – Procedural	– Accuracy – Precision – Applied training – Technical experience
4. Process data	See step 3	– Specialised – Structures – Automated – Medium variation – Procedural	– Numerical skills – Methodical – accurate – Applied training – Programming – Experience with tools
5. Analyse data	Internal and external service providers who know the possibilities, such as the service owner, process owner and the business and IT analysts	– See step 2	– See step 2
6. Present and use the information (reporting)	Internal and external service providers who know the possibilities and the main decision makers, such as the CSI manager, service manager, service owner, service level manager, process owner	– See step 1	– See step 1
7. Implement corrective actions	See step 6	– See step 2	– See step 2

The service manager must know a great deal about market analysis, be able to anticipate new market needs, formulate complex programs, guide personnel, and sell services.

CSI manager

Without a clear and unambiguous responsibility, improvement will not occur. As a result this new role is essential for a successful improvement program. The **CSI manager** is responsible for CSI in the organisation. The CSI manager manages the measuring, analysis, investigating and reporting of trends and initiates service improvement activities. In addition, they also make sure that sufficient CSI supporting resources are available. They are responsible for:

* Development of the CSI domain
* Awareness and communication of CSI throughout the organisation
* Allocating CSI roles
* Identifying and prioritising improvement opportunities to senior management together with the service owner
* Identifying monitoring requirements together with the service level manager
* Ensuring that the proper monitoring tools are installed
* Creating SIPs together with the service level manager
* Capturing baseline data to measure improvement against it
* Defining and reporting upon CSF, KPI and activity metrics
* Using supporting frameworks and models
* Making knowledge management an integral part of the daily routine
* Evaluating analysed data

The CSI manager must be able to lead projects throughout the organisation, build good relationships with the business and IT management, have a flair for improvement opportunities throughout the company, and be able to counsel personnel.

Service owner

It is crucial to appoint one person responsible for each service: this is the **service owner**. They are the central point of contact for a specific service. It does not matter where the underlying technological components, process or functions are located. The main responsibilities are:

* Owning and representing the service
* Understanding which components make up the service
* Measuring the performance and availability
* Attending Change Advisory Board (CAB) meetings if these changes are relevant to the service they represent
* Working with the CSI manager to identify and prioritise improvements
* Participating in internal and external service reviews
* Maintaining the service entry in the service catalogue
* Participating in the negotiation of SLA and OLA

Process owner

Having an owner is just as crucial to a process as a service owner is to a service. The **process owner** ensures that the organisation follows a process. They must be a senior manager with enough credibility, influence, and authority in the organisation departments which are part of the process. The process owner performs the essential role of process champion, design lead, advocate, coach, and protector. See also the section on "Service Design".

Other roles

Other roles which are important to CSI:

- **Service knowledge manager** – Designs and maintains a knowledge management strategy and implements this
- **Reporting analyst** – Evaluates and analyses data, and identifies trends; often cooperates with SLM roles (see Service Design); must have good communication skills because reporting is an essential element of communication
- **Communication responsibility** – Designs a communication strategy for CSI

9.7 Methods, techniques and tools

There are various methods and techniques to check whether planned improvements actually produce measurable improvements. One method or technique is not usually enough: you need to find the best mix for your organisation. Check whether the chosen methods and techniques are suitable to measure the results of your processes, document them thoroughly, and instruct personnel who will be using the method or technique.

Implementation review

To determine whether the improvements produce the desired effects, you have to ask whether the original problem situation has actually improved, and how the organisation has planned and implemented the improvement. The following questions help with this:

- Have we correctly assessed the present situation and have we properly formulated the problem?
- Have we taken the correct decisions with respect to our strategy?
- Have we adopted the strategy in the right way?
- Have we formulated the right CSI goals?
- Have the goals been reached?
- Do we now provide better IT services?
- What are the lessons learned and where are we now?

Assessments

An assessment compares the performance of an operational process against a performance standard. This can be an agreement in an SLA, a maturity standard, or a benchmark of companies in the same industry. By conducting assessments, IT organisations show their commitment to improvement in maturity.

Assessments are very well suited to answer the question "where are we now?", and to determine the extent of the gap with "where we want to be". A well-designed maturity assessment framework evaluates the viability of all aspects of the process environment including the people, process, and technology as well as factors a affecting overall process effectiveness in the business. Keep in mind that the desired performance or maturity level of a process depends on the impact that the process has on the customer's business processes.

First determine the relationship between business processes, IT services, IT systems, and components. CSI can separately assess the effectiveness and efficiency results for each component. This helps in identifying areas for improvement.

It is crucial to clearly define what is being assessed. Base this on the goals and the expected future use of assessment and assessment reports. An assessment can take place on three levels:
- **Process only** – Only assess process attributes based on the general principles and guidelines of the process framework which defines the subject process
- **People, process and technology** – Also assess skills, roles, and talents of managers and personnel who participate in the process; also assess the process-supporting technology
- **Full assessment** – Also assess the culture of acceptance within the organisation, the ability of the organisation to articulate a process strategy, the definition of a vision for the process environment as an "end-state", the structure and function of the process organisation, and so on

All these factors are compared to the maturity attributes of the selected maturity model.

Assessments are useful in the:
- **Planning phase** – As starting point (baseline) for process performance
- **Implementation phase (*do*)** – To check that the estimates are correct
- **Measurement phase (*check*)** – To complete the balance and to identify further possible improvements

Advantages of assessments:
- They can measure certain parts of a process independently of the rest and determine the impact of that specific component on the rest of the process
- They can be repeated

Disadvantages of assessments:
- They only offer a snapshot in time and do not give insight into the cultural dynamics of an organisation
- They can become a goal in themselves instead of a means to an end
- They are labour-intensive
- The results are still dependent on subjective assessors and therefore not entirely objective, even if the measurements are

This applies to both internal and external assessments. Table 9.6 gives an overview of the advantages and disadvantages of both forms.

Table 9.6 Internal versus external assessment

Internal assessment	
Advantages	**Disadvantages**
• No expensive consultants • Self-assessment sets are available for free • Promotes internal co-operation and communication • Promotes internal level of knowledge • Good starting point for CSI • Internal knowledge of existing environment	• Less objective • Disappointing acceptance of findings • Internal politics can get involved • Limited knowledge of skills • Labour intensive
External assessment	
Advantages	**Disadvantages**
• Objectivity • Expert ITIL knowledge • Wide experience with several IT organisations • Analytical skills • Credibility • Minimal impact on the provision of services	• High costs • Risk as to acceptance • Limited knowledge of existing environments • Insufficient preparation limits effectiveness

Benchmarks

A benchmark is a particular type of assessment: organisations compare (parts of) their processes with the performance of the same types of processes that are commonly recognised as "best practice". This can be done in four ways:
- **Internal** – Against an earlier starting point (baseline)
- **Internal** – Against another system or department
- **External** – Against industry standards
- **External** – Directly with similar organisations; this is only useful, however, if there are enough similar organisations in terms of environment, sector and geographical placement

The form you choose depends on the purpose of the benchmark:
- Measurements of costs (price) and performance of internal or external service providers
- Compare process performance with the existing industry standard

- Compare the financial performance of high-level IT costs with industry standard or other organisations
- Measure effectiveness in achieving the required customer satisfaction

To determine this you can set up an organisational profile, which consists of four key components:
- **Company information profile** – Basic information such as scope and type of organisation
- **Current assets** – Hardware such as desktops and servers
- **Current best practices** – Policy, procedures and tools and the degree to which they are used in the organisation
- **Complexity** – The number of end users and the quantity and type of technology in your organisation

In all cases a benchmark provides the following results:
- Represents performance
- Shows the gaps
- Shows the risk of not closing these gaps
- Helps set priorities
- Helps in communicating the information well

In this way organisations discover whether their processes are cost-effective, whether they meet customer needs, and how effective they are in comparison to other organisations. They become aware of the need to improve and the ways they can do so, for example in the areas of economies of scale, efficiency, and effectiveness. Management can then act on this. In the ideal case benchmarking forms part of a continual cycle of improvement and is repeated regularly.

A study into the performance of one's own organisation and other departments or organisations takes time. Setting up a benchmark database and visiting other organisations also involves costs.

Benchmarking is done in cooperation with:
- The business
- Users or consumers
- Internal service providers
- External service providers
- Users in "public domain"
- Benchmark your partners (other organisations who are involved in the comparison)

First look to see if there are any problem areas. Use the steps from the CSI improvement process, supported by (some of) the following techniques:
- Informal discussions with the business, personnel, or suppliers
- Focus groups
- Market research
- Quantitative research

- Surveys
- Questionnaires
- Re-engineering analysis
- Process mapping
- Quality control variation reports
- Financial ratio analysis

Two special forms of benchmarking are:

- **Process maturity comparison** – As opposed to an assessment, this is not a comparison with the maturity model, but the maturity level is compared with that of other organisations; for example, CMMI can be used as a maturity model
- **Total cost of ownership (TCO**™**)** – The sum of all the costs of the design, the introduction, operation, and improvement of services (developed by Gartner); it is often used to compare specific services in one organisation with those of another organisation

Balanced Scorecard (BSC™)

Kaplan and Norton developed the **Balanced Scorecard (BSC)** in the 1990s. Define a balanced scorecard for each business unit. Begin carefully: select two to four goals. Then you can extend this as a "waterfall" to the underlying components, such as the service desk. After successful implementation keep measuring regularly.

Gap analysis

This analysis naturally flows on from assessments and benchmarks. Having determined where the organisation is now, the gap analysis will determine the size of the gap with where the organisation wants to be. In this way light is shed on new opportunities for improvement. The *service gap model* in Figure 9.8 shows possible gaps or discrepancies.

Gap analyses can be the result of a benchmarking on service or process maturity investigations. They can be done on a strategic, tactical, or operational level. It gives an overview of the amount of resources and money which an organisation has to spend to reach specific goals.

SWOT analysis

A **SWOT analysis** looks at the *Strengths, Weaknesses, Opportunities, and Threats* of an organisation (component) or project. The organisation then answers the following questions:

- How can we profit from strong points?
- How can we remove weak points?
- How can we use opportunities optimally?
- How can we manage and eliminate threats?

Set your end goal before you perform a SWOT analysis. Look at which strong points help achieve a goal, which weaknesses prevent you from doing this, what external conditions promote the goal, and what external conditions prevent it.

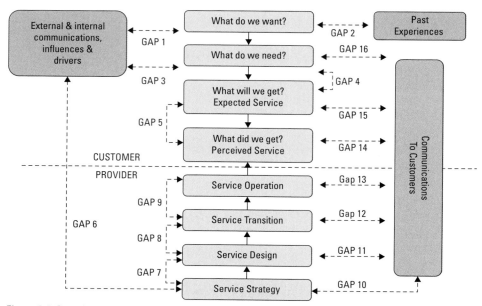

Figure 9.8 Sample service gap model

Source: The Cabinet Office

To arrive at a SWOT of the whole organisation, you can first make a SWOT for each organisation component or function and then integrate into a company SWOT. See Table 9.7 for sample aspects of SWOTs.

Table 9.7 Examples of aspects from SWOT analyses

Possible strengths	Possible weaknesses
• Core competences • Financial means • Recognised as a market leader • Proven management	• No clear strategic direction • Outdated facilities • Low profits • Little insight into performance
Possible opportunities	**Possible threats**
• Creation of new customer groups • Application of skills and knowledge for new products	• Foreign competition with lower prices • Lower market growth • Expensive legislation and regulation

Rummler-Brache swim-lane diagram

• Geary Rummler and Alan Brache introduced the idea of representing the relationships between processes and organisations or departments with "swim lanes" in a Rummler-Brache **swim-lane diagram**. This maps the flow of a process: from the customer through the department to the technology (Figure 9.9). The horizontal rows divide the separate organisations or departments from each other. Activities and decisions are connected through arrows to indicate the flow.

- The row in which these components are placed indicates which organisational component is responsible for the activity or decision.
- Because this instrument places the whole process within a recognisable structure of organisations, it is very useful as a communication tool with the management.

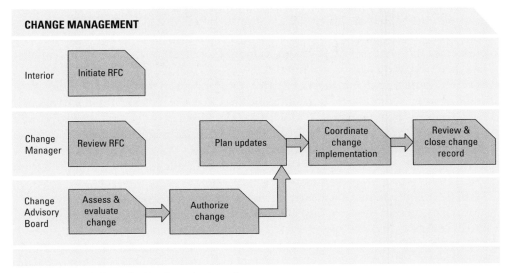

Figure 9.9 Sample Rummler-Brache swim-lane diagram

Source: The Cabinet Office

Tools

CSI needs different types of software to support, test, monitor, and report on the ITSM processes. As part of the assessment of "where do we want to be?" the requirements for enhancing tools will be addressed and documented. The need and sophistication of the tools required depend on the business need for IT services and to some extent the size of the organisation.

In any case, tools must monitor and analyse the most important components of a service, in a manner that supports the CSI process. They can also centralise, automate, and integrate the key processes. This then produces new data for trend analysis.

Tools to be used for CSI are for example:

- **IT service management suites** – Tools and suites compatible with the ITIL process framework providing significant levels of integration between the processes and their associated record types. This functionality creates a rich source of data and creates many of the inputs for CSI. The CMS is the foundation for the integration of all ITSM tool functionality and is a critical data source for CSI.
- **Event management** – Events are status messages from, for example, servers and systems; tools for event management assess these status reports for impact and origin, and categorise the reports

- **System and network management** – Monitors technology platforms; the tools generate error messages for event management, providing input to performance management
- **Automated incident and problem solving** – Proactive detection monitors, pre-programmed scripts that automatically repair the technology; they also record information for analysis for possible improvements
- **Knowledge management** – Databases with descriptions of earlier incidents and problems, and their proven solutions; also measurement of the use of the database and the effectiveness of the solution
- **Service request and fulfilment (service catalogue and workflow)** – Helps with defining a service catalogue and automates service requests and their settlement
- **Performance management** – Collects data about availability, capacity, and performance to develop availability and capacity information systems
- **Application and service performance monitoring** – Monitors the service of the technology from an end user perspective; the tools measure availability, reaction and transaction times and efficiency of the servers
- **Statistical analysis tools** – Central collection point for raw data from the above tools; the analysis instruments group these data logically, creating models for current services and making predictive models for future services
- **Software version control/software configuration management** – Creates an overview of all software for the development environment, thus providing the Definitive Media Library (DML)
- **Software test management** – Supports the test and roll-out activities of release management
- **Security management** – Protects against intruders and unauthorised use; all hardware and software that is under security management must automatically give a warning as soon as a security incident threatens
- **Project and portfolio management** – Registers new functionality and the services and systems that they support; the tools help to map the service portfolio and keep it up-to-date; they can also automate organisational aspects such as plans
- **Financial management** – Monitors the use of resources and services for the invoicing process
- **Business intelligence/reporting** – Collects data from all the above mentioned tools, with which it generates important information for the business

9.8 Implementation

Before you implement CSI you must make sure that:
- The critical roles of CSI manager, service owner, and reporting analyst have been filled
- Monitoring and reporting on technology metrics is in place
- Internal review meetings are scheduled
- External review meeting scheduled to follow internal review meetings

Communication forms an important part of any service improvement project. A communications plan is required which will need to deal with the responses and feedback from the target audience.

Define a communication plan that always states the messenger, what the message is, target audience, the timing, the frequency of communication, the method of communication, and the feedback mechanism.

CSI can be implemented through various approaches:
- **Service approach** – With this you define the issues with certain services; you create an action plan with the owner of the service: how are we going to remove the issue?
- **Lifecycle approach** – With this you look at the results of the various lifecycle phases and you look for possible improvements
- **Functional approach** – If many incidents occur with one specific function in an organisation, for example in the server group, you can remove as many problems in this function group as possible with a test project

See also "Basic concepts": Organisational Change and the PDCA Cycle.

Business case
The business case must make it clear whether it is useful to start with CSI. It must indicate what exactly will change in the intended future situation with respect to the starting situation. From a set **baseline** an organisation can estimate what the present situation provides and costs, and how much the improvement of the situation will provide and cost. Formulate this in the language that the business understands. In any case answer the following questions:
- **Where are we?** – Determine the present service levels.
- **What do we want?** – Determine the company vision, mission, goals, and objectives.
- **What do we need?** – Determine what services are essential for the fulfilment of the mission and set priorities based on this.
- **What can we afford?** – With the help of service level management (SLM) and financial management, set the budget for IT services and see what actions are feasible.
- **What will we get?** – Determine the required results together with the business
- **What did we get?** – Have Service Operation monitor the service levels and report on them.
- **Does it still meet our wants/needs?** – Look at further possible improvements with the business.

Answer these questions by testing. In the section "Processes and other activities" testing is discussed in detail.

For a business case, it is important to have an overview of the **costs** and benefits of CSI. Extra information about the measurement and estimation of costs and benefits can be found in the section "Processes and other activities" and in "Methods, techniques and tools".

Costs
When deciding on an improvement initiative, always keep an eye on the costs of development, operations, and on-going maintenance. Examples of this are:
- Labour costs
- Training costs
- Tools to process measurement data
- Assessments or benchmark studies
- Management time to follow progress
- Communication campaigns to create awareness and to change the culture

Benefits
Results of a service improvement plan can be expressed in terms of:
- **Improvements** – Measurable improvements with respect to the starting situation
- **Benefits** – Profit that is the result of improvements (usually in financial terms)
- **Return on Investment (ROI)** – The difference between the costs and benefits of the improvement
- **Value on Investment (VOI)** – ROI, plus the extra value that cannot be expressed in money or that only becomes clear in the long term. It is difficult to quantify extra value such as higher customer satisfaction; if there are enough "hard numbers", it still does not add much; a narrative appendix as to this qualitative value is more useful

Define both direct and indirect benefits and consider each group of **stakeholders** for each organisational level. Define the benefits such that they are measurable. Put the business first. Benefit for the business can mean:
- Shorter time to market
- Customer bonding
- Lower maintenance costs for the inventory
- Larger market share

CSI can provide the following benefits:
- **To the business**:
  - More reliable support for business processes through incident, problem, and change management
  - Higher productivity through increased quality and availability of IT services
  - The business knows what they can expect of the IT department and what the IT department expects of them
  - Procedures to ensure the continuity of IT service are oriented to the needs of the business
  - Better management information about business processes and IT services
  - The IT department has more knowledge of the business processes, so that it can respond better to the desires of the business
  - Quality projects, releases, and changes run according to plan and provide the agreed quality at the agreed costs
  - Minimal number of unused opportunities

○ Better relationship between the business and IT
○ Higher customer satisfaction
- **Financial**:
  ○ Efficient IT services
  ○ Cost-effective IT infrastructure and services
  ○ Cost reduction, for example though lower costs for the implementation of changes and less excess processes and equipment
  ○ Changes have less (financial) impact on the business
  ○ Services meet the requirements but do not over-perform
  ○ Better division of resources, such that expenditures for the continuity of IT services are in proportion with the importance of the business processes that they support
  ○ Cost structure is tuned to business needs
  ○ Minimal costs and risks with checks that legislation is followed
- **Innovative**:
  ○ More proactive development of technology and services through better information on the areas in which changes can lead to profits
  ○ The IT department reacts better to changes in demands from the business or the market and to new trends
  ○ A business which trusts their IT service providers that dare to "think big"
- **Internal benefits for the IT organisation**:
  ○ More competent IT department, less chance of errors
  ○ Integration of people and processes
  ○ More communication and teamwork (also with the business)
  ○ More productive and more motivated personnel
  ○ Defined roles and responsibilities
  ○ More effective processes, better use of resources
  ○ IT repeats and increases profit points through increased process maturity
  ○ Better metrics and management reports through structured approach to measurement and knowledge gathering
  ○ Better picture of and more trust in present and future IT improvement opportunities
  ○ Services and systems achieve feasible goals within a realistic schedule
  ○ Better direction of service providers
  ○ Better relationship with the business
  ○ Cost alignment with business needs

Critical Success Factors (CSFs)

A **Critical Success Factor** (CSF) is a necessary condition for a good result of a service or process. Critical success factors for CSI are:
- Appoint a CSI manager (see also "Organisation")
- Adoption of CSI by the whole organisation
- Constant visible management participation in CSI activities, for example by creating a vision and communicating about it
- Clear criteria for the prioritisation of improvement projects
- Adoption of the service cycle approach

- Sufficient funding
- Resource allocation – people are dedicated to the improvement effort, not just as an add-on to their already long list of tasks to perform
- Technology to support improvement activities
- Embrace service management processes and do not adapt it to meet personal needs and agendas

Challenges and risks
Introduction of CSI comes with the following challenges and risks:
- Lack of management commitment
- Poor relationship and communication between IT and the business
- Too little knowledge of the IT impact on the business and its important processes
- Too little knowledge of the business' priorities
- Lack of information, monitoring, and measurement
- Not using the information from reports
- Insufficient resources, budget, and time
- Immature service management processes
- Too little or no knowledge management (see also "Organisation")
- Trying to change everything at once
- Resistance against (cultural) changes
- Not enough business or IT objectives, strategies and policy
- Poor supplier management
- Not testing
- Tooling is too complex or insufficient
- Difference in used technology

Interfaces
CSI uses many data from the entire lifecycle of a service. The information that results from this, together with the demands of the business, the technical specifications, the opportunities of IT, the budget, trends and legislation, gives insight into the opportunities for the improvement of an organisation.

Service Level Management (SLM)
Service level management is the most important process for CSI: it discusses with the business what the IT organisation needs to measure and what the results should be. That is why this section begins with information on what SLM and CSI have in common. For more information about the service level management process see the Section about "Service Design".

After each phase of the lifecycle, test whether the improvement initiative has met its goals. This can be done using the **Post Implementation Review (PIR)** from the change management process.

Because steps 1 and 2 of the CSI improvement process lie primarily with SLM and CSI, an overview of the common ground between CSI and the other ITIL processes and the different Service Lifecycle phases is given starting from step 3 only. Service Operation also provides information about what *can* be measured before step 2.

In the light of CSI, the objective of SLM is to maintain and improve the quality of IT services. SLM does this by making a constant cycle of agreements, monitoring, and reporting about IT service levels.

In the CSI improvement process, SLM plays a role with:
- Identify the strategy for improvement:
  - Consult with the business as to what it would like
- Define what you will measure
  - See what has already been measured
  - Determine what can and should be measured (SLA, OLA and Underpinning Contracts)
- Data gathering (measuring):
  - Determine what happens with the data: who receives them, what analyses are needed?
- Data processing:
  - Evaluate the processed data from the business perspective
  - Consider how often the data must be processed and how often they must be reported on
- Data analysis:
  - Compare the Service Level achievements (performance, results) with the SLA
  - Identify and record trends to expose possible patterns
  - Determine the need for SIPs
  - The need to adjust existing OLA or Underpinning Contracts (UC)
- Presenting the information: (reporting)
  - Reporting to and communicating with the business
  - Organising internal and external service evaluations
  - Helping to prioritise activities
- Implementing corrective actions: (service improvement plan)
  - Together with problem and availability management, set up an SIP and ensure that the organisation carries out this plan

In this way SLM determines what the organisation measures and monitors; together with the business, it reports on the performance and signals new business demands. Using this information CSI identifies and prioritises improvement opportunities. This is the most important input for the SIP.

It is recommended that an annual budget is set for SIPs. SLM and CSI can then take quick action, which leads to a proactive attitude.

If an organisation outsources its Service Delivery processes, it must also negotiate regarding CSI and include this in the SLA. Otherwise the acting party will no longer be motivated to deliver more than is agreed upon in the contract.

Monitor and gather data (measurement, step 3)
In the Service Lifecycle, *Service Strategy* monitors the effect of the strategies, the standards, and the policies upon the design decisions.

Service Design monitors and collects information related to the design and modification of services and service management processes. This phase also tests whether the CSFs and KPIs agreed upon with the business are measurable and effective. They also determine what should be measured and set schedules and milestones for this.

Service Transition monitors and measures data about the actual usage of services and service management processes. It develops the monitoring procedures and sets measurement criteria for after implementation.

Service Operation measures the performance of the services and components in the production environment. Once again this forms input for the CSI improvement process: what can be measured and what do these data say?

Apart from SLM, availability management also plays an important role in step 3. This process:
- Creates metrics in consultation with the business to measure availability
- Determines which tools are needed to make these measurements
- Monitors and measures the performance of the infrastructure and frees up enough resources for this
- Provides data to CSI
- Updates availability plans

Capacity management also undertakes these actions; it does this in order to measure whether the IT organisation can provide the requested services. This can be done from three perspectives:
- **Business capacity management** – Answers the question "what do we need?" and "how to we measure that?" together with the business
- **Service capacity management** – Answers the question "what do we need?" from the service perspective and provides information about this to CSI
- **Component capacity management** – Looks at the components a service is comprised of and what needs to be measured to monitor this in its entirety

Incident management defines monitoring requirements to track events and incidents, preferably automated, before they cause problems. It also monitors the reaction, repair, and resolution time and the number of escalations. For example, the service desk monitors the number of reports, the average response time, and the percentage of callers who hang up prematurely.

Security management monitors and measures the security and records security incidents and problems.

And, finally, financial management monitors and measures the costs and keeps an eye on the budget. It also contributes to the reports as to the costs and ROI of improvement initiatives.

Process data (step 4)

Service Operation processes the data in logical groups. Within these groups availability management and capacity management process the data at the component level regarding availability and capacity. They work together with SLM to give these data an "end-to-end" perspective and use the agreed upon reporting form to do this.

Incident management and the service desk check and process data about incidents and service requests, and the KPIs related to this. Security management checks and processes data about security incidents and provides reports on them.

Analyse data (step 5)

Service Strategy analyses trends, looks at whether the strategies, policies, and standards introduced achieve their goal, and whether there are opportunities for improvement. *Service Design* analyses the results of design and project activities, and researches trends and opportunities for improvement. It also looks at whether the CSFs and KPIs set in step 2 are still adequate. *Service Operation* also analyses results, trends, and opportunities for improvement.

The most important Service Operation process for CSI is problem management. This process finds the underlying causes of problems, and these form important opportunities for improvement.

Availability management analyses performance and trends about components and service data. It compares data with earlier months, quarters, and years. It also looks at whether the correct information is being measured and whether SIPs are needed. It uses the following techniques:

- **Component Failure Impact Analysis (CFIA)** – An availability matrix updates which components are strategically important for each service and what role they play (Figure 9.10); a well-arranged configuration management database (CMDB) is required for this; identifies single points of failure
- **Fault Tree Analysis (FTA)** – Determines the chain of events that can lead to the failure of an IT service (Figure 9.11)
- **Service Failure Analysis (SFA)** – Looks at what a failure means for the business (impact) and what the business expects and aims at end-to-end availability improvement; based on this, CSI can determine and prioritise possible improvements
- **Technical Observation Post (TOP)** – A meeting of IT personnel with different specialisations to discuss one aspect of availability. The purpose of a TOP is to monitor events real-time as they occur with the specific aim of identifying improvement opportunities
- **Expanded Incident Lifecycle** – This is a powerful technique to analyse the incidents and for instance it calculates the mean time to restore a service (MTRS); see also the section on "maintainability" under Service Strategy

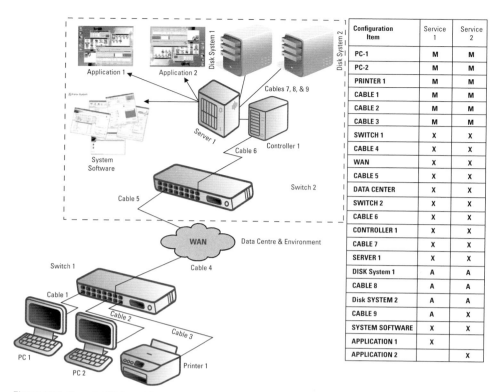

Configuration Item	Service 1	Service 2
PC-1	M	M
PC-2	M	M
PRINTER 1	M	M
CABLE 1	M	M
CABLE 2	M	M
CABLE 3	M	M
SWITCH 1	X	X
CABLE 4	X	X
WAN	X	X
CABLE 5	X	X
DATA CENTER	X	X
SWITCH 2	X	X
CABLE 6	X	X
CONTROLLER 1	X	X
CABLE 7	X	X
SERVER 1	X	X
DISK System 1	A	A
CABLE 8	A	A
Disk SYSTEM 2	A	A
CABLE 9	A	X
SYSTEM SOFTWARE	X	X
APPLICATION 1	X	
APPLICATION 2		X

Figure 9.10 Sample CFIA matrix

Source: The Cabinet Office

Capacity management analyses when which customer uses what services, how they use them, and how this influences the performance of one or more systems or components. This again provides improvement opportunities to CSI.

Capacity management tries to prevent problems proactively, by making extra storage capacity ready on time, for example. Often this is done by reproducing the situation in a model, and then asking a number of "what if" questions.

Incident management and the service desk can compare the collected data with earlier results and the agreed service levels. They can also propose SIPs or corrective actions.

Security management uses all the other processes to find the origin of security incidents and problems. It looks for trends and possible improvements in the area of monitoring and looks at whether security strategies produce the intended results.

Every improvement initiative must consult IT Service Continuity Management (ITSCM) to make sure that the IT services are not put at risk. **Risk management** plays a central role in this. It analyses what effects an improvement can have, while in

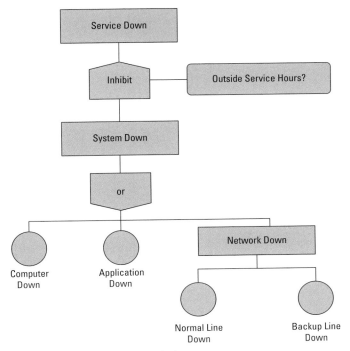

Figure 9.11 Sample fault tree analysis

Source: The Cabinet Office

turn CSI analyses the results of risk management activities, to discover opportunities for improvement. See also Service Design regarding risk management.

Present and use information (step 6)

Service Strategy presents results, trends, and recommendations for the improvement of adopted strategies, policies, and standards. *Service Design* does this for design improvements and project activities and *Service Transition* and *Service Operation* for service and service management processes.

Availability management, capacity management, incident management, service desk, problem management, and security management help with creating reports and prioritising corrective actions.

The knowledge management process is very important in CSI when presenting and using the information. This is the only way CSI can get a good overview of the knowledge of the organisation and the opportunities for improvement. It is also important in order to ensure continual improvement and to ensure that all the knowledge and experience gathered is shared and stored. For more information about knowledge management see also the section about "Service Transition".

Implement corrective actions (step 7)

Availability management, capacity management, incident management, service desk, problem management and security management perform incremental or corrective actions where approval from the business is not required.

Capacity management can also proceed by introducing **demand management** measures to influence the behaviour of the end user:

- Calculation of costs
- Making policy for the proper use of the services
- Communicating expectations
- Education about proper use
- Negotiating maintenance times
- Setting use restrictions, such as limiting the amount of storage space

As with all other changes in the lifecycle, CSI changes must go through the change, release, and deployment process. CSI must therefore submit a Request for Change (RFC) with change management and conduct a PIR after implementation. Also consider the updating of the CMDB by means of configuration management. After this, IT Service Continuity Management (ITSCM) must keep the continuity plan up-to-date.

Finally

The introduction of CSI is not simple. It requires conscious striving toward continual improvement as part of the culture and behaviour of the organisation, and a proactive attitude. In a world where the technology changes very quickly, such a proactive attitude is a big challenge; after all we are constantly controlled by the changes. In a situation of increasing outsourcing and professional development of IT service management, service quality is progressively becoming a distinguishing factor. To get "in control" and to achieve the desired quality it is preferable to work proactively. CSI is essential to this.

As with many other domains, a systematic approach is needed for this. Do not begin with a big-bang approach with all the processes at once, but first determine the biggest problem areas (for example with SWOT) and choose a well-considered approach for the improvements. Recognising the critical success factors is very important here.

Table 9.8 Overview of the Service Level Achievements accomplished

Period > Target	January	February	March	April	May	June	July	August
A						▓ (not achieved)	▒ (threatened)	▒ (threatened)
B	▒ (threatened)	▒ (threatened)	▒ (threatened)					
C								▓ (not achieved)
D				▒ (threatened)	▒ (threatened)	▒ (threatened)	▒ (threatened)	▓ (not achieved)
E								
F					▒ (threatened)	▒ (threatened)	▓ (not achieved)	▒ (threatened)
Legend:								
Goal achieved:								
Goal threatened:	▒							
Goal not achieved:	▓							

APPENDICES

A. References

Application Management. (2002). OGC. London: TSO.

Bernard, P. (2012) The IS Service Part 1 the Essentials. Van Haren Publishing

Bernard, P. (2012) The IS Service Part 2 the Handbook. Van Haren Publishing

Bernard, P. (2011) Passing the ITIL intermediate Exam. Van Haren Publishing

Business Perspective Volume 1. (2004). OGC. London: TSO.

Business Perspective Volume 2. (2006). OGC. London: TSO.

Cambridge Advanced Learner's Dictionary, http://dictionary.cambridge.org/

Cabinet Office. *ITIL. Continual Service Improvement* (2011). London: TSO.

Cabinet Office. *ITIL. Service Design* (2011). London: TSO.

Cabinet Office. *ITIL. Service Operation* (2011). London: TSO.

Cabinet Office. *ITIL. Service Strategy* (2011). London: TSO.

Cabinet Office. *ITIL. Service Transition* (2011). London: TSO.

Cambridge Advanced Learner's Dictionary, http://dictionary.cambridge.org/

Kaplan, R., & D. Norton (1992, January-February). The Balanced Scorecard - measures that drive performance. *Harvard Business Review*, Vol. 70, No. 1, p. 71-79.

Kaplan, R., & D. Norton (1993, September-October). Putting the Balanced Scorecard to work. *Harvard Business Review*, Vol. 71, No. 5, p. 134-142.

Kotter, J.P. (1996). *Leading Change.* Cambridge (MA): Harvard Business School Press.

Mintzberg, H. (1994). *The Rise and Fall of Strategic Planning: reconceiving roles for planning, plans, planners.* New York: The Free Press.

Nolan, R. (1973). Managing the computer resource: a stage hypothesis. *Communications of the ACM*, Vol. 16, Issue 7, July, p. 399 - 405.

Planning to Implement Service Management. (2002). OGC. London: TSO.

Pultorak D. et al *Passing the ITIL Foundation Exam*, Van Haren Publishing 2011

Rovers, M. ISO/IEC 20000-1:2011: A Pocket Guide. Van Haren Publishing 2011

Rummler, G. A., & A.P. Brache (1995, 2nd edition). *Improving Performance: How to Manage the White Space in the Organization Chart.* San Francisco: Jossey-Bass.

Security Management. (1999). OGC. London: TSO.

Service Delivery. (2001). OGC. London: TSO.

Service Support. (2000). Office of Government Commerce (OGC). London: TSO.

Software Asset Management. (2003). OGC. London: TSO.

Zeithaml, V.A., A. Parasuraman, & L. Berry (1990). *Delivering Quality Service.* New York: The Free Press. (SERVQUAL model)

Van Bon J. et al *ITIL A Pocket Guide 2011 Edition*, Van Haren Publishing 2011

Van Grembergen W., De Haes S., Guldentops E. (2003). *Structures, Processes and relational mechanisms for Information Technology Governance: Theories and practices, Strategies for Information Technology Governance*, book edited by Van Grembergen W., Idea Group Publishing.

B. ITIL 2011 summary of updates

B.1 Introduction

As outlined in the Mandate for Change (September 2009) and the Scope and Development Plan (February 2010), the ITIL guidance has been updated in response to:

- Issues raised through the change control log
- Advice from the change advisory board
- Feedback from the training community.

The project mandate was to correct errors, remove inconsistencies, and improve clarity and structure. The updated guidance also reflects the authoring team's responses to reviewer feedback received during the first and second public quality assurance reviews – with contributions from more than 100 reviewers.

Throughout the project, the authoring team have met regularly to discuss any issues as they occur. Adhering to a strict governance structure, any significant issues raised by the authoring team were escalated to the project board for assessment in their weekly meetings.

This document outlines global changes made across the suite and changes made specifically to the five core publications. It will provide you with a high-level overview of the updates that have occurred as part of the ITIL update project.

For a full list of all those that contributed to ITIL 2011 – including the authors, mentors and project board – please visit:

www.itil-officialsite.com/Publications/PublicationAcknowledgements.aspx

B.2 Global changes

The updated ITIL publications share a similar standard structure, to improve consistency and aid navigation. Some content has been reorganized to improve flow and readability, and ensure alignment across the suite – including clarification around interfaces, and inputs and outputs across the service lifecycle.

Terminology has been clarified and made consistent across the publications and the ITIL glossary.

Table 1 documents global updates made to all of the lifecycle publications.

Table B.1 Summary of global updates

AREA OF UPDATE	DESCRIPTION
Chapter 1	Chapter 1 (Introduction) contains generic content, which is the same across all five core publications. It provides an overview of the publication, the context of the publication in relation to the rest of the service lifecycle and best-practice guidance, and, lastly, a discussion about ITIL itself.
Chapter 2	Chapter 2, which looks at service management as a practice, is the same in each of the five core publications.
Chapter 6	Chapter 6 identifies the organizational roles and responsibilities that should be considered to manage each of the lifecycle stages (a stage per book) and the related practices. It includes generic roles, responsibilities, and competencies that apply across the service lifecycle, and specific aspects for the processes described in each publication.
Lifecycle interfaces, and inputs and outputs across the service lifecycle	A new table in Chapter 3 of each publication lists the inputs and outputs of the lifecycle to which the publication refers. Likewise a new appendix – Examples of inputs and outputs across the service lifecycle – has been added to each publication. It contains a table which identifies some of the major inputs and outputs between each stage to help users understand how the different lifecycle stages interact.
Related guidance appendix	This new appendix – in each of the core publications – includes frameworks, best practices, standards, models, and quality systems that complement and have synergy with the ITIL service lifecycle.
Roles	Roles have been made consistent across the publications, ensuring that activities apply only to one role.
Organization structures	It is now clear that organization structures given as examples are indicative rather than prescriptive.
Structure of processes	All processes have been given a common treatment, ensuring that each one has purpose and objectives; scope; value to business; policies, principles and basic concepts; process activities, methods and techniques; triggers, inputs, outputs and interfaces; information management; critical success factors and key performance indicators; and challenges and risks.
Product manager	All references to product manager have been replaced with service owner.
Capitalization	Excessive and inconsistent capitalization has been removed to aid readability.

B.3 ITIL Service Strategy

The concepts within the publication have been clarified, without changing the overall message. The updated publication includes more practical guidance and more examples where relevant.

The newly defined process of strategy management for IT services is responsible for developing and maintaining business and IT strategies, and there are now separate descriptions of business strategy and IT strategy. Financial management has been expanded, and business relationship management and demand management are now covered as processes.

Table B.2 Service Strategy

AREA OF UPDATE	DESCRIPTION
Service strategy processes	The processes have now been clearly named and defined: strategy management for IT services; service portfolio management; financial management for IT services; demand management; and business relationship management. Each process has been described using a standard template.
Business strategy and IT strategy	Business strategy and IT strategy are two different things, and ITIL Service Strategy now describes these separately and explains the relationship between the two: business strategy defines IT strategy, and IT strategy supports business strategy.
Strategy assessment, generation, and execution	More detailed guidance has been included on how an organization should go about assessing, generating, and executing its IT strategy, giving practical examples of how to proceed.
Value creation	Greater clarification is provided around how services add and realize value. New text has been included to describe how value is created, and how to differentiate between value added and value realized. A new table provides examples of utility and warranty.
Customers	It is now clearer how customers differ from users and consumers; how internal and external customers are differentiated; how business units and other IT departments as customers differ; and how IT performs its role as an external service provider.
Customer and service assets	Definitions of customer asset and service asset have been clarified, with an explanation around why these concepts are important and how they are used – including aligning service assets with customer outcomes. A new series of diagrams demonstrates the relationships between business outcomes, customer assets, service assets, constraints, and service management.
Strategy management for IT services	The newly defined process of strategy management for IT services is responsible for developing and maintaining business and IT strategies.
Financial management for IT services	The financial management for IT services process has been expanded to include some of the key elements included in the earlier ITIL publications which had been excluded in the 2007 edition of Service Strategy – such as accounting, budgeting and charging.
Business relationship management	Business relationship management is now covered as a process as well as a role. The differentiation between business relationship management for a Type I, II, and III service provider is better explained and clarified.

AREA OF UPDATE	DESCRIPTION
Governance	There is now more detail on governance, including a fuller definition of what governance means, the difference between governance and management, a governance framework, and how service management relates to governance.
Cloud computing	Some coverage has been added on how IT service management is impacted by the prevalence of cloud computing, and a new appendix has been added specifically covering service strategy and the cloud: characteristics, types, types of service, and components of cloud architecture.
Types of service management implementation	Coverage has been added regarding the types of service management implementation: even keel, trouble, growth, and radical change.
Organization	Some discussion on functions has been added and a logical organization structure for service management has been included, with supporting diagrams.

B.4 ITIL Service Design

Throughout the updated ITIL Service Design publication, there has been particular focus on alignment with ITIL Service Strategy.

A number of concepts and principles have been clarified, most significantly the flow and management of activity throughout the overall service design stage with the addition of the 'design coordination' process. Other significant clarifications include the five aspects of service design, the design of the service portfolio, and the terminology related to views of the service catalogue.

Table B.3 Service Design

AREA OF UPDATE	DESCRIPTION
Five aspects of service design	There is now consistency and clarity of references to the five aspects of service design.
Transition of a service from pipeline to catalogue to retired	The descriptions in the 2007 editions of Service Strategy and Service Design were unclear. In the 2011 edition, they have been updated to provide clarity on the definite transition points and the places for policy setting. A new status has been added to make policy setting easier.
Design coordination process	The design coordination process has been added to clarify the flow of activity in the service design lifecycle stage.
Service catalogue terminology	The service catalogue language has been revised with regard to the customer's view of the service catalogue, versus the technical or IT view.

B.5 ITIL Service Transition

The structure, content, and relationships of the configuration management system (CMS) and service knowledge management system (SKMS) have been clarified to help the reader to understand these key concepts.

There is new content explaining how a change proposal should be used. The evaluation process has been renamed 'change evaluation' and the purpose and scope have been modified to help clarify when and how this process should be used.

The service asset and configuration management process has additional content relating to asset management, and there are improvements in the flow and integration of a number of processes, including change management, release and deployment management, and change evaluation.

Table B.4 Service Transition

AREA OF UPDATE	DESCRIPTION
Change management	Top-level flowchart and section headings have been modified so that they are consistent with each other.
Change process model	The name 'change model' is now used consistently. Previously the description used the term 'change process model' but many places in Service Transition and the other publications used 'change model'.
Change proposal	More detail has been added to help clarify how and when a change proposal should be used.
Configuration record, configuration item (CI), CMS, SKMS	Many people were confused by the descriptions of a configuration record, CI, CMS and SKMS in the 2007 edition of Service Transition and wanted a clear and unambiguous explanation of these concepts.
Evaluation	The process name has been changed to 'change evaluation' and the purpose and scope have been clarified to show that this process is used for evaluating changes only.
Release and deployment management	Some sections have been reordered and a high-level process diagram has been provided showing how it all fits together.
Service asset and configuration management	Text has been added to explain the service asset management aspects better.

B.6 ITIL Service Operation

Process flows have been updated or added for all processes including request fulfilment, access management, and event management.

Key principles – including guidance around service requests and request models, and proactive problem management – have been clarified. The publication has been updated to explain how basic events flow into filters and rule engines to produce meaningful event information. The relationship between application management activities versus application development activities is also clarified.

Other improvements include an expanded section on problem analysis techniques, a procedure flow for incident matching, and further guidance for escalating incidents to problem management. In addition, the guidance for managing physical facilities has been expanded.

Table B.5 Service Operation

AREA OF UPDATE	DESCRIPTION
Service request	The concept of a service request has been significantly enhanced to provide a clearer definition, with examples and diagrams to illustrate how service requests link with the services they support. The relationship of service requests to request models and standard changes is also highlighted.
Request model	This concept has been expanded to clarify how each service request should be linked to a request model that documents the steps and tasks, and the roles and responsibilities needed to fulfil requests.
Event filtering and correlation	Additional clarification has been provided to illustrate how basic events flow into filters and rule engines to produce meaningful information.
Normal service operation	A clearer definition for this has now been included and added to the glossary.
Incident matching	A procedure has been added to provide examples of how incidents should initially be matched against known error records before escalation. A detailed procedure flow for matching incidents and escalating to problem management has been added.
Request fulfilment process flow	A new process flow now illustrates a suggested set of activities and steps for the request fulfilment process. This process flow also includes decision points for escalating requests to service transition as change proposals or incident management as incidents.
Problem analysis techniques	This section has been expanded to include more techniques for finding root causes. In addition, each technique now indicates the kinds of situations and incidents where it may be advantageous to use the particular technique described.
Problem investigation and analysis	A concept has been added to recreate problems when they are being investigated.
Mainframe and server management	The concept that the activities and procedures for managing mainframes are no different from servers has been added. How these activities might be carried out may differ, but the outcomes and kinds of management task are essentially the same.
Proactive problem management	The concept and description of activities for proactive problem management have been added to the problem management process.
Application management versus application development	The differences between application management and application development are now clarified. A diagram has been added to show the key activities that take place during each stage of the application management lifecycle to demonstrate how application management differs from application development.
Facilities management	This appendix has been greatly enhanced with additional information for managing physical facilities.

B.7 ITIL Continual Service Improvement

The seven-step improvement process and its relationship with the Plan-Do-Check-Act cycle (Deming Cycle) and knowledge management have been clarified. The continual service improvement (CSI) model has been re-named the CSI approach, and the concept of a CSI register has been introduced as a place to record details of all improvement initiatives within an organization.

Minor changes have been made throughout the publication to clarify the meaning and to improve readability. Particular emphasis has been placed on documenting the interfaces between CSI and other lifecycle stages.

Table B.6 Continual Service Improvement

AREA OF UPDATE	DESCRIPTION
Introduction of the CSI register	The CSI register is where all improvement opportunities are recorded. Each opportunity should be categorized as a small, medium or large undertaking. An indication of the amount of time it would take to complete the initiative should also be provided, along with the associated benefits. Together, this information will help produce a clear prioritized list of improvement initiatives. A full description of the CSI register is given in Chapter 3, and an example is provided in Appendix C.
Service measurement and service reporting	The treatment of service measurement and service reporting has been clarified. Because all processes have an element of measurement and reporting embedded within them, service measurement and service reporting are not considered to be processes. Therefore, these topics are covered in Chapters 3 and 5, rather than Chapter 4.
Seven-step improvement process	It is now clear that the seven-step process only contains seven steps. Some step names and activities have been amended, but the overall purpose of the process remains unchanged. The interface with the Deming Cycle and with knowledge management has been clarified.
The CSI approach	The CSI model has been re-named the CSI approach, because it is an approach to continual improvement and not a model.

B.8 ITIL glossary

The ITIL glossary has been aligned with the core publications, and reflects the updates made in those publications. There are around 55 new terms which have been added to the ITIL glossary, and approximately 30 terms have been deleted. Other terms have been updated – some more significantly than others – to reflect the content of the core publications.

The updated ITIL glossary can be found in English and other languages here:
    http://www.itil-officialsite.com/InternationalActivities/ITILGlossaries.aspx

All translated glossaries are being updated in line with the English version, and will be added to this web page as soon as they become available.

B.9 Continual improvement

The update project has addressed key issues identified in the Scope and Development Plan and change control log.

In the spirit of best practice, and the need to strive for continual improvement, any issues that you would like to raise for any of these publications can be registered in the change control log at:

　　　http://www.best-management-practice.com/changeLog

C. Glossary

C.1 ITIL Glossary

The ITIL glossary has been aligned with the core publications, and reflects the updates made in those publications. There are around 55 new terms which have been added to the ITIL glossary, and approximately 30 terms have been deleted. Other terms have been updated – some more significantly than others – to reflect the content of the core publications.

The updated ITIL glossary can be found in English and other languages here:
http://www.itil-officialsite.com/InternationalActivities/ITILGlossaries.aspx

All translated glossaries are being updated in line with the English version, and will be added to the above web page as soon as they become available.

Where a term is relevant to a particular phase in the Lifecycle of an IT service, or to one of the Core ITIL publications, this is indicated at the beginning of the definition. This glossary is based on the "**ITIL_2011_English_glossary_v1.0**" published in July 2011.

In order to simplify the text, all acronyms are "singular"; there is no "s" at the end to differentiate between singular or plural.

Again, in order to make the text more legible, excessive capitalisation has been removed and only the proper names, the product names, and the acronyms are capitalised.

C.2 Glossary

AREA OF UPDATE	DESCRIPTION
Acceptance	Formal agreement that an IT service, process, plan, or other deliverable is complete, accurate, reliable and meets its specified requirements. Acceptance is usually preceded by evaluation or testing and is often required before proceeding to the next stage of a project or process. See: service acceptance criteria.
Access management	(Service operation) the process responsible for allowing users to make use of IT services, data, or other assets. Access management helps to protect the confidentiality, integrity, and availability of assets by ensuring that only authorised users are able to access or modify the assets. Access management is sometimes referred to as rights management or identity management.
Account manager	(Service strategy) a role that is very similar to business relationship manager, but includes more commercial aspects. Most commonly used when dealing with external customers.
Accounting	(Service strategy) the process responsible for identifying actual costs of delivering IT services, comparing these with budgeted costs, and managing variance from the budget.
Accredited	Officially authorised to carry out a role; for example, an accredited body may be authorised to provide training or to conduct audits.
Active monitoring	(Service operation) monitoring of a configuration item or an IT service that uses automated regular checks to discover the current status. See: passive monitoring.
Activity	A set of actions designed to achieve a particular result. Activities are usually defined as part of processes or plans, and are documented in procedures.
Agreed service time	(Service design) a synonym for service hours, commonly used in formal calculations of availability. See: downtime.
Agreement	A document that describes a formal understanding between two or more parties. An agreement is not legally binding, unless it forms part of a contract. See: service level agreement, operational level agreement.
Alert	(Service operation) a warning that a threshold has been reached, something has changed, or a failure has occurred. Alerts are often created and managed by system management tools and are managed by the event management process.
Analytical modelling	(Service strategy) (Service design) (Continual service improvement) a technique that uses mathematical models to predict the behaviour of a configuration item or IT service. Analytical models are commonly used in capacity management and availability management. See: modelling.
Application	Software that provides functions that are required by an IT service. Each application may be part of more than one IT service. An application runs on one or more servers or clients. See: application management, application portfolio.
Application management	(Service design) (Service operation) the function responsible for managing applications throughout their lifecycle.
Application portfolio	(Service design) a database or structured document used to manage applications throughout their lifecycle. The application portfolio contains key attributes of all applications. The application portfolio is sometimes implemented as part of the service portfolio, or as part of the configuration management system.

AREA OF UPDATE	DESCRIPTION
Application service provider (ASP)	(Service design) an external service provider that provides IT services using applications running at the service provider's premises. Users access the applications by network connections to the service provider.
Application sizing	(Service design) the activity responsible for understanding the resource requirements needed to support a new application, or a major change to an existing application. Application sizing helps to ensure that the IT service can meet its agreed service level targets for capacity and performance.
Architecture	(Service design) the structure of a system or IT service, including the relationships of components to each other and to the environment they are in. Architecture also includes the standards and guidelines which guide the design and evolution of the system.
Assembly	(Service transition) a configuration item that is made up from a number of other CI; for example, a server CI may contain CI for CPU, disks, memory etc.; an IT service CI may contain hardware, software and other CI. See: component CI, build.
Assessment	Inspection and analysis to check whether a standard or set of guidelines is being followed, that records are accurate, or that efficiency and effectiveness targets are being met. See: audit.
Asset	(Service strategy) any resource or capability. Assets of a service provider include anything that could contribute to the delivery of a service. Assets can be one of the following types: management, organisation, process, knowledge, people, information, applications, infrastructure, and financial capital.
Asset management	(Service transition) asset management is the process responsible for tracking and reporting the value and ownership of financial assets throughout their lifecycle. Asset management is part of an overall service asset and configuration management process. See: asset register.
Asset register	(Service transition) a list of assets, which includes their ownership and value. The asset register is maintained by asset management.
Attribute	(Service transition) a piece of information about a configuration item. Examples are name, location, version number, and cost. Attributes of CI are recorded in the configuration management database (CMBD). See: relationship.
Audit	Formal inspection and verification to check whether a standard or set of guidelines is being followed, that records are accurate, or that efficiency and effectiveness targets are being met. An audit may be carried out by internal or external groups. See: certification, assessment.
Authority matrix	Synonym for RACI.
Automatic call distribution (ACD)	(Service operation) use of information technology to direct an incoming telephone call to the most appropriate person in the shortest possible time. ACD is sometimes called automated call distribution.
Availability	(Service design) ability of a configuration item or IT service to perform its agreed function when required. Availability is determined by reliability, maintainability, serviceability, performance, and security. Availability is usually calculated as a percentage. This calculation is often based on agreed service time and downtime. It is best practice to calculate availability using measurements of the business output of the IT service.

AREA OF UPDATE	DESCRIPTION
Availability management	(Service design) the process responsible for defining, analysing, planning, measuring and improving all aspects of the availability of IT services. Availability management is responsible for ensuring that all it infrastructure, processes, tools, roles, etc. Are appropriate for the agreed service level targets for availability.
Availability management information system (AMIS)	(Service design) a virtual repository of all availability management data, usually stored in multiple physical locations. See: service knowledge management system.
Availability plan	(Service design) a plan to ensure that existing and future availability requirements for IT services can be provided cost effectively.
Back-out	Synonym for remediation.
Backup	(Service design) (Service operation) copying data to protect against loss of integrity or availability of the original.
Balanced scorecard	(Continual service improvement) a management tool developed by Drs. Robert Kaplan (Harvard Business School) and David Norton. A balanced scorecard enables a strategy to be broken down into key performance indicators. Performance against the KPI is used to demonstrate how well the strategy is being achieved. A balanced scorecard has 4 major areas, each of which has a small number of KPI. The same 4 areas are considered at different levels of detail throughout the organisation.
Baseline	(Continual service improvement) a benchmark used as a reference point; for example: An ITSM baseline can be used as a starting point to measure the effect of a service improvement plan. • A performance baseline can be used to measure changes in performance over the lifetime of an IT service. • A configuration management baseline can be used to enable the IT infrastructure to be restored to a known configuration if a change or release fails.
Benchmark	(Continual service improvement) the recorded state of something at a specific point in time. A benchmark can be created for a configuration, a process, or any other set of data; for example, a benchmark can be used in: Continual service improvement, to establish the current state for managing improvements Capacity management, to document performance characteristics during normal operations See: benchmarking, baseline.
Benchmarking	(Continual service improvement) comparing a benchmark with a baseline or with best practice. The term benchmarking is also used to mean creating a series of benchmarks over time, and comparing the results to measure progress or improvement.
Best practice	Proven activities or processes that has been successfully used by multiple organisations. ITIL is an example of best practice.
Brainstorming	(Service design) a technique that helps a team to generate ideas. Ideas are not reviewed during the brainstorming session, but at a later stage. Brainstorming is often used by problem management to identify possible causes.
British standards institution (BSI)	The UK National Standards body, responsible for creating and maintaining British Standards. See: http://www.bsi-global.com for more information. See: ISO.

AREA OF UPDATE	DESCRIPTION
Budget	A list of all the money an organisation or business unit plans to receive, and plans to pay out, over a specified period of time. See: budgeting, planning.
Budgeting	The activity of predicting and controlling the spending of money. Consists of a periodic negotiation cycle to set future budgets (usually annual) and the day-to-day monitoring and adjusting of current budgets.
Build	(Service transition) the activity of assembling a number of configuration items to create part of an IT service. The term build is also used to refer to a release that is authorised for distribution; for example, server build or laptop builds. See: configuration baseline.
Build environment	(Service transition) a controlled environment where applications, IT services and other builds are assembled prior to being moved into a test or live environment.
Business	(Service strategy) an overall corporate entity or organisation formed of a number of business units. In the context of ITSM, the term business includes public sector and not-for-profit organisations, as well as companies do. An IT service provider provides IT services to a customer within a business. The IT service provider may be part of the same business as their customer (internal service provider), or part of another business (external service provider).
Business capacity management (BCM)	(Service design) in the context of ITSM, business capacity management is the activity responsible for understanding future business requirements for use in the capacity plan. See: service capacity management.
Business case	(Service strategy) justification for a significant item of expenditure. Includes information about costs, benefits, options, issues, risks, and possible problems. See: cost benefit analysis.
Business continuity management (BCM)	(Service design) the business process responsible for managing risks that could seriously affect the business. BCM safeguards the interests of key stakeholders, reputation, brand, and value creating activities. The BCM process involves reducing risks to an acceptable level and planning for the recovery of business processes should a disruption to the business occur. BCM sets the objectives, scope, and requirements for IT service continuity management.
Business continuity plan (BCP)	(Service design) a plan defining the steps required to restore business processes following a disruption. The plan will also identify the triggers for invocation, people to be involved, communications, etc. IT service continuity plans form a significant part of business continuity plans.
Business customer	(Service strategy) a recipient of a product or a service from the business; for example, if the business is a car manufacturer then the business customer is someone who buys a car.
Business impact analysis (BIA)	(Service strategy) BIA is the activity in business continuity management that identifies vital business functions and their dependencies. These dependencies may include suppliers, people, other business processes, IT services, etc. BIA defines the recovery requirements for IT services. These requirements include recovery time objectives, recovery point objectives, and minimum service level targets for each IT service.
Business objective	(Service strategy) the objective of a business process, or of the business as a whole. Business objectives support the business vision, provide guidance for the IT strategy, and are often supported by IT services.
Business operations	(Service strategy) the day-to-day execution, monitoring, and management of business processes.

AREA OF UPDATE	DESCRIPTION
Business perspective	(Continual service improvement) an understanding of the service provider and IT services from the point of view of the business, and an understanding of the business from the point of view of the service provider.
Business process	A process that is owned and carried out by the business. A business process contributes to the delivery of a product or service to a business customer; for example, a retailer may have a purchasing process which helps to deliver services to their business customers. Many business processes rely on IT services.
Business relationship management	(Service strategy) the process or function responsible for maintaining a relationship with the business. BRM usually includes: Managing personal relationships with business managers Providing input to service portfolio management Ensuring that the IT service provider is satisfying the business needs of the customers
Business relationship manager (BRM)	(Service strategy) a role responsible for maintaining the relationship with one or more customers. This role is often combined with the service level manager role. See: account manager.
Business service	An IT service that directly supports a business process, as opposed to an infrastructure service which is used internally by the IT service provider and is not usually visible to the business. The term business service is also used to mean a service that is delivered to business customers by business units; for example, delivery of financial services to customers of a bank, or goods to the customers of a retail store. Successful delivery of business services often depends on one or more IT services.
Business service management (BSM)	(Service strategy) (Service design) an approach to the management of IT services that considers the business processes supported and the business value provided. This term also means the management of business services delivered to business customers.
Business unit	(Service strategy) a segment of the business which has its own plans, metrics, income and costs. Each business unit owns assets and uses these to create value for customers in the form of goods and services.
Call	(Service operation) a call to the service desk from a user. A call could result in an incident or a service request being logged.
Call centre	(Service operation) an organisation or business unit which handles large numbers of incoming and outgoing telephone calls. See: service desk.
Call type	(Service operation) a category that is used to distinguish incoming requests to a service desk. Common call types are incident, service request, and complaint.
Capability	(Service strategy) the ability of an organisation, person, process, application, configuration item or IT service to carry out an activity. Capabilities are intangible assets of an organisation. See: resource.
Capability maturity model (CMM)	(Continual service improvement) the capability maturity model for software (also known as the CMM and SW-CMM is a model used to identify best practices to help increase process maturity. CMM was developed at the software engineering institute (SEI) of Carnegie Mellon University. In 2000, the SW-CMM was upgraded to CMMI® (Capability Maturity Model Integration). The SEI no longer maintains the SW-CMM model, its associated appraisal methods, or training materials.

AREA OF UPDATE	DESCRIPTION
Capability maturity model (CMMI)	(Continual service improvement) Capability Maturity Model® Integration (CMMI) is a process improvement approach developed by the Software Engineering Institute (SEI) of Carnegie Mellon University. CMMI provides organisations with the essential elements of effective processes. It can be used to guide process improvement across a project, a division, or an entire organisation. CMMI helps integrate traditionally separate organisational functions, set process improvement goals and priorities, provide guidance for quality processes, and provide a point of reference for appraising current processes. See: http://www.sei.cmu.edu/cmmi/ for more information. See: CMM, continuous improvement, maturity.
Capacity	(Service design) the maximum throughput that a configuration item or IT service can deliver whilst meeting agreed service level targets. For some types of CI, capacity may be the size or volume; for example, disks drive.
Capacity management	(Service design) the process responsible for ensuring that the capacity of IT services and the IT infrastructure is able to deliver agreed service level targets in a cost effective and timely manner. Capacity management considers all resources required delivering the IT service, and plans for short, medium, and long-term business requirements.
Capacity management information system (CMIS)	(Service design) a virtual repository of all capacity management data, usually stored in multiple physical locations. See: service knowledge management system.
Capacity plan	(Service design) a capacity plan is used to manage the resources required to deliver IT services. The plan contains scenarios for different predictions of business demand, and costed options to deliver the agreed service level targets.
Capacity planning	(Service design) the activity within capacity management responsible for creating a capacity plan.
Capital expenditure (CAPEX)	(Service strategy) the cost of purchasing something that will become a financial asset; for example, computer equipment, and buildings. The value of the asset is depreciated over multiple accounting periods.
Capital item	(Service strategy) an asset that is of interest to financial management because it is above an agreed financial value.
Capitalisation	(Service strategy) identifying major cost as capital, even though no asset is purchased. This is done to spread the impact of the cost over multiple accounting periods. The most common example of this is software development, or purchase of a software license.
Category	A named group of things that have something in common. Categories are used to group similar things together; for example, cost types are used to group similar types of cost; incident categories are used to group similar types of incident; CI types are used to group similar types of configuration item.
Certification	Issuing a certificate to confirm compliance to a standard. Certification includes a formal audit by an independent and accredited body. The term certification is also used to mean awarding a certificate to verify that a person has achieved a qualification.
Change	(Service transition) the addition, modification, or removal of anything that could have an effect on IT services. The scope should include all IT services, configuration items, processes, documentation, etc.
Change advisory board (CAB)	(Service transition) a group of people that advises the change manager in the assessment, prioritisation and scheduling of changes. This board is usually made up of representatives from all areas within the IT service provider, the business, and third parties such as suppliers.

AREA OF UPDATE	DESCRIPTION
Change case	(Service operation) a technique used to predict the impact of proposed changes. Change cases use specific scenarios to clarify the scope of proposed changes and to help with cost benefit analysis. See: use case.
Change history	(Service transition) information about all changes made to a configuration item during its life. Change history consists of all those change records that apply to the CI.
Change management	(Service transition) the process responsible for controlling the lifecycle of all changes. The primary objective of change management is to enable beneficial changes to be made, with minimum disruption to IT services.
Change model	(Service transition) a repeatable way of dealing with a particular category of change. A change model defines specific pre-defined steps that will be followed for a change of this category. Change models may be very simple, with no requirement for approval (e.g. password reset) or may be very complex with many steps that require approval (e.g. major software release). See: standard change, change advisory board.
Change record	(Service transition) a record containing the details of a change. Each change record documents the lifecycle of a single change. A change record is created for every request for change that is received, even those that are subsequently rejected. Change records should reference the configuration items that are affected by the change. Change records are stored in the configuration management system.
Change request	Synonym for request for change.
Change schedule	(Service transition) a document that lists all approved changes and their planned implementation dates. A change schedule is sometimes called a forward schedule of change, even though it also contains information about changes that have already been implemented.
Change window	(Service transition) a regular, agreed time when changes or releases may be implemented with minimal impact on services. Change windows are usually documented in SLA.
Charging	(Service strategy) requiring payment for IT services. Charging for IT services is optional, and many organisations choose to treat their IT service provider as a cost centre.
Chronological analysis	(Service operation) a technique used to help identify possible causes of problems. All available data about the problem is collected and sorted by date and time to provide a detailed timeline. This can make it possible to identify which events may have been triggered by others.
CI type	(Service transition) a category that is used to classify CI. The CI Type Identifies the required attributes and relationships for a configuration record. Common CI types include: hardware, document, user, etc.
Classification	The act of assigning a category to something. Classification is used to ensure consistent management and reporting. CI, incidents, problems, changes, etc. Are usually classified.
Client	A generic term that means a customer, the business or a business customer; for example, client manager may be used as a synonym for account manager. The term client is also used to mean: A computer that is used directly by a user; for example, a pc, handheld computer, or workstation The part of a client-server application that the user directly interfaces with, for example, an email client

AREA OF UPDATE	DESCRIPTION
Closed	(Service operation) the final status in the lifecycle of an incident, problem, change etc. When the status is closed, no further action is taken.
Closure	(Service operation) the act of changing the status of an incident, problem, change, etc. To closed.
CoBiT	(Continual service improvement) control objectives for information and related technology (COBIT) PROVIDE guidance and best practice for the management of it processes. CoBiT is published by the IT governance institute. See: http://www.isaca.org/ for more information.
Code of practice	A guideline published by a public body or a standards organisation, such as ISO or BSI. Many standards consist of a code of practice and a specification. The code of practice describes recommended best practice.
Cold standby	Synonym for gradual recovery.
Commercial off the shelf (COTS)	(Service design) application software or middleware that can be purchased from a third party.
Compliance	Ensuring that a standard or set of guidelines is followed, or that proper, consistent accounting or other practices are being employed.
Component	A general term that is used to mean one part of something more complex; for example, a computer system may be a component of an IT service, an application may be a component of a release unit. Components that need to be managed should be configuration items.
Component capacity management (CCM)	(Service design) (Continual service improvement) the process responsible for understanding the capacity, utilisation, and performance of configuration items. Data is collected, recorded, and analysed for use in the capacity plan. See: service capacity management.
Component CI	(Service transition) a configuration item that is part of an assembly; for example, a CPU, or memory CI may be part of a server CI.
Component failure impact analysis (CFIA)	(Service design) a technique that helps to identify the impact of CI failure on IT services. A matrix is created with IT services on one edge and CI on the other. This enables the identification of critical CI (that could cause the failure of multiple IT services) and of fragile IT services (that have multiple single points of failure).
Computer telephony integration (CTI)	(Service operation) CTI is a general term covering any kind of integration between computers and telephone systems. It is most commonly used to refer to systems where an application displays detailed screens relating to incoming or outgoing telephone calls. See: automatic call distribution, interactive voice response.
Concurrency	A measure of the number of users engaged in the same operation at the same time.
Confidentiality	(Service design) a security principle that requires that data should only be accessed by authorised people.
Configuration	(Service transition) a generic term, used to describe a group of configuration items that work together to deliver an IT service, or a recognisable part of an IT service. Configuration is also used to describe the parameter settings for one or more CI.
Configuration baseline	(Service transition) a baseline of a configuration that has been formally agreed and is managed through the change management process. A configuration baseline is used as a basis for future builds, releases, and changes.

AREA OF UPDATE	DESCRIPTION
Configuration control	(Service transition) the activity responsible for ensuring that adding, modifying or removing a CI is properly managed; for example, by submitting a request for change or service request.
Configuration identification	(Service transition) the activity responsible for collecting information about configuration items and their relationships, and loading this information into the CMDB. Configuration identification is also responsible for labelling the CI themselves, so that the corresponding configuration records can be found.
Configuration item (CI)	(Service transition) any component that needs to be managed in order to deliver an IT service. Information about each CI is recorded in a configuration record within the configuration management system and is maintained throughout its lifecycle by configuration management. A CI is under the control of change management. CI typically include IT services, hardware, software, buildings, people, and formal documentation such as process documentation and SLA.
Configuration management	(Service transition) the process responsible for maintaining information about configuration items required delivering an IT service, including their relationships. This information is managed throughout the lifecycle of the CI. Configuration management is part of an overall service asset and configuration management process.
Configuration management database (CMDB)	(Service transition) a database used to store configuration records throughout their lifecycle. The configuration management system maintains one or more CMDB, and each CMDB stores attributes of CI, and relationships with other CI.
Configuration management system (CMS)	(Service transition) a set of tools and databases that are used to manage an IT service provider's configuration data. The CMS also includes information about incidents, problems, known errors, changes and releases; and may contain data about employees, suppliers, locations, business units, customers and users. The CMS includes tools for collecting, storing, managing, updating, and presenting data about all configuration items and their relationships. The CMS is maintained by configuration management and is used by all IT service management processes. See: configuration management database, service knowledge management system.
Configuration record	(Service transition) a record containing the details of a configuration item. Each configuration record documents the lifecycle of a single CI. Configuration records are stored in a configuration management database.
Configuration structure	(Service transition) the hierarchy and other relationships between all the configuration items that comprise a configuration.
Continual service improvement (CSI)	(Continual service improvement) a stage in the lifecycle of an IT service and the title of one of the core ITIL publications. Continual service improvement is responsible for managing improvements to IT service management processes and IT services. The performance of the IT service provider is continually measured and improvements are made to processes, IT services, and it infrastructure in order to increase efficiency, effectiveness, and cost effectiveness. See: Plan-Do-Check-Act (P-D-C-A cycle).
Continuous availability	(Service design) an approach or design to achieve 100% availability. A continuously available IT service has no planned or unplanned downtime.
Continuous operation	(Service design) an approach or design to eliminate planned downtime of an IT service. Note that individual configuration items may be down even though the IT service is available.
Contract	A legally binding agreement between two or more parties.

AREA OF UPDATE	DESCRIPTION
Contract portfolio	(Service strategy) a database or structured document used to manage service contracts or agreements between an IT service provider and their customers. Each IT service delivered to a customer should have a contract or other agreement which is listed in the contract portfolio. See: service portfolio, service catalogue.
Control	A means of managing a risk, ensuring that a business objective is achieved, or ensuring that a process is followed. Example controls include policies, procedures, roles, raid, door-locks, etc. A control is sometimes called a countermeasure or safeguard. Control also means to manage the utilisation or behaviour of a configuration item, system, or IT service.
Control objectives for information and related technology (CobiT)	See: CobiT.
Control perspective	(Service strategy) an approach to the management of IT services, processes, functions, assets, etc. There can be several different control perspectives on the same IT service, process, etc., allowing different individuals or teams to focus on what is important and relevant to their specific role. Example control perspectives include reactive and proactive management within it operations, or a lifecycle view for an application project team.
Control processes	The ISO/IEC 20000 process group that includes change management and configuration management.
Core service	(Service strategy) an IT service that delivers basic outcomes desired by one or more customers. See: supporting service, core service package.
Core service package (CSP)	(Service strategy) a detailed description of a core service that may be shared by two or more service level packages. See: service package.
Cost	The amount of money spent on a specific activity, IT service, or business unit. Costs consist of real cost (money), notional cost such as people's time, and depreciation.
Cost benefit analysis	An activity that analyses and compares the costs and the benefits involved in one or more alternative courses of action. See: business case, net present value, internal rate of return, return on investment, and value on investment.
Cost centre	(Service strategy) a business unit or project to which costs are assigned. A cost centre does not charge for services provided. An IT service provider can be run as a cost centre or a profit centre.
Cost effectiveness	A measure of the balance between the effectiveness and cost of a service, process, or activity, a cost effective process is one which achieves its objectives at minimum cost. See: KPI, return on investment, value for money.
Cost element	(Service strategy) the middle level of category to which costs are assigned in budgeting and accounting. The highest level category is cost type; for example, a cost type of 'people' could have cost elements of payroll, personnel benefits, expenses, training, overtime, etc. Cost elements can be further broken down to give cost units; for example, the cost element 'expenses' could include cost units of hotels, transport, meals, etc.
Cost management	(Service strategy) a general term that is used to refer to budgeting and accounting, sometimes used as a synonym for financial management.

AREA OF UPDATE	DESCRIPTION
Cost type	(Service strategy) the highest level of category to which costs are assigned in budgeting and accounting; for example, hardware, software, people, accommodation, external and transfer. See: cost element, cost type.
Cost unit	(Service strategy) the lowest level of category to which costs are assigned, cost units are usually things that can be easily counted (e.g. Personnel numbers, software licenses) or things easily measured (e.g. CPU usage, electricity consumed). Cost units are included within cost elements; for example, a cost element of 'expenses' could include cost units of hotels, transport, meals, etc. See: cost type.
Countermeasure	Can be used to refer to any type of control. The term countermeasure is most often used when referring to measures that increase resilience, fault tolerance, or reliability of an IT service.
Course corrections	Changes made to a plan or activity that has already started to ensure that it will meet its objectives. Course corrections are made as a result of monitoring progress.
CRAMM	A methodology and tool for analysing and managing risks. CRAMM was developed by the UK Government, but is now privately owned. Further information is available from http://www.cramm.com/
Crisis management	The process responsible for managing the wider implications of business continuity. A crisis management team is responsible for strategic issues such as managing media relations and shareholder confidence, and decides when to invoke business continuity plans.
Critical success factor (CSF)	Something that must happen if a process, project, plan, or IT service is to succeed. KPI are used to measure the achievement of each CSFs; for example, a CSFs of 'protect IT services when making changes' could be measured by KPI such as 'percentage reduction of unsuccessful changes', 'percentage reduction in changes causing incidents', etc.
Culture	A set of values that is shared by a group of people, including expectations about how people should behave, ideas, beliefs, and practices. See: vision.
Customer	Someone who buys goods or services. The customer of an IT service provider is the person or group who defines and agrees the service level targets. The term customer is also sometimes used informally to mean user, for example, 'this is a customer-focused organisation'.
Customer portfolio	(Service strategy) a database or structured document used to record all customers of the IT service provider. The customer portfolio is the business relationship manager's view of the customers who receive services from the IT service provider. See: contract portfolio, service portfolio.
Dashboard	(Service operation) a graphical representation of overall IT service performance and availability. Dashboard images may be updated in real-time, and can also be included in management reports and web pages. Dashboards can be used to support service level management, event management, or incident diagnosis.
Data-to-information-to-knowledge-to-wisdom (DIKW)	A way of understanding the relationships between data, information, knowledge, and wisdom. DIKW shows how each of these builds on the others.

AREA OF UPDATE	DESCRIPTION
Definitive media library (DML)	(Service transition) one or more locations in which the definitive and approved versions of all software configuration items are securely stored. The DML may also contain associated CI such as licenses and documentation. The DML is a single logical storage area even if there are multiple locations. All software in the DML is under the control of change and release management and is recorded in the configuration management system. Only software from the DML is acceptable for use in a release.
Deliverable	Something that must be provided to meet a commitment in a service level agreement or a contract. Deliverable is also used in a more informal way to mean a planned output of any process.
Demand management	Activities that understand and influence customer demand for services and the provision of capacity to meet these demands. At a strategic level demand management can involve analysis of patterns of business activity and user profiles. At a tactical level it can involve use of differential charging to encourage customers to use IT services at less busy times. See: capacity management.
Deming cycle	Synonym for Plan-Do-Check-Act (P-D-C-A) cycle.
Dependency	The direct or indirect reliance of one process or activity upon another.
Deployment	(Service transition) the activity responsible for movement of new or changed hardware, software, documentation, process, etc., to the live environment. Deployment is part of the release and deployment management process. See: rollout.
Depreciation	(Service strategy) a measure of the reduction in value of an asset over its life. This is based on wearing out, consumption or other reduction in the useful economic value.
Design	(Service design) an activity or process that identifies requirements and then defines a solution that is able to meet these requirements. See: service design.
Detection	(Service operation) a stage in the incident lifecycle. Detection results in the incident becoming known to the service provider. Detection can be automatic, or can be the result of a user logging an incident.
Development	(Service design) the process responsible for creating or modifying an IT service or application. Also used to mean the role or group that carries out development work.
Development environment	(Service design) an environment used to create or modify IT services or applications. Development environments are not typically subjected to the same degree of control as test environments or live environments. See: development.
Diagnosis	(Service operation) a stage in the incident and problem lifecycles. The purpose of diagnosis is to identify a workaround for an incident or the root cause of a problem.
Diagnostic script	(Service operation) a structured set of questions used by service desk personnel to ensure they ask the correct questions, and to help them classify, resolve, and assign incidents. Diagnostic scripts may also be made available to users to help them diagnose and resolve their own incidents.
Differential charging	A technique used to support demand management by charging different amounts for the same IT service function at different times.

AREA OF UPDATE	DESCRIPTION
Direct cost	(Service strategy) a cost of providing an IT service which can be allocated in full to a specific customer, cost centre, project, etc., for example, cost of providing non-shared servers or software licenses. See: indirect cost.
Directory service	(Service operation) an application that manages information about it infrastructure available on a network, and corresponding user access rights.
Do nothing	(Service design) a recovery option. The service provider formally agrees with the customer that recovery of this IT service will not be performed.
Document	Information in readable form. A document may be paper or electronic. For example, a policy statement, service level agreement, incident record, diagram of computer room layout. See: record.
Downtime	(Service design) (Service operation) the time when a configuration item or IT service is not available during its agreed service time. The availability of an IT service is often calculated from agreed service time and downtime.
Driver	Something that influences strategy, objectives, or requirements. For example new legislation or the actions of competitors.
Early life support	(Service transition) support provided for a new or changed IT service for a period of time after it is released. During early life support the IT service provider may review the KPI, service levels, and monitoring thresholds, and provide additional resources for incident and problem management.
Economies of scale	(Service strategy) the reduction in average cost that is possible from increasing the usage of an IT service or asset. See: economies of scope.
Economies of scope	(Service strategy) the reduction in cost that is allocated to an IT service by using an existing asset for an additional purpose. For example delivering a new IT service from existing it infrastructure. See: economies of scale.
Effectiveness	(Continual service improvement) a measure of whether the objectives of a process, service, or activity have been achieved. An effective process or activity is one that achieves its agreed objectives. See: KPI.
Efficiency	(Continual service improvement) a measure of whether the right amount of resources has been used to deliver a process, service, or activity. An efficient process achieves its objectives with the minimum amount of time, money, people, or other resources. See: KPI.
Emergency change	(Service transition) a change that must be introduced as soon as possible. For example, to resolve a major incident or to implement a security patch. The change management process will normally have a specific procedure for handling emergency changes. See: emergency change advisory board (ECAB).
Emergency change advisory board (ECAB)	(Service transition) a sub-set of the change advisory board who make decisions about high impact emergency changes. Membership of the ECAB may be decided at the time a meeting is called, and depends on the nature of the emergency change.

AREA OF UPDATE	DESCRIPTION
Environment	(Service transition) a subset of the IT infrastructure that is used for a particular purpose. For example: live environment, test environment, build environment. It is possible for multiple environments to share a configuration item, for example, test and live environments may use different partitions on a single mainframe computer. Also used in the term physical environment to mean the accommodation, air conditioning, power system, etc. Environment is also used as a generic term to mean the external conditions that influence or affect something.
Error	(Service operation) a design flaw or malfunction that causes a failure of one or more configuration items or IT services. A mistake made by a person or a faulty process that impacts a CI or IT service is also an error.
Escalation	(Service operation) an activity that obtains additional resources when these are needed to meet service level targets or customer expectations. Escalation may be needed within any IT service management process, but is most commonly associated with incident management, problem management, and the management of customer complaints. There are two types of escalation, functional escalation, and hierarchic escalation.
e-Sourcing capability model for client organisations (ESCM-CL)	(Service strategy) a framework to help organisations guide their analysis and decisions on service sourcing models and strategies. ESCM-CL was developed by Carnegie Mellon University. See: eSCM-SP
e-Sourcing capability model for service providers (ESCM-SP)	(Service strategy) a framework assisting IT service providers develop their IT service management capabilities from a service sourcing perspective. ESCM-SP was developed by Carnegie Mellon University. See: eSCM-CL.
Estimation	The use of experience to provide an approximate value for a metric or cost. Estimation is also used in capacity and availability management as the cheapest and least accurate modelling method.
Evaluation	(Service transition) the process responsible for assessing a new or changed IT service to ensure that risks have been managed and to help determine whether to proceed with the change. Evaluation is also used to mean comparing an actual outcome with the intended outcome, or comparing one alternative with another.
Event	(Service operation) A change of state that has significance for the management of an IT service or other configuration item. The term is also used to mean an alert or notification created by any IT service, configuration item or monitoring tool. Events typically require IT operations personnel to take actions, and often lead to incidents being logged.
Event management	(Service operation) the process responsible for managing events throughout their lifecycle. Event management is one of the main activities of it operations.
Exception report	A document containing details of one or more KPI or other important targets that have exceeded defined thresholds. Examples include SLA targets being missed or about to be missed and a performance metric indicating a potential capacity problem.
Expanded incident lifecycle	(Availability management) detailed stages in the lifecycle of an incident. The stages are detection, diagnosis, repair, recovery, and restoration. The expanded incident lifecycle is used to help understand all contributions to the impact of incidents and to plan how these could be controlled or reduced.
External customer	A customer who works for a different business to the IT service provider. See: external service provider, internal customer.

AREA OF UPDATE	DESCRIPTION
External metric	A metric that is used to measure the delivery of IT service to a customer. External metrics are usually defined in SLA and reported to customers. See: internal metric.
External service provider	(Service strategy) an IT service provider which is part of a different organisation to their customer. An IT service provider may have both internal customers and external customers. See: Type III service provider.
External sourcing	Synonym for outsourcing.
Facilities management	(Service operation) the function responsible for managing the physical environment where the IT infrastructure is located. Facilities management includes all aspects of managing the physical environment, for example, power and cooling, building access management and environmental monitoring.
Failure	(Service operation) loss of ability to operate to specification, or to deliver the required output. The term failure may be used when referring to IT services, processes, activities, configuration items, etc. A failure often causes an incident.
Failure modes and effects analysis (FMEA)	An approach to assessing the potential impact of failures. FMEA involves analysing what would happen after failure of each configuration item, all the way up to the effect on the business. FMEA is often used in information security management and in IT service continuity planning.
Fast recovery	(Service design) a recovery option which is also known as hot standby. Provision is made to recover the IT service in a short period of time, typically less than 24 hours. Fast recovery typically uses a dedicated fixed facility with computer systems, and software configured ready to run the IT services. Immediate recovery may take up to 24 hours if there is a need to restore data from backups.
Fault	Synonym for error.
Fault tolerance	(Service design) the ability of an IT service or configuration item to continue to operate correctly after failure of a component part. See: resilience, countermeasure.
Fault tree analysis (FTA)	(Service design) (Continual service improvement) a technique that can be used to determine the chain of events that leads to a problem. Fault tree analysis represents a chain of events using Boolean notation in a diagram.
Financial management	(Service strategy) the function and processes responsible for managing an IT service provider's budgeting, accounting, and charging requirements.
First-line support	(Service operation) the first level in a hierarchy of support groups involved in the resolution of incidents. Each level contains more specialist skills, or has more time or other resources. See: escalation.
Fishbone diagram	Synonym for Ishikawa diagram.
Fit for purpose	An informal term used to describe a process, configuration item, IT service, etc., that is capable of meeting its objectives or service levels. Being 'fit for purpose' requires suitable design, implementation, control, and maintenance.
Fixed cost	(Service strategy) a cost that does not vary with IT service usage, for example, the cost of server hardware. See: variable cost.
Fixed facility	(Service design) a permanent building, available for use when needed by an IT service continuity plan. See: recovery option, portable facility.

AREA OF UPDATE	DESCRIPTION
Follow the sun	(Service operation) a methodology for using service desks and support groups around the world to provide seamless 24 * 7 services. Calls, incidents, problems, and service requests are passed between groups in different time sons.
Fulfilment	Performing activities to meet a need or requirement; for example, by providing a new IT service, or meeting a service request.
Function	A team or group of people and the tools or other resources they use to carry out one or more processes or activities – for example, the service desk. The term also has two other meanings: • An intended purpose of a configuration item, person, team, process or IT service. For example, one function of an email service may be to store and forward outgoing mails, while the function of a business process may be to despatch goods to customers. • To perform the intended purpose correctly, as in "The computer is functioning."
Functional escalation	(Service operation) transferring an incident, problem or change to a technical team with a higher level of expertise to assist in an escalation.
Gap analysis	(Continual service improvement) an activity which compares two sets of data and identifies the differences. Gap analysis is commonly used to compare a set of requirements with actual delivery. See: benchmarking.
Governance	Ensures that policies and strategy are actually implemented, and that required processes are correctly followed. Governance includes defining roles and responsibilities, measuring and reporting, and taking actions to resolve any issues identified.
Gradual recovery	(Service design) a recovery option which is also known as cold standby. Provision is made to recover the IT service in a period of time greater than 72 hours. Gradual recovery typically uses a portable or fixed facility that has environmental support and network cabling, but no computer systems. The hardware and software are installed as part of the IT service continuity plan.
Guideline	A document describing best practice that recommends what should be done. Compliance to a guideline is not normally enforced. See: standard.
Help desk	(Service operation) a point of contact for users to log incidents. A help desk is usually more technically focused than a service desk and does not provide a single point of contact for all interaction. The term help desk is often used as a synonym for service desk.
Hierarchic escalation	(Service operation) informing or involving more senior levels of management to assist in an escalation.
High availability	(Service design) an approach or design that minimises or hides the effects of configuration item failure on the users of an IT service. High availability solutions are designed to achieve an agreed level of availability and make use of techniques such as fault tolerance, resilience, and fast recovery to reduce the number of incidents, and the impact of incidents.
Hot standby	Synonym for fast recovery or immediate recovery.
Identity	(Service operation) a unique name that is used to identify a user, person, or role. The identity is used to grant rights to that user, person, or role. Example identities might be the username smithj or the role 'change manager'.
Immediate recovery	(Service design) a recovery option which is also known as hot standby. Provision is made to recover the IT service with no loss of service. Immediate recovery typically uses mirroring, load balancing and split site technologies.

AREA OF UPDATE	DESCRIPTION
Impact	(Service operation) (Service transition) a measure of the effect of an incident, problem, or change on business processes. Impact is often based on how service levels will be affected. Impact and urgency are used to assign priority.
Incident	(Service operation) an unplanned interruption to an IT service or a reduction in the quality of an IT service. Failure of a configuration item that has not yet affected service is also an incident; for example failure of one disk from a mirror set.
Incident management	(Service operation) the process responsible for managing the lifecycle of all incidents. The primary objective of incident management is to return the IT service to users as quickly as possible.
Incident record	(Service operation) a record containing the details of an incident. Each incident record documents the lifecycle of a single incident.
Indirect cost	(Service strategy) a cost of providing an IT service which cannot be allocated in full to a specific customer; for example, cost of providing shared servers or software licenses. Also known as overhead. See: direct cost.
Information security management (ISM)	(Service design) the process that ensures the confidentiality, integrity, and availability of an organisation's assets, information, data and IT services. Information security management usually forms part of an organisational approach to security management which has a wider scope than the IT service provider, and includes handling of paper, building access, phone calls etc., for the entire organisation.
Information security management system (ISMS)	(Service design) the framework of policy, processes, standards, guidelines, and tools that ensures an organisation can achieve its information security management objectives.
Information security policy	(Service design) the policy that governs the organisation's approach to information security management.
Information technology (IT)	The use of technology for the storage, communication or processing of information. The technology typically includes computers, telecommunications, applications, and other software. The information may include business data, voice, images, video, etc. Information technology is often used to support business processes through IT services.
Infrastructure service	An IT service that is not directly used by the business, but is required by the IT service provider, so they can provide other IT services; for example, directory services, naming services, or communication services.
Insourcing	Synonym for internal sourcing.
Integrity	(Service design) a security principle that ensures data and configuration items are only modified by authorised personnel and activities. Integrity considers all possible causes of modification, including software and hardware failure, environmental events and human intervention.
Interactive voice response (IVR)	(Service operation) a form of automatic call distribution that accepts user input, such as key presses and spoken commands, to identify the correct destination for incoming calls.
Intermediate recovery	(Service design) a recovery option which is also known as warm standby. Provision is made to recover the IT service in a period of time between 24 and 72 hours. Intermediate recovery typically uses a shared portable or fixed facility that has computer systems and network components. The hardware and software will need to be configured, and data will need to be restored, as part of the IT service continuity plan.

AREA OF UPDATE	DESCRIPTION
Internal customer	A customer who works for the same business as the IT service provider. See: internal service provider, external customer.
Internal metric	A metric that is used within the IT service provider to monitor the efficiency, effectiveness, or cost effectiveness of the IT service provider's internal processes. Internal metrics are not normally reported to the customer of the IT service. See: external metric.
Internal rate of return (IRR)	(Service strategy) a technique used to help make decisions about capital expenditure. IRR calculates a figure that allows two or more alternative investments to be compared. A larger IRR indicates a better investment. See: net present value, return on investment.
Internal service provider	(Service strategy) an IT service provider which is part of the same organisation as their customer. An IT service provider may have both internal customers and external customers. See: Type I service provider, Type II service provider, insource.
Internal sourcing	(Service strategy) using an internal service provider to manage IT services. See: service sourcing, Type I service provider, Type II service provider.
International organisation for standardisation (ISO)	The international organisation for standardisation (ISO) is the world's largest developer of standards. ISO is a non-governmental organisation which is a network of the national standards institutes of 156 countries. Further information about ISO is available from http://www.iso.org/
International standards organisation	See: international organisation for standardisation (ISO).
Internet service provider (ISP)	An external service provider that provides access to the internet. Most ISPs also provide other IT services such as web hosting.
Invocation	(Service design) initiation of the steps defined in a plan; for example initiating the IT service continuity plan for one or more IT services.
Ishikawa diagram	(Service operation) (Continual service improvement) a technique that helps a team to identify all the possible causes of a problem. Originally devised by Kaoru Ishikawa, the output of this technique is a diagram that looks like a fishbone.
ISO 9000	A generic term that refers to a number of international standards and guidelines for quality management systems. See: http://www.iso.org/ for more information. See: ISO.
ISO 9001	An international standard for quality management systems. See: ISO 9000, standard.
ISO/IEC 17799	(Continual service improvement) ISO code of practice for information security management. See: standard.
ISO/IEC 20000	ISO specification and code of practice for IT service management. ISO/IEC 20000 is aligned with ITIL best practice.
ISO/IEC 27001	(Service design) (Continual service improvement) ISO specification for information security management. The corresponding code of practice is ISO/IEC 17799. See: standard.
ISO/IEC 31000	Intended to be a family of standards relating to risk management; the purpose of ISO 31000:2009 is to provide principles and generic guidelines on risk management.

AREA OF UPDATE	DESCRIPTION
ISO/IEC 38500	The ISO/IEC standard relating to Corporate governance of information technology.
IT directorate	(Continual service improvement) senior management within a service provider charged with developing and delivering IT services. Most commonly used in UK Government departments.
IT infrastructure	All of the hardware, software, networks, facilities, etc., that are required to develop, test, deliver, monitor, control or support IT services. The term it infrastructure includes all of the information technology, but not the associated people, processes and documentation.
IT operations	(Service operation) activities carried out by IT operations control, including console management, job scheduling, backup and restore, and print and output management. It operations is also used as a synonym for service operation.
IT operations control	(Service operation) the function responsible for monitoring and control of the IT services and it infrastructure. See: operations bridge.
IT operations management	(Service operation) the function within an IT service provider which performs the daily activities needed to manage IT services and the supporting it infrastructure. It operations management includes it operations control and facilities management.
IT service	A service provided to one or more customers by an IT service provider. An IT service is based on the use of information technology and supports the customer's business processes. An IT service is made up from a combination of people, processes, and technology and should be defined in a service level agreement.
It service continuity management (ITSCM)	(Service design) the process responsible for managing risks that could seriously affect IT services. ITSCM ensures that the IT service provider can always provide minimum agreed service levels, by reducing the risk to an acceptable level and planning for the recovery of IT services. ITSCM should be designed to support business continuity management.
IT service continuity plan	(Service design) a plan defining the steps required recovering one or more IT services. The plan will also identify the triggers for invocation, people to be involved, communications, etc. The IT service continuity plan should be part of a business continuity plan.
IT service management (ITSM)	The implementation and management of quality IT services that meet the needs of the business. IT service management is performed by IT service providers through an appropriate mix of people, process, and information technology. See: service management.
IT Service Management Forum (itSMF)	The IT service management forum is an independent organisation dedicated to promoting a professional approach to IT service management. The itSMF is a not-for-profit membership organisation with representation in many countries around the world (itSMF chapters). The itSMF and its membership contribute to the development of ITIL and associated IT service management standards. See: http://www.itsmf.com/ for more information.
IT service provider	(Service strategy) a service provider that provides IT services to internal customers or external customers.
IT steering group (ISG)	A formal group that is responsible for ensuring that business and IT service provider strategies and plans are closely aligned. An IT steering group includes senior representatives from the business and the IT service provider.

AREA OF UPDATE	DESCRIPTION
ITIL	A set of best practice guidance for IT service management. ITIL is owned by the OGC and consists of a series of publications giving guidance on the provision of quality IT services, and on the processes and facilities needed to support them. See: http://www.itil.co.uk/ for more information.
Job description	A document which defines the roles, responsibilities, skills, and knowledge required by a particular person. One job description can include multiple roles, for example the roles of configuration manager and change manager may be carried out by one person.
Job scheduling	(Service operation) planning and managing the execution of software tasks that are required as part of an IT service. Job scheduling is carried out by IT operations management, and is often automated using software tools that run batch or online tasks at specific times of the day, week, month, or year.
Kano model	(Service strategy) a model developed by Noriaki Kano that is used to help understand customer preferences. The Kano model considers attributes of an IT service grouped into areas such as basic factors, excitement factors, performance factors, etc.
Kepner & Tregoe analysis	(Service operation) (Continual service improvement) a structured approach to problem solving. The problem is analysed in terms of what, where, when and extent. Possible causes are identified. The most probable cause is tested. The true cause is verified.
Key performance indicator (KPI)	(Continual service improvement) a metric that is used to help manage a process, IT service, or activity. Many metrics may be measured, but only the most important of these are defined as KPI and used to actively manage and report on the process, IT service, or activity. KPI should be selected to ensure that efficiency, effectiveness, and cost effectiveness are all managed. See: critical success factor.
Knowledge base	(Service transition) a logical database containing the data used by the service knowledge management system.
Knowledge management	(Service transition) the process responsible for gathering, analysing, storing and sharing knowledge and information within an organisation. The primary purpose of knowledge management is to improve efficiency by reducing the need to rediscover knowledge. See: data-to-information-to-knowledge-to-wisdom, service knowledge management system.
Known error	(Service operation) a problem that has a documented root cause and a workaround. Known errors are created and managed throughout their lifecycle by problem management. Known errors may also be identified by development or suppliers.
Known error database (KEDB)	(Service operation) a database containing all known error records. This database is created by problem management and used by incident and problem management. The known error database is part of the service knowledge management system.
Known error record	(Service operation) a record containing the details of a known error. Each known error record documents the lifecycle of a known error, including the status, root cause, and workaround. In some implementations a known error is documented using additional fields in a problem record.

AREA OF UPDATE	DESCRIPTION
Lifecycle	The various stages in the life of an IT service, configuration item, incident, problem, change, etc. The lifecycle defines the categories for status and the status transitions that are permitted. For example: The lifecycle of an application includes requirements, design, build, deploy, operate, and optimise. The expanded incident lifecycle includes detect, respond, diagnose, repair, recover, restore. The lifecycle of a server may include: ordered, received, in test, live, disposed, etc.
Line of service (LOS)	(Service strategy) a core service or supporting service that has multiple service level packages. A line of service is managed by a product manager and each service level package is designed to support a particular market segment.
Live	(Service transition) refers to an IT service or configuration item that is being used to deliver service to a customer.
Live environment	(Service transition) a controlled environment containing live configuration items used to deliver IT services to customers.
Maintainability	(Service design) a measure of how quickly and effectively a configuration item or IT service can be restored to normal working after a failure. Maintainability is often measured and reported as MTRS. Maintainability is also used in the context of software or IT service development to mean ability to be changed or repaired easily.
Major incident	(Service operation) the highest category of impact for an incident. A major incident results in significant disruption to the business.
Managed services	(Service strategy) a perspective on IT services which emphasises the fact that they are managed. The term managed services is also used as a synonym for outsourced IT services.
Management information	Information that is used to support decision-making by managers. Management information is often generated automatically by tools supporting the various IT service management processes. Management information often includes the values of KPI such as 'percentage of changes leading to incidents', or 'first time fix rate'.
Management of risk (M_o_R)	The OGC methodology for managing risks. M_o_R includes all the activities required to identify and control the exposure to risk which may have an impact on the achievement of an organisation's business objectives. See: http://www.m-o-r.org/ for more details.
Management system	The framework of policy, processes, and functions that ensures an organisation can achieve its objectives.
Manual workaround	A workaround that requires manual intervention. Manual workaround is also used as the name of a recovery option in which the business process operates without the use of IT services. This is a temporary measure and is usually combined with another recovery option.
Marginal cost	(Service strategy) the cost of continuing to provide the IT service. Marginal cost does not include investment already made; for example the cost of developing new software and delivering training.
Market space	(Service strategy) all opportunities that an IT service provider could exploit to meet business needs of customers. The market space identifies the possible IT services that an IT service provider may wish to consider delivering.

AREA OF UPDATE	DESCRIPTION
Maturity	(Continual service improvement) a measure of the reliability, efficiency, and effectiveness of a process, function, organisation, etc. The most mature processes and functions are formally aligned to business objectives and strategy, and are supported by a framework for continual improvement.
Maturity level	A named level in a maturity model such as the Carnegie Mellon Capability Maturity Model Integration.
Mean time between failures (MTBF)	(Service design) a metric for measuring and reporting reliability. MTBF are the average time that a configuration item or IT service can perform its agreed function without interruption. This is measured from when the CI or IT service starts working, until it next fails.
Mean time between service incidents (MTBSI)	(Service design) a metric used for measuring and reporting reliability. MTBSI are the mean time from when a system or IT service fails, until it next fails. MTBSI is equal to MTBF + MTRS.
Mean time to repair (MTTR)	The average time taken to repair a configuration item or IT service after a failure. MTTR is measured from when the CI or IT service fails until it is repaired. MTTR does not include the time required to recover or restore. MTTR is sometimes incorrectly used as a synonym for mean time to restore service.
Mean time to restore service (MTRS)	The average time taken to restore a configuration item or IT service after a failure. MTRS is measured from when the CI or IT service fails until it is fully restored and delivering its normal functionality. See: maintainability, mean time to repair.
Metric	(Continual service improvement) something that is measured and reported to help manage a process, IT service, or activity. See: KPI.
Middleware	(Service design) software that connects two or more software components or applications. Middleware is usually purchased from a supplier, rather than developed within the IT service provider. See: off the shelf.
Mission statement	The mission statement of an organisation is a short but complete description of the overall purpose and intentions of that organisation. It states what is to be achieved, but not how this should be done.
Model	A representation of a system, process, IT service, configuration item, etc., that is used to help understand or predict future behaviour.
Modelling	A technique that is used to predict the future behaviour of a system, process, IT service, configuration item, etc. Modelling is commonly used in financial management, capacity management, and availability management.
Monitor control loop	(Service operation) monitoring the output of a task, process, IT service, or configuration item; comparing this output to a predefined norm; and taking appropriate action based on this comparison.
Monitoring	(Service operation) repeated observation of a configuration item, IT service, or process to detect events and to ensure that the current status is known.
Near-shore	(Service strategy) provision of services from a country near the country where the customer is based. This can be the provision of an IT service, or of supporting functions such as service desk. See: on-shore, off-shore.
Net present value (NPV)	(Service strategy) a technique used to help make decisions about capital expenditure. NPV compares cash inflows to cash outflows. Positive NPV indicates that an investment is worthwhile. See: internal rate of return, return on investment.

AREA OF UPDATE	DESCRIPTION
Notional charging	(Service strategy) an approach to charging for IT services. Charges to customers are calculated and customers are informed of the charge, but no money is actually transferred. Notional charging is sometimes introduced to ensure that customers are aware of the costs they incur or as a stage during the introduction of real charging.
Objective	The defined purpose or aim of a process, an activity, or an organisation as a whole. Objectives are usually expressed as measurable targets. The term objective is also informally used to mean a requirement. See: outcome.
Off the shelf	Synonym for commercial off the shelf.
Office of public sector information (OPSI)	OPSI license the crown copyright material used in the ITIL publications. They are a UK Government department who provide online access to UK legislation, license the re-use of crown copyright material, manage the information fair trader scheme, maintain the government's information asset register, and provide advice and guidance on official publishing and crown copyright.
Off-shore	(Service strategy) provision of services from a location outside the country where the customer is based, often in a different continent. This can be the provision of an IT service, or of supporting functions such as service desk. See: on-shore, near-shore.
On-shore	(Service strategy) provision of services from a location within the country where the customer is based. See: off-shore, near-shore.
Operate	To perform as expected. A process or configuration item is said to operate if it is delivering the required outputs. Operate also means to perform one or more operations; for example, to operate a computer is to do the day-to-day operations needed for it to perform as expected.
Operation	(Service operation) day-to-day management of an IT service, system, or other configuration item. Operation is also used to mean any pre-defined activity or transaction; for example loading a magnetic tape, accepting money at a point of sale, or reading data from a disk drive.
Operational	The lowest of three levels of planning and delivery (strategic, tactical, operational). Operational activities include the day-to-day or short term planning or delivery of a business process or IT service management process. The term operational is also a synonym for live.
Operational cost	Cost resulting from running the IT services. Often repeating payments; for example personnel costs, hardware maintenance and electricity (also known as 'current expenditure' or 'revenue expenditure'). See: capital expenditure.
Operational expenditure (OPEX)	Synonym for operational cost.
Operational level agreement (OLA)	(Service design) (Continual service improvement) an agreement between an IT service provider and another part of the same organisation. An OLA supports the IT service provider's delivery of IT services to customers. The OLA defines the goods or services to be provided and the responsibilities of both parties; for example there could be an OLA: Between the IT service provider and a procurement department to obtain hardware in agreed times Between the service desk and a support group to provide incident resolution in agreed times See: service level agreement.

AREA OF UPDATE	DESCRIPTION
Operations bridge	(Service operation) a physical location where IT services and it infrastructure are monitored and managed.
Operations control	Synonym for it operations control.
Operations management	Synonym for it operations management.
Opportunity cost	(Service strategy) a cost that is used in deciding between investment choices. Opportunity cost represents the revenue that would have been generated by using the resources in a different way; for example the opportunity cost of purchasing a new server may include not carrying out a service improvement activity that the money could have been spent on. Opportunity cost analysis is used as part of a decision-making processes, but is not treated as an actual cost in any financial statement.
Optimise	Review, plan and request changes, in order to obtain the maximum efficiency and effectiveness from a process, configuration item, application, etc.
Organisation	A company, legal entity or other institution. Examples of organisations that are not companies include international standards organisation or itSMF. The term organisation is sometimes used to refer to any entity which has people, resources, and budgets; for example a project or business unit.
Outcome	The result of carrying out an activity; following a process; delivering an IT service, etc. The term outcome is used to refer to intended results, as well as to actual results. See: objective.
Outsourcing	(Service strategy) using an external service provider to manage IT services. See: service sourcing, Type III service provider.
Overhead	Synonym for indirect cost.
Pain value analysis	(Service operation) a technique used to help identify the business impact of one or more problems. A formula is used to calculate pain value based on the number of users affected, the duration of the downtime, the impact on each user, and the cost to the business (if known).
Pareto principle	(Service operation) a technique used to prioritise activities. The Pareto principle says that 80% of the value of any activity is created with 20% of the effort. Pareto analysis is also used in problem management to prioritise possible problem causes for investigation.
Partnership	A relationship between two organisations which involves working closely together for common goals or mutual benefit. The IT service provider should have a partnership with the business, and with third parties who are critical to the delivery of IT services. See: value network.
Passive monitoring	(Service operation) monitoring of a configuration item, an IT service, or a process that relies on an alert or notification to discover the current status. See: active monitoring.
Pattern of business activity (PBA)	(Service strategy) a workload profile of one or more business activities. Patterns of business activity are used to help the IT service provider understand and plan for different levels of business activity. See: user profile.
Percentage utilisation	(Service design) the amount of time that a component is busy over a given period of time; for example, if a CPU is busy for 1800 seconds in a one hour period, its utilisation is 50%.

AREA OF UPDATE	DESCRIPTION
Performance	A measure of what is achieved or delivered by a system, person, team, process or IT service.
Performance anatomy	(Service strategy) an approach to organisational culture that integrates, and actively manages, leadership and strategy, people development, technology enablement, performance management and innovation.
Performance management	(Continual service improvement) the process responsible for day-to-day capacity management activities. These include monitoring, threshold detection, performance analysis, and tuning, and implementing changes related to performance and capacity.
Pilot	(Service transition) a limited deployment of an IT service, a release, or a process to the live environment. A pilot is used to reduce risk and to gain user feedback and acceptance. See: test, evaluation.
Plan	A detailed proposal which describes the activities and resources needed to achieve an objective; for example, a plan to implement a new IT service or process. ISO/IEC 20000 requires a plan for the management of each IT service management process.
Plan-do-check-act (PDCA)	(Continual service improvement) a four stage cycle for process management, attributed to Dr. W Edwards Deming. Plan-do-check-act is also called the Deming cycle. Plan: design or revise processes that support the IT services Do: implement the plan and manage the processes Check: measure the processes and IT services, compare with objectives and produce reports Act: plan and implement changes to improve the processes
Planned downtime	(Service design) agreed time when an IT service will not be available. Planned downtime is often used for maintenance, upgrades and testing. See: change window, downtime.
Planning	An activity responsible for creating one or more plans; for example, capacity planning.
PMBoK	A project management standard maintained and published by the project management institute. PMBoK stands for project management body of knowledge. See: http://www.pmi.org/ for more information. See: PRINCE2.
Policy	Formally documented management expectations and intentions. Policies are used to direct decisions, and to ensure consistent and appropriate development and implementation of processes, standards, roles, activities, it infrastructure, etc.
Portable facility	(Service design) a prefabricated building, or a large vehicle, provided by a third party and moved to a site when needed by an IT service continuity plan. See: recovery option, fixed facility.
Post implementation review (PIR)	A review that takes place after a change or a project has been implemented. A PIR determines if the change or project was successful, and identifies opportunities for improvement.
Practice	A way of working or a way in which work must be done. Practices can include activities, processes, functions, standards, and guidelines. See: best practice.

AREA OF UPDATE	DESCRIPTION
Prerequisite for success (PFS)	An activity that needs to be completed or a condition that needs to be met, to enable successful implementation of a plan or process. A PFS is often an output from one process that is a required input to another process.
Pricing	(Service strategy) the activity for establishing how much customers will be charged.
PRINCE2	The standard UK Government methodology for project management. See: http://www.ogc.gov.uk/prince2/ for more information. See: PMBoK.
Priority	(Service transition) (Service operation) a category used to identify the relative importance of an incident, problem, or change. Priority is based on impact and urgency, and is used to identify required times for actions to be taken; for example, the SLA may state that priority 2 incidents must be resolved within 12 hours.
Proactive monitoring	(Service operation) monitoring that looks for patterns of events to predict possible future failures. See: reactive monitoring.
Proactive problem management	(Service operation) part of the problem management process. The objective of proactive problem management is to identify problems that might otherwise be missed. Proactive problem management analyses incident records, and uses data collected by other IT service management processes to identify trends or significant problems.
Problem	(Service operation) a cause of one or more incidents. The cause is not usually known at the time a problem record is created, and the problem management process is responsible for further investigation.
Problem management	(Service operation) the process responsible for managing the lifecycle of all problems. The primary objectives of problem management are to prevent incidents from happening, and to minimise the impact of incidents that cannot be prevented.
Problem record	(Service operation) a record containing the details of a problem. Each problem record documents the lifecycle of a single problem.
Procedure	A document containing steps that specify how to achieve an activity. Procedures are defined as part of processes. See: work instruction.
Process	A structured set of activities designed to accomplish a specific objective. A process takes one or more defined inputs and turns them into defined outputs. It may include any of the roles, responsibilities, tools and management controls required to reliably deliver the outputs. A process may define policies, standards, guidelines, activities and work instructions if they are needed.
Process control	The activity of planning and regulating a process, with the objective of performing the process in an effective, efficient, and consistent manner.
Process manager	A role responsible for operational management of a process. The process manager's responsibilities include planning and coordination of all activities required to carry out, monitor, and report on the process. There may be several process managers for one process; for example, regional change managers or IT service continuity managers for each data centre. The process manager role is often assigned to the person who carries out the process owner role, but the two roles may be separate in larger organisations.

AREA OF UPDATE	DESCRIPTION
Process owner	A role responsible for ensuring that a process is 'fit for purpose'. The process owner's responsibilities include sponsorship, design, change management, and continual improvement of the process and its metrics. This role is often assigned to the same person who carries out the process manager role, but the two roles may be separate in larger organisations.
Production environment	Synonym for live environment.
Profit centre	(Service strategy) a business unit which charges for services provided. A profit centre can be created with the objective of making a profit, recovering costs, or running at a loss. An IT service provider can be run as a cost centre or a profit centre.
Pro-forma	A template, or example document, contains example data that will be replaced with the real values when these are available.
Program/programme	A number of projects and activities planned and managed together to achieve an overall set of related objectives and other outcomes.
Project	A temporary organisation, with people and other assets required achieving an objective or other outcome. Each project has a lifecycle that typically includes initiation, planning, execution, closure, etc. Projects are usually managed using a formal methodology such as prince2.
Projected service outage (PSO)	(Service transition) a document that identifies the effect of planned changes, maintenance activities and test plans on agreed service levels.
Projects in controlled environments (PRINCE2)	See: PRINCE2
Qualification	(Service transition) an activity that ensures that it infrastructure is appropriate, and correctly configured, to support an application or IT service. See: validation.
Quality	The ability of a product, service, or process to provide the intended value. For example, a hardware component can be considered to be of high quality if it performs as expected and delivers the required reliability. Process quality also requires an ability to monitor effectiveness and efficiency, and to improve them if necessary. See: quality management system.
Quality assurance (QA)	(Service transition) the process responsible for ensuring that the quality of a product, service or process will provide its intended value.
Quality management system (QMS)	(Continual service improvement) the set of processes responsible for ensuring that all work carried out by an organisation is of a suitable quality to reliably meet business objectives or service levels. See: ISO 9000.
Quick win	(Continual service improvement) an improvement activity which is expected to provide a return on investment in a short period of time with relatively small cost and effort. See: Pareto principle.
RACI	(Service design) (Continual service improvement) a model used to help define roles and responsibilities. RACI stands for responsible, accountable, consulted, and informed. See: stakeholder.
Reactive monitoring	(Service operation) monitoring that takes action in response to an event. For example submitting a batch job when the previous job completes, or logging an incident when an error occurs. See: proactive monitoring.

AREA OF UPDATE	DESCRIPTION
Reciprocal arrangement	(Service design) a recovery option. An agreement between two organisations to share resources in an emergency; for example, computer room space, or use of a mainframe.
Record	A document containing the results or other output from a process or activity. Records are evidence of the fact that an activity took place and may be paper or electronic; for example, an audit report, an incident record, or the minutes of a meeting.
Recovery	(Service design) (Service operation) returning a configuration item or an IT service to a working state. Recovery of an IT service often includes recovering data to a known consistent state. After recovery, further steps may be needed before the IT service can be made available to the users (restoration).
Recovery option	(Service design) a strategy for responding to an interruption to service. Commonly used strategies are do nothing, manual workaround, reciprocal arrangement, gradual recovery, intermediate recovery, fast recovery, and immediate recovery. Recovery options may make use of dedicated facilities, or third party facilities shared by multiple businesses.
Recovery point objective (RPO)	(Service operation) the maximum amount of data that may be lost when service is restored after an interruption. Recovery point objective is expressed as a length of time before the failure; for example, a recovery point objective of one day may be supported by daily backups, and up to 24 hours of data may be lost. Recovery point objectives for each IT service should be negotiated, agreed and documented, and used as requirements for service design and IT service continuity plans.
Recovery time objective (RTO)	(Service operation) the maximum time allowed for recovery of an IT service following an interruption. The service level to be provided may be less than normal service level targets. Recovery time objectives for each IT service should be negotiated, agreed, and documented. See: business impact analysis.
Redundancy	Synonym for fault tolerance. The term redundant also has a generic meaning of obsolete, or no longer needed.
Relationship	A connection or interaction between two people or things. In business relationship management it is the interaction between the IT service provider and the business. In configuration management it is a link between two configuration items that identifies a dependency or connection between them; for example, applications may be linked to the servers they run on, IT services have many links to all the CI that contribute to them.
Relationship processes	The ISO/IEC 20000 process group that includes business relationship management and supplier management.
Release	(Service transition) a collection of hardware, software, documentation, processes or other components required to implement one or more approved changes to IT services. The contents of each release are managed, tested, and deployed as a single entity.
Release and deployment management	(Service transition) the process responsible for both release management and deployment.
Release identification	(Service transition) a naming convention used to uniquely identify a release. The release identification typically includes a reference to the configuration item and a version number; for example Microsoft Office 2003 SR2.

AREA OF UPDATE	DESCRIPTION
Release management	(Service transition) the process responsible for planning, scheduling and controlling the movement of releases to test and live environments. The primary objective of release management is to ensure that the integrity of the live environment is protected and that the correct components are released. Release management is part of the release and deployment management process.
Release process	The name used by ISO/IEC 20000 for the process group that includes release management. This group does not include any other processes. Release process is also used as a synonym for release management process.
Release record	(Service transition) a record in the CMDB that defines the content of a release. A release record has relationships with all configuration items that are affected by the release.
Release unit	(Service transition) components of an IT service that are normally released together. A release unit typically includes sufficient components to perform a useful function; for example one release unit could be a desktop pc, including hardware, software, licenses, documentation, etc.; a different release unit may be the complete payroll application, including IT operations procedures and user training.
Release window	Synonym for change window.
Reliability	(Service design) (Continual service improvement) a measure of how long a configuration item or IT service can perform its agreed function without interruption. Usually measured as MTBF or MTBSI. The term reliability can also be used to state how likely it is that a process, function, etc. will deliver its required outputs. See: availability.
Remediation	(Service transition) recovery to a known state after a failed change or release.
Repair	(Service operation) the replacement or correction of a failed configuration item.
Request for change (RFC)	(Service transition) a formal proposal for a change to be made. An RFC includes details of the proposed change, and may be recorded on paper or electronically. The term RFC is often misused to mean a change record, or the change itself.
Request fulfilment	(Service operation) the process responsible for managing the lifecycle of all service requests.
Requirement	(Service design) a formal statement of what is needed; for example, a service level requirement, a project requirement or the required deliverables for a process. See: statement of requirements.
Resilience	(Service design) the ability of a configuration item or IT service to resist failure or to recover quickly following a failure; for example, an armoured cable will resist failure when put under stress. See: fault tolerance.
Resolution	(Service operation) action taken to repair the root cause of an incident or problem, or to implement a workaround. In ISO/IEC 20000, resolution processes is the process group that includes incident and problem management.
Resolution processes	The ISO/IEC 20000 process group that includes incident management and problem management.
Resource	(Service strategy) a generic term that includes it infrastructure, people, money or anything else that might help to deliver an IT service. Resources are considered to be assets of an organisation. See: capability, service asset.

AREA OF UPDATE	DESCRIPTION
Response time	A measure of the time taken to complete an operation or transaction. Used in capacity management as a measure of it infrastructure performance, and in incident management as a measure of the time taken to answer the phone, or to start diagnosis.
Responsiveness	A measurement of the time taken to respond to something. This could be response time of a transaction, or the speed with which an IT service provider responds to an incident or request for change, etc.
Restoration of service	See: restore.
Restore	(Service operation) taking action to return an IT service to the users after repair and recovery from an incident. This is the primary objective of incident management.
Retire	(Service transition) permanent removal of an IT service, or other configuration item, from the live environment. Retired is a stage in the lifecycle of many configuration items.
Return on investment (ROI)	(Service strategy) (Continual service improvement) a measurement of the expected benefit of an investment. In the simplest sense it is the net profit of an investment divided by the net worth of the assets invested. See: net present value, value on investment.
Return to normal	(Service design) the phase of an IT service continuity plan during which full normal operations are resumed; for example, if an alternate data centre has been in use, then this phase will bring the primary data centre back into operation, and restore the ability to invoke IT service continuity plans again.
Review	An evaluation of a change, problem, process, project, etc. Reviews are typically carried out at predefined points in the lifecycle, and especially after closure. The purpose of a review is to ensure that all deliverables have been provided, and to identify opportunities for improvement. See: post implementation review.
Rights	(Service operation) entitlements, or permissions, granted to a user or role; for example the right to modify particular data, or to authorise a change.
Risk	A possible event that could cause harm or loss, or affect the ability to achieve objectives. A risk is measured by the probability of a threat, the vulnerability of the asset to that threat, and the impact it would have if it occurred.
Risk assessment	The initial steps of risk management. Analysing the value of assets to the business, identifying threats to those assets, and evaluating how vulnerable each asset is to those threats. Risk assessment can be quantitative (based on numerical data) or qualitative.
Risk management	The process responsible for identifying, assessing, and controlling risks. See: risk assessment.
Role	A set of responsibilities, activities, and authorities granted to a person or team. A role is defined in a process. One person or team may have multiple roles; for example, the roles of configuration manager and change manager may be carried out by a single person.
Rollout	(Service transition) synonym for deployment. Most often used to refer to complex or phased deployments or deployments to multiple locations.
Root cause	(Service operation) the underlying or original cause of an incident or problem.
Root cause analysis (RCA)	(Service operation) an activity that identifies the root cause of an incident or problem. RCA typically concentrates on it infrastructure failures. See: service failure analysis.

AREA OF UPDATE	DESCRIPTION
Running costs	Synonym for operational costs.
Scalability	The ability of an IT service, process, configuration item, etc. To perform its agreed function when the workload or scope changes.
Scope	The boundary, or extent, to which a process, procedure, certification, contract, etc. Applies; for example, the scope of change management may include all live IT services and related configuration items; the scope of an ISO/IEC 20000 certificate may include all IT services delivered out of a named data centre.
Second-line support	(Service operation) the second level in a hierarchy of support groups involved in the resolution of incidents and investigation of problems. Each level contains more specialist skills, or has more time or other resources.
Security	See: information security management.
Security management	Synonym for information security management.
Security policy	Synonym for information security policy.
Separation of concerns (SoC)	(Service strategy) an approach to designing a solution or IT service that divides the problem into pieces that can be solved independently. This approach separates 'what' is to be done from 'how' it is to be done.
Server	(Service operation) a computer that is connected to a network and provides software functions that are used by other computers.
Service	A means of delivering value to customers by facilitating outcomes customers want to achieve without the ownership of specific costs and risks.
Service acceptance criteria (SAC)	(Service transition) a set of criteria used to ensure that an IT service meets its functionality and quality requirements and that the IT service provider is ready to operate the new IT service when it has been deployed. See: acceptance.
Service analytics	(Service strategy) a technique used in the assessment of the business impact of incidents. Service analytics models the dependencies between configuration items, and the dependencies of IT services on configuration items.
Service asset	Any capability or resource of a service provider. See: asset.
Service asset and configuration management (SACM)	(Service transition) the process responsible for both configuration management and asset management.
Service capacity management (SCM)	(Service design) (Continual service improvement) the activity responsible for understanding the performance and capacity of IT services. The resources used by each IT service and the pattern of usage over time are collected, recorded, and analysed for use in the capacity plan. See: business capacity management, component capacity management.
Service catalogue	(Service design) a database or structured document with information about all live IT services, including those available for deployment. The service catalogue is the only part of the service portfolio published to customers, and is used to support the sale and delivery of IT services. The service catalogue includes information about deliverables, prices, contact points, ordering and request processes. See: contract portfolio.
Service continuity management	Synonym for IT service continuity management.

AREA OF UPDATE	DESCRIPTION
Service contract	(Service strategy) a contract to deliver one or more IT services. The term service contract is also used to mean any agreement to deliver IT services, whether this is a legal contract or an SLA. See: contract portfolio.
Service culture	A customer oriented culture. The major objectives of a service culture are customer satisfaction and helping the customer to achieve their business objectives.
Service design	(Service design) a stage in the lifecycle of an IT service. Service design includes a number of processes and functions and is the title of one of the core ITIL publications. See: design.
Service design package	(Service design) document(s) defining all aspects of an IT service and its requirements through each stage of its lifecycle. A service design package is produced for each new IT service, major change, or IT service retirement.
Service desk	(Service operation) the single point of contact between the service provider and the users. A typical service desk manages incidents and service requests, and also handles communication with the users.
Service failure analysis (SFA)	(Service design) an activity that identifies underlying causes of one or more IT service interruptions. SFA identifies opportunities to improve the IT service provider's processes and tools, and not just the IT infrastructure. SFA is a time constrained, project-like activity, rather than an on-going process of analysis. See: root cause analysis.
Service hours	(Service design) (Continual service improvement) an agreed time period when a particular IT service should be available; for example, 'Monday to Friday 08:00 to 17:00 except public holidays'. Service hours should be defined in a service level agreement.
Service improvement plan (SIP)	(Continual service improvement) a formal plan to implement improvements to a process or IT service.
Service knowledge management system (SKMS)	(Service transition) a set of tools and databases that are used to manage knowledge and information. The SKMS includes the configuration management system, as well as other tools and databases. The SKMS stores, manages, updates, and presents all information that an IT service provider needs to manage the full lifecycle of IT services.
Service level	Measured and reported achievement against one or more service level targets. The term service level is sometimes used informally to mean service level target.
Service level agreement (SLA)	(Service design) (Continual service improvement) an agreement between an IT service provider and a customer. The SLA describes the IT service, documents service level targets, and specifies the responsibilities of the IT service provider and the customer. A single SLA may cover multiple IT services or multiple customers. See: operational level agreement.
Service level management (SLM)	(Service design) (Continual service improvement) the process responsible for negotiating service level agreements, and ensuring that these are met. SLM is responsible for ensuring that all IT service management processes, operational level agreements, and underpinning contracts, are appropriate for the agreed service level targets. SLM monitors and reports on service levels, and holds regular customer reviews.
Service level package (SLP)	(Service strategy) a defined level of utility and warranty for a particular service package. Each SLP is designed to meet the needs of a particular pattern of business activity. See: line of service.

AREA OF UPDATE	DESCRIPTION
Service level requirement (SLR)	(Service design) (Continual service improvement) a customer requirement for an aspect of an IT service. SLRs are based on business objectives and are used to negotiate agreed service level targets.
Service level target	(Service design) (Continual service improvement) a commitment that is documented in a service level agreement. Service level targets are based on service level requirements, and are needed to ensure that the IT service design is 'fit for purpose'. Service level targets should be smart, and are usually based on KPI.
Service maintenance objective	(Service operation) the expected time that a configuration item will be unavailable due to planned maintenance activity.
Service management	Service management is a set of specialised organisational capabilities for providing value to customers in the form of services.
Service management lifecycle	An approach to IT service management that emphasises the importance of coordination and control across the various functions, processes, and systems necessary to manage the full lifecycle of IT services. The service management lifecycle approach considers the strategy, design, transition, operation, and continuous improvement of IT services.
Service manager	A manager who is responsible for managing the end-to-end lifecycle of one or more IT services. The term service manager is also used to mean any manager within the IT service provider. Most commonly used to refer to a business relationship manager, a process manager, an account manager, or a senior manager with responsibility for IT services overall.
Service operation	(Service operation) a stage in the lifecycle of an IT service. Service operation includes a number of processes and functions and is the title of one of the core ITIL publications. See: operation.
Service owner	(Continual service improvement) a role which is accountable for the delivery of a specific IT service.
Service package	(Service strategy) a detailed description of an IT service that is available to be delivered to customers. A service package includes a service level package and one or more core services and supporting services.
Service pipeline	(Service strategy) a database or structured document listing all IT services that are under consideration or development, but are not yet available to customers. The service pipeline provides a business view of possible future IT services and is part of the service portfolio which is not normally published to customers.
Service portfolio	(Service strategy) the complete set of services that are managed by a service provider. The service portfolio is used to manage the entire lifecycle of all services, and includes three categories: service pipeline (proposed or in development); service catalogue (live or available for deployment); and retired services. See: service portfolio management, contract portfolio.
Service portfolio management (SPM)	(Service strategy) the process responsible for managing the service portfolio. Service portfolio management considers services in terms of the business value that they provide.
Service potential	(Service strategy) the total possible value of the overall capabilities and resources of the IT service provider.
Service provider	(Service strategy) an organisation supplying services to one or more internal customers or external customers. Service provider is often used as an abbreviation for IT service provider. See: Type I service provider, Type II service provider, Type III service provider.

AREA OF UPDATE	DESCRIPTION
Service provider interface (SPI)	(Service strategy) an interface between the IT service provider and a user, customer, business process, or a supplier. Analysis of service provider interfaces helps to co-ordinate end-to-end management of IT services.
Service provisioning utilisation (SPO)	(Service strategy) analysing the finances and constraints of an IT service to decide if alternative approaches to service delivery might reduce costs or improve quality.
Service reporting	(Continual service improvement) the process responsible for producing and delivering reports of achievement and trends against service levels. Service reporting should agree the format, content, and frequency of reports with customers.
Service request	(Service operation) a request from a user for information, for advice, or for a standard change, or for access to an IT service; for example, to reset a password, or to provide standard IT services for a new user. Service requests are usually handled by a service desk, and do not require an RFC to be submitted. See: request fulfilment.
Service sourcing	(Service strategy) the strategy and approach for deciding whether to provide a service internally or to outsource it to an external service provider. Service sourcing also means the execution of this strategy. Service sourcing includes: Internal sourcing internal or shared services using Type I or Type II service providers Traditional sourcing full service outsourcing using a Type III service provider Multi-vendor sourcing prime, consortium or selective outsourcing using Type III service providers
Service strategy	(Service strategy) the title of one of the core ITIL publications. Service strategy establishes an overall strategy for IT services and for IT service management.
Service transition	(Service transition) a stage in the lifecycle of an IT service. Service transition includes a number of processes and functions and is the title of one of the core ITIL publications. See: transition.
Service utility	(Service strategy) the functionality of an IT service from the customer's perspective. The business value of an IT service is created by the combination of service utility (what the service does) and service warranty (how well it does it). See: utility.
Service validation and testing	(Service transition) the process responsible for validation and testing of a new or changed IT service. Service validation and testing ensures that the IT service matches its design specification and will meet the needs of the business.
Service valuation	(Service strategy) a measurement of the total cost of delivering an IT service, and the total value to the business of that IT service. Service valuation is used to help the business and the IT service provider agree on the value of the IT service.
Service warranty	(Service strategy) assurance that an IT service will meet agreed requirements. This may be a formal agreement such as a service level agreement or contract, or may be a marketing message or brand image. The business value of an IT service is created by the combination of service utility (what the service does) and service warranty (how well it does it). See: warranty.
Serviceability	(Service design) (Continual service improvement) the ability of a third party supplier to meet the terms of their contract. This contract will include agreed levels of reliability, maintainability, or availability for a configuration item.

AREA OF UPDATE	DESCRIPTION
Shift	(Service operation) a group or team of people who carry out a specific role for a fixed period of time; for example, there could be four shifts of it operations control personnel to support an IT service that is used 24 hours a day.
Simulation modelling	(Service design) (Continual service improvement) a technique that creates a detailed model to predict the behaviour of a configuration item or IT service. Simulation models can be very accurate but are expensive and time consuming to create. A simulation model is often created by using the actual configuration items that are being modelled, with artificial workloads or transactions. They are used in capacity management when accurate results are important. A simulation model is sometimes called a performance benchmark.
Single point of contact	(Service operation) providing a single consistent way to communicate with an organisation or business unit; for example, a single point of contact for an IT service provider is usually called a service desk.
Single point of failure (SPoF)	(Service design) any configuration item that can cause an incident when it fails, and for which a countermeasure has not been implemented. A SPoF may be a person, or a step in a process or activity, as well as a component of the IT infrastructure. See: failure.
Slam chart	(Continual service improvement) a service level agreement monitoring chart is used to help monitor and report achievements against service level targets. A slam chart is typically colour coded to show whether each agreed service level target has been met, missed, or nearly missed during each of the previous 12 months.
Smart	(Service design) (Continual service improvement) an acronym for helping to remember that targets in service level agreements and project plans should be specific, measurable, achievable, relevant, and timely.
Snapshot	(Service transition) the current state of a configuration as captured by a discovery tool. Also used as a synonym for benchmark. See: baseline.
Source	See: service sourcing.
Specification	A formal definition of requirements. A specification may be used to define technical or operational requirements, and may be internal or external. Many public standards consist of a code of practice and a specification. The specification defines the standard against which an organisation can be audited.
Stakeholder	All people who have an interest in an organisation, project, IT service, etc. Stakeholders may be interested in the activities, targets, resources, or deliverables. Stakeholders may include customers, partners, employees, shareholders, owners, etc. See: RACI.
Standard	A mandatory requirement. Examples include ISO/IEC 20000 (an international standard), an internal security standard for Unix configuration, or a national government standard for how financial records should be maintained. The term standard is also used to refer to a code of practice or specification published by a standards organisation such as ISO or BSI. See: guideline.

AREA OF UPDATE	DESCRIPTION
Standard change	(Service transition) a pre-approved change that is low risk, relatively common and follows a procedure or work instruction; for example, password reset or provision of standard equipment to a new employee. RFC are not required to implement a standard change, and they are logged and tracked using a different mechanism, such as a service request. See: change model.
Standard operating procedures (SOP)	(Service operation) procedures used by IT operations management.
Standby	(Service design) used to refer to resources that are not required to deliver the live IT services, but are available to support IT service continuity plans; for example, a standby data centre may be maintained to support hot standby, warm standby or cold standby arrangements.
Statement of requirements (SoR)	(Service design) a document containing all requirements for a product purchase, or a new or changed IT service. See: terms of reference.
Status	The name of a required field in many types of record. It shows the current stage in the lifecycle of the associated configuration item, incident, problem, etc.
Status accounting	(Service transition) the activity responsible for recording and reporting the lifecycle of each configuration item.
Storage management	(Service operation) the process responsible for managing the storage and maintenance of data throughout its lifecycle.
Strategic	(Service strategy) the highest of three levels of planning and delivery (strategic, tactical, operational). Strategic activities include objective setting and long-term planning to achieve the overall vision.
Strategy	(Service strategy) a strategic plan designed to achieve defined objectives.
Super user	(Service operation) a user who helps other users, and assists in communication with the service desk or other parts of the IT service provider. Super users typically provide support for minor incidents and training.
Supplier	(Service strategy) (Service design) a third party responsible for supplying goods or services that are required to deliver IT services. Examples of suppliers include commodity hardware and software vendors, network and telecom providers, and outsourcing organisations. See: underpinning contract, supply chain.
Supplier and contract management information system (SCMIS)	(Service design) a database or structured document used to manage supplier contracts throughout their lifecycle. The SCMIS contains key attributes of all contracts with suppliers, and should be part of the service knowledge management system.
Supplier management	(Service design) the process responsible for ensuring that all contracts with suppliers support the needs of the business, and that all suppliers meet their contractual commitments.
Supply chain	(Service strategy) the activities in a value chain carried out by suppliers. A supply chain typically involves multiple suppliers, each adding value to the product or service. See: value network.
Support group	(Service operation) a group of people with technical skills. Support groups provide the technical support needed by all of the IT service management processes. See: technical management.

AREA OF UPDATE	DESCRIPTION
Support hours	(Service design) (Service operation) the times or hours when support is available to the users. Typically these are the hours when the service desk is available. Support hours should be defined in a service level agreement, and may be different from service hours; for example, service hours may be 24 hours a day, but the support hours may be 07:00 to 19:00.
Supporting service	(Service strategy) a service that enables or enhances a core service; for example, a directory service or a backup service. See: service package.
SWOT analysis	(Continual service improvement) a technique that reviews and analyses the internal strengths and weaknesses of an organisation and the external opportunities and threats which it faces. SWOT stands for strengths, weaknesses, opportunities, and threats.
System	A number of related things that work together to achieve an overall objective; for example: A computer system including hardware, software and applications A management system, including multiple processes that are planned and managed together; for example a quality management system A database management system or operating system that includes many software modules that are designed to perform a set of related functions
System management	The part of IT service management that focuses on the management of it infrastructure rather than process.
Tactical	The middle of three levels of planning and delivery (strategic, tactical, operational). Tactical activities include the medium term plans required to achieve specific objectives, typically over a period of weeks to months.
Tag	(Service strategy) a short code used to identify a category; for example, tags ec1, ec2, ec3, etc. Might be used to identify different customer outcomes when analysing and comparing strategies. The term tag is also used to refer to the activity of assigning tags to things.
Technical management	(Service operation) the function responsible for providing technical skills in support of IT services and management of the IT infrastructure. Technical management defines the roles of support groups, as well as the tools, processes and procedures required.
Technical observation (TO)	(Continual service improvement) a technique used in service improvement, problem investigation, and availability management. Technical support personnel meet to monitor the behaviour and performance of an IT service and make recommendations for improvement.
Technical service	Synonym for infrastructure service.
Technical support	Synonym for technical management.
Tension metrics	(Continual service improvement) a set of related metrics, in which improvements to one metric have a negative effect on another. Tension metrics are designed to ensure that an appropriate balance is achieved.
Terms of reference (ToR)	(Service design) a document specifying the requirements, scope, deliverables, resources and schedule for a project or activity.
Test	(Service transition) an activity that verifies that a configuration item, IT service, process, etc., meets the IT specification or agreed requirements. See: service validation and testing, acceptance.
Test environment	(Service transition) a controlled environment used to test configuration items, builds, IT services, processes, etc.

AREA OF UPDATE	DESCRIPTION
Third party	A person, group, or business who is not part of the service level agreement for an IT service, but is required to ensure successful delivery of that IT service; for example a software supplier, a hardware maintenance company, or a facilities department. Requirements for third parties are typically specified in underpinning contracts or operational level agreements.
Third-line support	(Service operation) the third level in a hierarchy of support groups involved in the resolution of incidents and investigation of problems. Each level contains more specialist skills, or has more time or other resources.
Threat	Anything that might exploit vulnerability. Any potential cause of an incident can be considered to be a threat; for example, a fire is a threat that could exploit the vulnerability of flammable floor coverings. This term is commonly used in information security management and IT service continuity management, but also applies to other areas such as problem and availability management.
Threshold	The value of a metric which should cause an alert to be generated, or management action to be taken; for example, 'priority 1 incident not solved within 4 hours', 'more than 5 soft disk errors in an hour', or 'more than 10 failed changes in a month'.
Throughput	(Service design) a measure of the number of transactions, or other operations, performed in a fixed time; for example, 5,000 emails sent per hour or 200 disk i/o per second.
Total cost of ownership (TCO)	(Service strategy) a methodology used to help make investment decisions. TCO assesses the full lifecycle cost of owning a configuration item, not just the initial cost or purchase price. See: total cost of utilisation.
Total cost of utilisation (TCU)	(Service strategy) a methodology used to help make investment and service sourcing decisions. TCU assesses the full lifecycle cost to the customer of using an IT service. See: total cost of ownership.
Total quality management (TQM)	(Continual service improvement) a methodology for managing continual improvement by using a quality management system. TQM establishes a culture involving all people in the organisation in a process of continual monitoring and improvement.
Transaction	A discrete function performed by an IT service; for example, transferring money from one bank account to another. A single transaction may involve numerous additions, deletions, and modifications of data. Either all of these complete successfully or none of them is carried out.
Transition	(Service transition) a change in state, corresponding to a movement of an IT service or other configuration item from one lifecycle status to the next.
Transition planning and support	(Service transition) the process responsible for planning all service transition processes and coordinating the resources that they require. These service transition processes are change management, service asset and configuration management, release and deployment management, service validation and testing, evaluation, and knowledge management.
Trend analysis	(Continual service improvement) analysis of data to identify time related patterns. Trend analysis is used in problem management to identify common failures or fragile configuration items, and in capacity management as a modelling tool to predict future behaviour. It is also used as a management tool for identifying deficiencies in IT service management processes.

AREA OF UPDATE	DESCRIPTION
Tuning	The activity responsible for planning changes to make the most efficient use of resources. Tuning is part of performance management, which also includes performance monitoring and implementation of the required changes.
Type I service provider	(Service strategy) an internal service provider that is embedded within a business unit. There may be several Type I service providers within an organisation.
Type II service provider	(Service strategy) an internal service provider that provides shared IT services to more than one business unit.
Type III service provider	(Service strategy) a service provider that provides IT services to external customers.
Underpinning contract (UC)	(Service design) a contract between an IT service provider and a third party. The third party provides goods or services that support delivery of an IT service to a customer. The underpinning contract defines targets and responsibilities that are required to meet agreed service level targets in an SLA.
Unit cost	(Service strategy) the cost to the IT service provider of providing a single component of an IT service; for example, the cost of a single desktop pc, or of a single transaction.
Urgency	(Service transition) (Service design) a measure of how long it will be until an incident, problem, or change has a significant impact on the business; for example, a high impact incident may have low urgency, if the impact will not affect the business until the end of the financial year. Impact and urgency are used to assign priority.
Usability	(Service design) the ease with which an application, product, or IT service can be used. Usability requirements are often included in a statement of requirements.
Use case	(Service design) a technique used to define required functionality and objectives, and to design tests. Use cases define realistic scenarios that describe interactions between users and an IT service or other system. See: change case.
User	A person who uses the IT service on a day-to-day basis. Users are distinct from customers, as some customers do not use the IT service directly.
User profile (UP)	(Service strategy) a pattern of user demand for IT services. Each user profile includes one or more patterns of business activity.
Utility	(Service strategy) functionality offered by a product or service to meet a particular need. Utility is often summarised as 'what it does'. See: service utility.
Validation	(Service transition) an activity that ensures a new or changed IT service, process, plan, or other deliverable meets the needs of the business. Validation ensures that business requirements are met even though these may have changed since the original design. See: verification, acceptance, qualification, service validation, and testing.
Value chain	(Service strategy) a sequence of processes that creates a product or service that is of value to a customer. Each step of the sequence builds on the previous steps and contributes to the overall product or service. See: value network.
Value for money	An informal measure of cost effectiveness. Value for money is often based on a comparison with the cost of alternatives. See: cost benefit analysis.

AREA OF UPDATE	DESCRIPTION
Value network	(Service strategy) a complex set of relationships between two or more groups or organisations. Value is generated through exchange of knowledge, information, goods, or services. See: value chain, partnership.
Value on investment (VOI)	(Continual service improvement) a measurement of the expected benefit of an investment. VOI considers both financial and intangible benefits. See: return on investment (ROI).
Variable cost	(Service strategy) a cost that depends on how much the IT service is used, how many products are produced, the number and type of users, or something else that cannot be fixed in advance. See: variable cost dynamics.
Variable cost dynamics	(Service strategy) a technique used to understand how overall costs are impacted by the many complex variable elements that contribute to the provision of IT services.
Variance	The difference between a planned value and the actual measured value. Commonly used in financial management, capacity management and service level management, but could apply in any area where plans are in place.
Verification	(Service transition) an activity that ensures a new or changed IT service, process, plan, or other deliverable is complete, accurate, and reliable and matches its design specification. See: validation, acceptance, service validation, and testing.
Verification and audit	(Service transition) the activity responsible for ensuring that information in the CMDB is accurate and that all configuration items have been identified and recorded in the CMDB. Verification includes routine checks that are part of other processes; for example, verifying the serial number of a desktop PC when a user logs an incident. Audit is a periodic, formal check.
Version	(Service transition) a version is used to identify a specific baseline of a configuration item. Versions typically use a naming convention that enables the sequence or date of each baseline to be identified; for example, payroll application version 3 contains updated functionality from version 2.
Vision	A description of what the organisation intends to become in the future. A vision is created by senior management and is used to help influence culture and strategic planning.
Vital business function (VBF)	(Service design) a function of a business process which is critical to the success of the business. Vital business functions are an important consideration of business continuity management, IT service continuity management, and availability management.
Vulnerability	A weakness that could be exploited by a threat; for example, an open firewall port, a password that is never changed, or a flammable carpet. A missing control is also considered to be vulnerability.
Warm standby	Synonym for intermediate recovery.
Warranty	(Service strategy) a promise or guarantee that a product or service will meet its agreed requirements. See: service validation and testing, service warranty.
Work in progress (WIP)	A status indicating activities have started, but are not yet complete. It is commonly used as a status for incidents, problems, changes, etc.
Work instruction	A document containing detailed instructions that specify exactly what steps to follow to carry out an activity. A work instruction contains much more detail than a procedure and is only created if very detailed instructions are needed.

AREA OF UPDATE	DESCRIPTION
Workaround	(Service operation) reducing or eliminating the impact of an incident or problem for which a full resolution is not yet available; for example, by restarting a failed configuration item. Workarounds for problems are documented in known error records. Workarounds for incidents that do not have associated problem records are documented in the incident record.
Workload	The resources required delivering an identifiable part of an IT service. Workloads may be categorised by users, groups of users, or functions within the IT service. This is used to assist in analysing and managing the capacity, performance, and utilisation of configuration items and IT services. The term workload is sometimes used as a synonym for throughput.

D. Index

E. List of tables

F. List of figures